3 9153 00940152 4

W9-BNG-191

THE Hofstadter Aegis A MEMORIAL

THE HOFSTADTER AEGIS

A Memorial

Edited by Stanley Elkins
and Eric McKitrick

New York
Alfred · A · Knopf
1974

THIS IS A BORZOI BOOK
PUBLISHED BY ALFRED A. KNOPF, INC.

 Published in the United States by Alfred A. Knopf, Inc., New York, and simultaneously in Canada by Random House of Canada Limited, Toronto. Distributed by Random House, Inc., New York.

Library of Congress Cataloging in Publication Data:
Main entry under title
The Hofstadter aegis.
Includes bibliographical references.
CONTENTS: Meyers, M. Founding and revolution: a commentary on Publius-Madison. —Kerber, L. K. Daughters of Columbia: educating women for the Republic, 1787–1805 —Banner, J. M., Jr. The problem of South Carolina. [etc.]
1. United States—History—Addresses, essays, lectures. 2. Hofstadter, Richard, 1916–1970. I. Hofstadter, Richard, 1916–1970. II. Elkins, Stanley M., ed. III. McKitrick, Eric L., ed.
E178.6.H72 917.3'03 73–20440
ISBN 0–394–49107–6

Manufactured in the United States of America

FIRST EDITION

CONTENTS

Preface
vii

MARVIN MEYERS
Founding and Revolution:
A Commentary on Publius-Madison
3

LINDA K. KERBER
Daughters of Columbia: Educating Women for the Republic, 1787–1805
36

JAMES M. BANNER, JR.
The Problem of South Carolina
60

LAWRENCE W. LEVINE
"Some Go Up and Some Go Down":
The Meaning of the Slave Trickster
94

WILSON SMITH
Apologia pro Alma Matre: The College as Community in Ante-Bellum America
125

ERIC FONER
Thaddeus Stevens, Confiscation, and Reconstruction
154

Contents

JAMES MCLACHLAN
American Colleges and the Transmission of Culture: The Case of the Mugwumps
184

DOROTHY ROSS
The "New History" and the "New Psychology": An Early Attempt at Psychohistory
207

DAVID BURNER and THOMAS R. WEST
A Technocrat's Morality: Conservatism and Hoover the Engineer
235

OTIS L. GRAHAM, JR.
The Planning Ideal and American Reality: The 1930s
257

STANLEY ELKINS and ERIC MCKITRICK
Richard Hofstadter: A Progress
300

PAULA S. FASS
The Writings of Richard Hofstadter: A Bibliography
368

THE CONTRIBUTORS
383

INDEX OF NAMES
follows page
384

PREFACE

THE FOURTEEN authors of this volume, all historians, are without exception former graduate students of Richard Hofstadter. The decision to have it this way, made in the weeks immediately following his death, set in motion a certain logic which has imposed itself on the entire character of the book. The terms of the logic emerged from the nature of Richard Hofstadter's own interests and values, and from the special character of the relationship he had with his students.

The book has no overall "theme," if to have one required that specific topics in some field of particular concern to Richard Hofstadter be assigned to individual authors. For one thing, Professor Hofstadter himself never "assigned" anything to anyone. For another, his own interests were so exceptionally diverse, and their range so wide, that no collective undertaking would be a wholly appropriate memorial to him that did not reflect something of that same range and diversity. Consequently it seemed natural and right that the authors should choose their own topics, matters currently of concern to themselves. Each of the essays does, as it turns out, reflect one or another of his interests, too: education, slavery, politics, public careers, political and social ideas, and so on. But it just happened so, and is more a tribute to the inclusiveness of those interests than to the coerciveness of any given one of them.

Indeed, coerciveness in any form was the one quality almost totally missing from Richard Hofstadter's makeup. He had a kind of innate dignity that made it unnecessary for him to insist upon himself, and allowed him a natural modesty. There was a delicacy that prevented the making of personal claims upon others, and that excluded any sense of proprietorship over their work. It was the work itself that mattered, not his relationship to it. Discipleship was a thing he never asked for, probably because it never occurred to him. He thus encouraged—or rather just assumed—a degree of autonomy in his students that most professors, with the best will in the world, find hard to reconcile with the full pattern of their own role as teacher and preceptor. But what united Richard Hofstadter with his students was, again, the work. That they "ought" to be free to think for themselves was not a value he went about professing; he simply took for granted that they were.

For anyone coming under his aegis out of a setting in which other assumptions prevailed, all this had the most profound consequences. With his willingness to show his work to a student for criticism—the utter seriousness with which he told you that he could accept some of your comments but couldn't go along with others—he quite unaffectedly paid the supreme compliment of colleagueship. It was the same with your own work; you and he dealt with it as peers. The work was the leveler, and the great object—at once transcendent and impersonal—was that it should succeed.

There was, to be sure, another side. One was on one's own, and although help was there when one had to have it, anyone who needed repeatedly to be told what to do would encounter a Hofstadter who was fretful and somewhat out of his element. Some of the very professors who are most proprietary over their students' work can, undeniably, make superb directors of dissertations. Hofstadter in that sense never quite "directed" anyone. But for those who worked under his sponsorship he could do something better; in every nuance of his demeanor—in criticism or in praise—he acted out his respect for what you had under way. He thus accorded it the kind of legitimacy that counted—and you were free.

So the one "theme," if such it may be called, that this volume can have is a kind of Platonic standard of achievement that impels each to his best. We think that standard has been met. Most of the authors know each other well; they have passed their work about for criticism, and there has been no end of correspondence with the editors, whose hectoring has admittedly been excessive, often unreasonable, and probably un-Hofstadter-like. However that may be, each essay has been the product of much thought and effort; each has developed and grown and changed in deference to a standard we hold in common, thanks to him, and that is why the book has been so long in preparation.

The essays exhibit, as we have said, a striking variety.

Marvin Meyers has reexamined the effort made by James Madison, writing as "Publius" in *The Federalist,* to defend the drafting of a new constitution. Publius-Madison, Meyers says, achieved an exquisite tactical balance between conservatism and a bold appeal to the Revolutionary example, arguing on the one hand that the Revolution and the Constitution were both justified by "the absolute necessity of the case," but that prudence, on the other hand, counseled that neither experiment should be risked more than once.

The acute concern of Americans about the character of their future citizens, according to Linda Kerber, provided the setting for the first debates over the role of women in the new Republic and the kind of education they ought to have in order to play it. In the course of the debate, women acquired a new responsibility for the republic's moral climate; it was primarily this that justified their claim to something of greater substance in the way of education; but the price they paid for it was the surrender of other claims to rights that would not in some cases be gained for more than a century.

James Banner offers a comprehensive analysis of the "problem of South Carolina," and of what it was that made ante-bellum South Carolina different. Banner examines the historical conditions that retarded the development of two-party politics there, and considers the implications both for the Nullification crisis and, thirty years later, for South Carolina's primacy in the Secession movement.

Folklorists have long been fascinated by the Brer Rabbit tales from the ante-bellum plantation, with all their insights into the fantasy world of the slave. Lawrence Levine, arguing that the trickster was a much subtler and more complex figure than formerly imagined, examines the didactic function of the trickster tales for a people who had to survive in a world of unpredictable and amoral power. The lessons taught were rarely simple: the trickster was often the slave, but he might sometimes be the master as well.

Historians of education (with Richard Hofstadter himself in the vanguard) have been very hard on what they have seen as the intellectual sterility of the pre–Civil War American college. Wilson Smith disagrees. Smith considers the many sources of strength in the "hilltop" colleges: their relationship with the localities that helped support them, the hierarchies of prestige and respect they helped establish, and the opportunities they offered to poor but ambitious young men off the farm. But Smith's major concern—elusive though he admits it to be—is the sense of purpose and feeling of community he believes the old-time college instilled in both teachers and students.

Eric Foner, examining Thaddeus Stevens's urge to revolutionize the South—with primary emphasis on Stevens's efforts to bring about a general confiscation of large landholdings—provides a thorough case study in both the possibilities and the limits of radicalism in a bourgeois party.

Endless efforts have been made to determine the sources of the "Mugwump" reform impulse of the late nineteenth century, but about the only thing generally agreed on is that an overwhelming proportion of the

Mugwump leaders attended college. James McLachlan suggests, with a seemingly innocent simplicity: why not have a look at what they learned there? McLachlan points to two critical experiences, the senior course in moral philosophy (typically taught by the president) and the debates of the literary societies—and discovers a striking correlation between the attitudes and values exhibited in these performances and those the reformers urged upon their fellow citizens in later life.

James Harvey Robinson, according to Dorothy Ross, was one of the first historians to recognize that concepts then being developed in the field of psychology might also be of great use to the historian. But Robinson's own efforts, as Mrs. Ross shows, came to very little. His grasp of contemporary psychological theory was itself limited, as were his dogmatic convictions about the nature of historical change. Everything had to be fitted into his Darwinian presumption that all significant change, social as well as biological, could be explained through the mutation or sport—the unpredictable genius able to surmount the deadening force of habit and tradition.

David Burner and Thomas West, in assessing the career in engineering and business that preceded Herbert Hoover's emergence into public life, discover a man with a passionate commitment to efficiency and planning in both business and government, balanced by a strong faith in the importance of voluntary cooperation, who would never cease insisting that he was an old-fashioned liberal. He was, certainly, the model "Progressive," and it might be supposed that such a combination of qualities should have given him a good preparation for the crisis of the Depression. What he lacked, however, was a true feeling for community values and national morale, and the political sensitivity of the traditional conservative—qualities strikingly apparent in Hoover's successor, the squire of Hyde Park.

Despite all the talk during the New Deal period about national planning, little was accomplished, and much of what was—even at the level of fiscal management—was astonishingly inept. Otis Graham discusses the reasons, and describes the emergence of an unplanned alternative to planning, the "broker state."

Paula Fass, in compiling the most complete listing to date of Richard Hofstadter's writings, has performed a service of great value to anyone wishing to examine the whole body of Hofstadter's work.

Another kind of memorial to Richard Hofstadter might have been a book all about *him*. He would certainly have been polite about that, as he was about everything, but it would probably have given him little pleasure, being rather an invasion of his privacy. On the other hand, some consideration of his work would surely have interested him—and some sort of general assessment would in any case seem to be in order. We have assumed this, in addition to the editorial requirements of the volume, as our responsibility.

An appraisal of a man's work is all very well, but an occasion like the present one exerts heavy coercions. The act of personal tribute which it represents would seem to imply a strong case for giving any such essay at least some biographical dimension. The formative experiences of his early maturity, the turning points of his professional career, the persons he associated with, significant aspects of his character, the things he liked and didn't like—surely all such items, in the life of a man whose name had become as celebrated as Richard Hofstadter's, might be supposed to have some bearing on what he did to acquire that celebrity.

We have been urged, for instance, to say something about Hofstadter's political activities, both his early ones and those he engaged in later on. Or, to consider how a world view formed by the climate of the 1930s may have been significantly modified by that of the Cold War era. We might have made a point of certain elements of personality, preferences, and tastes. We might have looked for the sources of his extraordinary sense of paradox and irony, his latent pessimism, his skepticism about sweeping social remedies, or his feeling for the fragility of institutions and complex social arrangements.

We have undertaken none of this. For one thing, we had not the heart—nor, for another, the knowledge. Richard Hofstadter had been our friend for some twenty years, and of course we knew some of the details of his life, and had ready access to more. But who were we to say—this early—what was pertinent and what was not? There have already been a few brief, though highly sensitive, personal recollections, and we have noted them elsewhere.[1] But if any biographical study is undertaken—even in essay form—of this unusually complex man that will do him true justice, the time for it is not yet at hand, nor will we be the ones to do it.

We nonetheless believed there was another kind of justice that we could at least attempt. Richard Hofstadter was concerned always with mind, and with the functioning of mind in this culture. Accordingly we felt that it would not be inappropriate to write about *his* mind—that aspect of it publicly accessible in his writings—and of what he did with it. This effort in itself, even with virtually everything "personal" rigidly excluded by design, has been more demanding than we expected. Further ones, we hope, may be undertaken by others.

The debts we owe, both as editors and as authors, are extensive. A number of our colleagues and friends have treated this book as a high occasion, and have devoted an inordinate amount of time and attention to its contents. They include David Allmendinger, Robert Averitt, Jacques Barzun, Robert D. Cross, Kingsley Ervin, Ashbel Green, John Higham, Beatrice K. Hofstadter, Cecelia Kenyon, William E. Leuchtenburg, Robert McCaughey, Lionel Trilling, Allen Weinstein, R. Jackson Wilson, and C. Vann

[1] See page 301, note 1.

Woodward. A special note is due Professor Wilson, who set an example of colleagueship in extensive critical scrutiny that will stand as a model for us henceforth. Mrs. Hofstadter, who first asked us to assume this work, at once renounced all proprietorship over it while at the same time serving as a priceless resource, giving us needed information as well as exercising her formidable critical gifts on several of the essays. She and Mr. Green, moreover, assisted us with a number of difficult editorial decisions.

Stanley Elkins
Eric McKitrick

THE Hofstadter Aegis A MEMORIAL

MARVIN MEYERS

Founding and Revolution: A Commentary on Publius-Madison

IN 1787 the ghosts of ancient lawgivers mingled with the founders of the new American Republic. James Madison, under the Roman mask of Publius Valerius Publicola, readily recalled the example of a Lycurgus or Solon in his defense of the Philadelphia Convention. Yet Publius-Madison knew the vast distance separating the Revolutionary generation from their political ancestors. Indeed, all history seemed to him a graveyard of lost republican hopes, a long grim lesson in the perils of founding and maintaining free government. The Revolution of 1776 marked "a new and more noble course" for America and "for the whole human race." [1] The Convention of 1787 de-

[1] Jacob E. Cooke, ed., *The Federalist* (Cleveland and New York, 1961), No. 14, p. 89. All further references to this work cite simply the essay number and the pages of this edition. *N.B.* The present essay is designed as a close interpretation of "Publius-Madison" and thus focuses almost exclusively on his contributions to *The Federalist*. For a broader approach to Madison's thought from a similar point of view, together with a substantial selection of writings, see Marvin Meyers, *The Mind of the Founder: Sources of the Political Thought of James Madison* (Indianapolis and New York, 1973).

fined the terms on which the revolutionary enterprise could be secured and perpetuated. Both—not simply the first but the second as well—were grounded in the self-evident truths of Jefferson's Declaration and their necessary consequence: "whenever any form of government becomes destructive of these ends, it is the right of the people to alter or abolish it, and to institute new government, laying its foundations . . . in such form, as to them shall seem most likely to effect their safety and happiness."

The "simple voice of nature and reason"—of *Common Sense*—pronounced the first principle of founding. There simplicity ended. The American founding project, as Madison defined it in *The Federalist,* demanded extraordinary wisdom and judgment of a half-formed people who had just accomplished "a revolution which has no parallel in the annals of human society."[2] A novel constitutional design must provide what the lawgivers of all ages had failed to discover: "a Republican remedy for the diseases most incident to republican government."[3] An unprecedented form of union must cure the fatal weakness and confusion that post-Revolutionary America shared with all past confederacies.[4] In sum, a measure of popular liberty such as men had rarely known and never long sustained must be reconciled with that full measure of governmental power necessary to secure the rights, the safety, and the happiness of society.

The founding of the American Republic seemed a task for demigods. Modern republican teaching made it the business of men—first the chosen few of Philadelphia, then the broadly representative state conventions—meeting from day to day to resolve inevitable conflicts of interest and opinion by the painful process of deliberation and consent. The ancient way of calling on the gods was not after all so strange to Publius-Madison. If against great odds a good constitution should be established in America,

---

[2] No. 14, p. 89.
[3] No. 10, p. 65.
[4] No. 14, p. 89; Nos. 18–20, *passim;* No. 39, p. 257.

he wrote, men of pious reflection might well perceive in it "a finger of that Almighty hand which has been so frequently extended to our relief." [5]

Madison's contribution to *The Federalist* presents an extended commentary on the complex problems of founding that followed from the simple principles of nature and reason. At the threshold he had to face a profound dilemma. In principle, the right of the people to institute new government is joined to their right to alter or abolish old government. In fact, America had passed from Revolution to founding; and the bloody history of past republics taught the risk of entering upon an endless cycle of political creation and destruction. How, then, could one defend the work of founding without either inviting chaos or abandoning the fundamental right of the people to make and unmake the laws? Madison's subtle interweaving of political understanding with bold principle, of founding prudence with founding right, offers a revealing introduction to the reasoning of Publius and, beyond that, to the mind of the Revolutionary generation.

Philadelphia: The Right of Founding

Patrick Henry smelled a rat in Philadelphia and stayed home. The scent of conspiracy spread through the states during the momentous spring and summer of 1787. After the Convention adjourned and its work was revealed, suspicion became ugly fact for many Antifederalists. Convened by Congress for "the sole and express purpose" of recommending changes in the Articles of Confederation, a secret conclave of ambitious notables had betrayed their trust and formed a design to subvert the liberties of America. The enterprise of the Philadelphia Convention, its enemies charged, carried the taint of a counterrevolutionary coup.

[5] No. 37, p. 238.

In the pages of *The Federalist,* Publius-Madison assumed the main burden of proving the legitimacy of the Constitutional Convention and its plan. By what right did the Founders propose a new regime for America? As Madison recognized, the very existence of the Convention was extraconstitutional, although an act of Congress and the compliance of twelve states practically covered that defect.[6] His own instructions from Virginia, like those of other delegates, gave only the authority to devise, discuss, and report "such Alterations and farther Provisions as may be necessary to render the Federal Constitution adequate to the Exigencies of the Union."[7] This was, prima facie, a commission to reform, not transform, the Confederation. Moreover, by proposing to refer the new Constitution to state ratifying conventions and to ignore the rule of unanimity for amending the Articles, the Convention flagrantly violated the terms of the existing federal compact in the most important respect: it redefined the very source of political authority.

The gravity of that last offense could not escape such a man as Madison, bred in the tradition of the compact philosophy. To say as he did that the Congress after the fact condoned the departure, and that few critics chose to challenge it, established only the general acceptance of a doubtful act.[8] The revolutionary character of the recommendation for a radically new mode of ratification was undeniable, and Madison was prepared finally to meet head-on this question "of a very delicate nature": "On what principle the confederation, which stands in the solemn form of a compact among the states, can be superceded without the unanimous consent of the parties to it?" The answer could be found at once "by recurring to the absolute necessity of the case; to the great principle of self-preserva-

---

[6] No. 40, p. 266.

[7] Max Farrand, ed., *The Records of the Federal Convention of 1787,* rev. ed., III (New Haven, 1966), 559–561.

[8] *The Federalist,* No. 40, p. 263.

tion; to the transcendent law of nature and of nature's God, which declares that the safety and happiness of society are the objects at which all political institutions aim, and to which all such institutions must be sacrificed." [9]

The most popular and damaging attacks on the legitimacy of the Convention passed over the important theoretical issue of ratification to seize upon the sweeping charge of usurpation by an antirepublican cabal. Addressing his defense to sober judges—"our most considerate and virtuous citizens" [10]—Madison unfolded his full argument cautiously. Here as elsewhere in *The Federalist*, Madison gladly offered timid men a technical excuse for acting boldly. Even in Revolutionary America, innovators had to overcome a certain natural conservatism. After a decade of frustration in and out of Congress, Madison could have repeated with conviction Jefferson's lesson of 1776 (and Locke's of a century before): "all experience hath shown that mankind are more disposed to suffer while evils are sufferable than to right themselves by abolishing the forms to which they are accustomed." If a part of mankind—our *least* considerate and virtuous citizens, such as those who followed Captain Shays—sometimes showed too little toleration for necessary evils and customary forms, then it was all the more important to persuade moderate men by circumspect reasoning to support a fundamental reform capable of restraining factious rebels. Prudence was not the same as timidity; good order and procedural nicety were not interchangeable terms.

With some delicacy, then, Madison advanced toward an appeal to revolutionary principles which might, if overdrawn, alarm the sober or incite the reckless. Perhaps there was no irreconcilable conflict between the end of framing a national authority adequate to its responsibilities and the prescribed means of piecemeal amendments. Perhaps the great principles of the proposed Constitution could be

[9] No. 43, p. 297.
[10] No. 10, p. 257.

construed merely as "the expansion of principles which are found in the articles of Confederation." Perhaps. To sensible observers, however, "the aspect of an entire transformation" of the old regime was no illusion.[11] "Suppose then," Madison asked, "that the expressions defining the authority of the Convention, were irreconcilably at variance with each other; that a *national* and *adequate government* could not possibly, in the judgment of the Convention, be effected by *alterations* and *provisions* in the *articles of confederation,* which part of the definition ought to have been embraced, and which rejected?"[12] A common rule of construction, founded on plain reason and legal axioms, required that the end control the means. Considering above all else "the happiness of the people of America," the Convention rightly chose to create an adequate national government, even if this meant violating the Articles.[13] By this double-jointed argument, Madison at once placed the work of the Convention within the broad limits of its commission, construed according to familiar legal principles, and introduced a final standard of judgment—the happiness of the people—that led straight back to the revolutionary doctrine of the Declaration.

Then he paused to explain the obvious. There had been no coup at Philadelphia, nor any sort of change in laws and men. The Convention had met, debated, resolved, reported, and adjourned. The delegates claimed no right for themselves to create or destroy constitutions and governments. Their plan "is to be of no more consequence than the paper on which it is written" unless the people ratify it.[14] Acting for and under "this supreme authority," the Founders had only the duty to give wise counsel to their masters. Insofar as they passed the limits of their regular authority, they could find a sure defense in the ultimate

[11] No. 40, pp. 262–263.
[12] No. 40, p. 260.
[13] No. 40, pp. 259–260.
[14] No. 40, p. 264.

power of the people whose interests and will they served. Precisely because the Convention was a temporary instrument of popular sovereignty, it was obliged to look beyond the literal terms of its commission and, if necessary, the terms of the existing Federal compact itself. The approbation of the people would "blot out all antecedent errors and irregularities"; their disapproval "would destroy [the proposed plan] forever." [15] Again Madison comforted respectable citizens who prized standard forms of legality and legitimacy in order to nerve them for audacious decisions based finally on revolutionary principles. The Convention, being merely the author of a paper plan, was permitted and even obliged to stretch its counsels to the widest limits that the situation of the country required. The people shall be judge.

The extraordinary conduct of the Convention delegates flowed, then, from the extraordinary situation of their sovereign principals. For Madison, the exercise of popular sovereignty was neither an abstract formality nor a formless gush of spontaneous sentiment and energy. The Convention lacked authority to revolutionize the political order in its own right; the people at large could not act effectively for themselves. In the name of the people, and subject to their consent, the Founders were obliged to chart a new and more noble course. The history of revolutions, properly understood, pointed the way.

> They must have reflected, that in all great changes of established governments, forms ought to give way to substance; that a rigid adherence in such cases to the former, would render nominal and nugatory the transcendent and precious right of the people to 'abolish or alter their governments as to them shall seem most likely to effect their safety and happiness;' since it is impossible for the people spontaneously and universally, to move in concert towards their object; and it is therefore essential, that such

---

[15] No. 40, pp. 265–266.

> changes be instituted by some *informal and unauthorised propositions,* made by some patriotic and respectable citizen or number of citizens.[16]

It was the American Revolution in particular that offered the compelling precedent. On one side, those who attacked the Convention out of "an overscrupulous jealousy of danger to the rights of the people"[17] could not easily repudiate the example of the Revolution that had established American freedom. On the other, "our most considerate and virtuous citizens" who feared anarchy could accept the example of the Revolution that they themselves had led into the paths of order. Madison of course was one of them. He could speak for the Convention to its natural friends.

> They must have recollected that it was by this irregular and assumed privilege of proposing to the people plans for their safety and happiness, that the States were first united against the danger with which they were threatened by their antient government; that Committees and Congresses, were formed for concentrating their efforts, and defending their rights; and that *Conventions* were *elected* in *the several States*, for establishing the constitutions under which they are now governed; nor could it have been forgotten that no little ill-timed scruples, no zeal for adhering to ordinary forms, were any where seen, except in those who wished to indulge under these masks, their secret enmity to the substance contended for.[18]

Once more in 1787 America confronted a great crisis. The "hopes and expectations of the great body of citizens" were turned to the Convention. The Founders' choice was plain: they could exercise "a manly confidence in their country, by whose confidence they had been so peculiarly distinguished" and point out a system "capable in their judgment

[16] No. 40, p. 265.
[17] No. 1, p. 5.
[18] No. 40, p. 265.

of securing its happiness"; or they could take "the cold and sullen resolution" of sacrificing substance to forms and earn the condemnation of "the impartial world," of "the friends of mankind," and of "every virtuous citizen." [19]

The supreme object of the founding, Madison insisted, was "the real welfare of the great body of the people." [20] Thus founders were obliged when necessary to sacrifice means to ends, forms to substance, standing laws and institutions to the public good. They must make their formal instructions fit their broad responsibilities as agents of the people in the exercise of the highest sovereign power: forming a new regime for a new nation. Publius-Madison would happily persuade his gentle readers that the Convention acted well within its commission, that the new Constitution merely rearranged and strengthened the old, that established local institutions would retain ample rights and powers. Yet knowing the strength of old loyalties and habits, the prevalence of suspicion toward the "cabal" at Philadelphia, the real boldness of the Convention's innovations, Madison did not hesitate to seize upon the revolutionary principles and precedents that finally could sustain his case. However: short of a profound degeneration of the political order and of the American character, once would be enough. Founding, as the constructive phase of revolution, should be a unique, or at most a rare and extraordinary, event.

Successors: The Prudence of Founding

Publius-Madison argued with uncommon urgency that a second convention to accommodate the critics of the first would be futile and, in its consequences, fatal to the cause of Union and republican government. He did not retract his defense of the right of founding; rather he moved prudential considerations, never wholly out of sight, to the center of the case. Necessity justified the

[19] No. 40, p. 266.
[20] No. 45, p. 309.

"irregular and assumed privilege of proposing to the people plans for their safety and happiness" during the Revolution and again at Philadelphia.[21] Political crisis made its own laws, though by no means arbitrary ones. In the situation of 1787–1788, a cold formalism would have exposed the young republic to "the uncertainty of delay, and the hazard of events," and thus to dissolution and death.[22]

Critics of the Convention plan held contrary notions of its faults, offered conflicting remedies, and often proposed no real cure for the mortal diseases of the Confederation. Indeed, collectively they represented just that Babel of social interests, private opinions, and party animosities that the Convention had managed to resolve or reconcile by an almost miraculous exercise of wisdom, moderation, public spirit, and good will.[23] Assume the worst of the Convention and the best of its opponents, Publius-Madison suggested, with a wicked wit that lightened his Roman gravity for a moment, and imagine that the country called upon those most sagacious Antifederalists to form a new convention with full powers to revise the original work—"though it required some effort to view [the experiment] seriously even in fiction."

> . . . I leave it to be decided by the sample of opinions just exhibited, . . . whether the Constitution, now before the public, would not stand as fair a chance for immortality, as Lycurgus gave to that of Sparta, by making its change to depend on his own return from exile and death, if it were to be immediately adopted, and were to continue in force, not until a BETTER, but ANOTHER should be agreed upon by this new assembly of Lawgivers.[24]

Founding led the nation into treacherous waters, lighted only by the warning beacons of history. Masters of modern political philosophy, Machiavelli and Rousseau

---

[21] No. 40, p. 266.
[22] *Ibid.*
[23] No. 37, pp. 237–239.
[24] No. 38, p. 246.

among them, had argued that it could only be the work of one great genius, a mortal god.[25] Madison was more inclined to share Hamilton's preference for the "judicious reflections" of David Hume: "To balance a large state or society (says he) whether monarchical or republican, on general laws, is a work of so great difficulty, that no human genius, however comprehensive, is able by mere dint of reason and reflection, to effect it."[26] With or without the gifts of genius, a founding convention faced almost insuperable problems of its own.

The example of the Greeks—the appearance among them of single lawgivers—did not persuade Publius-Madison. On the contrary, it taught him "to admire the improvement made by America on the ancient mode of preparing and establishing regular plans of government." Indeed, how could sober and enlightened Americans think of imitating a country where the wisest and best lawgivers, in order to win popular consent for their reforms, had to wrap their laws in mystery, summon voices from on high or from the grave, bend reason to prejudice as Solon did, or, like Lycurgus, abandon country and life itself as a pledge of disinterested motives? Nonetheless, Greek history should warn Americans of "the hazards and difficulties" incident to their own founding experiments, and of "the great imprudence of unnecessarily multiplying them."[27] Modern experience only confirmed those ancient fears of founding by convention. The bleak record of Dutch efforts to reform "the baneful and notorious vices of their Constitution" weighed heavily for republicans amid the cumulative evidence of failure. "The history of almost all the great councils and consultations, held among mankind for reconciling their discordant opinions, assuaging their mutual jealousies, and adjusting their respective interests, is a

[25] See Machiavelli, *The Discourses,* Bk. I, ch. ix; Rousseau, *The Social Contract,* Bk. II, ch. vii.
[26] Publius-Hamilton quoting Hume in *The Federalist,* No. 85, p. 594.
[27] No. 38, p. 241.

history of factions, contentions, and disappointments; and may be classed among the most dark and degrading pictures which display the infirmities and depravities of the human character." The rare exceptions only served by contrast "to darken the gloom of the adverse prospect." In this dim light, Philadelphia seemed indeed a miracle.[28]

Like Hume, Madison called for modesty, moderation, and patience in the face of a task almost beyond the scope of human genius; for a reliance on judgment, experience, and time to amend the inevitable errors of the Founders—all of this after the first bold experiment had been launched.

Is it an unreasonable conjecture that the errors "which may be contained in the plan of the Convention are such as have resulted rather from the defect of antecedent experience on this complicated and difficult subject, than from a want of accuracy or care in the investigation of it; and consequently such as will not be ascertained until an actual trial shall have pointed them out?"[29] Madison fully expected that such errors would manifest themselves in time, not only for the reasons Hume had given but still more because the Constitution represented in some of its important features—the provisions affecting slavery, for example, or the equal allocation of Senate seats—an accommodation to present views and interests that deviated from fundamental principles of the republican regime. Views and interests would change with changing circumstances, above all, perhaps, with the new conditions created by the operation of the Constitution itself upon American society. Nor could one exclude the possibility of further progress in the science of politics, as in all the arts and sciences of modern civilization. If Americans could claim the merit of discovering valuable principles and forms of popular government unknown to their ancient and modern teachers, perhaps future lawgivers standing

---

[28] No. 37, pp. 238–239.
[29] No. 48, pp. 241–242.

on their shoulders would discern still greater possibilities. Madison did not press the point.[30]

Granting the continual growth of experience and knowledge, the inevitable change of circumstances, and of course the inalienable right of future generations to alter or abolish forms of government, Madison nonetheless approached the question of future constitutional revision most delicately. The constitutional foundations of the American Republic were designed to endure for ages. Prudent adaptation and technical adjustment, rather than basic reconstruction, would be the likely tasks of later generations. Madison's strong case against an immediate second convention applied, with somewhat less severity, to any frequent and substantial revision of the fundamental law. It was hard for him to imagine a convention after Philadelphia that would not shake the political order and threaten the achievement of the Founders. Only the people could judge revolutions and constitutions; but one should not ask too much of them, too often.

Madison granted that the provision of "a constitutional road to the decision of the people . . . for certain great and extraordinary occasions" followed necessarily from republican principles.[31] Here was a lawful way to change the fundamental laws without recourse to "irregular and assumed privilege." But "great and extraordinary occasions" meant one thing, regular reviews of the fundamental law quite another. The distinction became fully apparent as Madison turned his attention to Jefferson's plan for occasional conventions to mend breaches in the Constitution, and to the equally misguided provision in Pennsylvania's state constitution of 1776 for septennial appeals to the people on constitutional issues through a Council of Censors.

Jefferson's scheme raised "insuperable objections."

---

[30] See No. 10 *passim;* No. 14, pp. 83–85, 88–89; No. 38, p. 241; No. 39, pp. 250–257; No. 47, pp. 324–327; No. 63, pp. 426–428.
[31] No. 49, p. 339.

It would almost certainly fail in its special object of "maintaining the constitutional equilibrium" among the three great departments of government.[32] Whatever the substantive result might be, however, simply making the experiment involved grave dangers. Frequent conventions called by any two branches of government threatened to open an abyss, for constitutional questions penetrated to the roots of sovereignty and loyalty. The "honorable determination . . . to rest all our experiments on the capacity of mankind for self-government"[33]—and for establishing and changing the foundations of government—did not rest on blind faith in the people. Madison meant a rational confidence, with conditions. Those conditions grew out of his understanding of the springs of political conduct. No passage of *The Federalist* tells more of Madisonian prudence than his critique of his friend Jefferson:

> As every appeal to the people would carry an implication of some defect in the government, frequent appeals would in great measure deprive the government of that veneration, which time bestows on every thing, and without which perhaps the wisest and freest governments would not possess the requisite stability. If it be true that all governments rest on opinion, it is no less true that the strength of opinion in each individual, and its practical influence on his conduct, depend much on the number which he supposes to have entertained the same opinion. The reason of man, like man himself is timid and cautious, when left alone; and acquires firmness and confidence, in proportion to the number with which it is associated. When the examples, which fortify opinion, are *antient* as well as *numerous*, they are known to have a double effect. In a nation of philosophers, this consideration ought to be disregarded. A reverence for the laws, would be sufficiently inculcated by the voice of an enlightened reason. But a nation of philosophers is as

[32] No. 49, pp. 339, 341.

[33] No. 39, p. 250.

> little to be expected as the philosophical race of kings wished for by Plato. And in every other nation, the most rational government will not find it a superfluous advantage, to have the prejudices of the community on its side.[34]

The classic version of the dissolution of government envisioned wild and bloody scenes of revolutionary mobs led by incendiary demagogues. The classic-American nightmare, peopled by Captain Shays and his "desperate debtors," could be—and was—used to shock respectable and complacent readers of *The Federalist* into awareness of the urgent need for creating a new order by extraordinary means.[35] Revolutionary founding was the alternative to revolutionary chaos. Contemplating Jefferson's proposed conventions, however, Madison projected a quite different threat of dissolution, far less dramatic, far more subtle. Continual questioning of the regime would gnaw at the vital prejudices of the community, the common faith that made men loyal citizens, until America—the real America and no imaginary "nation of philosophers"—slowly dissolved into its disconnected, self-regarding elements. There would be men but no citizens; a country but no nation; a dead body of laws. The danger for America was most extreme because free republics above all other forms of government "rest on opinion" in principle as well as practice.

The slow and quiet descent from questioning to systematic doubt to alienation was not the worst consequence of such frequent conventions as Jefferson projected. More serious still, Madison maintained, was "the danger of disturbing the public tranquility by interesting too strongly the public passions. . . ." The Revolution and the founding had been extraordinary occasions, and the manner in which they were met had done "much honour to the virtue and intelligence of the people of America." Nevertheless,

---

[34] No. 49, p. 340.

[35] Quoted phrase adapted from Hamilton's No. 6, p. 31; but Madison obviously has Shaysites in mind in No. 10, No. 51, and elsewhere.

Madison cautioned, such experiments "are of too ticklish a nature to be unnecessarily multiplied." [36] The bitter quarrel between Federalists and Antifederalists was a warning that even under the most favorable conditions the possibility of establishing "good government" by "reflection and choice" [37] would hang in doubt. The danger would become still more formidable in future conventions: "The *passions* . . . not *the reason,* of the public, would sit in judgment. But it is the reason of the public alone that ought to controul and regulate the government. The passions ought to be controuled and regulated by the government." [38] Jefferson's innocence in calling for such conventions contained the seeds of disaster, a point Madison believed to have been confirmed by Pennsylvania's Council of Censors and the violent partisanship that had erupted within it.[39]

The new order of the Founders, however, once established, offered a stable framework within which differences might be negotiated and the equilibrium of governmental departments maintained. The remedies it provided presupposed at once the rightful sovereignty of the people, their capacity for self-government, and the inevitable workings of passion, prejudice, and interest in human conduct. Making a virtue of necessity, Madison called for the multiplication of interests, views, and parties in society and government to the point that no one of them could impose its self-serving judgment on the rest; and for the establishment of a political order in which "the private interest of every individual, may be a centinel over the public rights." [40] "This policy of supplying by opposite and rival interests, the defect of better motives," he wrote, "might be traced through the whole system of human affairs, private as well as public." [41]

---

[36] No. 49, pp. 340–341.
[37] No. 1, p. 3. (Hamilton's words.)
[38] No. 49, p. 343.
[39] No. 50, pp. 344–346.
[40] No. 51, pp. 349, 351–353.
[41] No. 51, p. 349.

Yet those same influences, that same diversity of interests which can bring stability to a government already established, are likely to tear a constitutional convention apart: ". . . although this variety of interests . . . may have a salutary influence on the administration of the government when formed; yet everyone must be sensible of the contrary influence which must have been experienced in the task of forming it." [42] Why this self-evident "contrary influence" on founding?

One is left to infer Madison's meaning from other passages of *The Federalist.* First, he argued, questions of fundamental law, of the character of the regime, are vastly more difficult to settle by compromise of contending views and interests than are the ordinary issues of public policy. They involve the very terms on which men choose to live together in political society and submit life, liberty, and property to a common rule and judge. They stir the deepest hopes and fears, unleash the greatest passions.[43] Moreover, the inherent complexity of the founding task—viewing the whole of society at once, encompassing all its diversities of condition and culture, balancing the variety of political forms and functions in a working system, anticipating long-run change and providing for its consequences: this must strain human capacity to its outer limits and open endless sources of division.[44]

The first founding, one would think, should be the most vulnerable to contending interests and jealousies, since men at the beginning would not yet see the common ground that underlay their ordinary differences, feel the benefits of citizenship, revere the law embodying their own consent, respect the equal rights of fellow citizens, which might in turn prepare them to accept the sacrifice of a part of their desires to secure the rest—to subordinate short-run interests to the safety and happiness of their society over years and generations. That Madison nevertheless focused

[42] No. 51, p. 349; No. 37, pp. 237–238.
[43] See Nos. 38, 49, 50, *passim.*
[44] See Nos. 37–38 *passim.*

his fears on future tests of founding suggests his great reliance on favorable historical circumstances: on proximity to the common revolutionary struggle uniting minds and hearts, on the extremity of the crisis of 1787 compelling men to agree upon a rational if imperfect solution or face political death. No doubt, too, this emphasis reflects his estimate of the original founders, that extraordinary body called by the doubting Thomas Jefferson "an assembly of demigods," [45] as compared to any probable successors.[46]

Madison intended to save the constitutional convention for extreme situations in which revolutionary principles or their equivalent within the Constitution would apply. A desperate national crisis, as he perceived it, justified the work at Philadelphia. Nothing less would warrant a repetition. With some reluctance he later led the first Congress in drafting amendments that became the Bill of Rights. Yet this was the most cautious of available approaches to constitutional revision, using governmental channels and minimizing the direct appeal to the people. Indeed he viewed this course of action as the best way to avoid a second convention or a still more dangerous recourse to extralegal methods of reform.[47] In the troubled times of 1798–1800 he did see a grave national crisis; he appealed to the people of Virginia and America for a "recurrence to fundamental principles," and included a new federal convention among the proper means that might save the republic from Federalist tyranny. For Madison, it seemed to be 1787 again, perhaps 1776. Once more revolutionary thoughts flowed freely.[48]

But however such later evidence may affect our under-

---

[45] Jefferson to John Adams, Aug. 30, 1787, in *The Adams-Jefferson Letters*, I (Chapel Hill, N.C., 1959), 196.

[46] See above.

[47] Madison to Jefferson, Oct. 17, 1788, in Meyers, *Mind of the Founder*, pp. 203–209; Speech in Congress, June 8, 1789, *ibid.*, pp. 210–228.

[48] "Report on the Virginia Resolutions," *ibid.*, pp. 297–349.

standing, Madison in the name of Publius seemed to exhaust his arguments for constitutional conventions in defending the first founders. Beyond Philadelphia, prudence suggested that constitutional construction within the original frame of government would represent the necessary and proper continuation of founding by other means. Lawgiving, Madison believed, was not completed with a stroke of the pen and a formal act of ratification. It would not be revised solely or chiefly by another stroke, another act, although the natural and legal right to do so remained complete. The shape and quality of the de facto Constitution as it emerged out of the play of interests and opinions, passions and judgments, institutions and powers, would define the achievement of the Philadelphia Convention.

The regime projected in 1787 left ample room for ad hoc constructive lawgiving and gave sufficient means for realizing the public good, the safety and happiness of society. Without "recurring more or less to the doctrine of *construction* or *implication*" the legislature would be paralyzed and the Constitution "would be a dead letter." To limit legislation to cases of expressly delegated power would only leave Congress with the old dilemma of abandoning "all real authority" or construing the limitation to mean nothing. To enumerate in the Constitution every act necessary and proper for carrying out the broad objects of public policy would be patently absurd.

> The attempt would have involved a complete digest of laws on every subject to which the Constitution relates; accommodated too not only to the existing state of things, but to all the possible changes which futurity may produce: For in every new application of a general power, the *particular powers,* which are the means of attaining the *object* of the general power, must always necessarily vary with that object; and be often properly varied whilst the object remains the same.[49]

[49] *The Federalist,* No. 44, pp. 303–305.

In short, the legislature would necessarily fill in the broad outlines of the Constitution, adapting it to the inevitable and imperfectly predictable "changes which futurity may produce": changes in the situation of the country and thus in the practical meaning of the objects of the general powers of government. Abuses of that great trust would be controlled by executive veto, judicial review, or in the last resort "by the election of more faithful representatives." [50] As always, this last was the sovereign remedy.

In this revision of the Constitution from within, no small matters were at stake and no mere mechanical balance of governmental agencies would determine the result. Thus the assumption of constructive powers involved the very form and function of the national government, and this in turn involved the very form and function of the Union. Finally, the great forces inherent in the Founders' complex republican form of popular government would shape the operative meaning of the fundamental law. Checks and balances, the rivalries of state and national governments, the competition of interests and parties, would work out "the sum of the differences": a reasonable approximation of justice serving both private rights and "the permanent and aggregate interests of the community." [51] Enlightened statesmen and skilled judges would point the way. But the decisive judgment, in revision as in founding, would come from the ultimate source of political authority prescribed by Revolutionary and republican principles: the voice of the people.

This was the fixed point and the invariable test of the system. "The first question," Madison proposed,

> . . . is, whether the general form and aspect of the government be strictly republican? It is evident that no other form would be reconcilable with the genius of the people of America; with the fundamental principles of the revolution; or with that honorable

---

[50] No. 44, p. 305.

[51] No. 10, p. 57 and *passim;* No. 51 *passim.*

> determination, which animates every votary of freedom, to rest all our experiments on the capacity of mankind for self-government. If the plan of the Convention therefore be found to depart from the republican character, its advocates must abandon it as no longer defensible.[52]

The judgment of the people on the original work of founding was vulnerable enough to error; more dangerous still were the disintegrative forces of passion and faction and doubt that would be loose if future conventions should be allowed to reopen fundamental questions of the regime. The prudence of founding rested on just such perceptions; Madison was quite aware that the people acting within the forms of the Constitution—even the best of constitutions—might become their own worst enemies before sober second thought took over. Yet he could not deny the legitimacy of popular sovereignty. Madison could maintain the conviction, moreover, that popular judgment on great public questions would on the whole and in the long run prove sound.

Madison's discussion of the case for a new Union with expanding powers rode roughshod over Antifederalist objections. The ends and means of popular government, founded on Revolutionary principles, must decide the issue. His rhetoric rose to an uncommonly high pitch:

> . . . if, in a word the Union be essential to the happiness of the people of America, is it not preposterous, to urge as an objection to a government without which the objects of the Union cannot be attained, that such a government may derogate from the importance of the Governments of the individual states? Was then the American revolution effected, was the American confederacy formed, was the precious blood of thousands spilt, and the hard earned substance of millions lavished, not that the people of America should enjoy peace, liberty and safety; but that . . . particular municipal establishments,

[52] No. 39, p. 250.

> might enjoy a certain extent of power, and be arrayed with certain dignities and attributes of sovereignty? We have heard of the impious doctrine in the old world that the people were made for Kings, not Kings for people. Is the same doctrine to be revived in the new, in another shape, that the solid happiness of the people is to be sacrificed to the views of political institutions of a different form? It is too early for politicians to presume on our forgetting that the public good, the real welfare of the great body of the people is the supreme object to be pursued; and that no form of government whatever, has any other value, than as it may be fitted for the attainment of this object.[53]

The ends of the regime—"peace, liberty and safety," "solid happiness," "the real welfare of the great body of the people"—are precisely of the sort that the people themselves can judge, case by case. Not ingenious theory but ordinary experience, the felt burdens and benefits of government, will instruct their choice. Thus, looking to the prospective development of the constitutional order with reference to the same question of growing central power, Madison concluded: "If . . . the people should in future become more partial to the federal than to the state governments, the change can only result, from such manifest and irresistable proofs of a better administration, as will overcome all their antecedent propensities. And in that case, the people ought not surely to be precluded from giving most of their confidence where they may discover it to be most due. . . ." [54]

Degeneration: Revolution Reconsidered

The original founding—the one that had occurred at Philadelphia—rested for its legitimacy on Revolutionary

[53] No. 45, p. 309.
[54] No. 46, p. 317.

principle. Short of necessity, prudence recommended to Publius-Madison no further tests of founding by convention, even when the laws permitted. Chronic revolution, or more probably some silent course of dissolution, could well become the lawless law of the land. Construction (to be later known as "broad construction"), which was the continuation of founding by other means, offered a salutary way of reforming law within the Constitution, consistent with that principle of popular sovereignty underlying both the founding and the Republic that it had made. Madison found every reason to expect that the future would fulfill the ends of founding in the spirit of the laws.

Antifederalists were still more certain that this misbegotten Constitution would quickly degenerate into oligarchy or tyranny. In their unclassical view, aristocracy, monarchy, or merely national consolidation would be no less corrupt forms of government. Once the people of the states were seduced or badgered into giving their consent, the counterfeit robes of republican and federal virtue would fall away to reveal the beast, Leviathan. Publius-Madison was himself enough of a neo-Roman to acknowledge the cyclical theory of constitutional decay, enough of a modern republican and federalist to suspect that power could corrupt, and quite enough of a political realist to see the practical importance first of listening to such familiar prophecies of doom and then of answering them. Much of his defense of the Convention and its work in *The Federalist* was designed expressly to demonstrate first the wholly popular and sufficiently federal nature of the new regime, and then its capacity to maintain that character, if not indefinitely, at least for the foreseeable future. Prophetic powers he firmly disclaimed, for either himself or others.

The heart of the problem, present and prospective, was simply that: "In framing a government which is to be administered by men over men, the great difficulty lies in this: You must first enable the government to controul the governed; and in the next page, oblige it to controul itself."[55] Men, not angels; men, not philosophers.[56] Within the frame of the Constitution, government must have ample and efficient power to control the people under the rule of law. Voting, supplemented by a complex system of balances in society and government, must secure the people against usurpation and tyranny. What if the controls should fail? Envisioning the worst fate of the new Republic, the inevitable doom pronounced by Antifederalist prophets, Madison was drawn back to the problem of revolution.

The Antifederalists professed to foresee all manner of antirepublican perversions to which the new Constitution was susceptible; these would bring about a dissolution of government and society and would in turn necessitate and justify a second revolution. Publius-Madison, on the other hand, insisted that ratification of this Constitution was precisely the way in which these very perversions were best prevented. No second revolution need occur: nearly every page of *The Federalist* is dedicated to showing how the causes which might render one necessary would be removed.

Publius's reply to the charge that Congress would become an instrument of class oppression epitomizes this view and puts it all on the very highest republican ground. The constitutional provisions governing the election, organization, powers, and duties of the House of Representatives, all taken together, go to establish between rulers and ruled a "communion of interests and sympathy of sentiments of which few governments have furnished examples; but without which every government degenerates into tyranny." Was it really conceivable that a House so designed would endeavor to exempt its members, or any favored class, from the operation of the laws? No: in the Lockean philosophy to which all subscribed, there could be no civil society worthy of the name without equal laws

[55] No. 51, p. 349.
[56] *Ibid.;* No. 49, p. 340.

binding legislature, prince, and people all alike. Standing as guarantee and restraint was "the genius of the whole system, the nature of just and constitutional laws, and above all the vigilant and manly spirit which actuates the people of America, a spirit which nourishes freedom, and in return is nourished by it.

"If this spirit shall ever be so debased as to tolerate a law not obligatory on the legislature as well as on the people, the people will be prepared to tolerate anything but liberty." [57] With this, the very possibility and even the value of republican government were called into question. Madison did not doubt that there was "a degree of depravity in mankind" which required a "degree of circumspection and distrust." But did it require that much? "Were the pictures which have been drawn by the political jealousy of some among us, faithful likenesses of the human character, the inference would be that there is not sufficient virtue among men for self-government; and that nothing less than the chains of despotism can restrain them from destroying and devouring one another." [58]

Among innumerable horrors, the one that most obsessed the Antifederalists was the "inevitable" perversion of the new regime by national usurpation of state powers. Madison pursued the argument with its own logic. Suppose against all reason that the balances built into the political order failed, that the natural attachment of the people to their states somehow was overcome, that the state governments acting singly could not arrest the progress of the evil.

> But ambitious encroachments of the Fœderal Government . . . would not excite the opposition of a single state or of a few states only. They would be signals of general alarm. Every Government would espouse the common cause. A correspondence would be opened. Plans of resistance would be concerted. One spirit would animate and conduct the whole.

---

[57] No. 57, pp. 386–387.
[58] No. 55, p. 378.

> The same combination in short would result from an apprehension of the fœderal, as was produced by the dread of a foreign yoke; and unless the projected innovations should be voluntarily renounced, the same appeal to a trial of force would be made. . . .[59]

Grant, for the moment, "the visionary supposition that the Fœderal Government may previously accumulate a military force for the projects of ambition." [60] Yet the power of an armed people, with their own local governments to organize and direct them, would overwhelm any standing army that a jealous imagination could invent.

Madison thus allowed himself to glimpse the possibility of legitimate revolutionary resistance to national usurpation, and affirmed his confidence in the capacity of Americans to maintain their rights, even against the (imaginary) hireling legions of a federal despot. If the government were to degenerate into a tyranny, it could only be because the people themselves were corrupt beyond redemption. They would then neither care for liberty nor know how to use and keep it. On that profoundly antirepublican assumption, they would be no more capable of recovering their rights by revolution, and restoring "all things to their pristine order," [61] than they would be of governing themselves under a good republican constitution.

Candor as well as political strategy directed Madison to consider another source of perversion and a more direct road to revolution. The kind of despotism the Antifederalists feared was not, in his view, among "the diseases most incident to Republican Government" or, indeed, to federal systems. It was, on the contrary, "instability, injustice, and confusion"—the evils characteristic of popular misrule—that had destroyed past republics and driven the American Confederacy itself to the edge of catastrophe.[62] A justified

[59] No. 46, p. 320.
[60] *Ibid.*
[61] No. 63, p. 429.
[62] No. 10, pp. 56–57, 65.

Revolutionary impulse—"the absolute necessity of the case," "the great principle of self-preservation" [63]—had led a desperate people to demand a radical remedy. It had been the task of the Founders to guide that Revolutionary impulse into wise constructive courses.

One way or another, men would find a remedy for the "instability, injustice, and confusion" of a faction-ridden polity, as they had always found an escape from the inconvenience of the state of nature. And republican remedies were not the only kind: men might be brought to the point of embracing almost any cure that seemed to promise a decent, orderly, and reasonably comfortable civil existence, even though "liberty be lost in the pursuit." [64]

The case of Rhode Island might well be one that could turn out either way. "It can be little doubted," Madison predicted, "that if the state of Rhode Island was separated from the confederacy, and left to itself, the insecurity of rights under the popular form of government within such narrow limits, would be displayed by such reiterated oppressions of factious majorities, that some power altogether independent of the people would soon be called for by the voice of the very factions whose misrule had proved the necessity of it." [65] The wild Rhode Islanders would find themselves in a state of anarchy, no better than "a state of nature where the weaker individual is not secured against the violence of the stronger"; and sooner or later they would be prepared—the stronger parties no less than the weaker—to buy social peace and security at almost any price. Grave Publius may finally have cracked a smile as he suggested that the most fanatical of American democrats and localists—so fearful for their republican and federal virtue that they would not even send a delegate to Philadelphia—would soon be calling king or nobles to their rescue. And the summons would come not merely from the victims of popular frenzy but from the very

[63] No. 43, p. 297.
[64] No. 51, p. 352.
[65] *Ibid.*

villains frightened by their own powers of destruction. Yet Madison was quite serious: if this response to chaos could be expected in Rhode Island, of all places, it would do as much to prove the universality of his argument as would his analogy to the state of nature, the original condition of all mankind.[66]

Madison undoubtedly thought that the road to revolution passed most commonly through the despoiled estates of "our most considerate and virtuous citizens, equally the friends of public and private faith, and of public and personal liberty. . . ." These would feel immediately "the superior force of an interested and over-bearing majority," and they would echo their "distrust of public engagements, and alarm for private rights" from "one end of the continent to the other." Under popular government, such oppression of the few by the many, the legal majority, could operate within perverted forms of the law. But also, as Shays and Company made alarmingly clear, it could take the path of violent mob action incited by demagogues. Driven to the wall, substantial citizens might well become alienated from the republic and seek justice—that justice which consists in the keeping of contractual promises, the securing of private rights and possessions, the fair treatment of the party of the few by the government of the many, the rule of law and the maintenance of public order: seek it "until it be obtained, or until liberty be lost in the pursuit."

Yet Madison's appeal was, after all, not to a beleaguered few but to public opinion. For in the last analysis the primary source of revolution lay not so much in the distresses of a minority as in the experience of the great body of the people. It was *their* safety, their happiness, that would be threatened by instability, injustice, and confusion, by political anarchy and impotence no less than by usurpation and tyranny. It was not so paradoxical that the people could be at once their own enemies—though never

[66] No. 10, p. 57.

intentionally or permanently—and their own healers. Their recourse lay either in the Constitution or in something far more drastic.[67]

Somehow the Antifederalists, with all their alarums, failed to understand that the dominant side of human nature in America was really its conservative side. But Publius-Madison understood it. Pressing his appeal to the good sense of the people against political evils that were largely the result of popular influence, he declared that bills of attainder, ex post facto laws, and laws impairing the obligation of contract were "contrary to the first principles of the social compact, and to every principle of sound legislation." [68] And if the people drunk might drive the propertied and learned classes to despair and rebellion unless they could find security within a well-made constitution, the people sober would see themselves among the chief victims of their own folly, support in time the means and agents of stability in government, favor useful constitutional reforms, and failing these, withdraw their own allegiance from a republic that could not banish speculative exploiters, give a regular course to *their* business. Long before the Jacksonians, Madison discovered the argument that excessive and arbitrary legislative interference with private rights and interests—even by popular representatives—could profit the few at the expense of the many.[69]

The clincher, finally, was that along with liberty must go energy—a principle supported no less by Publius-Madison than by Publius-Hamilton. Fully acknowledging the demands of "the genius of Republican liberty" for popular sovereignty, frequent elections, short terms of office, and a government of numerous representatives, Madison firmly insisted on the parallel conclusion:

> Energy in Government is essential to that security against external and internal danger, and to that prompt and salutary execution of the laws, which

[67] No. 63, pp. 424–425.
[68] No. 44, pp. 301–302.
[69] No. 62, pp. 421–422.

> enter into the very definition of good Government. Stability in Government is essential to national character, and to the advantages annexed to it, as well as to *that repose and confidence in the minds of the people, which are among the chief blessings of civil society.* An irregular and mutable legislation, is not more an evil in itself, than it is odious to the people; and it may be pronounced with assurance, that the people of this country, enlightened as they are, with regard to the nature, and interested, as the great body of them are, in the effects of good Government, will never be satisfied, till some remedy be applied to the vicissitudes and uncertainties, which characterize the state administrations.[70]

Such a people, properly informed and led, would be a consequential force for establishing the new regime and preserving it against dissolution by chaotic or despotic tendencies. It went without saying that such a people would also be a potential force for fundamental change should the new order prove as feeble, erratic, and incompetent as the old.

1776 marked a noble and necessary Revolution, 1787 a wise and necessary act of founding based on revolutionary right. The well-tempered and well-balanced Republic of the Founders offered every rational hope that America would prudently continue founding by constructive means in the spirit of the laws, and would arrest any tendency toward despotic or aristocratic degeneration. A free people commanding sovereign power and bearing arms would maintain their essential rights and interests against corrupt rulers of every sort by every means within the laws or even, in the last resort, by revolutionary resistance such as they had carried through triumphantly in 1776. The same people in another character, the sober and enlightened citizens of America seeking their own safety and

[70] No. 37, pp. 233–234. Emphasis added.

repose and solid happiness, would, at least on second thought, repudiate those blind passions and momentary interests driving them into the fatal paths of instability, injustice, and confusion. The state of nature inevitably passing over into a state of war had been and always would be intolerable: for the strong as well as the weak, the many as well as the few. The "great principle of self-preservation," "the transcendent law of nature and of nature's God," at once explained and justified revolution, explained and justified the universal forming of civil society and the particular founding of the new American Republic.

None of this meant for Publius-Madison a guarantee of eternal social peace and order under the silent operation of the laws of the Republic. He was quite as ready as Hamilton to arm the magistrate with a sharp sword to cut down either antirepublican reaction or domestic violence in the states. Suppressing local insurrection by national force raised difficult questions, though Montesquieu's *Spirit of the Laws* served as an enlightened guide. "At first view it might not seem to square with the republican theory, to suppose either that a majority have not the right, or that a minority will have the force to subvert a government; and consequently that the fœderal interposition can never be required but when it would be improper. But," Madison quickly added in the authentic voice of neo-Publius, "theoretic reasoning in this, as in most other cases, must be qualified by the lessons of practice." [71]

What Madison's appeal to the "practical" amounted to here was a special kind of argument by analogy using salutary prejudice to counter harmful prejudice: why should not federal power be available for the protection of state rights? "Why may not illicit combinations for purposes of violence be formed as well by a majority of a State, especially a small State, as by a majority of a county or a district of the same State; and if the authority of the State ought in the latter case to protect the local mag-

[71] No. 43, p. 293.

istracy, ought not the fœderal authority in the former support the State authority?" [72] Yet whoever the insurgent force might be, it would be far better that "the superintending power" should repress the violence; and the standing threat of national interposition would "generally prevent the necessity of exerting it." This view of a superintending power enforcing order in the provinces, joined to his similar argument for national guardianship of republican forms against local ambition and intrigue, forms a deeper impression of Madison's vision: that of a national society so closely knit that a single principle of government and a uniform condition of social peace must pervade the whole. Under the normal and expected workings of the Constitution this would occur through free choice, good habit, and salutary prejudice. When necessary, it could be imposed by force.[73]

For the extreme case of general mass insurrection, the final conflict, Publius-Madison offered no remedy or hope beyond the plan of the Founders for establishing a good republican regime in America. Just or unjust—and Madison had strongly indicated that only intolerable misrule could drive great masses over a broad country to revolution—such a popular uprising would leave government no serious political choice. All that could be said was that "the Fœderal Constitution . . . diminishes the risk of a calamity, for which no possible constitution can provide a cure." [74]

In short, while government had now been provided with all the powers needed to perform its ambitious tasks, Publius-Madison nonetheless recognized the impossibility of defending the Founders' work by force against a hostile society. A popular regime at war with the people is a contradiction. The decisive answer to the problem of revolution is a constitution that will attach the people to their country and their laws by the benefits it confers, the

[72] *Ibid.*
[73] No. 43, pp. 293–295.
[74] No. 43, p. 295.

burdens it lifts. Men are not angels or philosophers, a truth that applies to both rulers and ruled. There are no nations governing and governed by reason and virtue alone. The task of founding is to make the ordinary stuff of human nature—the interests and passions and prejudices as well as the saving gifts of intellect and character and spirit—serve the common good, the safety and happiness of society. Without the guidance and restraint of wise laws, the same human qualities will spread injustice and undermine the very basis of social life, "the necessary confidence between man and man." [75] They will reduce society to a state of war, drive government toward tyranny, and make enemies of fellow citizens and friends.

For Publius-Madison, the founding was a gentle revolution to end all revolutions, so far as the eye of reason and experience could see, and to give freedom and self-government a new life in America and ultimately "for the whole human race." [76]

---

[75] No. 44, pp. 300–302.
[76] No. 14, p. 89.

LINDA K. KERBER

Daughters of Columbia: Educating Women for the Republic, 1787–1805

"I EXPECT TO SEE our young women forming a new era in female history," wrote Judith Sargent Murray in 1798.[1] Her optimism was part of a general sense that all possibilities were open in the post-Revolutionary world; as Benjamin Rush put it, the first act of the republican drama had only begun. The experience of war had given words like "independence" and "self-reliance" personal as well as political overtones; among the things that ordinary folk had learned from wartime had been that the world could, as the song had it, turn upside down. The rich could quickly become poor, wives might suddenly have to manage family businesses; women might even, as the famous Deborah Gannett had done, shoulder a gun. Political theory taught that republics rested on the virtue of their citizens; revolutionary experience taught that it was useful to be prepared for a wide range of unusual possibilities.[2]

[1] *The Gleaner*, III (Boston, 1798), 189.

[2] Montesquieu's comment that republics differed from other political systems by the reliance they placed on

A desire to explore the possibilities republicanism now opened to women was expressed by a handful of articulate, urban, middle-class men and women. While only a very few writers—Charles Brockden Brown, Judith Sargent Murray, Benjamin Rush—devoted extensive attention to women and what they might become, many essayists explored the subject in the periodical literature. In the fashion of the day, they concealed their identity under pseudonyms like "Cordelia," "Constantia," or, simply, "A Lady." These expressions came largely from Boston, New York, and Philadelphia: cities which were the centers of publishing. The vitality of Philadelphia, as political and social capital, is well known; the presence of so many national legislators in the city, turning up as they did at dances and dinner parties, was no doubt intellectually invigorating, and not least for the women of Philadelphia. In an informal way, women shared many of the political excitements of the city. Philadelphia was the home of the Young Ladies' Academy, founded in 1786, with explicitly fresh ideas about women's education, and an enrollment of more than a hundred within two years; Benjamin Rush would deliver his "Thoughts upon Female Education" there. The first attempt at a magazine expressly addressed to women was made by the Philadelphia *Lady's Magazine and Repository*. Two of the most intense anonymous writers—"Sophia" and "Nitidia"—wrote for Philadelphia newspapers. And after the government moved to Washington, Joseph Dennie's *Port Folio* solicited "the assistance of the ladies," and published essays by Gertrude Meredith, Sarah Hall, and Emily Hopkinson. Boston and New York were not far behind in displaying similar interests: in New York, Noah Webster's *American Magazine* included in its prospectus a specific appeal for female contributors; the *Boston Weekly Magazine* was careful to publish the speeches at the annual "Exhibition" of Susanna Rowson's Young Ladies' Academy.

Most journalists' comments on the role and functions

virtue is explored in Howard Mumford Jones, *O Strange New World* (New York, 1964), p. 431.

of women in the republic merged, almost imperceptibly, into discussions of the sort of education proper for young girls. A pervasive Lockean environmentalism was displayed; what people were was assumed to be dependent on how they were educated. "Train up the child in the way he should grow, and when he is old he will not depart from it"; the biblical injunction was repeatedly quoted, and not quoted idly. When Americans spoke of what was best for the child they were also speaking—implicitly or explicitly—of their hopes for the adult. Charles Brockden Brown, for example, is careful to provide his readers with brief accounts of his heroines' early education. When we seek to learn the recipe for Murray's "new era in female history" we find ourselves reading comments on two related themes: how young women are to be "trained up," and what is to be expected of them when they are old.

If the republic were to fulfill the generous claims it made for the liberty and competence of its citizens, the education of young women would have to be an education for independence rather than for an upwardly mobile marriage. The periodicals are full of attacks on fashion, taking it for an emblem of superficiality and dependence. The Philadelphia *Lady's Magazine* criticized a father who prepared his daughters for the marriage market: "You boast of having given your daughters an education which will enable them 'to shine in the first circles.' . . . They sing indifferently; they play the harpsichord indifferently; they are mistresses of every common game at cards . . . they . . . have just as much knowledge of dress as to deform their persons by an awkward imitation of every new fashion which appears. . . . Placed in a situation of difficulty, they have neither a head to dictate, nor a hand to help in any domestic concern." [3] Teaching young girls to dress well was part of the larger message that their primary lifetime goal must be marriage; in this context, fashion became a feature of sexual politics. "I have sometimes been led,"

[3] August 1792, pp. 121–123.

remarked Benjamin Rush, "to ascribe the invention of ridiculous and expensive fashions in female dress entirely to the gentlemen in order to divert the ladies from improving their minds and thereby to secure a more arbitrary and unlimited authority over them." [4] In the marriage market, beauty, flirtatiousness, and charm were at a premium; intelligence, good judgment, and competence (in short, the republican virtues) were at a discount. The republic did not need fashion plates; it needed citizens—women as well as men—of self-discipline and of strong mind. The contradiction between the counsel given to young women and their own self-interest, as well as the best interests of the republic, seemed obvious. The marriage market undercut the republic.[5]

Those who addressed themselves to the problem of the proper education for young women used the word "independence" frequently. Sometimes it was used in a theoretical fashion: How, it was asked, can women's minds be free if they are taught that their sphere is limited to

---

[4] "Thoughts upon Female Education, Accommodated to the Present State of Society, Manners, and Government in the United States of America" (Philadelphia and Boston, 1787). Reprinted in Frederick Rudolph, ed., *Essays on Education in the Early Republic* (Cambridge, Mass., 1865), p. 39.

[5] "The greater proportion of young women are trained up by thoughtless parents, in ease and luxury, with no other dependence for their future support than the precarious chance of establishing themselves by marriage: for this purpose (the men best know why) elaborate attention is paid to external attractions and accomplishments, to the neglect of more useful and solid acquirements. . . . [Marriage is the] *sole* method of procuring for themselves an establishment." *New York Magazine*, August 1797, p. 406. For comment on the marriage market, see letter signed "A Matrimonial Republican" in Philadelphia *Lady's Magazine*, July 1792, pp. 64–67; "Legal Prostitution, Or Modern Marriage," Boston *Independent Chronicle*, October 28, 1793. For criticism of fashion, see *American Magazine*, December 1787, p. 39; July 1788, p. 594; *American Museum*, August 1788, p. 119; *Massachusetts Mercury*, August 16, 1793; January 16, 1795.

clothing, music, and needlework? Often the context of independence is economic and political: it seemed appropriate that in a republic women should have greater control over their own lives. "The *dependence* for which women are uniformly educated" was deplored; it was pointed out that the unhappily married woman would quickly discover that she had "neither liberty nor property." [6]

The idea that political independence should be echoed by a self-reliance which would make women as well as men economically independent appears in its most developed form in a series of essays Judith Sargent Murray published in the *Massachusetts Magazine* between 1792 and 1794, and collected under the title *The Gleaner* in 1798. Murray insisted that instruction in a manual trade was especially appropriate in a republic, and decried the antiegalitarian habit of assuming that a genteel and impractical education was superior to a vocational one. She was critical of fathers who permitted their sons to grow up without knowing a useful skill; she was even more critical of parents who "pointed their daughters" toward marriage and dependence. This made girls' education contingent on a single event; it offered them a single image of the future. "I would give my daughters every accomplishment which I thought proper," Murray wrote, "and to crown all, I would early accustom them to habits of industry and order. They should be taught with precision the art economical; they should be enabled to procure for themselves the necessaries of life; independence should be placed within their grasp." Repeatedly Murray counseled that women should be made to feel competent at something: "A woman *should reverence herself.*" [7]

Murray scattered through the *Gleaner* essays brief fictional versions of self-respecting women, in the charac-

[6] *New York Magazine*, August 1797, p. 406; Philadelphia *Universal Asylum and Columbian Magazine*, July 1791, p. 11.
[7] Murray, *Gleaner*, I, 168, 193.

ters of Margaretta, Mrs. Virgilius, and Penelope Airy. In his full-length novel *Ormond,* published in 1799, Charles Brockden Brown imagined a considerably more developed version of a competent woman. Constantia Dudley is eminently rational. When her father is embezzled of his fortune she, "her cheerfulness unimpaired," sells "every superfluous garb and trinket," her music and her books; she supports the family by needlework. Constantia never flinches; she can take whatever ill fortune brings, whether it is yellow fever or the poverty that forces her to conclude that the only alternative to starvation is cornmeal mush three times a day for three months. Through it all, she resists proposals of marriage, because even in adversity she scorns to become emotionally dependent without love.[8]

Everything Constantia does places her in sharp contrast to Helena Cleves, who also "was endowed with every feminine and fascinating quality." Helena has had a genteel education; she can paint, and sing, and play the clavichord, but it is all fashionable gloss to camouflage a lack of real mental accomplishment and self-discipline. What Brown called "exterior accomplishments" were acceptable so long as life held no surprises, but when Helena meets disaster, she is unprepared to maintain her independence and her self-respect. She falls into economic dependence upon a "kinswoman"; she succumbs to the "specious but delusive" reasoning of Ormond, and becomes his mistress. He takes advantage of her dependence, all the while seeking in Constantia a rational woman worthy of his intelligence; eventually, in despair, Helena kills herself.[9]

The argument that an appropriate education would steel girls to face adversity is related to the conviction that all citizens of a republic should be self-reliant. But the argument can be made independent of explicit republican ideology. It may well represent the common sense of a

---

[8] Charles Brockden Brown, *Ormond; Or the Secret Witness,* ed. by Ernest Marchand (New York, 1799; reprinted 1937, 1962), p. 19.

[9] *Ibid.,* pp. 98–99.

revolutionary era in which the unexpected was very likely to happen; in which large numbers of people had lived through reversals of fortune, encounters with strangers, physical dislocation. Constantia's friend Martinette de Beauvais has lived in Marseilles, Verona, Vienna, and Philadelphia; she had dressed like a man and fought in the American Revolution; after that she was one of the "hundreds" of women who took up arms for the French.[10] Constantia admires and sympathizes with her friend; nothing in the novel is clearer than that women who are not ready to maintain their independence in a crisis, as Constantia and Martinette do, risk sinking, like Helena, into prostitution and death.

The model republican woman was competent and confident. She could ignore the vagaries of fashion; she was rational, benevolent, independent, self-reliant. Writers who spoke to this point prepared lists of what we would now call role models: heroines of the past offered as assurance that women could indeed be people of accomplishment. There were women of the ancient world, like Cornelia, the mother of the Gracchi; rulers like Elizabeth of England and the Empress Catherine of Russia; a handful of Frenchwomen: Mme. de Genlis, Mme. Maintenon, and Mme. Dacier; and a long list of British intellectuals: Lady Mary Wortley Montagu, Hannah More, Elizabeth Carter, Mrs. Knowles (the Quaker who had bested Dr. Johnson in debate), Mary Wollstonecraft, and the Whig historian Catharine Macaulay.[11] Such women were ru-

---

[10] "It was obvious to suppose that a woman thus fearless and sagacious had not been inactive at a period like the present, which called forth talents and courage without distinction of sex, and had been particularly distinguished by female enterprise and heroism." *Ibid.*, p. 170.

[11] For examples of such lists, see: Murray, *Gleaner,* III, 200–219; John Blair Linn, *The Powers of Genius: A Poem in Three Parts* (Philadelphia, 1802); Philadelphia *Weekly Magazine,* August 4, 11, 1798; *Port Folio,* February 12, 1803; September 27, 1806; Philadelphia *Minerva,* March 14, 1795. For the admiration expressed by Abigail Adams and Mercy Otis Warren for Catharine

mored to exist in America; they were given fictional embodiment by Murray and Brown. Those who believed in these republican models demanded that their presence be recognized and endorsed, and that a new generation of young women be urged to make them patterns for their own behavior. To create more such women became a major educational challenge.

Writers were fond of pointing out that the inadequacies of American women could be ascribed to early upbringing and environmental influences. "Will it be said that the judgment of a male of two years old, is more sage than that of a female of the same age?" asked Judith Sargent Murray. "But . . . as their years increased, the sister must be wholly domesticated, while the brother is led by the hand through all the flowery paths of science." The *Universal Asylum* published a long and thoughtful essay by "A Lady" which argued that "in the nursery, strength is equal in the male and female." When a boy went to school, he immediately met both intellectual and physical challenge; his teachers instructed him in science and language, his friends dared him to fight, to run after a hoop, to jump a rope. Girls, on the other hand, were "committed to illiterate teachers, . . . cooped up in a room, confined to needlework, deprived of exercise." Thomas Cooper defined the problem clearly: "We first keep their minds and then their persons in subjection," he wrote. "We educate women from infancy to marriage, in such a way as to debilitate both their corporeal and their mental powers. All the accomplishments we teach them are directed not to their future benefit in life but to the amusement of the male sex; and having for a series of years, with much assiduity, and

Macaulay, see Abigail Adams to Isaac Smith, Jr., April 20, 1771; Abigail Adams to Catharine Sawbridge Macaulay, n.d., 1774; Mercy Otis Warren to Abigail Adams, January 28, 1775; in L. H. Butterfield, ed., *Adams Family Correspondence,* I (Cambridge, Mass., 1963), 76–77, 177–179, 181–183. For the circle of English "bluestockings," in the 1780s, see M. G. Jones, *Hannah More* (Cambridge, 1952), pp. 41–76.

sometimes at much expense, incapacitated them for any serious occupation, we say they are not fit to govern themselves." [12]

Schemes for the education of the "rising generation" proliferated in the early republic, including a number of projects for the education of women. Some, like those discussed in the well-known essays of Benjamin Rush and Noah Webster, were theoretical; others took the form of admitting girls to boys' academies or establishing new schools for girls. There were not as many as Judith Sargent Murray implied when she said: "Female academies are everywhere establishing," but she was not alone in seeing schools like Susanna Rowson's Young Ladies' Academy and the Young Ladies' Academy of Philadelphia as harbingers of a trend. One pamphlet address, written in support of the Philadelphia Academy, expressed the hope that it would become "a great national seminary" and insisted that although "stubborn prejudices still exist . . . we must (if open to conviction) be convinced that *females* are fully capable of sounding the most profound depths, and of attaining to the most sublime excellence in every part of science." [13]

Certainly there was a wide range of opinion on the content and scope of female education in the early republic. Samuel Harrison Smith's essay on the subject, which won the American Philosophical Society's 1797 prize for the best plan for a national system of education, began by proposing "that every male child, without excep-

---

[12] *Massachusetts Magazine,* II (March 1790), 133; *Universal Asylum* and *Columbian Magazine,* July 1791, p. 9; Thomas Cooper, "Propositions Respecting the Foundation of Civil Government," in *Political Arithmetic* (Philadelphia [?], 1798), p. 27. See also *Boston Weekly Magazine,* May 21, 1803, pp. 121–122; *American Museum,* January 1787, p. 59; Philadelphia *Lady's Magazine,* June 1792.

[13] J. A. Neale, "An Essay on the Genius and Education of the Fair Sex," Philadelphia *Minerva,* April 4, March 21, 1795.

tion, be educated."[14] At the other extreme was Timothy Dwight, the future president of Yale, who opened his academy at Greenfield Hill to girls and taught them the same subjects he taught to boys, at the same time and in the same rooms.[15] But Dwight was the exception. Most proposals for the education of young women agreed that the curriculum should be more advanced than that of the primary schools but somewhat less than that offered by colleges and even conventional boys' academies. Noah Webster thought women should learn speaking and writing, arithmetic, geography, belles-lettres; "A Reformer" in the *Weekly Magazine* advocated a similar program, to which practical instruction in nursing and cooking were added. Judith Sargent Murray thought women should be able to converse elegantly and correctly, pronounce French, read history (as a narrative substitute for novels, rather than for its own interest or value), and learn some simple geography and astronomy.[16] The best-known proposal was Benjamin Rush's; he too prescribed reading,

---

[14] *Remarks on Education: Illustrating the Close Connection between Virtue and Wisdom* (Philadelphia, 1798), reprinted in Rudolph, *Essays on Education*, p. 211. Smith did acknowledge that female instruction was important, but commented that concepts of what it should be were so varied that he feared to make any proposals, and despaired of including women in the scheme he was then devising. "It is sufficient, perhaps, for the present, that the improvement of women is marked by a rapid progress and that a prospect opens equal to their most ambitious desires" (p. 217). The other prizewinner, Samuel Knox, proposed to admit girls to the primary schools in his system, but not to the academies or colleges. Knox's essay, "An Essay on the Best System of Liberal Education," may be found in Rudolph, *Essays on Education*, pp. 271–372.

[15] Charles E. Cunningham, *Timothy Dwight: 1752–1817: A Biography* (New York, 1942), pp. 154–163.

[16] Noah Webster, "Importance of Female Education," in *American Magazine*, May 1788, pp. 368, 369. This essay was part of his pamphlet *On the Education of Youth in America* (Boston, 1790), conveniently reprinted in Rudolph, *Essays on Education*, pp. 41–78. *Weekly Magazine*, April 7, 1798; Murray, *The Gleaner*, I, 70–71.

grammar, penmanship, "figures and bookkeeping," geography. He added "the first principles of natural philosophy," vocal music (because it soothed cares and was good for the lungs) but not instrumental music (because, except for the most talented, it seemed a waste of valuable time), and history (again, as an antidote to novel reading).

Rush offered his model curriculum in a speech to the Board of Visitors of the Young Ladies' Academy of Philadelphia, later published and widely reprinted under the title "Thoughts upon Female Education Accommodated to the Present State of Society, Manners and Government in the United States of America." The academy claimed to be the first female academy chartered in the United States; when Rush spoke, on July 28, 1787, he was offering practical advice to a new school. Rush linked the academy to the greater cause of demonstrating the possibilities of women's minds. Those who were skeptical of education for women, Rush declared, were the same who opposed "the general diffusion of knowledge among the citizens of our republics." Rush argued that "female education should be accommodated to the state of society, manners, and government of the country in which it is conducted." An appropriate education for American women would be condensed, because they married earlier than their European counterparts; it would include bookkeeping, because American women could expect to be "the stewards and guardians of their husbands' property," and executrices of their husbands' wills. It would qualify them for "a general intercourse with the world" by an acquaintance with geography and chronology. If education is preparation for life, then the life styles of American women required a newly tailored educational program.[17]

[17] Benjamin Rush, "Thoughts upon Female Education," in Rudolph, *Essays on Education,* pp. 25–40. See also the comments of the Reverend James Sproat, a member of the Board of Visitors, June 10, 1789, in *The Rise and Progress of the Young Ladies' Academy of Philadelphia; Containing an Account of a Number of Public Examinations and Commencements; the Charter and*

The curriculum of the Young Ladies' Academy (which one of the Board of Visitors called "abundantly sufficient to complete the female mind") included reading, writing, arithmetic, English grammar, composition, rhetoric, and geography. It did not include the natural philosophy Rush hoped for (although Rush did deliver a dozen lectures on "The Application of the Principles of Natural Philosophy, and Chemistry, to Domestic and Culinary Purposes"); it did not include advanced mathematics or the classics.[18]

In 1794 the Young Ladies' Academy published a collection of its graduation addresses; one is struck by the scattered observations of valedictorians and salutatorians that reading, writing, and arithmetic were not enough. Priscilla Mason remarked in her 1793 graduation address that while it was unusual for a woman to address "a promiscuous assembly," there was no impropriety in women's becoming accomplished orators. What had prevented them, she argued, was that "our high and mighty Lords . . . have denied us the means of knowledge, and then reproached us for the want of it. . . . They doom'd the sex to servile or frivolous employments, on purpose to degrade their minds, that they themselves might hold unrivall'd, the power and pre-eminence they had usurped." Academies

Bye-Laws; Likewise, a Number of Orations delivered by the Young Ladies, and several by the Trustees of Said Institution (Philadelphia, 1794), p. 24.

[18] Benjamin Say, "Address," December 4, 1789, in *Rise and Progress of the Young Ladies' Academy,* p. 33; Benjamin Rush, *Syllabus of Lectures, Containing the Application of the Principles of Natural Philosophy . . .* (Philadelphia, 1787). Rush, of course, was waging his own crusade against the classics as inappropriate in a republic; he argued elsewhere that to omit Latin and Greek would have the beneficial effect of diminishing "the present immense disparity which subsists between the sexes, in the degrees of their education and knowledge." When his contemporaries omitted the classics from the female curriculum it was usually because they thought women's minds were not up to it. Rush, "Observations upon the Study of the Latin and Greek Languages," in *Essays, Literary, Moral and Philosophical* (Philadelphia, 1798), p. 44.

like hers enabled women to increase their knowledge, but the forums in which they might use it were still unavailable: "The Church, the Bar, and the Senate are shut against us."[19]

So long as the propriety of cultivating women's minds remained a matter for argument, it was hard to press a claim to public competence; Priscilla Mason was an exception. Rush had concluded his advice to the Young Ladies' Academy by challenging his audience to demonstrate "that the cultivation of reason in women is alike friendly to the order of nature and the private as well as the public happiness." But meeting even so mild a challenge was difficult; "bluestocking" was not a term of praise in the early republic. "Tell me," wrote the Philadelphian Gertrude Meredith angrily, ". . . do you imagine, from your knowledge of the young men in this city, that ladies are valued according to their mental acquirements? I can assure you that they are not, and I am very confident that they never will be, while men indulge themselves in expressions of contempt for one because she has a *bare elbow,* for another because she . . . never made a *good pun, nor smart repartee.* . . . [Would they] not titter . . . at her expense, if a woman made a Latin quotation, or spoke with enthusiasm of Classical learning?"[20] When Gertrude Meredith visited Baltimore, she found that her mildly satirical essays for the *Port Folio* had transformed her into a formidable figure: "Mrs. Cole says she should not have been more distressed at visiting Mrs. Macaulay the authoress than myself as she had heard I *was so sensible,* but she was very glad to find I was so free and easy. You must allow," she concluded dryly, "that this compliment was elegantly turned." A similar complaint was made by an essayist whom we know only as "Sophia":

[19] Priscilla Mason, "Oration," May 15, 1793, in *Rise and Progress of the Young Ladies' Academy*, pp. 90–95. See also the valedictory oration by Molly Wallace, June 12, 1792, *ibid.*, pp. 73–79.
[20] Letter signed M.G., "American Lounger," *Port Folio*, April 7, 1804.

> A woman who is conscious of possessing, more intellectual power than is requisite in superintending the pantry, and in adjusting the ceremonials of a feast, and who believes she, in conforming to the will of the giver, in improving the gift, is by the wits of the other sex denominated a learned lady. She is represented as disgustingly slovenly in her person, indecent in her habits, imperious to her husband, and negligent of her children. And the odious scarecrow is employed, exactly as the farmer employs his unsightly bundle of rags and straw, to terrify the simple birds, from picking up the precious grain, which he wishes to monopolize. After all this, what man in his sober senses can be astonished, to find the majority of women as they really are, frivolous and volatile; incapable of estimating their own dignity, and indifferent to the best interests of society. . . ? [21]

These women were not creating their own paranoid images of discouragement. The same newspapers for which they wrote often printed other articles insisting that intellectual accomplishment is inappropriate in a woman, that the intellectual woman is not only invading a male province, but must herself somehow be masculine. "Women of masculine minds," wrote the Boston minister John Sylvester John Gardiner, "have generally masculine manners, and a robustness of person ill calculated to inspire the tender passion." Noah Webster's *American Magazine*, which in its prospectus had made a special appeal to women writers and readers, published the unsigned comment: "If we picture to ourselves a woman . . . firm in resolve, unshaken in conduct, unmoved by the delicacies of situation, by the fashions of the times, . . . we immediately change the idea of the sex, and . . . we see under the form of a woman the virtues and qualities of a man." Even the *Lady's Magazine*, which had promised to

[21] Gertrude Meredith to David Meredith, May 3, 1804, Meredith Papers, Historical Society of Pennsylvania; Philadelphia *Evening Fireside*, April 6, 1805.

demonstrate that "the FEMALES of Philadelphia are by no means deficient in *those talents,* which have immortalized the names of a *Montagu,* a *Craven,* a *More,* and a *Seward,* in their inimitable writings," published a cautionary tale, whose moral was that although "learning in men was the road to preferment . . . consequences very opposite were the result of the same quality in women." Amelia is a clergyman's only daughter; she is taught Latin and Greek, with the result that she becomes "negligent of her dress," and "pride and pedantry grew up with learning in her breast." Eventually she is avoided by both sexes, and becomes emblematic of the fabled "white-washed jackdaw (who, aiming at a station from which nature had placed him at a distance, found himself deserted by his own species, and driven out of every society)." For conclusion there was an explicit moral: "This story was intended (at a time when the press overflows with the productions of female pens) . . . to admonish them, that . . . because a few have gained applause by studying the dead languages, all womankind should [not] assume their Dictionaries and Lexicons; else . . . (as the Ladies made rapid advances towards manhood) we might in a few years behold a sweepstakes rode by women, or a second battle at Odiham, fought with superior skill, by Mesdames Humphries and Mendoza." [22]

[22] *New-England Palladium,* September 18, 1801; *American Magazine,* February 1788, p. 134; *Lady's Magazine,* January 1793, pp. 68–72. (The "battle at Odiham" refers to a famous bare-knuckle prize fight, one of the earliest major events in the history of boxing, fought in 1788 by Daniel Mendoza and Richard Humphries in Hampshire, England.) Other attacks on female pedantry, which express the fear that intellectual women will be masculine, are found in the *American Magazine,* March 1788, pp. 244–245 ("To be lovely you must be content to be women . . . and leave the masculine virtues, and the profound researches of study to the province of the other sex"); *New-England Palladium,* September 4, 18, December 4, 1801, March 5, 9, 1802; Benjamin Silliman, *Letters of Shahcoolen, a Hindu Philosophy, Residing in Philadelphia; To His Friend, El*

The prediction that accomplishment would unsex women was coupled with the warning that educated women would abandon their proper sphere; the female pedant and the careful housekeeper were never found in the same person. The most usable cautionary emblem for this seems to have been Mary Wollstonecraft, whose life and work linked criticism of women's status with free love and political radicalism. Mary Wollstonecraft's *Vindication of the Rights of Women* was her generation's most coherent statement of what women deserved and what they might become. The influence of any book is difficult to trace, and although we know that her book was reprinted in Philadelphia shortly after its publication in 1792, it would be inaccurate to credit Wollstonecraft with responsibility for raising in America questions relating to the status of women. It seems far more likely that she verbalized effectively what a larger public was already thinking or was willing to hear; "In very many of her sentiments," remarked the Philadelphia Quaker Elizabeth Drinker, "she, as some of our friends say, *speaks my mind.*" [23]

Wollstonecraft's primary target was Rousseau, whose definition of woman's sphere was a limited one: "The empire of women," Rousseau had written, "is the empire of softness, of address, of complacency; her commands are caresses; her menaces are tears." Wollstonecraft perceived that to define women in this way was to condemn them to "a state of perpetual childhood"; she deplored the "false system of education" which made women "only anxious to inspire love, when they ought to cherish a nobler ambi-

Hassan, an Inhabitant of Delhi (Boston, 1802), pp. 23–24, 62; *American Museum,* December 1788, p. 491; *Boston Weekly Magazine,* March 24, 1804, p. 86 ("War-like women, learned women, and women who are politicians, equally abandon the circle which nature and institutions have traced round their sex; they convert themselves into men").

[23] *Extracts from the Journal of Elizabeth Drinker, from 1759 to 1807, A.D.,* ed. by Henry D. Biddle (Philadelphia, 1889), p. 285. The entry is dated April 22, 1796.

tion, and by their abilities and virtues exact respect." Women's duties were different from those of men, but they similarly demanded the exercise of virtue and reason; women would be better wives and mothers if they were taught that they need not depend on frivolity and ignorance. Wollstonecraft ventured the suggestion that women might study medicine, politics, and business, but whatever they did, they should not be denied civil and political rights, they should not have to rely on marriage for assurance of economic support, they should not "remain immured in their families groping in the dark." [24]

If, in some quarters, Mary Wollstonecraft's work was greeted as the common sense of the matter, in others it was met with hostility. The *Vindication* was a popular subject of satire, especially when, after the author's death in childbirth in 1797, William Godwin published a *Memoir* revealing that she had lived with other men, and with Godwin himself before her pregnancy and their marriage. Critics were then freed to discount her call for reform as the self-serving demand of a woman of easy virtue, as Benjamin Silliman did throughout his *Letters of Shahcoolen.* Timothy Dwight, who had taken the lead in offering young women education on a par with young men, shuddered at Wollstonecraft and held "the female philosopher" up to ridicule in "Morpheus," a political satire which ran for eight installments in the *New-England Palladium.*[25] Dwight called Wollstonecraft "an unchaste woman," "a sentimental lover," "a strumpet"; as Silliman had done, he linked her radical politics to free love. " 'Away with all monopolies,' " Dwight has her say. " 'I hate these exclusive rights; these privileged orders. I am for having everything

[24] Mary Wollstonecraft, *A Vindication of the Rights of Woman, With Strictures on Political and Moral Subjects* (New York, 1891), pp. 23, 149–156.

[25] *New-England Palladium,* November 24, 27, December 8, 11, 15, 1801; March 2, 5, 9, 1802. Identification of Dwight as author is made by Robert Edson Lee, "Timothy Dwight and the Boston *Palladium,*" *New England Quarterly,* XXXV (1962), 229–239.

free, and open to all; like the air which we breathe. . . .' "

" 'Love, particularly, I suppose, Madam [?]' "

" 'Yes, brute, love, if you please, and everything else.' "[26] Even Charles Brockden Brown's feminist tract *Alcuin* concluded with a long gloss on the same theme: to permit any change in women's status was to imply the acceptance of free love. Alcuin, who has been playing the conservative skeptic, concludes that once it is established that marriage "has no other criterion than custom," it becomes simply "a mode of sexual intercourse." His friend Mrs. Carter protests energetically that free love is not at all what she wanted; " 'because I demand an equality of conditions among beings that equally partake of the same divine reason, would you rashly infer that I was an enemy to the institution of marriage itself?' " Brown lets her have the last word, but he does not make Alcuin change his mind.[27]

Dwight had one final charge to make against Wollstonecraft; he attacked her plea that women emerge from the confines of their families. " 'Who will make our puddings, Madam?' " his protagonist asks. When she responds: " 'Make them yourself,' " he presses harder: " 'Who shall nurse us when we are sick?' " and, finally, " 'Who shall nurse our children?' " The last question reduces the fictional Mary to blushes and silence.[28]

It would not, however, reduce Rush, or Murray, or Brown, to blushes and silence. (Nor, I think, would it have so affected the real Mary Wollstonecraft.) They had neither predicted that women would cease their housewifely duties nor demanded that women should. Priscilla Mason's demand that hitherto male professions be opened to women was highly unusual, and even she apologized for it before she left the podium. There were, it is true, some other hints that women might claim the privileges and duties of

[26] *New-England Palladium,* March 9, 1802.

[27] Charles Brockden Brown and Lee R. Edwards, *Alcuin: A Dialogue* (New York, 1971), pp. 44–88.

[28] *New-England Palladium,* March 9, 1802.

male citizens of the republic. In *Alcuin*, Mrs. Carter explains her intense political disappointment through the first two chapters, arguing that Americans had been false to their own revolutionary promises in denying political status to women. "If a stranger questions me concerning the nature of our government, I answer, that in this happy climate all men are free: the people are the source of all authority; from them it flows, and to them, in due season, it returns . . . our liberty consists in the choice of our governors: all, as reason requires, have a part in this choice, yet not without a few exceptions . . . females . . . minors . . . the poor . . . slaves. . . . I am tired of explaining this charming system of equality and independence." St. George Tucker, commenting on Blackstone, acknowledged that women were taxed without representation; like "aliens . . . children under the age of discretion, idiots, and lunatics," American women had neither political nor civil rights. "I fear there is little reason for a compliment to our laws for their respect and favour to the female sex," Tucker concluded. As Tucker had done, John Adams acknowledged that women's experience of the republic was different from men's; he hesitantly admitted that the republic claimed the right "to govern women without their consent." For a brief period from 1790 to 1807, New Jersey law granted the franchise to "all free inhabitants," and on occasion women exercised that right; it is conceivable that New Jersey might have stood as a precedent for other states. Instead, New Jersey's legislature rewrote its election law; the argument for political competence was taken no further.[29]

---

[29] Brown, *Alcuin*, pp. 32–33; St. George Tucker, *Blackstone's Commentaries: With Notes of Reference, to the Constitution and Laws, of the Federal Government of the United States, and of the Commonwealth of Virginia*, II (Philadelphia, 1803), 145, 445; John Adams to James Sullivan, May 26, 1776, in *The Works of John Adams*, ed. by Charles Francis Adams, IX (1856), 375–

All of these were hesitant suggestions introduced into a hostile intellectual milieu in which female learning was equated with pedantry and masculinity. To resist those assumptions was to undertake a great deal; it was a task for which no one was ready; indeed, it is impossible to say that anyone really wanted to try. Instead, the reformers would have been quick to reply, with Brown's Mrs. Carter, that they had no intention of abandoning marriage; that they had every intention of making puddings and nursing babies; that the education they demanded was primarily to enable women to function more effectively within their traditional sphere, and only secondarily to fulfill demands like Priscilla Mason's that they emerge from it. People were complaining that American women were boring, frivolous, spending excessive amounts of money for impractical fashions; very well, a vigorously educated woman would be less likely to bore her husband, less likely to be a spendthrift, better able to cope with adverse fortune. Judith Sargent Murray versified an equation:

Where'er the maiden Industry *appears,*
A thrifty contour every object wears;
And when fair order *with the nymph combines,*
Adjusts, directs, and every plan designs,
Then Independence *fills her peerless seat,*
And lo! the matchless trio is complete.

Murray repeatedly made the point that the happiness of the nation depended on the happiness of families; and that the "felicity of families" is dependent on the presence of women who are "properly methodical, and economical in their distributions and expenditures of time." She denied

379; Edward Raymond Turner, "Women's Suffrage in New Jersey: 1790–1807," *Smith College Studies in History,* I (1916), 165–187. Opposition to woman suffrage apparently surfaced after women voted as a bloc in an unsuccessful attempt to influence the outcome of an Essex County election in 1797.

that "the present enlarged plan of female education" was incompatible with traditional notions of women's duties: she predicted that the "daughters of Columbia" would be free of *"invidious and rancorous passions"* and "even the semblance of pedantry"; "when they become wives and mothers, they will fill with honour the parts allotted them." [30]

Rarely, in the literature of the early Republic, do we find any objection to the notion that women belong in the home; what emerges is the argument that the Revolution had enlarged the significance of what women did in their homes. Benjamin Rush's phrasing of this point is instructive; when he defined the goals of republican women, he was careful not to include a claim to political power: "The equal share that every citizen has in the liberty and the possible share he may have in the government of our country make it necessary that our ladies should be qualified to a certain degree by a peculiar and suitable education, *to concur in instructing their sons in the principles of liberty and government.*" The Young Ladies' Academy promised "not wholly to engross the mind" of each pupil, "but to allow her to prepare for the duties in life to which she may be destined." Miss P. W. Jackson, graduating from Mrs. Rowson's Academy, explained what she had learned of the goals of the educated woman: "A woman who is skilled in every useful art, who practices every domestic virtue . . . may, by her precept and example, inspire her brothers, her husband, or her sons, with such a love of virtue, such just ideas of the true value of civil liberty . . . that future heroes and statesmen, who arrive at the summit of military or political fame, shall *exaltingly declare, it is to my mother I owe this elevation.*" By their household management, by their refusal to countenance vice, crime, or cruelty in their suitors and husbands, women had the power to direct the moral development of the male citizens of the republic. The influence women

---

[30] *Gleaner,* I, 161, 12, 29, 191, 190.

had on children, especially on their sons, gave them ultimate responsibility for the future of the new nation.[31]

This constellation of ideas, and the republican rhetoric which made it convincing, appears at great length in the Columbia College commencement oration of 1795. Its title was "Female Influence"; behind the flowery rhetoric lurks a social and political message:

> Let us then figure to ourselves the accomplished woman, surrounded by a sprightly band, from the babe that imbibes the nutritive fluid, to the generous youth just ripening into manhood, and the lovely virgin. . . . Let us contemplate the mother distributing the mental nourishment to the fond smiling circle, by means proportionate to their different powers of reception, watching the gradual openings of their minds, and studying their various turns of temper. . . . Religion, fairest offspring of the skies, smiles auspicious on her endeavours; the Genius of Liberty hovers triumphant over the glorious scene. . . . Yes, ye fair, the reformation of a world is in your power. . . . Reflect on the result of your efforts. Contemplate the rising glory of confederated America. Consider that your exertions can best secure, increase, and perpetuate it. The solidity and stability of the liberties of your country rest with you; since Liberty is never sure, 'till Virtue reigns triumphant. . . . Already may we see the lovely daughters of Columbia asserting the importance and the honour of their sex. It rests with you to make this retreat [from the corruptions of Europe] doubly peaceful, doubly happy, by banishing from it those crimes and corruptions, which have never yet failed of giving rise to tyranny, or anarchy. While you thus keep our country virtuous, you maintain its independence. . . .[32]

---

[31] Rush, "Thoughts upon Female Education," in Rudolph, *Essays on Education,* p. 28 (my italics); "On Female Education," *Port Folio,* May 1809, p. 388; *Boston Weekly Magazine,* October 29, 1803.

[32] *New York Magazine,* May 1795, pp. 301–305.

Defined this way, the educated woman ceased to threaten the sanctity of marriage; the bluestocking need not be masculine. In this awkward—and in the 1790s still only vaguely expressed—fashion, the traditional womanly virtues were endowed with political purpose. A pivotal political role was assigned to the least political inhabitants of the Republic. Ironically, the same women who were denied political identity were counted on to maintain the republican quality of the new nation. "Let the ladies of a country be educated properly," Rush said, "and they will not only make and administer its laws, but form its manners and character." [33]

When Americans addressed themselves to the matter of the role of women, they found that those who admired bluestockings and those who feared them could agree on one thing: in a world where moral influences were fast dissipating, women as a group seemed to represent moral stability. Few in the early republic demanded, in a sustained way, substantial revisions in women's political or legal status; few spoke to the nascent class of unskilled women workers. But many took pride in the assertion that properly educated republican women would stay in the home and, from that vantage point, would shape the characters of their sons and husbands in the direction of benevolence, self-restraint, and responsible independence. They refuted charges of free love and masculinization; in doing so they created a justification for woman as household goddess so deeply felt that one must be permitted to suspect that many women of their generation were *refusing* to be household goddesses.[34] They began to make the argument for intelligent household management that Catharine Beecher, a generation later, would enshrine in her *Treatise on Domestic Economy* as woman's highest

---

[33] Rush, "Thoughts upon Female Education," in Rudolph, *Essays on Education*, p. 36.

[34] See, for example, *Boston Weekly Magazine*, December 18, 1802; *Weekly Magazine*, March 3, 1798; *Port Folio*, February 12, 1803, March 3, 1804, April 20, 1805.

goal. The Daughters of Columbia became, in effect, the Mothers of the Victorians. Whether Judith Sargent Murray, Charles Brockden Brown, or Benjamin Rush would have approved the ultimate results of their work is hard to say.

JAMES M. BANNER, JR.

The Problem of South Carolina[1]

I

HISTORIANS AGREE that the political culture of South Carolina differed from that of every other state. No other southern state appeared quite so dedicated to the preservation of slavery and its distinctive way of life. None other responded so dramatically to threats from the North. South Carolina nullified alone and seceded first. One man —John C. Calhoun—dominated politics there to a degree unparalleled elsewhere. In no other state was national authority at such a discount. Nowhere else in the South did the "fire-eaters" gain such an early ascendancy and maintain such a lasting hold.

Why should this have been so? The complexities and fears of race, the difficulties of a staple-crop plantation economy, and such a natural enemy as malaria are often offered as reasons. Yet such conditions, though perhaps more intense in the Palmetto State, were shared by other southern states before 1860 and will therefore not entirely

[1] I have benefited immensely in the preparation of this essay from the aid and criticism of W. W. Abbot, O. Vernon Burton, William W. Freehling, Sheldon Hackney, and Richard P. McCormick.

do to distinguish South Carolina. Much of the explanation lies rather within the realm of politics itself, which ought to be given its due, more often than it is, as a force which helps shape, as well as results from, the environing culture. With the exception of South Carolina, all southern states managed, if only for a decade or two before the Civil War, to create and maintain a two-party system. With the exception of South Carolina, an experience with sustained competitive party politics formed part of the public life of the South.[2]

In contrast to the other states, North and South, South Carolina possessed what is best seen as a no-party system with an occasional inclination toward temporary one-party dominance. Under such a system, no party has a genuine capacity to govern. Two or more groups of office-seekers and officeholders vie to attract voters, influence events, and command each other's attention; but none can offer the sustained, organized, and effective challenge which make for a full-fledged party or which make the system a functioning one- or two-party order. As it was, South Carolina's Unionist, Whig, and National Democratic oppositions were just strong enough at critical junctures to keep alive political debate, speak up for the ideals of national unity and constitutionalism, and provide an entry point, however narrow, for national influence—but never to create an enduring party. And the Democrats, for their part, though they tended personally to dominate state politics, shape most public issues, and control the state government, always reverted to casual and informal operations

[2] The two most recent studies of South Carolina, both of which stress the pervading influence of race fear upon state politics, are William W. Freehling, *Prelude to Civil War: The Nullification Controversy in South Carolina, 1816–1836* (New York, 1965), and Steven A. Channing, *Crisis of Fear: Secession in South Carolina* (New York, 1970). On two-party politics everywhere in the ante-bellum South save South Carolina, see Richard P. McCormick, *The Second American Party System: Party Formation in the Jacksonian Era* (Chapel Hill, N.C., 1966), Part V.

soon after the periodic crises which gave them a fleeting experience with unity and organization.[3]

This is not to deny that South Carolinians were able to create partisan machinery appropriate to their unstable and discontinuous party situation.[4] But if we take parties

---

[3] The problem is that almost all the attributes of what political scientists call no-party, one-party, and two-party systems existed in South Carolina from time to time without coherence or continuity. In the three decades before 1860, situations of factional chaos and widespread absence of competition (features of no-party systems), the insurmountable sway of a single party (as in one-party rule), and the bitter, organized strife between Nullifiers and Unionists (as in two-party states) were to be found—but all without durability. On types of parties and party systems, see Samuel P. Huntington, "Social and Institutional Dynamics of One-Party Systems," Clement H. Moore, "The Single Party as Source of Legitimacy," and Hugh D. Price, "Rise and Decline of One-Party Systems in Anglo-American Experience," in Samuel P. Huntington and Clement H. Moore, eds., *Authoritarian Politics in Modern Society: The Dynamics of Established One-Party Systems* (New York, 1970), pp. 3–98; V. O. Key, Jr., *American State Politics: An Introduction* (New York, 1956), *passim;* Maurice Duverger, *Political Parties: Their Organization and Activity in the Modern State,* 3d ed. (New York, 1963), pp. 63–71; Avery Leiserson, *Parties and Politics: An Institutional and Behavioral Approach* (New York, 1958), p. 64; William N. Chambers, *Political Parties in a New Nation: The American Experience, 1776–1809* (New York, 1963), pp. 45–53, 107, 144–147; Chambers, "Party Development and the American Mainstream," in Chambers and Walter D. Burnham, eds., *The American Party Systems: Stages of Political Development* (New York, 1967), p. 5; McCormick, *Second American Party System,* pp. 9–12; Sigmund Neumann, "Toward a Comparative Study of Political Parties," in Neumann, ed., *Modern Political Parties: Approaches to Comparative Politics* (Chicago, 1956), pp. 395, 400–401.

[4] Details on party organization and activity in South Carolina during the era of the first party system will be found, among other places, in Noble E. Cunningham, Jr., *The Jeffersonian Republicans: The Formation of Party Organization, 1789–1801* (Chapel Hill, N.C., 1957), pp. 160–161, 188–189; Cunningham, *The Jeffersonian Republicans in Power: Party Operations, 1801–*

to be institutions with strong programmatic commitments, clear partisan identities, durable organizations, and sustained leadership and electoral support, then no fully developed party or party system ever emerged in the state.[5] Nor did episodes of political ferment—like the Nullification crisis of 1832 and the first Secession crisis of 1850—prove anything more than temporary spurs to party growth. For these crisis situations defined the limits and capacities of the organizations they called forth; and no obstacle to institutional endurance was harder to overcome than the independence of crisis-time parties from normal party lines—of Nullifiers and Unionists from Democrats in 1832, of Secessionists and Co-Operationists from Democrats and Whigs in 1850. Along with the failure of continuous party competition, it was this constant reshuffling of partisan symbols, issues, and allegiances in South Carolina which discouraged party growth.[6]

1809 (Chapel Hill, N.C., 1963), pp. 189–190, 200–202, 275–276; Lisle A. Rose, *Prologue to Democracy: The Federalists in the South, 1789–1800* (Lexington, Ky., 1968), pp. 128 n., 196–197, 229–230, 248, 253–254, 267–277; John Harold Wolfe, *Jeffersonian Democracy in South Carolina* (Chapel Hill, N.C., 1940), pp. 119–121, 149, 157–161, 182–184, 259–260; and Elizabeth Cometti, "John Rutledge, Jr., Federalist," *Journal of Southern History,* XIII (May 1947), 186–219.

[5] In these terms, even the sometimes dominant state Democratic party fails fully to qualify as a party. As for the Unionist and Nullifier "parties" in the 1830s, the Whig party later, and such ephemeral "parties" as the States Rights Democratic party, the Nullifier Democratic party, and the States Rights Free Trader party—most of them created for the occasion and bearing through their names and adherents an alliance with the Democracy—they seem scarcely to deserve the formal designation of "party."

[6] Nevertheless, all these crisis "parties" managed to create machinery to organize the state and get out the vote. They convened legislative caucuses which presented nominees for governor, set up state central committees for the occasion, called mass meetings of their followers, established party-related pressure and propaganda associations under central statewide direction, built regional and district committee systems and delegate

The problem of South Carolina, in short, was not exclusively its society but also its politics, not only its parties but also its party system. What remains to be understood is why a no-party system existed in South Carolina when other states with roughly similar characters were creating two-party political orders. A no less compelling question is how this party system affected the carrying out of tasks,

---

structures, founded partisan and electioneering newspapers, and held statewide delegate conventions. All of these, of course, were temporary expedients.

For information on party organization and electioneering in South Carolina in the four decades before the Civil War, see Chauncey S. Boucher, *The Nullification Controversy in South Carolina* (New York, 1916); Boucher, "The Secession and Co-Operation Movements in South Carolina, 1848–1852," *Washington University Studies,* V (April 1918), 67–138; Boucher, "South Carolina and the South on the Eve of Secession, 1852 to 1860," *ibid.,* VI (April 1919), 81–144; Boucher, "The Annexation of Texas and the Bluffton Movement in South Carolina," *Mississippi Valley Historical Review,* VI (June 1919), 3–33; James Petigru Carson, *Life, Letters, and Speeches of James Louis Petigru: The Union Man of South Carolina* (Washington, D.C., 1920); Arthur C. Cole, *The Whig Party in the South* (Washington, D.C., 1913); Avery O. Craven, *The Growth of Southern Nationalism, 1848–1861* (Baton Rouge, 1953); Freehling, *Prelude to Civil War;* Philip M. Hamer, *The Secession Movement in South Carolina, 1847–1852* (Allentown, Pa., 1918); "Letters on the Nullification Movement in South Carolina, 1830–1834," *American Historical Review,* VI (July 1901), 736–765; Lillian A. Kibler, *Benjamin F. Perry, South Carolina Unionist* (Durham, N.C., 1946); Benjamin F. Perry, *Reminiscences of Public Men,* 2 vols. (Philadelphia, and Greenville, S.C., 1883–1889); J. Fred Rippy, *Joel R. Poinsett, Versatile American* (Durham, N.C., 1935); N. W. Stephenson, "Southern Nationalism in South Carolina in 1851," *American Historical Review,* XXXVI (Jan. 1931), 314–335; Laura A. White, "The National Democrats in South Carolina, 1852 to 1860," *South Atlantic Quarterly,* XXVIII (Oct. 1929), 370–389; White, *Robert Barnwell Rhett: Father of Secession* (New York, 1931); Charles M. Wiltse, *John C. Calhoun, Nullifier, 1829–1839* (Indianapolis, 1949); Wiltse, *John C. Calhoun, Sectionalist, 1840–1850* (Indianapolis, 1951).

such as the election of public officials and the linking of nation and states, deemed fundamental to American federalism.[7]

II

To begin with, South Carolina's provincial history was comparatively free from the kinds of civil strife which elsewhere became a normal ingredient of colonial existence and an important stimulus to the formation of party systems later on. Historians of colonial South Carolina agree that after 1740 no major internal divisions disturbed the province and that the two episodes most likely to have caused some permanent schism—the Great Awakening of the 1740s and the Regulator movement of the 1760s—had no lasting class or sectional consequences. Provincial energies instead became embroiled in a bitter and protracted constitutional struggle between the royal governor and his council on the one hand and the colonial House of Assembly on the other. Such crises of course occurred elsewhere in British North America, but what was unusual about this one was its failure to create enduring factional division, and, in addition, its monopolizing quality. It was not a political struggle for office and spoils but a constitutional battle pitting against each other two groups isolated in separate legislative branches and fighting for stakes too high to allow factional falling-out—a battle, in Robert Weir's words, which "took on the aspects of a contest

[7] In taking up such questions, one must necessarily treat political parties both as offsprings of independent, "fundamental" social forces (that is, as dependent variables) and, from a perspective less often adopted, as autonomous institutions which have their own dynamics and which enforce their own requirements upon the larger society (that is, as independent variables). Just as South Carolina's exceptionalism helped shape her political and party systems, so her party system helped create and define her racial and exclusive politics.

between the united representatives of one society and the representatives of an outside power." The contest so affected and absorbed all other political issues that South Carolina lived through a unique and critically long period of domestic political solidarity.[8]

Thus South Carolina entered the Revolution with little exposure to the critical formative experiences of internal dispute and compromise which help fashion political talent. Moreover, the comparatively minor, though sharp, domestic divisions of the Revolution and the Confederation in South Carolina made it all the easier, then and later, to view the events of the revolutionary era as part of a constitutional struggle against a hostile external force and little else. By the 1780s, then, two subtle but critical predispositions had come into being: one, a tendency to view division as unnatural as well as dangerous; and two, an inclination to treat opposition more as an external and constitutional challenge than as a political threat.

At the same time, the social and political implications of the state's disproportionately large slave population began to emerge. From the 1730s on, the presence of black

---

[8] M. Eugene Sirmans, *Colonial South Carolina: A Political History, 1663–1763* (Chapel Hill, N.C., 1966), pp. 200–207, 223–224, 231–233; Robert A. Weir, "'The Harmony We Were Famous For': An Interpretation of Pre-Revolutionary South Carolina Politics," *William and Mary Quarterly*, 3d ser., XXVI (Oct. 1969), 495–501. See also Richard Maxwell Brown, *The South Carolina Regulators* (Cambridge, Mass., 1963), p. 141; Jack P. Greene, "Changing Interpretations of Early American Politics," in Ray Allen Billington, ed., *The Reinterpretation of Early American History: Essays in Honor of John Edwin Pomfret* (San Marino, Calif., 1966), pp. 164–165, 177; and Greene, *The Quest for Power: The Lower Houses of Assembly in the Southern Colonies, 1689–1776* (Chapel Hill, N.C., 1963), pp. 38–39. The best brief description of colonial South Carolina society is Carl Bridenbaugh, *Myths and Realities: Societies of the Colonial South* (Baton Rouge, 1952), chaps. 2 and 3. On South Carolina during the Revolutionary era, see Charles G. Singer, *South Carolina in the Confederation* (Philadelphia, 1941).

chattels, who by 1776 in some parishes outnumbered the whites by as much as seven to one, had served along with the dominant British authority to unite the white colonists. However, once British political rule ended, the slaves' presence assumed the major unifying role and exerted among the minority whites an extraordinary and irresistible bent toward ideological conformity and communal and political solidarity. After 1820, no other state claimed so high a ratio of blacks to whites. And although fewer than 10 percent of the whites owned slaves in 1850, in no other state, save Louisiana, did the slave population become so evenly distributed territorially.[9] Fear of servile revolt tended therefore to be more common and intense everywhere in South Carolina than anywhere else in the South. And the San Domingo revolution of Toussaint L'Ouverture, the Charleston revolt of Denmark Vesey, Nat Turner's rebellion in Virginia, the recurring Charleston fires of the 1820s, and

---

[9] Weir, "'The Harmony We Were Famous For,'" pp. 482–483; David D. Wallace, *The History of South Carolina,* 4 vols. (New York, 1934), II, 418; Rosser H. Taylor, *Ante-Bellum South Carolina: A Social and Cultural History* (Chapel Hill, N.C., 1942), p. 8; and Charles S. Sydnor, *The Development of Southern Sectionalism, 1819–1848* (Baton Rouge, 1948), p. 5. In 1820 the tidewater parishes of Georgetown, Charleston, Colleton, and Beaufort had 126,000 blacks and 30,000 whites. Excluding Charleston City, blacks outnumbered whites in the four parishes by six to one. *Ibid.*, p. 11. After 1810, Louisiana's black population, including free blacks, surpassed the white population but never to the degree of South Carolina's from 1820 on. In 1860, two-thirds of the parishes of both states contained black majorities; in Mississippi, only one-half did so. Extrapolated from U.S. Bureau of the Census, *A Compendium of the Ninth Census* (Washington, D.C., 1870), pp. 8–18, 52–55, 88–89.

The figure for South Carolina slave ownership is somewhat misleading in indicating only slave owners. Since most of these would have been males with families, probably at least as much as 25 to 30 percent of the state's adult white population, including women and adult children at home, lived in households with slaves and thus had close contact with slavery. This says nothing of those affected by slavery in other ways.

the typical and universal acts of slave resistance and violence did nothing to dampen this endemic anxiety. In such a charged setting, discord and division among the whites became deeply feared; every effort was made to maintain unity of purpose; deeply shared beliefs and commitments came to define narrowly what was and what was not legitimate in the way of politics and discourse; and a tradition—one is inclined to say an entire culture—of conformity thus came into being.

The existence of slavery also worked in other ways than through fear to bind whites together. As W. J. Cash and others have observed, by enabling every white to assume a minimal class superiority and to oppose any exploitation of his labor, the blacks' presence gave poor whites a sense of affinity with their "betters" based on race which purely class interests could never have done.[10] Not only did this sense of class position work for ideological uniformity among the whites, but it also sharply diminished the consciousness of existing social and economic tensions, which might have taken the form of political conflict, and maintained for an unusual length of time the deference of less fortunate whites toward the more privileged planter class. All in all, this was not an atmosphere in which competitive politics were likely to be tolerated, much less to flourish.

Yet however valid V. O. Key's assertion that "whatever phase of the southern political process one seeks to understand, sooner or later the trail of inquiry leads to the Negro," other factors quite as significant as slavery impeded the growth of two-party politics.[11] For one, the ethnic and cultural differences which almost everywhere else helped establish and sustain political divisions were generally fewer and less intense in South Carolina than elsewhere in the nation and, during the half-century before

---

[10] W. J. Cash, *The Mind of the South* (New York, 1941), pp. 35–43.

[11] V. O. Key, Jr., *Southern Politics.* (New York, 1949), p. 5.

the Civil War, were diminishing. Such differences as those between the Anglican gentry in the tidewater parishes and the Scotch-Irish Presbyterians and German and Swiss Calvinists and Lutherans in the middle and upcountry districts did of course make themselves felt.[12] Moreover, Charleston and a few smaller towns contained differentiated white populations of rich and poor, merchants and mechanics, tradesmen, sailors, and professionals. But as time passed, the white immigrant groups were absorbed into the larger society. In addition, the gradual diffusion of the low-country aristocracy into the interior brought about greater association and intermarriage among the English and other stocks and stimulated the rise to maturity and power of the backcountry society (of which Calhoun was the leading exemplar). Moreover, the limited variety of South Carolina town and city society could not nourish or institutionalize cultural and political differences against such other forces as race solidarity. Finally, South Carolina was not struck as were many other states after 1830 by a flood of German and Irish immigrants. Their absence not only eliminated many of the typical sources of urban politics but also blunted the rise of a distinctive town and urban life outside Charleston.[13] In short, the arena of ethnocultural politics, so conducive to party competition elsewhere, was considerably narrower in South Carolina, and its limits helped greatly to reduce the number and complexity of public issues throughout the state.

The lessening of ethnic and religious division was related to the long-run decline in internal sectional antagonism. Such antagonisms were at one time consider-

---

[12] Bridenbaugh, *Myths and Realities*, chaps. 2 and 3; and Taylor, *Ante-Bellum South Carolina*, p. 150.

[13] Of South Carolina's total 1850 population, black and white, only 1 percent were foreign-born. Even more strikingly, only 2 percent of the American native-born residing in South Carolina had been born outside the state. J. Potter, "The Growth of Population in America, 1700–1860," in D. V. Glass and D. E. C. Eversley, eds., *Population in History* (London, 1965), p. 682.

able. After the Revolution, sectional conflicts with ethnic and religious overtones, such as the fight over ratification, had become so sharp that one authority on the South has written that by the early nineteenth century, in contrast to provincial tranquillity, intrastate sectionalism in South Carolina was "more pronounced than in any of the other South Atlantic states."[14] Yet within thirty years of Jefferson's election, the decline of coastal rice culture, the onset of the great cotton booms, the interior sweep of plantation agriculture, and legislative reapportionment had greatly weakened, if not entirely ended, these regional schisms.

Their demise was not due, however, to the superior strength of the backcountry. For though the inland districts contained 80 percent of the state's white population, they had never been strong enough to exact major and lasting concessions from the dominant tidewater parishes. The constitution of 1790 had given the interior greater legislative representation than before and had also established the permanent capital at its piedmont site in Columbia. Yet, according to William A. Schaper, under the 1790 frame of government "a little more than one-fifth of the white population imposed a government upon the other four-fifths."[15]

---

[14] Thomas P. Abernethy, *The South in the New Nation, 1789–1819* (Baton Rouge, 1961), pp. 438–439. See also Gordon S. Wood, *The Creation of the American Republic, 1776–1787* (Chapel Hill, N.C., 1969), pp. 278–282.

[15] William A. Schaper, *Sectionalism and Representation in South Carolina*, in *Annual Report of the American Historical Association for the Year 1900*, 2 vols. (Washington, D.C., 1901), I, 379; and Abernethy, *South in the New Nation*, p. 28. On the 1790 constitution, see *ibid.*, p. 32; Wolfe, *Jeffersonian Democracy in South Carolina*, pp. 44–46. Malapportionment at this time is discussed by Schaper, *Sectionalism and Representation*, p. 379; Fletcher M. Green, *Constitutional Development in the South Atlantic States, 1776–1860* (Chapel Hill, N.C., 1930), pp. 121–122, 197; and David D. Wallace, *South Carolina: A Short History, 1520–1948* (Chapel Hill, N.C., 1951), p. 356. On an unsuccessful reappor-

If this were so, how were sectional grievances kept from breaking forth as they had in the 1760s? One reason was that cotton, demanded by new markets, moved swiftly upcountry after the Revolution onto plantations owned by low-country magnates. Slaves accompanied cotton. And whereas for fifty years after the Revolution the generally slaveless upcountry farmers had demanded a more just legislative representation of the interior districts, by the 1820s their calls had been stilled, in part through the growing ideological comity everywhere in white South Carolina, in part by a timely shift in the basis of legislative apportionment.[16] An 1808 amendment to the state constitution gave a majority of the membership in both houses of the legislature to the upcountry districts. Yet however designed to benefit the western regions, the amendment was not drawn to place more power in the hands of small farmers and tradesmen. Instead, the planter class, regrouping in central South Carolina on upland cotton plantations added to low-country holdings, had simply outmaneuvered the yeoman farmers and preserved its hold through reapportionment. As South Carolina's black population spread inland and as the area around Columbia developed a plantation economy similar to that of the tidewater, it was no sacrifice of the planters' interests to give a greater proportion of legislative seats to the inland districts.[17]

---

tionment attempt in 1794, see Rose, *Prologue to Democracy,* p. 104, and Wolfe, *Jeffersonian Democracy in South Carolina,* pp. 52–53.

[16] On the upcountry spread of tidewater culture, see Schaper, *Sectionalism and Representation,* pp. 384–395, 400–408, 434–437; and Rose, *Prologue to Democracy,* pp. 57–59.

[17] The reapportionment of 1808 is analyzed in Wolfe, *Jeffersonian Democracy in South Carolina,* pp. 219–220; Taylor, *Ante-Bellum South Carolina,* p. 6; and Freehling, *Prelude to Civil War,* p. 90. See also Thomas Cooper and Daniel McCord, eds., *The Statutes at Large of South Carolina,* 10 vols. (Columbia, S.C., 1836–1841), V, 594–595.

The results, however inadvertent, were profound. After 1830, although sectional antagonisms continued to break out over representation and taxation, sectional strife only temporarily shattered political solidarity; it never created the basis of lasting political competition. Furthermore, as the potentially volatile piedmont-plain schism was submerged under race fear and reduced by constitutional change, the ruling gentry could more easily unite the state against external enemies. And finally, as the nonplantation backcountry became a smaller and smaller part of the state, its political role became steadily weaker, so that in most elections after 1830, including that to the malapportioned Nullification Assembly in 1832, the upcountry of the yeoman farmer was at a great disadvantage. "There never was a time until the reconstruction days," Schaper has concluded, "that the black belt, or the greater low country, did not absolutely control the government of the state."[18]

Under some circumstances, the homogenizing effects of race fear, ethnic integration, and sectional peace might have been less keenly felt. A major city, for instance, is often a staging area of class strife and a spur to sectional politics, roles which Charleston might reasonably have been expected to fill. Long after the capital moved to Columbia in 1790 and well past the Civil War, she re-

[18] Schaper, *Sectionalism and Representation,* pp. 436–437. On the persistence of sectional schism, despite its submergence in race fear, see Key, *Southern Politics,* pp. 135–142; Wallace, *Short History,* pp. 424–425; Schaper, *Sectionalism and Representation,* pp. 424–426; and Boucher, "Secession and Co-Operation Movements," 132–134 n. Attempts at further reapportionment after 1808 are covered in Schaper, *Sectionalism and Representation,* pp. 437–446, and indicated in Cooper and McCord, eds., *Statutes of South Carolina,* VI, 117, 384–385. The effect of malapportionment at the time of the Nullification crisis is dealt with by Schaper, *Sectionalism and Representation,* pp. 441–443, and Chauncey S. Boucher, "Sectionalism, Representation, and the Electoral Question in Ante-Bellum South Carolina," *Washington University Studies,* IV, 2 (Oct. 1916), 12–13.

mained the state's only political center and only real city. She supported the only concentrated middle-class population of professionals, shopkeepers, and artisans in the state and of all towns was ethnically and economically the most varied.[19] No interior Pittsburgh challenged her economic preeminence, no Albany her political might, no Newport her social glitter, no Concord her cultural claims.

But as with so much else in South Carolina, Charleston was a city apart and her role ambiguous. For one thing, she was located in the heart of the tidewater black belt; her life and moods, dominated by the "peculiar institution," rendered all typical urban divisions subversive perils. Furthermore, as Charleston's aristocracy fastened its hold ever more tightly on the state through the inexorable inland advance of cotton culture, the city and its low-country hinterlands, by effectively keeping control of state politics, did the opposite of what a city might have done: they reinforced, rather than undermined, a homogeneity of view and of politics.

After all, few Charlestonians were fully urban. Their style of life was redolent of the landed gentry, their values marked by plantation slave owning, their political views a "country" ideology which depreciated the norms of merchant capitalism and scorned the reigning national political ways typified by Jackson's "Kitchen Cabinet" and Martin Van Buren. Charleston was a city at one with the surrounding land. If there were differences between leaders of the city and rural populations, they were differences at most of policy and power and rarely ever of value or world view. It was the country gentlemen who provided

---

[19] In 1850, as compared with Charleston City's 42,984 inhabitants, Columbia, the state's second largest community, had only 6,000 residents, followed by Camden, with 1,333. Not more, and probably less, than 15 percent of South Carolina's 1850 population lived in towns of more than 2,000. Taylor also reports 40-odd occupations in Charleston in 1831. Taylor, *Ante-Bellum South Carolina,* pp. 23–24, 75.

the models for the state's population, who ruralized the city rather than becoming citified by it.

The intimacy of city and country life in South Carolina was further reinforced by the cycle of Charleston's existence, which periodically brought together the city and country folk as in no other American community. Most of the state's leading families kept a permanent residence there, and many of them remained throughout the year. But more important, Charleston was also the city seat of the low and upcountry slave masters who joined the city in May for the relatively pestilence-free high social season. Liberated for a time from the loneliness and anxiety of their plantations, they were thrown in upon each other for a few months annually to share their hopes and fears and to find mutual reinforcement of attitude and conviction. Upon returning in the autumn to their country seats, what information and sentiments they carried away from the city tended to become the ruling ideology of the entire state. This annual cycle was like the highs and lows of malarial fever, at one time or another during the year drawing to the city every leading figure for renewal, ideas, and the inspiration to maintain solidarity in the face of the slave and the outside world and then casting him back to the outlands. In subtle but unmistakable ways, Charleston played a major part in unifying and reinforcing opinion and making more difficult the emergence and durability of differing political views.

If parties seem to flourish best under the conditions and spurs of urban life, their existence is also tied closely to the vitality of voluntary association in general. For throughout our history, political parties, before they have been anything else, have been associations of people coming together without coercion, organizations nurtured by older traditions of congregational and corporate communion and sustained by the widening experiences of men and women in many sorts of freely chosen joint activities. Parties, like other voluntary associations, have seemed to flourish best in towns and cities, where a kind of critical mass of people may be found to support activities beyond the family and government, where some leisured and comfortable citizens devote part of their lives to public affairs without taking up full-time political careers, and where voluntary action can gain and re-create the kind of reinforcement and replication it seems to need in order to survive. Voluntary action also requires a generous appraisal of what is legitimate in a society—that is, a fair degree of toleration if not also a rough kind of democracy. In addition, voluntary association flourishes best where no rigid distinction is drawn between what is considered public and private activity. For by their nature, voluntary associations designed for peaceful ends are quasi-public, composed of private citizens acting in behalf of group or public needs and seeking to accomplish legitimate purposes for one reason or another considered outside the competence or power of public authority (which thus must itself not be too powerful). Finally, the prosperity of voluntary associations, and thus of political parties, is enhanced when large numbers of citizens possess a sense of their own competence to effect change and when society allows a certain flexibility in the roles a citizen may play in the community.

Now it seems apparent that voluntary associations in South Carolina never enjoyed such conditions of encouragement and, what is more, that for a state with a city of comparable size and similar density of white population, South Carolina probably had fewer voluntary associations than most other states. Whether in fact this was so, and why there were fewer, would require a separate essay to explore. A low and diffused white population, the homogeneity of white society, the absence of many town centers, the historic weakness of local government, a powerful legislative rule, and the commanding influence of Charleston no doubt played a major part in discouraging their existence. So too did well-maintained class lines, the assumption that competence resided primarily among the great planters and their agents (best exemplified in the property-holding qualifications for officeholding), and the discountenancing of public action unless called into being by the community's leading men. Nor was the toleration of spontaneous and extraofficial organization likely to be great in a society which deeply feared dissent—all of which is to say that any movement toward political association had to struggle against serious historical and cultural odds.

In addition to all these factors—the hobgoblin of race, the comparative social homogeneity of the state, declining sectional schism, the sway of Charleston, and the weakness of voluntary initiative—many of which existed elsewhere but not so directly or intensively, an incipient system of party opposition eventually came up against some insuperable legal and institutional obstacles, which by the 1830s were unique to South Carolina. Among them, probably the most difficult to overcome was the epicentral political position of the state legislature. None other in antebellum America wielded such power. Its commanding authority arose in the first place from its choice of the governor. No other American legislature retained this power as long as South Carolina's did—until 1860. The governor was a creature of the legislature; and no matter his personal authority, once in office he was an impotent figure, lacking the powers of veto and appointment, ineligible to succeed himself after a short two-year term, and empowered primarily to command the militia and call special sessions. An aggressive gubernatorial aspirant might court legislative backing and, if elected, might seek to advance legislation or promote appointments; but without power or tenure, he could never be fully independent of the planter-dominated legislative majority which chose him, nor could he successfully set about creating a "governor's party," much less a stable political organization.

Furthermore, the absence of a statewide popular election for governor impeded the formation of electoral coalitions across the state and the partisan machinery to stimulate and maintain them. Under these circumstances, the leadership of state government never became the goal in South Carolina of great ambitions, as in Martin Van

Buren's New York or Salmon Chase's Ohio, and men of talent instead sought careers in the federal Cabinet and Congress. None of this was lost on the state's astute and powerful oligarchy. If the election of governor were given to the people, Calhoun warned in 1838, the pollution of high politics by popular influence would result. "Two violent parties would spring up" to seek federal aid and patronage; then federal influence would triumph, tidewater and upcountry would divide, and the republic would give way to a democracy.[20]

No less of a deterrent effect on party formation was the retention by the legislature through 1865, alone among all others after 1832, of the choice of presidential electors. By the late 1830s in other states, the presidential contest, opened now to popular suffrage, had demonstrated its capacity to intrude deeply upon the popular consciousness, to disturb oligarchic rule, and to bring about the organization of electoral coalitions and party organizations everywhere. But, as appreciated by the defenders of legislative election, it was in the nature of the presidency to seem even more remote and irrelevant than the state governorship when not subject to popular choice. It was also characteristic of elections to the state legislatures not to be much affected by presidential politics, even when, as occasionally occurred in South Carolina, legislative candidates aligned themselves publicly with one or another national party. Thus to prohibit popular elections of the president was, as conservative and particularistic interests meant it to be, to isolate the citizenry from external political

[20] Calhoun to A. H. Pendleton, November 19, 1838, in J. Franklin Jameson, ed., "Correspondence of John C. Calhoun," in *Annual Report of the American Historical Association for the Year 1899*, 2 vols. (Washington, D.C., 1900), II, 419–421. See also Chauncey S. Boucher, "Representation and the Electoral Question in Ante-Bellum South Carolina," Mississippi Valley Historical Association *Proceedings*, IX, 1 (1915–1916), 110–124. On the powers of the governor, see Ralph A. Wooster, *The People in Power: Courthouse and Statehouse in the Lower South, 1850–1860* (Knoxville, 1969), p. 49.

concerns, to discourage the rise of competing statewide coalitions vying for support, and in effect to keep the state at one with itself.[21]

Even more important, the South Carolina legislature possessed the power to elect or appoint by joint ballot all other state officers and court clerks and many local officials, some of whom were permitted by law to occupy seats in the legislature concurrently. This did not prevent South Carolinians from having a more intimate association with local government than with any other level of officialdom in the state, nor the legislature from gradually increasing the number of local offices to be filled by the citizens' suffrage. But local government in South Carolina was an institution over which voters exerted at most an indirect and diluted influence. Its officials normally bowed to the wishes of a majority of the legislature, most of whose members came from other regions of the state and a majority of whom represented plantation sentiment. Moreover, since colonial days, South Carolina county government had been splintered among many boards and officers, thus dividing accountability. "Power was focused," Charles Sydnor has written, "at one point in the state rather than at small points all over it; and the great power of the legislature was not counterbalanced by local institutions responsible either to the few or the many in the parish or county. Hence, the legislature could in some measure impose unity upon the state, using its power to break down local opposition groups." A system better calculated to stifle local initiative and suppress political opposition could

[21] William Goodman, *The Two-Party System in the United States*, 3d ed. (Princeton, 1964), pp. 158–159; McCormick, *Second American Party System*, pp. 28–29; and Henry Jones Ford, *The Rise and Growth of American Politics: A Sketch of Constitutional Development* (New York, 1898), pp. 159–161. Attempts made in South Carolina during the 1840s and 1850s to gain a popular choice of presidential electors all failed owing to planter resistance and ideological pressures. Boucher, "Representation and Electoral Question," pp. 114 ff., and Wallace, *Short History*, p. 518.

hardly be conceived within the confines of republican government.[22]

With the presidency, the governorship, and most local offices cut off from public ballot, the only genuinely popular elections open to the average white male in South Carolina were elections for the legislature and—largely because they were mandated by the federal constitution and could not be abridged by state law—for Congress. By their nature, however, neither House nor legislative balloting was likely to promote party formation. Legislative seats, if contested at all, normally fell under the control of local factions with little stable association with factions elsewhere. Control of the Assembly, except in times of high political fever such as the early 1830s, rarely became an issue; nor was leadership in the legislature so concentrated that coordinated campaigns across district lines seemed necessary. Moreover, district boundaries, congressional as well as legislative, divided the electorate rather than consolidating it into a general statewide mass.

As for the congressional races, the component civil divisions of districts tended to change after each decennial census, making difficult the formation of lasting partisan organizations and alliances. And districts were gerrymandered so as to carve up groups and regions which might otherwise coalesce to form distinct voting blocs. Nevertheless, as the national parties competed after 1828 for control of the House, congressional contests repre-

---

[22] Sydnor, *Development of Southern Sectionalism*, pp. 34–38, 43–44, 288. See also Sirmans, *Colonial South Carolina*, pp. 250–252; Schaper, *Sectionalism and Representation*, pp. 325–327, 332, 380, 382–383, 426, 437; Columbus Andrews, *Administrative County Government in South Carolina* (Chapel Hill, N.C., 1933), pp. 5, 18–19; and Cooper and McCord, eds., *Statutes of South Carolina*, V, 351–353, 408–412, 569–570, 674–675; VI, 338–339. On the right to sit concurrently in the legislature while holding appointive office, see the South Carolina Constitution of 1790, Art. I, Sec. 21, in Francis Newton Thorpe, *The Federal and State Constitutions . . .*, 7 vols. (Washington, D.C., 1909), VI, 3258–3269.

sented the only significant aperture through which national politics might penetrate the barrier of legislative dominance and stir popular interest. Under these conditions, one might expect to find much party competition for South Carolina House seats and perhaps even competition tied, through the adoption of national party labels and slogans, to national campaigns for House majorities. Such were the traditions and ideology of South Carolina politics, however, that neither competition nor national party relations emerged to any great extent. The norm of solidarity was too difficult to break.

We look at competition for office, especially in frequently held elections, as a sign of party formation. Similarly, party labels are usually an index not only to party identification but also to the capacity of national politics to invade a state political system. Yet in the 144 congressional races held in the state between 1824 and 1860, 78—or more than one-half—offered no contest to the voters. Moreover, 128, or 71 percent, of the 180 candidates whose party affiliations are known during the same period considered themselves Democrats. Of the rest, only 18, or 10 percent, were Whigs.[23] So strong were the institu-

[23] These figures, like those in the succeeding paragraphs, are extrapolated in part from data made available by the Inter-University Consortium for Political Research. The data were supplied in partially checked form, and the Consortium bears no responsibility for either the analyses or interpretations presented here. I have found, however, that in the case of South Carolina, the voting data for the 1830s has been entered in the Consortium records with the incorrect congressional district designations, which I have corrected in my own calculations from information derived from Cooper and McCord, eds., *Statutes of South Carolina, passim,* and especially from the Edgefield (S.C.) *Advertiser*, October 18, 1838, and November 5, 1840. Moreover, I have supplemented the Consortium data with voting statistics taken from Philip F. Wild, "South Carolina Politics, 1816–1833" (unpublished PhD dissertation, University of Pennsylvania, 1949), pp. 231, 301, 373, 531; Patrick S. Brady, "Political Culture in the Early American Republic: The Case of South Carolina" (unpublished Ph.D. dissertation,

tional and cultural constraints against competition that in the most open and popular elections in ante-bellum South Carolina only faint glimmerings of two-party competition were to be seen.

Nevertheless, judging from voting statistics available for the period between 1824 and 1860, South Carolinians took up the franchise under competitive circumstances in proportions which bear favorable comparison with electoral participation everywhere else in the nation during the era of the second-party system. An 1810 amendment to the state constitution had confirmed the gradual liberalization of voting rules and practices after 1760 by extending the suffrage in legislative and congressional elections, with a few minor exceptions, to all adult white males.[24] Under

---

University of California, Santa Barbara, 1972), pp. 90–91; Kibler, *Perry*, pp. 168–169 and 222–225; and *The Whig Almanac and United States Register* (New York, 1854–1855), 1851, p. 60. A thorough search through extant South Carolina newspapers would no doubt turn up additional voting data.

Regarding the figures on House candidacies, 29 percent of the House candidates between 1824 and 1860 cannot now be identified by party affiliation at all, and 34 of the 180 identified candidates carried party labels, such as "States Rights Nullifier" and "Union," which put them clearly in neither the Democratic nor the Whig camp, as did such labels as "Nullifier Democrat" and "States Rights Whig." Moreover, since 12 percent of the House races had more than two candidates entered, taken with the 78 no-contest elections only one-third of the races were strictly two-way.

[24] Colonial voting rules and practices are analyzed in Albert E. McKinley, *The Suffrage Franchise in the Thirteen English Colonies in America* (Philadelphia, 1905), pp. 141, 151; Greene, *Quest for Power*, p. 186; Brown, *South Carolina Regulators*, pp. 138–139; and Schaper, *Sectionalism and Representation*, pp. 349–353. In South Carolina, alone of the southern colonies, nonfreehold taxpayers could vote. Voting practices and regulations from the 1760s through 1810 are examined by Chilton Williamson, *American Suffrage from Property to Democracy, 1760–1860* (Princeton, 1960), pp. 11, 35–36, 83–86, 123, 132–133, 272; George C. Rogers, Jr., *Charleston in the Age of the Pinckneys* (Norman, Okla., 1969),

such conditions of universal white manhood suffrage, participation ranged between 69.3 percent and 82.9 percent of the adult white males in the five elections after 1824 for which complete statewide tallies exist. Put another way, the ante-bellum voting peaks in statewide elections of one-half the other twenty-three states were below South Carolina's 83 percent high point. More significantly, in the forty-two congressional races (forty of them pitting two or more candidates against each other) for which statistics are available, the median level of voter participation was 68.7 percent, with voting levels rising as high as 94.5 percent in individual districts.[25] In view of the impossibility of achieving strict comparability between voting activity in occasional congressional races in one state and in repeated gubernatorial and presidential contests elsewhere, these tallies must be evaluated with care. But it is clear that when stimulated to do so by competition among candidates, if not among durable parties, the qualified voters of

---

p. 51; Fletcher M. Green, "Democracy in the Old South," *Journal of Southern History,* XII (Feb. 1946), 8–9, 11; Green, *Constitutional Development,* pp. 86–87, 201–202; Wallace, *Short History,* p. 360; and Wolfe, *Jeffersonian Democracy in South Carolina,* p. 240.

[25] These figures are derived from data cited in note 22, supra, as well as from U.S. census data. I have taken the figures upon which the comparisons of state voting activity are based from McCormick, *Second American Party System, passim.* Comparisons of this sort are fraught with difficulty, but McCormick's own figures make them no easier. Part of the difficulty results from the fact that his figures are based upon presidential and gubernatorial votes, whereas the only popular voting in South Carolina occurred in congressional races; this reduces the comparability of South Carolina statistics with those of other states. But more important, McCormick himself fails to describe his figures consistently, taking a participation figure of 97 percent as "highly suspicious" but accepting one of 94 percent as accurate. I have assumed a certain level of inaccuracy to be characteristic of all ante-bellum voting data and therefore have accepted all of McCormick's figures as valid for purposes of comparison. *Ibid.,* pp. 123, 245, 290.

South Carolina voted with the same ease and roughly the same willingness as the voters of the other states.[26]

Legal and practical electoral democracy, however, does not create a democratic political culture. Ante-bellum South Carolina politics may have rested on a democratic electoral base, but the state's political system remained, as it always had, in the hands of an oligarchy, protected by high propertyholding qualifications for office, enjoying wide appointive powers, and holding sway by that blend of aristocratic and demagogic tactics so common to conservative and closed societies. This is not, however, to say that the leading political figures of the state ran roughshod over docile and obedient subjects. On the contrary, given the state's broad electoral foundation in congressional and legislative races, coupled with the absence of an intervening party structure, an access to, if not a dependence on, the average elector more direct than anywhere else was paradoxically the result. Under such conditions, racial extremism was almost irresistible and "fire-eating" demagoguery took the place of genuine electoral competition and party politics. It was in such a no-limits situation that Nullification flourished and Secession won out.

III

The existence after 1828 of a sharp discontinuity of party systems between South Carolina on the one hand and the

26 Because legislative elections occurred at the same date and place as congressional elections, these figures of participation might reflect interest in the legislative contests. Returns from legislative elections, however, remain too fragmentary to permit reliable comparisons of turnouts. Moreover, in those few instances in which balloting for the House took place separately—namely, in the springs of 1833, 1843, and 1853, when congressional elections were postponed until census figures had become available and reapportionment might take place—voting levels were not comparably lower than in the normal case of joint balloting.

nation and the remaining states on the other suggests that a link is to be found between these out-of-phase party systems and the two great failures of American federalism —Nullification and Secession—in which South Carolina played the central role.[27] Historians have at least implicitly recognized the inappropriateness of party terminology by depicting these conflicts as "Andrew Jackson versus South Carolina" and "South Carolina versus the United States": they cannot be understood as Democrats versus Whigs or Democrats versus Republicans. It is not, however, necessary to argue that these crises arose solely, or even principally, from the collision of different party orders. Nor, since none of the southern states, with the exception of border state Kentucky, possessed two-party systems in 1832 (as they would by 1836), will it do to argue that the lack of a two-party system caused South Carolina to adopt the Ordinance of Nullification or that, alternatively, by possessing one, the state would not have nullified the Tariff of 1828. Rather, it seems likely that a two-party system in the state would have softened the sectional character of the clash and brought about a definition of the issues in party, not particularistic, terms. Instead, the same conditions which created a no-party situation gave abnormal dimensions to the Nullification crisis and affected the manner and ability of Jackson's administration to deal with it. And here, a brief comparison of Nullification with an earlier threat to the Union—the crisis in Massachusetts over the War of 1812—is instructive.[28]

---

[27] Although space limitations preclude a consideration of the Secession crisis, the approach adopted here should be useful in considering the problems facing the Buchanan administration on the eve of the Civil War.

[28] Although political scientists seem uniformly to agree that political parties affect the functioning of the federal system of government—both by enhancing and by impeding its operations—few have done much in specifying their effects. In fact, the entire problem of parties and federalism has been largely unexplored by students of politics. Only hints are to be found in Daniel J. Elazar, *American Federalism: A View from the States*

The chronicle of intensifying nullificationist and secessionist sentiment in Massachusetts needs no retelling;[29] but it would be well to examine the mechanisms which dampened the disunionist impulse there. To begin with, the obstructionist tactics which are so often described as the actions of an entire section were instead the actions of a party, and the nation's minority party at that. In Massachusetts, where Federalists were dominant during the war, a strong core of the party remained unionist throughout; and an energetic and strong Republican party, rooted in the dissenting sects and among the aggrieved and ambitious—possessing, that is, a powerful and distinct social base—challenged the Federalists at every turn. Therefore, as neither party could afford to forget, the dynamics and opportunities of political opposition were always in play.[30]

(New York, 1966); Elazar, *The American Partnership: Intergovernmental Cooperation in the Nineteenth-Century United States* (Chicago, 1962); Elazar, "Federalism and Intergovernmental Relations," in Elazar et al., *Cooperation and Conflict: Readings in American Federalism* (Itasca, Ill., 1969), pp. 2–20; Morton Grodzins, "American Political Parties and the American System," *Western Political Quarterly*, XIII (Dec. 1960), 974–998; Grodzins, "Centralization and De-Centralization in the American Federal System," in *A Nation of States: Essays on the American Federal System*, ed. by Robert A. Goldwin (Chicago, 1961), pp. 1–23; Key, *American State Politics;* E. E. Schattschneider, *Party Government* (New York, 1942); and David B. Truman, "Federalism and the Party System," in *Federalism: Mature and Emergent*, ed. by Arthur W. Macmahon (New York, 1955), pp. 115–136.

[29] This matter has been dealt with by Samuel Eliot Morison, *The Life and Letters of Harrison Gray Otis, Federalist, 1765–1848*, 2 vols. (Boston, 1913), and James M. Banner, Jr., *To the Hartford Convention: The Federalists and the Origins of Party Politics in Massachusetts, 1789–1815* (New York, 1970).

[30] On the role and function of party opposition, see especially Richard Hofstadter, *The Idea of a Party System: The Rise of Legitimate Opposition in the United States, 1780–1840* (Berkeley, 1969), and David E. Apter, "Some Reflections on the Role of a Political Opposition in New Nations," *Comparative Studies in Society and*

By 1812, the Republican minority had already established its institutional shape, gained the legitimacy of time and electoral victory, and won a kind of protected place in the Old Puritan Commonwealth. As for the Federalists, they commanded broad support among the populace and through skillful propaganda and the exploitation of existing public belief were successful in representing themselves as the arbiters and defenders of New England's best interests. They also possessed, in such men as Harrison Gray Otis, leaders of great political skill who gradually came to identify their public careers and the interests of their section with the future of their party—which they willingly served.

But there was more to the limits on Federalist action than the leaders' concern for votes and the party's future. Equally influential was the restraint of party opposition, the external partisan checks offered by the Republican challenge. Among the administration's few advantages was the existence in the nation's most disloyal quarter of a two-party system mature enough to provide a crucially needed device for holding the obstructionist opposition in check and allowing the war to be prosecuted more or less on Republican terms.

The key to the Republicans' political leverage was the opportunity, normally offered by a two-party system but taking on heightened significance and utility in times of crisis, to place the opposition on the defensive. In time of war, parties are likely to sniff out disloyalty and treason, as well as mere skulduggery or stupidity, in the work of opposition. And inasmuch as the Federalists avowed their contempt of the War of 1812, the Republicans had an inestimable advantage: their loyalty was proven, not only be-

History, IV (Jan. 1962), 154–168. A superb case study of the effects of party opposition upon political leadership is Eric L. McKitrick, "Party Politics and the Union and Confederate War Efforts," in *The American Party Systems,* ed. by Chambers and Burnham, pp. 117–151.

cause they displayed it, but ipso facto by their membership in the party of war. In contrast, the Federalists were to be suspected of treason unless proven otherwise, and their party was to be considered throughout the war—and with much good reason—as the party of disloyalty and obstruction. Thus, in an age of deep antiparty bias, the Republicans placed an insurmountable burden of proof on their opponents by branding opposition to the war as the unprincipled work of party. Patriotism came to have critical implications for the manner in which political force could be threatened and used, and for the Republicans the inclination to make patriotism and politics serve each other provided constant moral incentive to party action. In fact, the Republicans of Massachusetts, usually taken to be the rather hapless dependents of the party of Virginia aristocrats, were central to Madison's war effort. The existence of a local and "native" opposition party, possessing deep and stable social roots and a developed and active party organization, kept war and loyalist sentiment alive in the opposition stronghold, afforded appointment opportunities which helped undergird the state's feeble loyalism, aided in the recruitment of federal troops and the agitation for local defense, and provided accurate intelligence on the activities of seditious Federalists. The Republican party was the indispensable local agent of a president in crisis about whose partisan and national fidelity there was never a question.

Twenty years later, the Nullification crisis confronted the exuberantly partisan Andrew Jackson with political difficulties as exquisite as those which faced Madison earlier. The difference was that Jackson had fewer means with which to deal with them. For one thing, national and state party systems had become so discontinuous that the Nullifiers no longer considered themselves part of the larger political and constitutional system. For another, the traditional factional alignments in South Carolina had been thrown into confusion. Benjamin F. Perry recalled later that "there was in the new organization of parties, a complete amalgamation of all parties and distinctions." [31] What is more, Jackson was called upon to confront men whose party support he might need in the future. The principles of opposition politics may thus have been in play, but not in the way to which partisans of the administration were accustomed. The crisis, after all, could not very well be defined as the work of party when the Nullifiers had been Democrats almost to a man. It was almost inevitable, therefore, that both antagonists should portray their conflict in constitutional terms: party terms had lost their political relevance.

As if facing the challenge of his own party brethren was not awkward enough, Jackson's interests were thrown into the hands of South Carolina Unionists such as Benjamin F. Perry and the proto-Whig "loyalist" James L. Petigru—deeply conservative men who, unlike the less cautious radicals, meant to have no truck with democracy, who were unconcerned to create an enduring local opposition party, and whose political instincts were often anti-"Jacksonian" and considerably more retrograde than those of the Nullifiers. Moreover, Unionist strength in South Carolina, unlike Republican strength in Massachusetts earlier, possessed a narrower and more fractionated social base than did the Nullifier coalition. The Unionist "party," William Freehling has written, "was a motley coalition of disparate types," composed of upcountry yeoman farmers long impatient with tidewater rule, East Bay merchants disdainful of the planter life, and aristocratic lowland lawyers and planters who feared the egalitarian and sectional demands of the backcountry population. The disparateness of the coalition was reflected in the ideological divisions among the Unionists themselves. They differed over the constitutionality of the Tariff of 1828, the very nub of Nullification. And as if such fundamental disagreement made unity of action unlikely enough, some Charleston

[31] Perry, *Reminiscences*, II, 208.

unionists threatened in 1832 to bolt to the Whig standard of Henry Clay.[32]

Adding to the Unionists' troubles was their inability to gain legitimacy within the state. Time was not in their favor. As a group, they had not been offering candidates for many months before the Nullification crisis broke out and did not have the opportunity, as had the Massachusetts Republicans for at least fifteen years before 1814, to evolve a coherent party ideology and a representative political structure. Theirs was also a coalition of the moment, called into being in response to a single issue and lacking its members' institutional commitment after the issue which created it had been resolved.[33]

Had time not been working against Jackson, he might have encouraged the Unionists in party formation and forced the Nullifiers permanently into an opposition stance within the Whig party. One incentive was the federal patronage, and the criterion of appointment was to be "unionism," as it had been "patriotism" in Massachusetts. Some of Jackson's Unionist allies tried to move quickly to reward fidelity to the president and to prevent office from passing through Nullifier hands.[34] Yet the South Carolina patronage always raised sensitive party issues, inasmuch as a Unionist was as likely to be Whiggish or anti-Jackson as he was Democratic. Moreover, federal posts in South Carolina had always been few, most federal appointees had, under the older dispensation of rewarding "character," served through a succession of administrations, and removals had been virtually nonexistent. Calhoun's 1849 boast that in South Carolina "party organization, party discipline, party

---

[32] Freehling, *Prelude to Civil War,* p. 237.

[33] On the exclusion of Unionists from public affairs after the Nullification crisis, see George C. Rogers, Jr., *The History of Georgetown County, South Carolina* (Columbia, S.C., 1970), pp. 162, 250, and chap. 4 *passim.*

[34] See, e.g., James L. Petigru to William Elliott, November 18, 1832, Carson, *Petigru,* pp. 105–106.

proscription—and their offspring, *the spoils principle,* have been unknown" was accurate history.[35]

But the problem went deeper still. The Nullifiers, often threatening to bolt to the Whigs, never could do so and thus robbed Jackson of another chance to work the levers of two-party competition. It is difficult to see how the Nullifiers could under any circumstances have felt comfortable within the party of nationalism and tariffs. And as for Webster and Clay, these two Whig stalwarts always doubted Calhoun's appeal throughout the South and feared the effects upon northern opinion of any association with him.[36]

Nevertheless, in this confusing political landscape, the Nullifiers possessed high political skills, if not a modern party sensibility; and the Unionists' difficulties ideally suited the Nullifiers' ends. They created campaign committees, rallied the voters, and organized the state as it had never been organized before. Once in control of the legislature, they exploited its centralized authority to rid the state of official Unionist influence. Yet they failed to create formal or lasting party machinery. And their scorn for the very acts they were called upon by the crisis to perform stands in sharp contrast to the rapid, permanent, and almost total capitulation of the Massachusetts Federalists to the democratic mode soon after 1800.

Now the Nullifiers, like the Unionists, lacked a deep commitment to political democracy. But that will not explain their failure to sustain their organizing endeavors. Their lack of staying power resulted partly from the absence of an opposition strong and entrenched enough to keep them up to the mark. Part can be attributed to the

---

[35] Carl Russell Fish, *The Civil Service and the Patronage* (Cambridge, Mass., 1904), pp. 84, 98, 126 n.; Harold S. Schultz, *Nationalism and Sectionalism in South Carolina, 1852–1860* (Durham, N.C., 1950), pp. 54–55.

[36] E. Malcolm Carroll, *Origins of the Whig Party* (Durham, N.C., 1925), pp. 53–55; Cole, *Whig Party in the South*, pp. 15–16, 42–45; Wiltse, *John C. Calhoun, Nullifier*, p. 234.

single-mindedness of the Nullifier campaign, a single-issue movement bound to disintegrate with the passing of the crisis. Much, however, must be laid to their party inexperience, which, when coupled with their profound ideological distrust of parties in any form, created an almost primordial aversion to open political action in normal times.

One does not know precisely in what way an antiparty ideology and a lifetime spent within South Carolina's no-party system reinforced each other. But Calhoun's case, never so typical as here, suggests the effect of such a heritage upon a man second to none in poltical ambition.[37] Henry A. Wise, Calhoun's contemporary, once remarked that the Great Nullifier was "a giant of intellect, who was a child in party tactics." [38] Yet where was the political and ideological schooling in South Carolina which might have made Calhoun a party wizard? Without a competitive two-party system, how was he to gain the sense of give and take, of the courtesies and accommodations so necessary to normal political transactions—which the likes of Van Buren had absorbed in their bones in the chaotic world of Empire State politics? Only early in his public career, when he sought election to Congress, did Calhoun face the common electorate. Thereafter, like almost every other officeholder in the state, he was beholden to the omnipotent legislature.[39] With no cause to go to the people, with no

[37] The best single review of Calhoun's party thought is William W. Freehling, "Spoilsmen and Interests in the Thought and Career of John C. Calhoun," *Journal of American History,* LII (June 1965), 25–42. See also Louis Hartz, "South Carolina vs. the United States," in *America in Crisis: Fourteen Crucial Episodes in American History,* ed. by Daniel Aaron (New York, 1952), pp. 73–89.

[38] Quoted in Wiltse, *Calhoun, Nationalist,* p. 244; see also pp. 270–271. Others shared this view. Beverly Tucker thought Calhoun "certainly the most unskilled leader of a party that ever wielded a truncheon." Quoted in Joseph G. Rayback, *Free Soil: The Election of 1848* (Lexington, Ky., 1970), p. 32 n.

[39] Compare the case of the radical James H. Hammond, whose 1834 race for Congress was "the only popular

institutional career to design and protect, he needed rather to keep his eyes sharply on his rivals like William Smith who competed not for the people's suffrage, nor for party preferment, but for the support of the legislators in Columbia.

Such circumstances led Calhoun to react almost instinctively to political threat in the increasingly anachronistic manner of eighteenth-century factional politics. No better example of this is to be found than his pathetic assault on Van Buren, his archrival for the presidency, in the infamous "Peggy Eaton Affair" of 1829. Through his starchy wife, Calhoun used the pretext of Mrs. Eaton's questionable past to snub her husband, the Secretary of War, in order to bring on a showdown with her debonair champion, the Secretary of State. What the contretemps revealed, however, was not simply the political rivalry of two ambitious men, but also the clash of political standards and of political styles. Raised in a society where "honor" and "integrity" were valued as the touchstones of public careers, Calhoun was lost in a "Jacksonian" setting which prized "service" and "effectiveness" above all. Jackson demanded party loyalty—or loyalty to himself and his administration, which came to the same thing; Calhoun maladroitly insisted upon moral etiquette and justification by character and tone.

In the end, the failure of Calhoun and his followers to understand and accept the revolution in political standards and conduct that had taken place proved Jackson's major difficulty: South Carolina, the last refuge of the antiparty tradition, would not govern itself by the political code of the rest of the nation. The transfer from personal to institutionalized power so necessary to party government had not occurred there, nor would two divergent party systems accommodate each other. Not the challenge of opposition, but only the threat of force, coupled with a

election Hammond ever had to stand." Elizabeth Merritt, *James Henry Hammond, 1807–1864* (Baltimore, 1923), p. 31.

timely tariff compromise, could discipline the Nullifiers.

Almost thirty years later, another Democratic administration faced a secessionist South Carolina. Only this time, the situation, though analogous to 1832, was worse. Unlike the Whigs then, the opposition Republicans in 1860 lacked a single tie within her borders. In fact, the old Democracy had been supplanted by a new secessionist party whose members claimed no allegiance to the party of Jefferson, Jackson, and Stephen A. Douglas. Buchanan's failing authority was not really at fault. No Andrew Jackson could this time prevent disunion. South Carolina had moved irrevocably outside the bounds of the American party system—and Secession was the result. This was the problem of South Carolina.

LAWRENCE W. LEVINE

"Some Go Up and Some Go Down": The Meaning of the Slave Trickster [1]

FOR THE HISTORIAN interested in slave culture, folk tales constitute a crucial source. Although few black tales were collected until the decades following the Civil War, their distribution was so widespread throughout the South, their content so similar, and their style and function so uniform that it is evident they were not a sudden post-emancipation creation. "All over the South the stories of Br'er Rabbit are told," Octave Thanet reported in 1892. "Everywhere not only ideas and plots are repeated, but the very words often are the same; one gets a new vision of the power of oral tradition." [2] The variations in patterns of mobility, educational and vocational opportunities, cultural expression, and life styles brought about by emancipation produced inevitable changes in black folklore. Still,

[1] The research for this essay was supported by National Institute of Mental Health Grant No. MH18732–02. My work has profited greatly from the criticisms of my Berkeley colleagues Alan Dundes, Robert Middlekauff, Irwin Scheiner, and Kenneth Stampp.

[2] Octave Thanet, "Folk-Lore in Arkansas," *Journal of American Folklore* [cited hereafter as *JAF*], 5 (April–June 1892), 122.

throughout the remainder of the nineteenth century—and well into the twentieth in many parts of the South—the large body of slave tales remained a vital and central core of Afro-American expression.

As with other aspects of their verbal art, slaves established in their tales important points of continuity with their African past. This is not to say that slave tales in the United States were necessarily African. Scholars will need more complete indices of African tale types and motifs than now exist before they can determine the origin of slave tales with any definitiveness. Comparison of slave tales with those guides to African tales that do exist reveals that a significant number were brought directly from Africa; a roughly similar percentage were tales common in both Africa and Europe, so that while slaves may have brought the tale type with them, its place in their lore could well have been reinforced by their contact with whites; and, finally, a third group of tales were learned in the New World both through Euro-American influence and through independent creation.[3]

Unfortunately, extended debate concerning the exact point of origin of these tales has taken precedence over analysis of their meaning and function. Cultural continuities with Africa were not dependent upon importation and perpetuation of specific folk tales in their pristine form. It was in the place that tales occupied in the lives of the slaves, the meaning slaves derived from them, and the ways in which slaves used them culturally and psychically that the clearest resemblances with their African past

[3] The following African tale type and motif indices were used in this comparison: Erastus Ojo Arewa, "A Classification of the Folktales of the Northern East African Cattle Area by Types" (unpublished Ph.D. dissertation, University of California, Berkeley, 1966); Winifred Lambrecht, "A Tale Type Index for Central Africa" (unpublished Ph.D. dissertation, University of California, Berkeley, 1967); Kenneth Wendell Clarke, "Motif-Index of the Folk-Tales of Culture-Area V West Africa" (unpublished Ph.D. dissertation, Indiana University, 1958).

could be found. Thus, although Africans brought to the New World were inevitably influenced by the tales they found there and frequently adopted white tale plots, motifs, and characters, what is most important is not the mere fact of these borrowings but their nature. Afro-American slaves did not borrow indiscriminately from the whites among whom they lived. A careful study of their folklore reveals that they tended to be most influenced by those patterns of Euro-American tales which in terms of functional meaning and aesthetic appeal had the greatest similarity to the tales with deep roots in their ancestral homeland. Regardless of where slave tales came from, the essential point is that with respect to language, delivery, details of characterization, and plot, slaves quickly made them their own and through them revealed much about themselves and their world. These processes can be illustrated through an examination of the slaves' animal trickster tales.

I

Contrary to the stereotype established by such early collectors and popularizers of slave tales as Joel Chandler Harris, slave lore was not monopolized by the adventures of Brer Rabbit and his fellow creatures. Afro-American slaves, like their African progenitors, told a wide variety of tales covering many aspects of life and experience and fulfilling a myriad of needs. Slaves related human as well as animal trickster tales; they told Bible stories, explanatory tales, moralistic and didactic tales, supernatural tales and legends, humorous anecdotes, and stories featuring local traditions and personal experiences. The range of slave tales was narrow in neither content nor focus. In spite of this, it is not surprising or accidental that the tales most easily and abundantly collected in Africa and among Afro-Americans in the New World were animal trickster tales. Because of their overwhelmingly paradigmatic character, animal tales were, of all the narratives of social protest or psychological release, among the easiest to relate both within and especially outside the group.

The propensity of Africans to utilize their folklore quite consciously to gain psychological release from the inhibitions of their society and their situation is by now well known, but it needs to be reiterated here if the popularity and function of animal trickster tales is to be understood. After listening to a series of Ashanti stories that included rather elaborate imitations of afflicted people—an old woman dressed in rags and covered with sores, a leper, an old man suffering from the skin disease yaws—which called forth roars of laughter from the audience, the English anthropologist R. S. Rattray suggested that it was unkind to ridicule such subjects. "The person addressed replied that in everyday life no one might do so, however great the inclination to laugh might be. He went on to explain that it was so with many other things: the cheating and tricks of priests, the rascality of a chief—things about which every one knew, but concerning which one might not ordinarily speak in public. These occasions gave every one an opportunity of talking about and laughing at such things; it was 'good' for every one concerned, he said." Customs such as these led Rattray to conclude "beyond a doubt, that West Africans had discovered for themselves the truth of the psychoanalysts' theory of 'repressions', and that in these ways they sought an outlet for what might otherwise become a dangerous complex."[4]

Certainly this was at the heart of the popularity of animal trickster tales. Whether it is accurate to assert, as Rattray has done, that the majority of "beast fables" were derived from the practice of substituting the names of animals for the names of real individuals whom it would have been impolitic or dangerous to mention, there can be no question that the animals in these tales were easily recognizable representations of both specific actions and gen-

[4] R. S. Rattray, *Akan-Ashanti Folk Tales* (Oxford, 1930), pp. x–xii.

eralized patterns of human behavior. "In the fable," Léopold Senghor has written, "the animal is seldom a totem; it is this or that one whom every one in the village knows well: the stupid or tyrannical or wise and good chief, the young man who makes reparation for injustice. Tales and fables are woven out of everyday occurrences. Yet it is not a question of anecdotes or of 'material from life'. The facts are images and have paradigmatic value." [5] The popularity of these tales in Africa is attested to by the fact that the Akan-speaking peoples of the West Coast gave their folk tales the generic title *Anansesem* (spider stories), after the spider trickster Anansi, whether he appeared in the story or not, and this practice was perpetuated by such New World Afro-American groups as the South American Negroes of Surinam who referred to all their stories, whatever their nature, as *Anansitori,* or the West Indian blacks of Curaçao who called theirs *Cuenta de Nansi.*[6]

For all their importance, animals did not monopolize the trickster role in African tales; tricksters could, and did, assume divine and human form as well. Such divine tricksters as the Dahomean Legba or the Yoruban Eshu and Orunmila did not survive the transplantation of Africans to the United States and the slaves' adaptation to Christian religious forms. Human tricksters, on the other hand, played an important role in the tales of American slaves. By the nineteenth century, however, these human tricksters were so rooted in and reflective of their new cultural and social setting that outside of function they bore increasingly little resemblance to their African counterparts. It was in the animal trickster that the most easily perceivable correspondence in form and usage between African and Afro-American tales can be found. In both cases the

[5] Janheinz Jahn, *Muntu: An Outline of the New African Culture* (New York, 1961), p. 221.

[6] Rattray, *Akan-Ashanti Folk Tales,* p. xiii; Melville J. and Frances S. Herskovits, *Suriname Folk-Lore* (New York, 1936), p. 138; *Standard Dictionary of Folklore, Mythology and Legend* (New York, 1949–1950), I, 52–53.

primary trickster figures of animal tales were weak, relatively powerless creatures who attain their ends through the application of native wit and guile rather than power or authority: the Hare or Rabbit in East Africa, Angola, and parts of Nigeria; the Tortoise among the Yoruba, Ibo, and Edo peoples of Nigeria; the Spider throughout much of West Africa including Ghana, Liberia, and Sierra Leone; Brer Rabbit in the United States.[7]

In their transmutation from their natural state to the world of African and Afro-American tales, the animals inhabiting these tales, though retaining enough of their natural characteristics to be recognizable, were almost thoroughly humanized. The world they lived in, the rules they lived by, the emotions that governed them, the status they craved, the taboos they feared, the prizes they struggled to attain, were those of the men and women who lived in this world. The beings that came to life in these stories were so created as to be human enough to be identified with but at the same time exotic enough to allow both storytellers and listeners a latitude and freedom that came only with much more difficulty and daring in tales explicitly concerning human beings.

This latitude was crucial, for the one central feature of almost all trickster tales is their assault upon deeply ingrained and culturally sanctioned values. This of course accounts for the almost universal occurrence of trickster

[7] Other primary animal trickster figures in Africa whose geographical distribution is less clear-cut include Antelope, Squirrel, Wren, Weasel, and Jackal. Ruth Finnegan, *Oral Literature in Africa* (Oxford, 1970), pp. 344–354; Richard A. Waterman and William R. Bascom, "African and New World Negro Folklore," *Standard Dictionary of Folklore, Mythology and Legend,* I, 18–24; A. B. Ellis, "Evolution in Folklore: Some West African Prototypes of the 'Uncle Remus' Stories," *Popular Science Monthly,* 48 (Nov. 1895), 93–104. For a refutation of the once widely held thesis that the slaves' rabbit trickster was borrowed from the North American Indians, see Alan Dundes, "African Tales Among the North American Indians," *Southern Folklore Quarterly,* 29 (Sept. 1965), 207–219.

tales, but it has not rendered them universally identical. The values people find constraining and the mechanisms they choose to utilize in their attempts at transcending or negating them are determined by their culture and their situation. "It is very well to speak of 'the trickster,'" Melville and Frances Herskovits have noted, "yet one need but compare the Winnebago trickster [of the North American Indians] . . . with Legba and Yo in Dahomey to find that the specifications for the first by no means fit the second." [8] The same may be said of the slave trickster in relation to the trickster figures of the whites around them. Although animal trickster tales do not seem to have caught strong hold among American whites during the eighteenth and the first half of the nineteenth centuries, there were indigenous American tricksters from the tall, spare New Englander Jonathan, whose desire for pecuniary gain knew few moral boundaries, to the rough roguish confidence men of southwestern tales. But the American process that seems to have been most analogous in function to the African trickster tale was not these stories so much as the omnipresent tales of exaggeration. In these tall tales Americans were able to deal with the insecurities produced by forces greater than themselves not by manipulating them, as Africans tended to do, but by overwhelming them through the magnification of the self epitomized in the unrestrained exploits of a Mike Fink or Davy Crockett. "I'm . . . half-horse, half-alligator, a little touched with the snapping turtle; can wade the Mississippi, leap the Ohio, ride upon a streak of lightning, and slip without a scratch down a honey locust; can whip my weight in wildcats, . . . hug a bear too close for comfort, and eat any man opposed to Jackson," the latter would boast.[9]

---

[8] Melville J. and Frances S. Herskovits, *Dahomean Narrative* (Evanston, 1958), pp. 99–101.

[9] Constance Rourke, *American Humor* (New York, 1931), chaps. 1–2; Jesse Bier, *The Rise and Fall of American Humor* (New York, 1968), chaps. 1–2; Richard M. Dorson, *American Folklore* (Chicago, 1959),

It is significant that mythic strategies such as these played almost no role in the lore of nineteenth-century slaves; not until well after emancipation do tales of exaggeration, with their magnification of the individual, begin to assume importance in the folklore of Afro-Americans. Nor did the model of white trickster figures seem to have seriously affected the slave whose own tricksters remained in a quite different mold—one much closer to the cultures from which they had come. In large part African trickster tales revolved around the strong patterns of authority so central to African cultures. As interested as they might be in material gains, African trickster figures were more obsessed with manipulating the strong and reversing the normal structure of power and prestige. Afro-American slaves, cast into a far more rigidly fixed and certainly a more alien authority system, could hardly have been expected to neglect a cycle of tales so ideally suited to their needs. This is not to argue that slaves in the United States continued with little or no alteration the trickster lore of their ancestral home. The divergences were numerous: divine trickster figures disappeared; such important figures as Anansi the spider were at best relegated to the dim background; sizable numbers of European tales and themes found their way into the slave repertory. But we must take care not to make too much of these differences. For instance, the fact that the spider trickster retained its importance and its Twi name, Anansi, among the Afro-Americans of Jamaica, Surinam, and Curaçao, while in the United States Anansi lived only a peripheral existence in such tales as the Aunt Nancy stories of South Carolina and Georgia, has been magnified out of proportion by some students. "The sharp break between African and American tradition," Richard Dorson has written, "occurs at the West Indies, where Anansi the spider dominates hundreds of cantefables, the tales that inclose songs. But no Anansi stories are found in

chap. 2; James T. Pearce, "Folk-Tales of the Southern Poor-White, 1820–1860," *JAF*, 63 (Oct.–Dec. 1950), 398–412.

the United States."[10] The decline of the spider trickster in the United States can be explained by many factors from the ecology of the United States in which spiders are less ubiquitous and important than in either Africa or those parts of the New World in which the spider remained a central figure, to the particular admixture of African peoples in the various parts of the Western Hemisphere. Anansi, after all, was but one of many African tricksters and in Africa itself had a limited influence. Indeed, in many parts of South America where aspects of African culture endured overtly with much less alteration than occurred in the United States, Anansi was either nonexistent or marginal.[11]

What is more revealing than the life or death of any given trickster figure is the retention of the trickster tale itself. Despite all of the changes that took place, there persisted the mechanism, so well developed throughout most of Africa, by means of which psychic relief from arbitrary authority could be secured, symbolic assaults upon the powerful could be waged, and important lessons about authority relationships could be imparted. Afro-Americans in the United States were to make extended use of this mechanism throughout their years of servitude.

[10] Dorson, *American Folklore,* p. 185. In fact, as this essay demonstrates, Anansi stories were present in the nineteenth-century United States in small numbers. Not until the twentieth-century influx of West Indians into the United States are Anansi tales found with any regularity, as the manuscripts of the Federal Writers' Project, New York File, Archive of Folk Song (Library of Congress), indicate. Even then, of course, the spider remains a minor figure in United States black folklore.

[11] For an indication of the distribution of Anansi stories in South America, see Terrence Leslie Hansen, *The Types of the Folktale in Cuba, Puerto Rico, the Dominican Republic, and Spanish South America* (Berkeley, 1957).

II

In its simplest form the slaves' animal trickster tale was a cleanly delineated story free of ambiguity. The strong assault the weak, who fight back with any weapons they have. The animals in these tales have an almost instinctive understanding of each other's habits and foibles. Knowing Rabbit's curiosity and vanity, Wolf constructs a tar-baby and leaves it by the side of the road. At first fascinated by this stranger and then progressively infuriated at its refusal to respond to his friendly salutations, Rabbit strikes at it with his hands, kicks it with his feet, butts it with his head, and becomes thoroughly enmeshed. In the end, however, it is Rabbit whose understanding of his adversary proves to be more profound. Realizing that Wolf will do exactly what he thinks his victim least desires, Rabbit convinces him that of all the ways to die the one he is most afraid of is being thrown into the briar patch, which of course is exactly what Wolf promptly does, allowing Rabbit to escape.[12]

This situation is repeated in tale after tale: the strong attempt to trap the weak but are tricked by them instead. Fox entreats Rooster to come down from his perch, since all the animals have signed a peace treaty and there is no longer any danger: "I don' eat you, you don' boder wid me. Come down! Le's make peace!" Almost convinced by this good news, Rooster is about to descend when he thinks

[12] The tar-baby story appears in virtually every collection of black tales in this period. For examples, see Thaddeus Norris, "Negro Superstitions," *Lippincott's Magazine*, 6 (July 1870), 94–95; William Owens, "Folk-Lore of the Southern Negroes," *ibid.*, 20 (Dec. 1877), 750–751; Charles C. Jones, *Negro Myths From the Georgia Coast* (Boston, 1888), pp. 7–11; Louis Pendleton, "Notes on Negro Folk-Lore and Witchcraft in the South," *JAF*, 3 (July–Sept. 1890), 201; *Southern Workman*, 23 (Aug. 1894), 149–150; A. M. H. Christensen, *Afro-American Folk Lore* (New York, 1969; orig. pub. 1892), pp. 62–72.

better of it and tests Fox by pretending to see a man and a dog coming down the road. "Don' min' fo' comin' down den," Fox calls out as he runs away. "Dawg ain't got no sense, yer know, an' de man got er gun." [13] Spotting a goat lying on a rock, Lion is about to surprise and kill him when he notices that Goat keeps chewing and chewing although there is nothing there but bare stone. Lion reveals himself and asks what he is eating. Overcoming the momentary paralysis which afflicts most of the weak animals in these tales when they realize they are trapped, Goat saves himself by saying in his most terrifying voice: "Me duh chaw dis rock, an ef you dont leff, wen me done . . . me guine eat you." [14]

At its most elemental, then, the trickster tale consists of a confrontation in which the weak use their wits to evade the strong. Mere escape, however, does not prove to be victory enough, and in a significant number of these tales the weak learn the brutal ways of the more powerful. Fox, taking advantage of Pig's sympathetic nature, gains entrance to his house during a storm by pleading that he is freezing to death. After warming himself by the fire, he acts exactly as Pig's instincts warned him he would. Spotting a pot of peas cooking on the stove, he begins to sing:

Fox and peas are very good,
But Pig and peas are better.

Recovering from his initial terror, Pig pretends to hear a pack of hounds, helps Fox hide in a meal barrel, and pours the peas in, scalding Fox to death.[15] In one tale after another the trickster proves to be as merciless as his stronger opponent. Wolf traps Rabbit in a hollow tree and sets it on fire, but Rabbit escapes through a hole in the back and

[13] Elsie Clews Parsons, *Folk-Lore of the Sea Islands, South Carolina* (Memoirs of the American Folklore Society, XVI, 1923), p. 78.
[14] Jones, *Negro Myths,* p. 35.
[15] *Southern Workman,* 22 (June 1898), 125.

reappears, thanking Wolf for an excellent meal, explaining that the tree was filled with honey which melted from the heat. Wolf, in his eagerness to enjoy a similar feast, allows himself to be sealed into a tree which has no other opening, and is burned to death. "While eh duh bun, Buh Wolf bague an pray Buh Rabbit fuh leh um come out, but Buh Rabbit wouldnt yeddy [hear] um."[16] The brutality of the trickster in these tales was sometimes troubling ("Buh Rabbit . . . hab er bad heart," the narrator of the last story concluded), but more often it was mitigated by the fact that the strong were the initial aggressors and the weak really had no choice. The characteristic spirit of these tales was one not of moral judgment but of vicarious triumph. Storytellers allowed their audience to share the heartening spectacle of a lion running in terror from a goat or a fox fleeing a rooster; to experience the mocking joy of Brer Rabbit as he scampers away through the briar patch calling back to Wolf, "Dis de place me mammy fotch me up,—dis de place me mammy fotch me up"; to feel the joyful relief of Pig as he turns Fox's song upside down and chants:

Pigs and peas are very good,
But Fox and peas are better.

Had self-preservation been the only motive driving the animals in these stories, the trickster tale need never have varied from the forms just considered. But Brer Rabbit and his fellow creatures were too humanized to be content with mere survival. Their needs included all the prizes human beings crave and strive for: wealth, success, prestige, honor, sexual prowess. Brer Rabbit himself summed it up best in the tale for which this essay is named:

> De rabbit is de slickest o' all de animals de Lawd ever made. He ain't de biggest, an' he ain't de loudest but he sho' am de slickest. If he gits in trouble he gits out by gittin' somebody else in. Once he fell down a deep well an' did he holler and cry? No

---

[16] Jones, *Negro Myths*, pp. 97–99.

> siree. He set up a mighty mighty whistling and a singin', an' when de wolf passes by he heard him an' he stuck his head over an' de rabbit say, "Git 'long 'way f'om here. Dere ain't room fur two. Hit's mighty hot up dere and nice an' cool down here. Don' you git in dat bucket an' come down here." Dat made de wolf all de mo' onrestless and he jumped into the bucket an' as he went down de rabbit come up, an' as dey passed de rabbit he laughed an' he say, "Dis am life; some go up and some go down." [17]

There could be no mistaking the direction in which Rabbit was determined to head. It was in his inexorable drive upward that Rabbit emerged not only as an incomparable defender but also as a supreme manipulator, a role that complicated the simple contours of the tales already referred to.

In the ubiquitous tales of amoral manipulation, the trickster could still be pictured as much on the defensive as he was in the stories which had him battling for his very life against stronger creatures. The significant difference is that now the panoply of his victims included the weak as well as the powerful. Trapped by Mr. Man and hung from a sweet gum tree until he can be cooked, Rabbit is buffeted to and fro by the wind and left to contemplate his bleak future until Brer Squirrel happens along. "This yer my cool air swing," Rabbit informs him. "I taking a fine swing this morning." Squirrel begs a turn and finds his friend surprisingly gracious: "Certainly, Brer Squirrel, you do me proud. Come up here, Brer Squirrel, and give me a hand with this knot." Tying the grateful squirrel securely in the tree, Rabbit leaves him to his pleasure—and his fate. When Mr. Man returns, "he take Brer Squirrel home and cook him for dinner." [18]

---

[17] Federal Writers' Project, Mississippi File, Archive of Folksong (Library of Congress).

[18] Emma M. Backus, "Folk-Tales From Georgia," *JAF*, 13 (Jan.–March 1900), 22–24.

However, it was primarily advancement not preservation that led to the trickster's manipulations. Among a slave population whose daily rations were at best rather stark fare and quite often a barely minimal diet, it is not surprising that food proved to be the most common symbol of enhanced status and power. In his never ending quest for food the trickster was not content with mere acquisition which he was perfectly capable of on his own; he needed to procure the food through guile from some stronger animal. Easily the most popular tale of this type pictures Rabbit and Wolf as partners in farming a field. They have laid aside a tub of butter for winter provisions, but Rabbit proves unable to wait or to share. Pretending to hear a voice calling him, he leaves his chores and begins to eat the butter. When he returns to the field he informs his partner that his sister has just had a baby and wanted him to name it. "Well, w'at you name um?" Wolf asks innocently. "Oh, I name um Buh Start-um," Rabbit replies. Subsequent calls provide the chance for additional assaults on the butter and additional names for the nonexistent babies: "Buh Half-um," "Buh Done-um." After work, Wolf discovers the empty tub and accuses Rabbit, who indignantly denies the theft. Wolf proposes that they both lie in the sun, which will cause the butter to run out of the guilty party. Rabbit agrees readily, and when grease begins to appear on his own face he rubs it onto that of the sleeping Wolf. "Look, Buh Wolf," he cries, waking his partner, "de buttah melt out on you. Dat prove you eat um." "I guess you been right," Wolf agrees docilely, "I eat um fo' trute."[19] In some versions the animals propose a more hazardous ordeal by fire to discover the guilty party. Rabbit successfully jumps over

[19] For examples of the many versions of this tale, see Christensen, *Afro-American Folk Lore*, pp. 73–80; Guy B. Johnson, *Folk Culture on St. Helena Island, South Carolina* (Chapel Hill, N.C., 1930), pp. 138–140; Jones, *Negro Myths*, pp. 53–57; A. M. Bacon and Elsie Clews Parsons, "Folk-Lore from Elizabeth City County, Virginia," *JAF*, 35 (July–Sept. 1922), 253–256.

the flames but some innocent animal—Possum, Terrapin, Bear—falls in and perishes for Rabbit's crime.[20]

In most of these tales the aggrieved animal, realizing he has been tricked, desperately tries to avenge himself by setting careful plans to trap Rabbit, but to no avail. Unable to outwit Rabbit, his adversaries attempt to learn from him, but here too they fail. Seeing Rabbit carrying a string of fish, Fox asks him where they came from. Rabbit confesses that he stole them from Man by pretending to be ill and begging Man to take him home in his cart which was filled with fish. While riding along, Rabbit explains, he threw the load of fish into the woods and then jumped off to retrieve them. He encourages Fox to try the same tactic and Fox is beaten to death, as Rabbit knew he would be, since Man is too shrewd to be taken in the same way twice.[21]

And so it goes in story after story. Rabbit cheats Brer Wolf out of his rightful portion of a cow and a hog they kill together.[22] He tricks Brer Fox out of his part of their joint crop year after year "until he starved the fox to death. Then he had all the crop, and all the land too."[23] He leisurely watches all the other animals build a house in which they store their winter provisions and then sneaks in, eats the food, and scares the others, including Lion, away by pretending to be a spirit and calling through a horn in a ghostly voice that he is a "better man den ebber bin yuh befo."[24] He convinces Wolf that they ought to sell their

[20] See, for instance, Joel Chandler Harris, *Uncle Remus: His Songs and His Sayings* (New York, 1880), pp. 80–86; Elsie Clews Parsons, "Tales From Guilford County, North Carolina," *JAF*, 30 (April–June 1917), 192–193; Richard Smith, "Richard's Tales," *Publications of the Texas Folk-Lore Society*, 25 (1953), 220–224.

[21] Jones, *Negro Myths*, pp. 102–105; Parsons, *Folk-Lore of the Sea Islands*, p. 39.

[22] *Southern Workman*, 25 (Sept. 1896), 185–186; (Oct. 1896), 205.

[23] Bacon and Parsons, "Folk-Lore from Elizabeth City County, Virginia," 277–278.

[24] Jones, *Negro Myths*, pp. 49–53.

own grandparents for a tub of butter, arranges for his grandparents to escape so that only Wolf's remain to be sold, and once they are bartered for the butter he steals that as well.[25]

The many tales of which these are typical make it clear that what Rabbit craves is not possession but power and this he acquires not simply by obtaining food but by obtaining it through the manipulation and deprivation of others. It is not often that he meets his match, and then generally at the hands of an animal as weak as himself. Refusing to allow Rabbit to cheat him out of his share of the meat they have just purchased, Partridge samples a small piece of liver and cries out, "Br'er Rabbit, de meat bitter! Oh, 'e bitter, bitter! bitter, bitter! You better not eat de meat," and tricks Rabbit into revealing where he had hidden the rest of the meat. "You is a damn sha'p feller," Partridge tells him. "But I get even wid you." [26] Angry at Frog for inviting all the animals in the forest but him to a fish dinner, Rabbit frightens the guests away and eats all the fish himself. Frog gives another dinner, but this time he is prepared and tricks Rabbit into the water. "You is my master many a day on land, Brer Rabbit," Frog tells him just before killing and eating him, "but I is you master in the water." [27]

It is significant that when these defeats do come, most often it is not brute force but even greater trickery that triumphs. Normally, however, the trickster has more than his share of the food. And of the women as well, for sexual prowess is the other basic sign of prestige in the slaves' tales. Although the primary trickster was occasionally depicted as a female—Ol' Molly Hare in Virginia, Aunt Nancy or Ann Nancy in the few surviving spider stories [28]—in general women played a small role in slave

[25] Christensen, *Afro-American Folk Lore,* pp. 73–80.

[26] *Ibid.,* pp. 104–107; Parsons, *Folk-Lore of the Sea Islands,* pp. 30–31.

[27] Backus, "Folk-Tales from Georgia," p. 25.

[28] For examples, see Anne Virginia Culbertson, *At the Big House* (Indianapolis, 1904); Emma M. Backus,

tales. They were not actors in their own right so much as attractive possessions to be fought over. That the women for whom the animals compete are frequently the daughters of the most powerful creatures in the forest makes it evident that the contests are for potency as well as pleasure. When Brer Bear promises his daughter to the best whistler in the forest, Rabbit offers to help his only serious competitor, Brer Dog, whistle more sweetly by slitting the corners of his mouth, which in reality makes him incapable of whistling at all. If Rabbit renders his adversaries figuratively impotent in their quest for women, they often retaliate in kind. In the story just related, Dog chases Rabbit, bites off his tail, and nothing more is said about who wins the woman.[29] More often, though, Rabbit is successful. In the most well known and symbolically interesting courting tale, Rabbit and Wolf vie for the favors of a woman who is pictured as either equally torn between her two suitors or leaning toward Wolf. Rabbit alters the contest by professing surprise that she could be interested in Wolf, since he is merely Rabbit's riding horse. Hearing of this, Wolf confronts Rabbit, who denies ever saying it and promises to go to the woman and personally refute the libel as soon as he is well enough. Wolf insists he go at once, and the characteristic combination of Rabbit's deceit and Wolf's seemingly endless trust and gullibility allows Rabbit to convince his adversary that he is too sick to go with him unless he can ride on Wolf's back with a saddle and bridle for support. The rest of the story is inevitable. Approaching the woman's house Rabbit tightens the reins, digs a pair of spurs into Wolf, and trots him around crying,

---

"Animal Tales from North Carolina," *JAF,* 11 (Oct.–Dec. 1898), 288–289; Bacon and Parsons, "Folk-Lore from Elizabeth City County, Virginia," 266; Joel Chandler Harris, *Seven Tales of Uncle Remus* (Atlanta, 1948), tale 7.

[29] *Southern Workman,* 27 (April 1898), 76.

"Look here, girl! what I told you? Didn't I say I had Brother Wolf for my riding-horse?" [30] It was in many ways the ultimate secular triumph in slave tales. The weak doesn't merely kill his enemy: he mounts him, humiliates him, reduces him to servility, steals his woman, and, in effect, takes his place.

Mastery through possessing the two paramount symbols of power—food and women—did not prove to be sufficient for Rabbit. He craved something more. Going to God himself, Rabbit begs for enhanced potency in the form of a larger tail, greater wisdom, bigger eyes. In each case God imposes a number of tasks upon Rabbit before his wishes will be fulfilled. He must bring God a bag full of blackbirds, the teeth of a rattlesnake or alligator, a swarm of yellowjackets, the "eyewater" (tears) of a deer. Rabbit accomplishes each task by exploiting the animals' vanity. He tells the blackbirds that they cannot fill the bag and when they immediately prove they can, he traps them. He taunts the snake, "dis pole *swear* say you aint long as him." When Rattlesnake insists he is, Rabbit ties him to the stick, ostensibly to measure him, kills him, and takes his teeth. Invariably Rabbit does what is asked of him but finds God less than pleased. In some tales he is chased out of Heaven. In others God counsels him, "Why Rabbit, ef I was to gi' you long tail aint you see you'd 'stroyed up de whol worl'? Nobawdy couldn' do nuttin wid you!" Most commonly God seemingly complies with Rabbit's request and gives him a bag which he is to open when he returns home. But Rabbit cannot wait, and when he opens the bag prematurely

[30] For various versions of this widely popular tale, see Owens, "Folk-Lore of the Southern Negroes," p. 753; Jones, *Negro Myths*, pp. 27–31; *Southern Workman*, 23 (Aug. 1894), 149–150; Mrs. William Preston Johnston, "Two Negro Tales," *JAF*, 9 (July–Sept. 1896), 194–196; Bacon and Parsons, "Folk-Lore from Elizabeth City County, Virginia," pp. 265–266; Parsons, *Folk-Lore of the Sea Islands*, pp. 53–55.

"thirty bull-dawg run out de box, an' bit off Ber Rabbit tail again. An' dis give him a short tail again." [31]

The rabbit, like the slaves who wove tales about him, was forced to make do with what he had. His small tail, his natural portion of intellect—these would have to suffice, and to make them do he resorted to any means at his disposal: means which may have made him morally tainted but which allowed him to survive and even to conquer. In this respect there was a direct relationship between Rabbit and the slaves, a relationship which the earliest collectors and interpreters of these stories understood well. Joel Chandler Harris, as blind as he could be to some of the deeper implications of the tales he heard and retold, was always aware of their utter seriousness. "Well, I tell you dis," Harris had Uncle Remus say, "ef deze yer tales wuz des fun, fun, fun, en giggle, giggle, giggle, I let you know I'd a-done drapt um long ago." From the beginning Harris insisted that the animal fables he was collecting were "thoroughly characteristic of the negro," and commented that "it needs no scientific investigation to show why he selects as his hero the weakest and most harmless of all animals, and brings him out victorious in contests with the bear, the wolf, and the fox." [32] Harris's interpretations were typical. In the preface to her important 1892 collection of black tales, Abigail Christensen noted, "It must be remembered that the Rabbit represents the colored man. He is not as large nor as strong, as swift, as wise, nor as handsome as the elephant, the alligator, the bear, the deer, the serpent, the fox, but he is 'de mos' cunnin' man dat go on fo' leg' and by this cunning he gains success. So the negro, without education or wealth, could only hope to succeed by stratagem." [33] In that same year Octave Thanet, in an

---

[31] Christensen, *Afro-American Folk Lore,* pp. 36–41; Jones, *Negro Myths,* pp. 99–102; Parsons, *Folk-Lore of the Sea Islands,* pp. 14–19.

[32] *Nights with Uncle Remus* (Boston, 1883), p. 330; *Uncle Remus: His Songs and His Sayings,* p. xiv.

[33] Christensen, *Afro-American Folk Lore,* pp. ix–xiv.

article on Arkansas folklore, concluded, "Br'er Rabbit, indeed, personifies the obscure ideals of the negro race. . . . Ever since the world began, the weak have been trying to outwit the strong; Br'er Rabbit typifies the revolt of his race. His successes are just the kind of successes that his race have craved." [34]

These analyses of the animal trickster tales have remained standard down to our own day.[35] They have been advanced not merely by interpreters of the tales but by their narrators as well. Prince Baskin, one of Mrs. Christensen's informants, was quite explicit in describing the model for many of his actions:

> You see, Missus, I is small man myself; but I aint nebber 'low no one for to git head o' me. I allers use my sense for help me 'long jes' like Brer Rabbit. 'Fo de wah ol' Marse Heywood mek me he driber on he place, an' so I aint hab for work so hard as de res'; same time I git mo' ration ebery mont' an' mo' shoe when dey share out de cloes at Chris'mus time. Well, dat come from usin' my sense. An' den, when I ben a-courtin' I nebber 'lowed no man to git de benefit ob me in dat. I allers carry off de purties' gal, 'cause, you see, Missus, I know how to play de fiddle an' allers had to go to ebery dance to play de fiddle for dem.[36]

More than half a century later, William Willis Greenleaf of Texas echoed Baskin's admiration: "De kinda tales dat allus suits mah fancy de mo'es' am de tales de ole folks used to tell 'bout de ca'iens on of Brothuh Rabbit. In de early days Ah heerd many an' many a tale 'bout ole Brothuh

[34] Thanet, "Folk-Lore in Arkansas," p. 122.

[35] See, for instance, John Stafford, "Patterns of Meaning in Nights with Uncle Remus," *American Literature*, 18 (May 1946), 89–108; Louise Dauner, "Myth and Humor in the Uncle Remus Fables," *ibid.*, 20 (May 1948), 129–143; Bernard Wolfe, "Uncle Remus and the Malevolent Rabbit," *Commentary* (July 1949), 31–41; Marshall Fishwick, "Uncle Remus vs. John Henry: Folk Tension," *Western Folklore*, 20 (April 1961), 77–85.

[36] Christensen, *Afro-American Folk Lore*, pp. 1–5.

Rabbit what woke me to de fac' dat hit tecks dis, dat an' t'othuh to figguh life out—dat you hafto use yo' haid fo mo'n a hat rack lack ole Brothuh Rabbit do. Ole Brothuh Rabbit de smaa'tes' thing Ah done evuh run 'crost in mah whole bawn life." [37]

This testimony—and there is a great deal of it—documents the enduring identification between black storytellers and the central trickster figure of their tales. Brer Rabbit's victories became the victories of the slave. This symbolism in slave tales allowed them to long outlive slavery itself. So long as the perilous situation and psychic needs of the slave continued to characterize large numbers of freedmen as well, the imagery of the old slave tales remained both aesthetically and functionally satisfying. By ascribing actions to semi-mythical actors, Negroes were able to overcome the external and internal censorship that their hostile surroundings imposed upon them. The white master could believe that the rabbit stories his slaves told were mere figments of a childish imagination, that they were primarily humorous anecdotes depicting the "roaring comedy of animal life." Blacks knew better. The trickster's exploits, which overturned the neat hierarchy of the world in which he was forced to live, became their exploits; the justice he achieved, their justice; the strategies he employed, their strategies. From his adventures they obtained relief; from his triumphs they learned hope.

To deny this interpretation of slave tales would be to ignore much of their central essence. The problem with the notion that slaves completely identified with their animal trickster hero whose exploits were really protest tales in disguise is that it ignores much of the complexity and ambiguity inherent in these tales. This in turn flows from the propensity of scholars to view slavery as basically a relatively simple phenomenon which produced human products conforming to some unitary behavioral pattern. Too

---

[37] J. Mason Brewer, *Dog Ghosts and Other Texas Negro Folk Tales* (Austin, 1958), p. 50.

frequently slaves emerge from the pages of historians' studies either as docile, accepting beings or as alienated prisoners on the edge of rebellion. But if historians have managed to escape much of the anarchic confusion so endemic in the "peculiar institution," slaves did not. Slaveholders who considered Afro-Americans to be little more than subhuman chattels converted them to a religion which stressed their humanity and even their divinity. Masters who desired and expected their slaves to act like dependent children also enjoined them to behave like mature, responsible adults, since a work force consisting only of servile infantiles who can make no decisions on their own and can produce only under the impetus of some significant other is a dubious economic resource, and on one level or another both masters and slaves understood this. Whites who considered their black servants to be little more than barbarians, bereft of any culture worth the name, paid a fascinated and flattering attention to their song, their dance, their tales, and their forms of religious exercise. The life of every slave could be altered by the most arbitrary and amoral acts. They could be whipped, sexually assaulted, ripped out of societies in which they had deep roots, and bartered away for pecuniary profit by men and women who were also capable of treating them with kindness and consideration and who professed belief in a moral code which they held up for emulation not only by their children but often by their slaves as well. It would be surprising if these dualities which marked the slaves' world were not reflected in both the forms and the content of their folk culture. In their religious songs and sermons slaves sought certainty in a world filled with confusion and anarchy; [38] in their supernatural folk beliefs they sought power and control in a world filled with arbitrary forces greater than themselves; and in their tales they sought understanding of a world in which, for better or worse, they were forced to live. All the

[38] See Lawrence W. Levine, "Slave Songs and Slave Consciousness," in Tamara Hareven, ed., *Anonymous Americans* (Englewood Cliffs, N.J., 1971), pp. 99–130.

forms of slave folk culture afforded their creators psychic relief and a sense of mastery. Tales differed from the other forms in that they were more directly didactic in intent and therefore more compellingly and realistically reflective of the irrational and amoral side of the slaves' universe. It is precisely this aspect of the animal trickster tales that has been most grossly neglected.

III

Although the vicarious nature of slave tales was undeniably one of their salient features, too much stress has been laid on it. These were not merely clever tales of wish-fulfillment through which slaves could escape from the imperatives of their world. They could also be painfully realistic stories which taught the art of surviving and even triumphing in the face of a hostile environment. They underlined the dangers of acting rashly and striking out blindly, as Brer Rabbit did when he assaulted the tar-baby. They pointed out the futility of believing in the sincerity of the strong, as Brer Pig did when he allowed Fox to enter his house. They emphasized the necessity of comprehending the ways of the powerful, for only through such understanding could the weak endure. This lesson especially was repeated endlessly. In the popular tales featuring a race between a slow animal and a swifter opponent, the former triumphs not through persistence, as does his counterpart in the Aesopian fable of the Tortoise and the Hare—which always remained more popular among whites than blacks—but by outwitting his opponent and capitalizing on his weaknesses and short-sightedness. Terrapin defeats Deer by placing relatives along the route with Terrapin himself stationed by the finish line. The deception is never discovered, since to the arrogant Deer all terrapins "am so much like one anurrer you cant tell one from turrer." "I still t'ink Ise de fas'est runner in de worl'," the bewildered Deer complains after the race. "Maybe you air," Terrapin responds, "but I kin head you off wid sense." [39] Rabbit too understands the myopia of the powerful and benefits from Mr. Man's inability to distinguish between the animals by manipulating Fox into taking the punishment for a crime that Rabbit himself commits. "De Ole Man yent bin know de diffunce tween Buh Rabbit an Buh Fox," the storyteller pointed out. "Eh tink all two bin de same animal." [40] For black slaves whose individuality was so frequently denied by the whites above them, this was a particularly appropriate and valuable message.

In many respects the lessons embodied in the animal trickster tales ran directly counter to those of the moralistic tales so popular among ante-bellum slaves. Friendship, held up as a positive model in the moralistic tales, was pictured as a fragile reed in the trickster tales. In the ubiquitous stories in which a trapped Rabbit tricks another animal into taking his place, it never occurs to him simply to ask for help. Nor when he is being pursued by Wolf does Hog even dream of asking Lion for aid. Rather he tricks Lion into killing Wolf by convincing him that the only way to cure his ailing son is to feed him a piece of half-roasted wolf liver.[41] The animals in these stories seldom ask each other for disinterested help. Even more rarely are they caught performing acts of altruism—and with good reason. Carrying a string of fish he has just caught, Fox comes upon the prostrate form of Rabbit lying in the middle of the road moaning and asking for a doctor. Fox lays down his fish and hurries off to get help—with predictable results; "Ber Fox los' de fish. An' Ber Rabbit got de fish an' got

[39] Various versions of this ubiquitous tale can be found in Owens, "Folk-Lore of the Southern Negroes," p. 751; Christensen, *Afro-American Folk Lore,* p. 79; Sadie E. Stewart, "Seven Folk-Tales from the Sea Islands, S.C.," *JAF,* 32 (July–Sept. 1919), 394; Jones, *Negro Myths,* pp. 5–6; B. A. Botkin, ed., *Lay My Burden Down* (Chicago, 1945), p. 23; Backus, "Animal Tales from North Carolina," pp. 284–285; Parsons, *Folk-Lore of the Sea Islands,* p. 79.

[40] Jones, *Negro Myths,* p. 105.

[41] Christensen, *Afro-American Folk Lore,* pp. 101–103.

better. Dat's da las' of it." [42] Brer Rooster learns the same lesson when he unselfishly tries to help a starving Hawk and is rewarded by having Hawk devour all of his children.[43]

Throughout these tales the emphasis on the state of perpetual war between the world's creatures revealed the hypocrisy and meaninglessness of their manners and rules. Animals who called each other brother and sister one moment were at each other's throats the next. On his way to church one Sunday morning, Rabbit meets Fox and the usual unctuous dialogue begins. "Good-mornin', Ber Rabbit!" Fox sings out. "Good-mornin', Ber Fox!" Rabbit sings back. After a few more pleasantries, the brotherliness ends as quickly as it had begun and Fox threatens, "Dis is my time, I'm hungry dis mornin'. I'm goin' to ketch you." Assuming the tone of the weak supplicant, Rabbit pleads, "O Ber Fox! leave me off dis mornin'. I will sen' you to a man house where he got a penful of pretty little pig, an' you will get yer brakefus' fill." Fox agrees and is sent to a pen filled not with pigs but hound dogs who pursue and kill him. Reverting to his former Sabbath piety, Rabbit calls after the dogs, "Gawd bless yer soul! dat what enemy get for meddlin' Gawd's people when dey goin' to church." "I was goin' to school all my life," Rabbit mutters to himself as he walks away from the carnage, "an' learn every letter in de book but *d*, an' D was death an' death was de en' of Ber Fox." [44]

Such stories leave no doubt that slaves were aware of the need for role playing. But animal tales reveal more than this; they emphasize in brutal detail the irrationality and anarchy that rules man's universe. In tale after tale violence and duplicity are pictured as existing for their own sake. Rabbit is capable of acts of senseless cruelty performed for no discernible motive. Whenever he comes across an alligator's nest "didn' he jes scratch the aigs out

---

[42] Parsons, *Folk-Lore of the Sea Islands*, p. 44.
[43] Jones, *Negro Myths*, pp. 11–14.
[44] Parsons, *Folk-Lore of the Sea Islands*, pp. 66–67.

fur pure meaness, an' leave 'em layin' around to spile."[45] In an extremely popular tale Alligator confesses to Rabbit that he doesn't know what trouble is. Rabbit offers to teach him and instructs him to lie down in the broom grass. While Alligator is sleeping in the dry grass, Rabbit sets it on fire all around him and calls out, "Dat's trouble, Brer 'Gator, dat's trouble youse in."[46] Acts like this are an everyday occurrence for Rabbit. He sets Tiger, Elephant, and Panther on fire, provokes Man into burning Wolf to death, participates in the decapitation of Raccoon, causes Fox to chop off his own finger, drowns Wolf and leaves his body for Shark and Alligator to eat, boils Wolf's grandmother to death and tricks Wolf into eating her.[47] These actions often occur for no apparent reason. When a motive is present there is no limit to Rabbit's malice. Nagged by his wife to build a spring house, Rabbit tricks the other animals into digging it by telling them that if they make a dam to hold the water back they will surely find buried gold under the springbed. They dig eagerly and to Rabbit's surprise actually do find gold. "But Ole Brer Rabbit never lose he head, that he don't, and he just push the rocks out the dam, and let the water on and drown the lastest one of them critters, and then he picks up the gold, and of course Ole Miss Rabbit done get her spring house."[48] It is doubtful, though, that she was able to enjoy it for very long, since in another tale Rabbit coolly sacrifices his wife and little children in order to save himself from Wolf's vengeance.[49]

Other trickster figures manifest the identical amorality. Rabbit himself is taken in by one of them in the popu-

[45] Johnston, "Two Negro Tales," pp. 196–198.
[46] Christensen, *Afro-American Folk Lore*, pp. 54–57; Zora Neale Hurston, *Mules and Men* (Philadelphia, 1935), pp. 141–142.
[47] *Southern Workman*, 25 (April 1896), 82; Bacon and Parsons, "Folk-Lore from Elizabeth City County, Virginia," pp. 252–253, 277; Jones, *Negro Myths*, pp. 73–81; Harris, *Nights with Uncle Remus*, pp. 314–319.
[48] Emma M. Backus, "Tales of the Rabbit from Georgia Negroes," *JAF*, 12 (April–June 1899), 111–112.
[49] Christensen, *Afro-American Folk Lore*, pp. 26–35.

lar tale of the Rooster who tucked his head under his wing and explained that he had his wife cut his head off so he could sun it. "An' de rabbit he thought he could play de same trick, so he went home an' tol' his ol' lady to chop his head off. So dat was de las' of his head." [50] All tricksters share an incapacity for forgetting or forgiving. In a North Carolina spider tale, Ann Nancy is caught stealing Buzzard's food and saves herself only by obsequiously comparing her humble lot to Buzzard's magnificence, stressing "how he sail in the clouds while she 'bliged to crawl in the dirt," until he takes pity and sets her free. "But Ann Nancy ain't got no gratitude in her mind; she feel she looked down on by all the creeters, and it sour her mind and temper. She ain't gwine forget anybody what cross her path, no, that she don't, and while she spin her house she just study constant how she gwine get the best of every creeter." In the end she invites Buzzard to dinner and pours a pot of boiling water over his head, "and the poor old man go bald-headed from that day." [51] At that he was lucky. When Rabbit's friend Elephant accidentally steps on Rabbit's nest, killing his children, Rabbit bides his time until he catches Elephant sleeping, stuffs leaves and grass in his eyes, and sets them on fire.[52] Hare, unable to forgive Miss Fox for marrying Terrapin instead of himself, sneaks into her house, kills her, skins her, hangs her body to the ceiling, and smokes her over hickory chips.[53]

The unrelieved violence and brutality of these tales can be accounted for easily enough within the slave-as-trickster, trickster-as-slave thesis. D. H. Lawrence's insight that "one sheds one's sicknesses in books" is particularly applicable here. Slave tales which functioned as the bondsmen's books were a perfect vehicle for the channelization

---

[50] Elsie Clews Parsons, "Folk-Tales Collected at Miami, Florida," *JAF*, 30 (April–June 1917), 226.
[51] Backus, "Animal Tales from North Carolina," pp. 288–289.
[52] Jones, *Negro Myths*, pp. 91–93.
[53] *Southern Workman*, 26 (1897), 58.

of the slaves' "sicknesses": their otherwise inexpressible angers, their gnawing hatreds, their pent-up frustrations. On one level, then, the animal trickster tales were expressions of the slaves' unrestrained fantasies: the impotent become potent, the brutalized are transformed into brutalizers, the undermen inherit the earth. But so many of these tales picture the trickster in such profoundly ambivalent or negative terms, so many of them are cast in the African mold of not depicting phenomena in hard-and-fast, either-or, good-evil categories, that it is difficult to fully accept Bernard Wolfe's argument that it is invariably "the venomous American slave crouching behind the Rabbit." [54] Once we relax the orthodoxy that the trickster and the slave are necessarily one, other crucial levels of meaning and understanding are revealed.

"You nebber kin trus Buh Rabbit," a black storyteller concluded after explaining how Rabbit cheated Partridge. "Eh all fuh ehself; an ef you listne ter him tale, eh gwine cheat you ebry time, an tell de bigges lie dout wink eh yeye." [55] Precisely what many slaves might have said of their white masters. Viewed in this light, trickster tales were a prolonged and telling parody of white society. The animals were frequently almost perfect replicas of whites as slaves saw them. They occasionally worked but more often lived a life filled with leisure-time activities: they fished, hunted, had numerous parties and balls, courted demure women who sat on verandas dressed in white. They mouthed lofty platitudes and professed belief in noble ideals but spent much of their time manipulating, oppressing, enslaving one another. They surrounded themselves with meaningless etiquette, encased themselves in rigid hierarchies, dispensed rewards not to the most deserving but to the most crafty and least scrupulous. Their world was filled with violence, injustice, cruelty. Though they might possess great power, they did not always wield

[54] Wolfe, "Uncle Remus and the Malevolent Rabbit," p. 36.

[55] Jones, *Negro Myths*, pp. 128–129.

it openly and directly but often with guile and indirection. This last point especially has been neglected; the strong and not merely the weak could function as trickster. Jenny Proctor remembered her Alabama master who was exceedingly stingy and fed his slaves badly: "When he go to sell a slave, he feed that one good for a few days, then when he goes to put 'em on up the auction block he takes a meat skin and greases all round that nigger's mouth and makes 'em look like they been eating plenty meat and such like and was good and strong and able to work." [56]

Slave tales are filled with instances of the strong acting as tricksters: Fox asks Jaybird to pick a bone out of his teeth, and once he is in his mouth, Fox devours him; Buzzard invites eager animals to go for a ride on his back, then drops them to their deaths and eats them; Wolf constructs a tar-baby in which Rabbit almost comes to his end; Elephant, Fox, and Wolf all pretend to be dead in order to throw Rabbit off guard and catch him at their "funerals"; Fox tells Squirrel that he had a brother who could jump from the top of a tall tree right into his arms, and when Squirrel proves he can do the same, Fox eats him.[57] Tales like these, which formed an important part of the slaves' repertory, indicate that the slave could empathize with the tricked as well as the trickster. Again the didactic function of these stories becomes apparent. The slaves' interest was not always in being like the trickster but often in avoiding being like his victims from whose fate they could learn valuable lessons. Although the trickster tales could make a mockery of the values preached by the moralistic tales—friendship, hard work, sincerity—there were also impor-

[56] Botkin, *Lay My Burden Down*, p. 91.

[57] Emma M. Backus and Ethel Hatton Leitner, "Negro Tales from Georgia," *JAF*, 25 (April–June 1912), 127–128; Owens, "Folk-Lore of the Southern Negroes," 752; Bacon and Parsons, "Folk-Lore from Elizabeth City County, Virginia," pp. 262–264; Christensen, *Afro-American Folk Lore*, pp. 19–22, 62–72; Backus, "Folk-Tales from Georgia," pp. 24–25; *Southern Workman*, 28 (March 1899), 113.

tant lines of continuity between the moralistic tales and the trickster stories. Animals were taken in by the trickster most easily when they violated many of the lessons of the moralistic tales: when they were too curious, as Alligator was concerning trouble; too malicious, as Wolf was when he tried to kill Rabbit by the most horrible means possible; too greedy, as Fox and Buzzard were when their hunger for honey led to their deaths; overly proud and arrogant, as Deer was in his race with Terrapin; unable to keep their own counsel, as Fox was when he prematurely blurted out his plans to catch Rabbit; obsessed with a desire to be something other than what they are, as the Buzzard's victims were when they allowed their desire to soar in the air to overcome their caution.

The didacticism of the trickster tales was not confined to tactics and personal attributes. They also had important lessons to teach concerning the nature of the world and of the beings who inhabited it. For Afro-American slaves, as for their African ancestors, the world and those who lived in it were pictured in naturalistic and unsentimental terms. The vanity of human beings, their selfishness, their propensity to do anything and betray anyone for self-preservation, their drive for status and power, their basic insecurity, were all pictured in grim detail. The world was not a rational place in which order and justice prevailed and good was dispensed. The trickster, as Louise Dauner has perceived, often functioned as the eternal "thwarter," the symbol of "the irrational twists of circumstance." His remarkably gullible dupes seldom learned from their experience at his hands any more than human beings learn from experience. There was no more escape from him than there is escape from the irrational in human life.[58] The trickster served as agent of the world's irrationality and as reminder of man's fundamental helplessness. Whenever animals became too bloated with their power or importance or sense

[58] Dauner, "Myth and Humor in the Uncle Remus Fables," p. 135.

of control, the trickster was on hand to remind them of how things really were. No animal escaped these lessons; not Wolf, not Lion, not Elephant, indeed, not the trickster himself. Throughout there is a latent yearning for structure, for justice, for reason, but they are not to be had, in this world at least. If the strong are not to prevail over the weak, neither shall the weak dominate the strong. Their eternal and inconclusive battle served as proof that man is part of a larger order which he scarcely understands and certainly does not control.

If the animal trickster functioned on several different symbolic levels—as black slave, as white master, as irrational force—his adventures were given coherence and continuity by the crucial release they provided and the indispensable lessons they taught. In the exploits of the animal trickster, slaves mirrored in exaggerated terms the experiences of their own lives. It can be argued, of course, that slave tales, by channelizing the bondsmen's discontent, reducing their anxieties, and siphoning off their anger, served the master as well as the slave. In a sense they did, and the fact that tales and songs were often encouraged by the masters may indicate a gleaning of this fact on their part as well. But in terms of the values they inculcated, the models of action they held up for emulation, the disrespect and even contempt they taught concerning the strong, the psychic barriers they created against the inculcation of the white world's values, it would be difficult to maintain that they should be viewed largely as a means of control. What the tales gave to the masters with one hand they more than took back with the other. They encouraged trickery and guile, they stimulated the search for ways out of the system, they inbred a contempt for the powerful and an admiration for the perseverance and even the wisdom of the undermen. In short, they constituted an intragroup lore which must have intensified feelings of distance from the world of the slaveholder.

WILSON SMITH

Apologia pro Alma Matre: The College as Community in Ante-Bellum America

THE SENSE OF COMMUNITY in the nineteenth-century liberal arts college awaits its own historian. Amid the many studies of American higher education none is devoted primarily to this obvious but perplexing trait of the hilltop college. To answer fully the many questions that come to mind about the feeling and significance of corporate life in the old-time colleges is surely to write a book. If such a sense really existed, was it universal and constant, or only transitory, seasonal, or happenstance? Who or what created and carried it? Was it elusive or fragile? What flavor and force did it give to college life? In these few pages I shall approach the inquiry only in a preliminary and tentative fashion. First, I want to say briefly why the concept of community is a pressing question for anyone concerned with the nineteenth-century roots of some current problems in American higher education. Then at greater length I shall reconsider some aspects of college life before 1860, with an emphasis on the idea of community.

Throughout the recent time of trouble in American colleges and universities appeals for the restoration of a sense of community were numerous, and the stimuli ranged all the way from sentimental nostalgia to practical purposiveness. Here are some examples. A prominent alumnus of Amherst College, speaking to his classmates fifty years after their graduation, declared: "The College really may have lost the sense of unity, of community, which we shared when we found ourselves all together listening in one room [to President Alexander Meiklejohn during the compulsory 8 o'clock morning chapels], however too repetitive the process may have been. . . . One felt an inner lift from the uncompromising, undeviating directness of his [Meiklejohn's] insistence on the search for the truth no matter where that search might lead."[1] At the same meeting in 1972 a professor of history distinguished a new sense of community in Amherst College from the older ideal of a "Place Apart" where "some older sense of the wholeness of life could be preserved." He represented the new vision of community as one "which would genuinely respect and nourish diversity [of race, sex, religion, and college preparatory background in the student body] while maintaining some common sense of purpose, a vision of an institution which could leave space for individuality while preserving the integrity of the institution."[2] A sociologist at Princeton University had his own definition of academic community. "There are those who say that real life goes on outside the university. But that is only one ephemeral form of life. The underlying reality is to be found in libraries and other cultural repositories; it lies in the formulated understandings and recreations of the experienced life, rather than in the experience itself."[3] A pro-

[1] Francis T. P. Plimpton, "Address to the Fifty-Year Class," *Amherst,* XXV (Summer 1972), 16–17.
[2] Theodore P. Greene, "A Sesquicentennial 'Sermon,'" *ibid.,* pp. 13–15.
[3] Melvin M. Tumin, "What a University Is—vs. Some New Proposals," *University, A Princeton Quarterly,* No. 54 (Fall 1972), pp. 13–18.

fessor of philosophy at Columbia University said: "Only in terms of an ultimate goal, of which we all share intimations, do we constitute a community. Only in our service to our common end, glimpsed in our finer moments, are we a *uni*versity rather than a *pluri*versity. . . . Our purpose [of contributing to improving the quality of human life] constitutes us as colleagues, as a community of ethical individuals, not a mere aggregation of social roles." [4] Finally, a former foundation head, spokesman for excellence in American education and watchman of the public interest in Washington, warned: "If the college or university is to preserve its character as a community . . . it will have to have a considerable measure of internal coherence and morale. And that means that trustees, administration, faculty, and students are going to have to admit that they are all part of one community—distasteful as that may be to some of them—and they are going to have to ask what they can do individually and collaboratively to preserve the integrity and coherence of that community and to regain command of its future." [5] Without claiming more of a central historic theme from these statements than they intend, one can place them in the tradition that has prized if not idealized the corporate endeavor of teaching and learning since the time of the medieval universities.

But what did critics of American higher education in the 1960s tell the historian? Did they reject the picture of our nineteenth-century colleges as communities just as firmly as they rejected modern university arrangements? It seems not. They implied that a sense of community did exist in the old-time colleges, though not of a sort that contributed to the advancement of American higher education. They tended to see the colleges as petty communities

[4] Joseph L. Blau, "Memory's Vision," address delivered February 13, 1972, at Columbia University's Annual Commemoration Service; excerpted in *Columbia Reports,* VI (April 1972), 5.

[5] John W. Gardner, "Agenda for the Colleges and Universities," in Alvin C. Eurich, ed., *Campus 1980* (New York, 1968), p. 8.

of the mind that were intellectually inflexible, dogmatic, and authoritarian because of their denominational or evangelical Protestant sponsorship. Others called them "undemocratic" institutions, truly closed communities, where students were either "gentlemen in waiting," following an older elitist tradition, or "journeymen *apprentices* for upward mobility" in accordance with a newer one that served only the white middle classes.[6] They believed that the flowering of the American university after the Civil War, together with the painful gaining of academic freedom over the opposition of denominational interests, was a signal victory for higher education. Here they agreed with most of the friendly observers of university development and with what has become the established interpretation of university history in Western culture. But the sharpest critics of academic life went further. They concluded that the triumph of the university (until its fall from grace, as they saw it, in this century) should logically relegate the earlier colleges to a mildly interesting but intellectually inferior place in American educational history. To them, the old colleges are irrelevant—except as a dire warning—to a historical understanding of modern needs.

These varying judgments reveal the perennial problem of imposing visions of the future upon limited knowledge of the past. Yet modern educational leaders and critics alike can scarcely be expected to clarify the idea of academic community if historical definitions of it are few and analyses fewer. The *total* life and environment of the old-time college must be understood if we are to undertake such analyses with any success. Histories of American higher education are just beginning to reach a point where

---

[6] See, e.g., Kenneth Keniston, "The Faces in the Lecture Room," and Martin Meyerson, "The Ethos of the American College Student: Beyond the Protests," in Robert S. Morison, ed., *The Contemporary University: U.S.A.* (Boston, 1967), pp. 323–324, 273–274; Christopher Jencks and David Riesman, *The Academic Revolution* (Garden City, N.Y., 1968), p. 91.

this understanding may be possible.[7] Most college histories assume that some pervading feeling of unity about corporate institutional life can be discerned, before the day of fraternities and organized athletics, in the religious life and spirit of the place. This may seem rather a truism, yet it seems less so when one reflects that the kind of unity that is achieved through religious motives and common worship has been a thing seen on few modern campuses for many a year.

Beyond the religious, other contexts for community suggest other questions. What features of their cultural setting, of their economic existence, or of their geographical location in either urban or remote places may have made for community? Or were college communities more typically characterized by factions or subgroups? Did the ideal of community amount to no more than a collection of smaller communities—church governing bodies, trustees, administration, faculty, students, townspeople—professing some common aim? If some external unifying purpose did operate upon the college, what was its source? Or are these only fruitless questions? Were most colleges so financially weak and short-lived, so racked by petty dissensions among students, faculty, trustees, or townspeople, so raw like the surrounding country, or so filled with virtually unlettered and violent students that a sense of community was generally unrealized, unknown, unattainable?

The public rhetoric of college leaders rarely gives us precise definitions. But it does help us to perceive institutional meanings, and the changes that occur in these over time. In 1905, William Louis Poteat of Wake Forest College voiced the standard account of the purposes and character of the small liberal arts college.

> In its external aspect, the college is the promoter and conservator of the liberal arts, those subjects

---

[7] See especially Douglas Sloan, "Harmony, Chaos, and Consensus: The American College Curriculum," *Teachers College Record*, LXXIII (Dec. 1971), 221–251.

> which engage the interest of enlightened minds; it is the guardian of the culture of mankind; it is the apparatus by which each generation is brought up into sympathetic appreciation of the total achievement of the race. In its internal aspect, the college is a body of associates in pursuit of the higher things of life, a brotherhood in which character takes form in the atmosphere of culture, in which mind comes to its own in the process of dealing with the finest products of mind—a mutual benefit society yielding dividends in efficiency and character. . . . For the college is at once the minister and the symbol of the supremacy of the ideal world, and the note of idealism shares with the note of fellowship the dominance of college life.[8]

Poteat's concept of the small liberal arts college did not become popular until after the Civil War. Judging from their advertisements during the Gilded Age, most hilltop colleges were beginning to acquire the secular idealism and the feeling of cultural security which came from the institution's seeing itself as a "Place Apart," a sanctuary (if one wishes) for the Genteel Tradition.

Before the 1850s, academic rhetoric generally did not define the college as a distinct "community." The college was usually characterized as a "school" in its surrounding community. For example, in 1837, Jasper Adams claimed that the faculty is "held by the public to be chiefly responsible for the good conduct of the institution. It is the department through which it is practically known to the community, and on which it must principally depend for character and usefulness." [9] In his famous *Thoughts on the*

---

[8] William Louis Poteat, *Youth and Culture* (Wake Forest, 1938), pp. 12–13.

[9] Jasper Adams, "On the Relation Subsisting between the Board of Trustees and Faculty of a University," *American Institute of Instruction, Lectures . . . at Worcester, Mass., August, 1837* (Boston, 1838); quoted in Richard Hofstadter and Wilson Smith, eds., *American Higher Education: A Documentary History*, I (Chicago, 1961), 313.

Present Collegiate System in the United States (1842), Francis Wayland called for the college to become "the grand centre of intelligence to all classes and conditions of men, diffusing among all the light of every kind of knowledge, and approving itself to the best feelings of every class of the community." The object of a college, he asserted, is "the intellectual cultivation of the community." [10] Excited over the question of appointing Oliver Wolcott Gibbs to the chair of chemistry at Columbia College in 1854, George Templeton Strong, the great diarist and Columbia trustee, demanded: "For whom are we 'Trustees of Columbia College' if not for the community?" [11]

The semantic distinction between college and community in these authoritative words fades when their context is brought to mind. "Community" was there, but in a different way, and the colleges—the denominational colleges in particular—saw themselves as its instruments. They were the training schools and the recruiting agencies for the larger community. Recalling the earliest days of Oberlin College, James Harris Fairchild in 1871 viewed the relationship between the town of Oberlin and its new college in a way characteristic of many a similar situation in the Jacksonian era. He wrote: "The school was to be surrounded by a Christian community, united in the faith of the gospel and in self-denying efforts to establish and build up and sustain the school. Families were to be gathered from different parts of the land to organize a community devoted to this object." [12] The idea of their colleges as exclusive places apart where there existed superior idealism, a select fellowship of students, and more intense piety than among ordinary God-fearing citizens would have been abhorrent to most old-time church college people. Such an

---

[10] Quoted in *ibid.*, I, 373, 343.

[11] Allan Nevins and Milton Halsey Thomas, eds., *The Diary of George Templeton Strong,* II (New York, 1952), 153.

[12] J. H. Fairchild, *Oberlin, Its Origin, Progress, and Results* (Oberlin, 1871), p. 3.

idea would have meant to stand the natural order of things on end. The "school" was meant to "serve" the outside community by codifying and inculcating the community's own best principles, and thus to function as an integral part of civic life. Denominational colleges were designed to be the effective arm of the church in a Christian republic.

During the great period of college founding and growth after 1815, church and interdenominational agencies increasingly emphasized this singular community relationship between western and southern colleges and their nearby citizenry. Enthusiastic religious leaders and eastern ecclesiastical imperialists designed colleges as the ground floor in their whole structure of expanding literacy, piety, and moralism. The various tract, missionary, and Bible societies which they headed were to be "grounded only on a thorough and liberal popular enlightenment." [13] "We need the West!" proclaimed spokesmen for the Home Missionary movement: for men (whom "the narrow East cannot supply"), for money, for strong home support to overseas missions, and for protection against Roman Catholicism.[14] Only an "efficient" Protestant college, they warned, can "counteract" a Catholic college. Protestant graduates would lead in civic affairs, in the ministry, and in teaching the unlettered western masses. Without a steady supply of college-educated teachers to fill the schools, the western world—"this sea of incoherent and vehement mind [where] every wind of opinion has been let loose, and is struggling

[13] Truman Marcellus Post, "Plea for Western Colleges," in *The First Report of the Society for the Promotion of Collegiate and Theological Education at the West* (New York, 1844), Appendix; quoted in H. Shelton Smith, Robert T. Handy, and Lefferts A. Loetscher, eds., *American Christianity: An Historical Interpretation with Representative Documents,* II (New York, 1963), 52.

[14] *The Home Missionary* (Feb. 1855), quoted in Peter G. Mode, *Source Book and Bibliographical Guide for American Church History* (Menasha, Wis., 1921; reprinted Boston, 1964), pp. 435–436. See also Lyman Beecher, *A Plea for Colleges* (Cincinnati, 1838) and his *A Plea for the West* (Cincinnati, 1835).

for the mastery"—would fall to "the powers of darkness." [15] The ultimate aim was the stable community. "We want principles of stability, we want a system of permanent forces, we want deep, strong and constant influences, that shall take from the changefulness and excitability of the western mind, by giving it the tranquility of depth, and shall protect it from delusive and fitful impulses, by enduing it with a calm, profound and pure reason." [16]

Less sectarian (or more secular) college leaders like Francis Wayland of Brown University and Philip Lindsley of Nashville made similar pleas for stable educated communities in a tranquil republic. Wayland proposed that colleges devise curricula for farmers and mechanics, merchants and manufacturers, so that "the division of the community into classes" would be "annihilated." "Why should it be supposed," he asked, "that all higher education should be engrossed exclusively by the professions?" [17] In similar Jeffersonian tones Lindsley said: "I look to a well educated independent yeomanry as the sheet anchor of the Republic." He predicted that the university "will gradually create and collect a literary society among us. Such a society exists in every city and village in our country, where the university has been fairly domesticated, and nowhere else." [18] To sectarian and Jeffersonian educators alike, the raising of the community standard of intellect everywhere was a moral enterprise of great national promise.

But we need to know a great deal more than we do about the working ideals themselves, and about the kind of community they created among those who promoted them. Some of the impulses for this devotion to institutions of learning in nineteenth-century America are well enough understood. Much has been written, for example, of

[15] Post, "Plea for Western Colleges," in Smith, Handy, and Loetscher, eds., *American Christianity*, II, 49–53; *The Home Missionary* in Mode, *Source Book*, p. 435.
[16] Post, "Plea for Western Colleges," p. 51.
[17] Quoted in Hofstadter and Smith, *Documentary History*, I, 372.
[18] Quoted in *ibid.*, I, 377, 248–249.

the Puritan educational heritage, as well as of the evangelical motives behind the setting up of new colleges.[19] Rather less has been written of such matters as the various forms of voluntary effort that went into these enterprises, or about the models of prestige and emulation that towns and regions saw in successful colleges.[20] Yet in none of the literature do we see much of an effort to explore these themes as daily operating—and unifying—attitudes. The historian who unfolds this story in detail will serve us well.

If what has been sketched thus far sets the problem of the college and its surrounding community, there remains the question of the college as a community in itself. This now appears to be one of the most perplexing issues of our educational past, perplexing because of the very ambivalence of the demands which the old-time college made upon itself. Though the college was alert to its reciprocal function with the external community, it was also aware that it had special communal needs of its own. The cultivation of individual character was one of its aims, as important as the cultivation of mind. But this, as well as learning, required a certain protection. Where was the line to be drawn between the sacred and the worldly, between the demands of mental achievement of any kind and those of social equality, or between individual integrity and conformity to mass

---

[19] One seldom-cited work that tries to do for the social place of the church colleges what Bernard Bailyn claims that Edward Eggleston's *Transit of Civilization from England to America in the Seventeenth Century* (1900) tried to do for the role of education in the history of American culture is Peter G. Mode, *The Frontier Spirit in American Christianity* (New York, 1923), chap. 4, "The Small Colleges."

[20] "Philip Lindsley on the Condition of the Colleges, 1837," Hofstadter and Smith, *Documentary History*, I, 247; Donald R. Come, "The Influence of Princeton on Higher Education in the South before 1825," *William and Mary Quarterly*, 3d ser., II (Oct. 1945), 359–396.

norms? The college must have been as aware of its own position as a small sanctuary of rational culture in a vast, often irrational young republic as it was committed by contract and belief to the sometimes less than rational causes of its sponsoring denomination. Many a phenomenon of group effort and behavior in ante-bellum college life —the revivals; the curricular experiments in manual labor; the debating and social clubs which in the South defended slavery and in the North espoused free soil; even the periodic student rebellions—might well be read in the light of the various tensions these aims produced. Did such tensions serve to fragment the college community, or did they enhance its awareness of itself *as* a community? The latter effect, to me, is the more plausible.

The college's general educational purpose in society could not have failed to sharpen this self-awareness as a community. The members of such a community could perceive with greater acuteness than most of their fellow citizens the precarious condition of learning in Jacksonian America. Though drawn from the mainstream of American life, and destined to be reabsorbed into it after their student years, they nevertheless constituted a minority whose experience allowed them to look upon their society with a certain detachment. The old-time college graduate was not quite the man Tocqueville was describing when he pointed to the American individualist, forgetful of ancestors and unmindful of descendants, separated by democracy from both, and being thrown back "forever on himself alone." He was in fact furnished with the implements of an academic tradition, much of it ancient and venerable. These had been given him by the college, which asked in return not mainly loyalty (though that too would come in time) but rather his use of them to fashion a better society ("an American Zion"), to introduce a little more order there, and to give clearer form to his own aspirations. That the implements were conferred with the blessings of a clerical professoriat may not be of primary importance. More important, perhaps, are the questions of how these teachers imparted the secular furnishings of the liberal arts, how their intellectual success with students and alumni is to be discovered and assessed, and what sorts of limitations were imposed on the college by the "outside world." To follow these out is to get at the cultural context of higher education in ante-bellum America.

Another line of inquiry, open but unexplored, that bears on the problem of community has to do with the nature of the loyalties which the old-time college inspired. One very clear expression of this was the voluntary effort—the religious, civic, and charitable enterprise—that went into the founding and building of the church colleges.[21] The tales of farmers' wives contributing their butter-and-egg money for putting up the first building, of all the citizens in a new college town pitching in to level the land and to begin the construction, of people from the surrounding region, as well as people from the sponsoring denomination, pledging their resources to continue the institution—all are an essential part of educational history.[22] This sense of community achieved through extramural charity and philanthropy, when it operated best, was an example of what most struck Tocqueville when he exclaimed: "In no country in the world has the principle of association been more successfully used or applied to a greater variety of objects than in America." [23]

Rather less easy to get at and appraise are the loyalties

---

[21] Merle Curti and Roderick Nash, *Philanthropy in the Shaping of American Higher Education* (New Brunswick, N.J., 1965), chap. 3.

[22] *Ibid.*, p. 52; Stanley King, *A History of the Endowment of Amherst College* (Amherst, 1951), chap. 2; William S. Tyler, *A History of Amherst College* (New York, 1895), pp. 17–18.

[23] Alexis de Tocqueville, *Democracy in America*, ed. by Phillips Bradley, I (New York, 1945), 198. "In the United States associations are established to promote the public safety, commerce, industry, morality, and religion. There is no end which the human will despairs of attaining through the combined power of individuals united into a society." *Ibid.*, p. 199.

that were felt and expressed by students. They frequently show through in recollection. The son of an untutored blacksmith in South Carolina, who became a justice of the United States Supreme Court, recalled a quarter-century after his graduation from Nassau Hall: "To minds which acquire a taste for intellectual improvement the days of a college life are among the happiest spent on earth." [24] Then there are the sentiments that must have been inspired at commencement time, "the grand literary festival of the state," [25] when student prizes were awarded, declamations made, and forensic skills displayed. There is loyalty to the student's college class, which was the most obvious demonstration of "school spirit" before the day of fraternities and organized sports.[26] And what of the poor and pious farm boy who received scholarship funds to prepare himself for the ministry or for missionary work: what was the nature of *his* loyalty? Finally, one wonders about the various emotional by-products of the religious revival, so frequent an occurrence in the church colleges. Might not one such effect have been a special kind of loyalty to the place where it was experienced?

Nevertheless it would be fatuous to claim loyalty as a universal student sentiment. One might, indeed, gather quite the opposite from the words of Francis Wayland:

> A graduate leaves his College when his course is completed, and his connexion with it and his interest in it cease. We have no centre [like London] to which talent of all kinds tends. A class, as soon as it leaves the . . . College, is scattered in a few days to every State and Territory in the union. The College or University forms no integral and necessary

[24] Quoted in Donald G. Morgan, *Justice William Johnson: The First Dissenter* (Columbia, S.C., 1954), p. 20.
[25] Philip Lindsley, "Commencement Address, 1837," in Hofstadter and Smith, *Documentary History,* I, 248.
[26] Frederick Rudolph, *Mark Hopkins and the Log: Williams College, 1836–1872* (New Haven, 1956), pp. 82–83.

> part of the social system. It plods on its weary way solitary and in darkness. . . .[27]

Though Wayland was not arguing the absence of undergraduate loyalty, he does seem to have felt that alumni loyalty left something to be desired. It was Wayland's own region, on the other hand, that Philip Lindsley referred to when he declared:

> The office of a trustee is regarded as a most honourable distinction. . . . The office of president and professor is universally looked up to as the highest and most respectable which can be obtained by the aspiring candidates for honourable rank in society. No political or professional station takes precedence of these. . . . On all public solemnities and celebrations also, the principals of universities and colleges appear in the first or highest rank. Thus, the people are taught to respect and reverence the literary character, and the literary institution, and the literary professor, and the whole teaching corps of the Commonwealth.[28]

It does seem, in any event, that loyalty to the antebellum college tended to reside more within the mixed context of religious faith and institutional utility—commitment to the collegiate reinforcement of one's religious upbringing, and the access, for example, that college gave to secular or sectarian vocations—than would be the case in later nineteenth-century schools. This assumption should make more important our efforts to examine the quality of these loyalties in the old college and to understand the fluctuating conditions under which they altered and grew.

Recent educational critics have impeached the quality of teaching and the harmony of student life in the pre-Civil War colleges. They use as evidence much that historians have been telling us and much that comes from

---

[27] *Thoughts on the Present Collegiate System in the United States* (Boston, 1842), pp. 40–41.

[28] "Commencement Address, 1837," quoted in Hofstadter and Smith, *Documentary History,* I, 247.

old-time college people themselves. A great deal of this is certainly justified. Yet even here, the incomplete record we have of old-time college people, and the still-limited stage of our understanding of the psychology of earlier individual and group life, to me make it highly desirable that we hold the account open. I am concerned for the time being not with those elements of the college situation that divided the community but with those that held it together.

One does not have to defend the college curriculum in order to argue that teaching was probably better than such a jaundiced witness as Henry Adams has led us to believe.[29] Adams, of course, was not the only critic; there were George Ticknor before him at Harvard, Andrew Dickson White later at Yale, and still later Andrew F. West of Princeton.[30] We have, on the other hand, the testimony of Nicholas Longworth Anderson in Adams's own class at Harvard[31] and the memorials to esteemed teachers throughout the old republic.[32] We so far have only a few

---

[29] Henry Adams, *The Education of Henry Adams* (Boston, 1918, and various editions), chap. 4. See also Ernest Samuels, *The Young Henry Adams* (Cambridge, Mass., 1948), chap. 1.

[30] Hofstadter and Smith, *Documentary History*, I, 265–273; Andrew D. White, *Autobiography*, I (New York, 1905), 17–22, 26–34, 288–289; Andrew F. West, *Short Papers on American Liberal Education* (New York, 1907), pp. 52–56. Dean West's complaint about the poor teaching of new PhD's was directed to their overspecialized preparation for academic life; he espoused a broad liberal arts background for young professors that was precisely in the old-time college curricular tradition.

[31] Isabel Anderson, ed., *The Letters and Journals of General Nicholas Longworth Anderson: Harvard—Civil War—Washington, 1854–1892* (New York, 1942), pp. 24–84.

[32] The literature on the teaching abilities of nineteenth-century men, though generally favorable to their classroom effectiveness, is more abundant for some teachers than for others. Essential guides are *The Reminiscences of James Burrill Angell* (New York, 1912), pp. 22–38, for Wayland; Codman Hislop, *Eliphalet Nott* (Middletown, Conn., 1971), pp. 238–239, 565; Ralph Henry

published student diaries, notebooks, and alumni memoirs to indicate, however inconclusively, that these teachers and others less well known brought the "outside" world of their own knowledge into classroom exchanges with students.[33]

Gabriel, *Religion and Learning at Yale* (New Haven, 1958), chap. 6 for Silliman; John F. Fulton and Elizabeth H. Thomson, *Benjamin Silliman, 1779–1864: Pathfinder in American Science* (New York, 1947), pp. 145, 154, 161–163, 238, 241, 271; Frank Freidel, *Francis Lieber: Nineteenth-Century Liberal* (Baton Rouge, 1947); Dumas Malone, *The Public Life of Thomas Cooper* (New Haven, 1926); Daniel W. Hollis, *South Carolina College* (Columbia, S.C., 1951), pp. 88, 94, 178–179, 188, for Cooper and Lieber; John Edwin Pomfret, "Philip Lindsley, Pioneer Educator of the Old Southwest," in Willard Thorp, ed., *The Lives of Eighteen from Princeton* (Princeton, 1946), pp. 158–177; Thomas Jefferson Wertenbaker, *Princeton, 1746–1896* (Princeton, 1946), pp. 223–225, 243–244, on Henry and Dod; Robert S. Fletcher, *History of Oberlin College from Its Foundation through the Civil War,* 2 vols. (Oberlin, 1943), *passim,* for Finney and Mahan; Rudolph, *Mark Hopkins and the Log.* These and other memorable teachers who served for a time as college presidents are discussed in George P. Schmidt, *The Old Time College President* (New York, 1930). That the sensitive, if not imaginative classroom instruction from these men in the Jacksonian period was thought to be nearer the norm than the exception is indicated by the model teaching code put forward in the first normal school. Here the aim was not to embark upon radical new teaching methods but rather to standardize what were already considered the best methods of instruction. Cyrus Peirce wrote to Henry Barnard in 1841 that he was above all concerned with "the *art of Teaching,*" so that example and precept would be stressed, as well as classroom exchanges between students and teachers, to get at the *ideas* of the subject in terms the student could understand. Arthur O. Norton, ed., *The First State Normal School in America: The Journals of Cyrus Peirce and Mary Swift* (Cambridge, Mass., 1926), pp. l–liii.

[33] Alumni memoirs are of course more abundant than student diaries. Memoirs are reliable, I believe, when they appear to be generally accurate with regard to other opinions bearing upon circumstances in the writer's younger life or when their descriptions are supported by the contemporaneous accounts of others. I

The charge of bad teaching in the denominational colleges does not, I think, take full account of the missionary and evangelical tone of these institutions. If that tone sanctified, it must by the same token have enlivened, much of the teaching. Church colleges, and even some of the state universities in their earliest years, had a latter-day Puritan sense of purpose (by which I do not mean only grim determination); they conveyed the enthusiasm of their founders. Indeed, founders and first faculty members were often identical. Denominational colleges possessed the same promotional spirit that was spurring many new secular, corporate endeavors. The college was the mission training ground, and it would be well to think of the older students in particular as the trainees—rather than the heathen, as we might be led to suppose from the stress in some accounts on problems of discipline. Corporate zeal, religious fervor, or steady piety would have done much to keep studies and teaching from dullness—and to keep most professors plugging away at their jobs. Recurring revivals, prayer days, or visiting preachers served periodically to bring fac-

---

see no reason to consider memoirs or autobiographies invariably unreliable because they are written in later years. Many student diaries and notebooks, or correspondence reposing in college archives, should be published. Among those that I have found useful are R. C. Beatty, ed., *Journal of a Southern Student, 1846–1848, with Letters of a Later Period, by Giles Patterson* (Nashville, 1944); James C. White, "An Undergraduate's Diary, 1849–1853," *Harvard Graduates' Magazine,* XXI (March–June 1913), 423–430, 636–651; George F. Whicher, ed., *Remembrance of Amherst: An Undergraduate's Diary, 1846–1848* (New York, 1946); Allan Nevins and Milton Halsey Thomas, eds., *The Diary of George Templeton Strong* (New York, 1952), Vols. I and II; Laura Hadley Moseley, ed., *Diary (1843–1852) of James Hadley, Tutor and Professor of Greek in Yale College, 1845–1872* (New Haven, 1951); Albert C. Sewall, *Life of Prof. Albert Hopkins* (New York, 1879), which is larded with selections from the diary of Hopkins, who was in the Williams College class of 1826; John Hall, ed., *Forty Years' Familiar Letters of James W. Alexander, D.D.* (New York, 1860).

ulty and students alike to a renewed seriousness of purpose. And though it may be true that the mortality rate among church colleges before the Civil War was fairly high, it is surely true that a community—in the American experience especially—need not always be defined by its permanence.

A sustaining psychology of spirited enterprise particularly characterizes rural and western academic communities. I include here the middle and far western new state universities as well as, say, a Williams College in the western reaches of Massachusetts. Their curricula may often have been prescriptive or dogmatic, or in Morton White's sense, formalistic. But this need hardly mean that the teaching was boring. Under an experienced or enthusiastic instructor it could be quite otherwise for poor farmers' sons imbued with the Puritan work ethic, who took pride in attending college, who were having a new world of learning opened to them, and who, in their daily relationships with professors or with any adult, were in any case more formal than students today. Even so, warm faculty-student relationships were sometimes developed: we are told of students on the college farm at Oberlin leaning on their hoes to discuss philosophy—quite informally—with their professors.[34]

One of the best examples I have found to illustrate keen student receptivity to teaching comes out of the early twentieth century at a secular university. It is legitimate, I think, because this institution was still new enough to have students in the humanities who were similar to those of the older rural colleges. Young Leonard Bacon came from a distinguished line of Connecticut clergymen. There was a

[34] J. H. Fairchild, *Oberlin: The Colony and the College, 1833–1883* (Oberlin, 1883), p. 255; Asa Mahan, *Autobiography: Intellectual, Moral, and Spiritual* (London, 1882), pp. 261–275. Washington Gladden claimed that at Williams College in 1856 "every student . . . was personally known by every member of the faculty, and the personal interest of the teachers in the students was as paternal as the students would permit." *Recollections* (Boston, 1909), p. 70.

Yale education behind him and his forefathers. Of his reaction to students in his first English class at the University of California in 1910 he recalls:

> By the time my first recitation hour came to an end I saw that there was a sharp distinction between college students East and West. The average eastern undergraduate at least in my time, behaved a good deal as if college was his unquestioned right and he could do what he pleased with his own. In comparison with the Westerner, he was a good deal better prepared for, and a good deal less interested in, the intellectual matters to which he from time to time directed his wavering attention. Generally his background was better too, and not infrequently he had had opportunities to travel, to hear music, and to visit the theater, which had not necessarily enriched his mind. Of these last the Californian knew almost nothing. But he was correspondingly, if superficially, eager, a delightful shock to a tyro [teacher]. . . . The western undergraduate was honestly curious, and wanted the outline of a subject anyhow, whether or no his interest was deep enough to dig into the details. To him the university was a palace of art, a focus of the desirable, in which it was difficult but creditable to remain. A boy who had had opportunities so slender that he has noticed it himself, and who has escaped from the hay-presses of Modesto, is apt to be impressed by white colonnades and academic omniscience in a manner inconceivable beside the waters of the Charles or the Quinnipiac. This amiable weakness had at least one satisfactory result from the standpoint of a beginning teacher, namely that certain problems in the instruction of adolescence scarcely ever arose. The maintenance of order just didn't have to be thought about. One took courtesy and discipline for granted. And such scenes as occasionally occurred at Harvard or Yale were unknown. To hold attention seemed as easy as shooting birds sitting, and by no means so immoral. A teacher's principal difficulty was to

> know his subject well enough not to take the edge off such innocent enthusiasm.[35]

Textbooks in "practical" subjects and the teaching of them may have seemed more stimulating than "literary" studies to students who insisted upon a ready connection between lessons and earning a future living in the Jacksonian era. Champions of the traditional curriculum, who found their best apologia in the Yale Report of 1828—a report that is not as "conservative" as sometimes depicted [36] —insisted that the most "useful" way to educate boys was to engage them daily in "disciplining" their minds by thinking about, and then logically ordering and reciting, textbook materials. Throughout the North, however, local or regional groups of citizens called for "practical" college studies. Old-time college people had an answer for them. Indeed, the challenge to the traditional or "literary" curriculum, which was rarely inflexible anyway, often came in the Jacksonian era from college people themselves. There is no indication that some new kind of academic man sprang up overnight to teach "practical" subjects. These were usually proposed and offered by the very men who too readily are portrayed with unchanging educational views. Francis Wayland's famous "new system" at Brown in the 1850s was really inspired by Eliphalet Nott's "Parallel Scientific Course" introduced to Union College in 1828 (and anticipated there in the catalog of 1815). After Wayland came thirty college presidents who by 1845, as Union alumni, were injecting Nott's utilitarian and partly Jeffersonian curricular ideas into their institutions.[37] A "prac-

---

[35] *Semi-Centennial: Some of the Life and Part of the Opinions of Leonard Bacon* (New York, 1939), pp. 106–107.

[36] Most of the Yale Report of 1828 is reprinted in Hofstadter and Smith, *Documentary History,* I, 275–291. For trenchant remarks on the anachronistic reading of the Report by modern educators, see George E. Peterson, *The New England College in the Age of the University* (Amherst, 1946), pp. 213–214.

[37] Hislop, *Nott,* pp. 226–233. Some of the institutions where parallel "scientific" and "literary" courses were

tical" course, poorly taught, could be just as boring as a poorly taught course in the classics. Career expectations and emotional commitment could make a student just as susceptible to even passable teaching in a practical course as the religious student was susceptible to decent teaching on the "literary" side of the curriculum. In short, subject matter and the caliber of teaching in the rural college classroom are not the same, and should not be confused.

Still, the reports of cowed, apathetic, or rebellious students cannot be excluded from the story. Students rioted for many reasons, some well founded and some capricious—for the excessive disciplining of a fellow student who may have broken a parietal rule, for bad food in the commons, out of evangelical and humanitarian opposition to slavery in the 1830s, for the pleasure of harassing tutors and proctors who were viewed as overstrict campus policemen, or sometimes just from spring fever or for the hell of it.[38] One may, if one chooses, almost chart the growth of our older colleges and universities by their periodic riots and rebellions. Some institutional histories have a tendency to do precisely this, while failing to describe what occurred intellectually in study, classroom, or debating society. A serious probing into the psychology of student riots in the old-time colleges, and the reasons for them, remains to be done. Most large-scale rioting took place at the older established institutions, particularly at

---

introduced, though not always satisfactorily or permanently, were Union, University of North Carolina, Transylvania, Trinity, University of Nashville, Hobart (Geneva), University of Vermont, Amherst, Bowdoin, Columbia, New York University at its founding, Wesleyan, Lafayette, Oberlin, Norwich, University of Rochester, and of course Brown. See R. Freeman Butts, *The College Charts Its Course* (New York, 1939), pp. 131–137.

[38] Standard summaries of student rebellions may be found in John S. Brubacher and Willis Rudy, *Higher Education in Transition: An American History: 1836–1956* (New York, 1958), pp. 50–56, and in George P. Schmidt, *The Liberal Arts College: A Chapter in American Cultural History* (New Brunswick, 1957), chap. 4.

Harvard, Yale, the College of New Jersey, Virginia, and South Carolina, where students generally were younger and better off than those in rural newer colleges. When unrest did occur in hinterland church colleges, it was born infrequently out of serious expressions of social reform, like the Lane Seminary "revolt" at Cincinnati in 1833 (which was really a voluntary departure of older students from the seminary), but more typically out of a later, post–Civil War preference for frivolous "college life over hard study.

Here the matter of social, regional, and family background bears directly upon the questions of student rebelliousness, seriousness of purpose, and receptivity to decent teaching. We know, for example, that planters' sons from the South led or participated in rebellions against college laws at Nassau Hall in the first two decades of the nineteenth century.[39] The records of suspension, rustication, or expulsion of southern boys from Princeton and other strictly run colleges indicate that they were lackadaisical about their studies, if not given to pranks, vandalism, or what was considered flagrant rule breaking by presidents and faculties. Rebelliousness also marked the student careers of some scions of famous New England families.[40] Violence has been attributed to the students' not being treated as responsible citizens of their college communities, contrary to the status their parents may have led them to expect. Rioting at Union College, for example, virtually disappeared under the paternal but liberal administration of Eliphalet Nott, yet only after it had taken Nott five years to learn that a "parental system" implied "affection as well as obligation."[41] Unrest among students from southern slaveholding families may also be ascribed to their exaggerated ideas of "gentlemanly" conduct and to the anti-

---

[39] Wertenbaker, *Princeton,* chap. 5; Brubacher and Rudy, *Higher Education,* p. 53.

[40] Samuel Eliot Morison, *Three Centuries of Harvard, 1636–1936* (Cambridge, Mass., 1936), pp. 209–210.

[41] Hislop, *Nott,* p. 178.

intellectualism that often went with it. Student unrest may perhaps best be considered with reference to the violence-prone character of nineteenth-century American society as a whole, and to the conflicting forces at work within Jacksonian culture.[42]

Yet rioting and organized violence were not such widespread and recurring phenomena within the rural colleges from about 1810 to the Civil War as has been contended. At small and usually struggling new institutions most students were too mature, purposeful, or career-minded to riot.[43] At times, almost all of them were playful, rude, boisterous, and prank-loving.[44] There were even occasional instances of deadly violence: a duel, a shooting, or a stabbing. But the records of Williams, Hamilton, Vermont, Knox, Illinois, Oberlin, Western Reserve, Kenyon, Union, and several other hinterland colleges in this era show virtually no student uprisings that parallel the famed "Bread and Butter" and "Conic Section" rebellions at Yale in 1828 and 1830 or the "Great Rebellion" at Harvard in 1823. Andrew Dickson White's little Geneva College (Hobart) in

[42] Brubacher and Rudy, *Higher Education*, p. 55.

[43] The first "genuine student prank" at Knox College was not recorded until 1859, almost two decades after the college began. The college's historian attributes "the sobriety and seriousness" of the Knox campus to the maturity of the students and to the interruption of their course of studies for a year from the need to work or teach. Some of the students were in attendance over a span of seven to nine years rather than the usual four, including time spent in the academy or preparatory department. In 1848 the median age of upperclassmen was twenty-three years. Over the next three years the ages of freshmen averaged twenty, and for three years thereafter at least eighteen and a half. Hermann R. Muelder, *Fighters for Freedom: The History of Anti-Slavery Activities of Men and Women Associated with Knox College* (New York, 1959), pp. 333–334.

[44] Despite student riots in the first decade of the nineteenth century at Williams College, Frederick Rudolph asserts: "An unbounded sense of playfulness rather than major rioting . . . was more characteristic of the Williams student." *Mark Hopkins and the Log*, p. 119.

1849 is sometimes held up as a clear example of rowdyism, violence, and chaos in a small college. It is an exception among the hilltop colleges. The student body comprised only about forty sons of Protestant Episcopal churchmen, most of them from urban and wealthy backgrounds. Unlike White, they thought themselves rusticated, repressed, and able to wreak havoc because the college was totally dependent upon their parents for its income. They had neither the evangelical religious background nor the rural upbringing of most hilltop college students; nor did they have to pay or work their own way into or through college.[45] Amherst, Bowdoin, Brown, DePauw, Dickinson, Lafayette, Miami, and Williams each experienced at least one student rebellion in the long span of years between 1800 and 1875.[46] But these incidents came mostly after the late 1850s. The larger number of revivals than riots and the great periods of relative calm at these and other institutions between 1810 and 1860 suggest that rebelliousness is hardly to be taken as a typical student characteristic.[47]

---

[45] White, *Autobiography,* I, 17–22. Contrast the social background of Geneva College students with that of poor farm boys in most of the rural colleges, typified by the account of Samuel Willard of Illinois College found in Charles Henry Rammelkamp, *Illinois College, A Centennial History, 1829–1929* (New Haven, 1928), pp. 83–84.

[46] Frederick Rudolph, *The American College and University: A History* (New York, 1962), p. 98.

[47] *Ibid.*, pp. 80–85. In a chapter which best catches student tone in the old western church colleges, Peter Mode emphasized the religious spirit of the college community and the fact that the colleges turned out to be not the theological seminaries that their founders sometimes intended but ministerial recruiting stations where undergraduates decided for ministerial careers. Mode, *Frontier Spirit,* pp. 70–72.

I do not suggest that a computation of college riots in this period set against an enumeration of college revivals would necessarily prove the absence or presence of the sense of college community. Rioting sometimes was symptomatic of student demand for an improved college community, not for its destruction. There were instances too of students actively supporting

Students at the rural church colleges in that period seem to have been generally more like the California young people whom Leonard Bacon faced in 1910 than like the rioters in the lore of Princeton, Yale, Harvard, and Virginia. Even at Harvard and Yale there was always a large number, on some occasions possibly a majority, who nipped incipient rebellion in the bud or even threatened the troublemakers. At Yale they were called "blue skins" and at Harvard "blacks," in contrast to the rowdy "high fellows." [48] A few of these quiet students, like George Ripley and Thomas Wilson Dorr, became active radicals in later life, while many student rebels in the older eastern schools, North and South, went on to orthodox and uneventful careers. The memoirs of a "blue skin" at Yale indicate that he and his kind were motivated by studiousness, by piety, or by fear of the tyranny that disturbers of the campus peace might bring down upon them.[49]

Despite scanty records of student social backgrounds from the early nineteenth century, it seems clear that college youth then came largely from rural or small-town Protestant families.[50] Their piety, their poverty in college,

---

college authority against the threat of the extramural community, although the town-gown antagonisms of European university history were generally absent from early nineteenth-century American colleges. See George B. Manhart, *DePauw Through the Years,* I (Greencastle, Ind., 1962), 52–53.

[48] Julian M. Sturtevant, *An Autobiography* (New York, 1896), pp. 94–98; Morison, *Three Centuries of Harvard,* p. 231.

[49] Sturtevant, *Autobiography,* pp. 94–98.

[50] Mode, *Frontier Spirit,* p. 69; Brubacher and Rudy, *Higher Education,* pp. 39–41. Limited archival records on student social backgrounds need not close this question. Local civic and church records of students' parents can tell us much. A recent study of midwestern voting behavior before the Civil War indicates how the "pietistic perspective" of religious people provided "an amorphous bond of unity" that underlay the structure of their political behavior. Their "bond" of piety meant that social norms connected with religious values were an integral part of their daily experience. Many of

and the cultural similarity which tied family beliefs to the aims of the college served to forestall rebelliousness. This was also true of students at the new western state universities.[51] A college founded in the 1820s or 1830s often experienced a generation of serious-minded students, compliant with college authority, who gradually gave way by the 1860s to a breed considerably less intent upon the formal course of studies. At a rural college like Williams, students whom Nathaniel Hawthorne described in 1838 as "great, unpolished bumpkins, who had grown up as farmer-boys" and who came in their "black ill-cut broadcloth" from "the hills and woods in this neighborhood," were by the 1860s becoming sophisticated "trumps" and were embarrassed by country language and manners.[52] New rural colleges—east, west, and south—witnessed some social distinction within their student bodies, but it was based more upon the degree of one's public religious conviction or the seriousness with which one took the school's educational purposes than upon wealth or family social standing. There was also a kind of institutional social democracy which enhanced a spirit of fellowship. Julian Sturtevant, a president of Illinois College, described this condition even at Yale, where he remembered his fellow students as "a

---

these people fought for and founded church colleges precisely because of their "pietistic perspective" wherein there was an overt connection between holiness and behavior. Paul Kleppner, *The Cross of Culture: A Social Analysis of Midwestern Politics, 1850–1900* (New York, 1970), pp. 73, 89. For similar findings among evangelical groups in Michigan, see Ronald P. Formisano, *The Birth of Mass Political Parties: Michigan, 1827–1861* (Princeton, 1971), p. 79 and *passim.*

[51] Merle Curti and Vernon Carstensen, *The University of Wisconsin, A History, 1848–1925*, Vol. I (Madison, 1949), chap. 6; Winton U. Solberg, *The University of Illinois, 1867–1894: An Intellectual and Cultural History* (Urbana, 1968), pp. 168–169; Harry A. Kersey, Jr., *John Milton Gregory and the University of Illinois* (Urbana, 1968), pp. 84–85; Allan Nevins, *Illinois* (New York, 1917), pp. 67–68, 90.

[52] Rudolph, *Mark Hopkins and the Log*, pp. 65–66.

strange medley. The families of merchant princes of New York, Boston, and Philadelphia; of aristocratic cotton planters; of hard-handed New England farmers; of Ohio backwoodsmen, and even the humblest sons of daily toil were there, sitting at the same tables. However distasteful this might be to many, there was no help for it . . . Yale College in 1822 was the most democratic portion of American society." [53]

Found in the pages of American biographical dictionaries are "successful" nineteenth-century alumni who often held cordial memories of their colleges. It is tempting

[53] Sturtevant, *Autobiography,* pp. 94–98. John Todd's appeal for collegiate giving in 1847 claimed: "Our Colleges are *chiefly* and *mainly* institutions designed for the poor and those in moderate circumstances, and not for the rich. . . . We have no institutions in the land more truly *republican* than our Colleges." *Plain Letter Addressed to a Parishioner in Behalf of the Society for Collegiate and Theological Education at the West* (New York, 1847), p. 22.

"Whatever the reason may be, the fact is, that by far the greatest part of able and faithful ministers and missionaries have arisen from the middle and laboring classes of society. . . . It was in the school of poverty that they were disciplined to great undertakings. . . . The worth of such men, and the need of them, in an age of enterprise and of great moral revolution, like the present, cannot be too highly estimated. . . . The proper business of [education] societies is, by a wise and wholesome patronage, to increase the number of *self made men. . . .*" "Address" of the Presbyterian Education Society, November 1831; quoted in Mode, *Source Book,* p. 386.

I stress that statements such as these are indicative of a pattern; they are not quantitative fact, even though by now it is generally assumed that college graduates were leaders in nineteenth-century American society to a greater degree than their small number in the total population would suggest. Cf. P. M. G. Harris, "The Social Origins of American Leaders: The Demographic Foundations," *Perspectives in American History,* III (1969), 159–344; George Wilson Pierson, *The Education of American Leaders: Comparative Contributions of U.S. Colleges and Universities* (New York, 1969).

to consult only them for a definition of the college as a community. College attendance, however, was not an automatic door to success and eminence then, any more than it is now, and such men are not the only kind we should examine when it is a question of what else the colleges of that day did to promote a common sense of identity among students. There is much on this that we do not know and that remains to be explored. To what extent did college attendance confirm and reinforce the standards of the environing society? In what measure, on the other hand, did it give one resources for resisting the psychological coercions of a democratic culture, for imposing a kind of order on chaotic surroundings, for developing one's own form of spiritual autonomy? The colleges were in many a sense weak and fumbling enterprises. Some of them simply vanished.[54] But that they made no difference at all, except for the worse, is to me not an acceptable premise. That they did matter, and that their people were in some way united in community, has been the argument of this essay.

To write in memory of a truly exceptional man and historian must be to write with candor, if with nothing else. This essay has not tried to assess the old-time college com-

[54] The mortality rate of denominational colleges before the Civil War was probably not as high as Donald G. Tewksbury's well-known monograph has led us to believe. Natalie A. Naylor finds that in Pennsylvania alone the mortality rate among degree-granting colleges with a four-year college level curriculum was below 27 percent, rather than the 48 percent Tewksbury gives for Pennsylvania. Naylor concludes: "The oft-cited 80 or 81 per cent mortality figure for ante-bellum colleges derived from Tewksbury's data is exaggerated and misleading. Most of the bona fide colleges—those which actually offered college-level instruction and conferred degrees—did survive." Natalie A. Naylor, "The Ante-Bellum College Movement: A Reappraisal of Tewksbury's *The Founding of American Colleges and Universities*," *History of Education Quarterly,* XIII (Fall 1973), 261–274.

munity primarily with modern intellectual or institutional standards. American educational premises, if not our codes of moral authority and of group behavior, have so changed that attempts by large, modern secular institutions to regain the spirit of a bygone college community may well be futile.[55] For some the knowledge that struggling colleges once possessed a sense of corporate unity when they possessed little else may be the only message here. For the historian of education there may be something more. It has much to do with Richard Hofstadter's view of educational history. We are indebted to him for many insights, but especially for having revealed to us the side of the old college that was repressive of free inquiry. His portrayal of the old academic mentality in all its narrowness stands as a reminder of how dogma may bury libertarian traditions. Yet I think that Richard Hofstadter would have looked tolerantly, though perhaps skeptically, upon examinations of the other side, the social side of the nineteenth-century colleges, which he would have conceded was important to their existence as institutions. For he was one of the first to insist that the role of education be examined within the total context of American history.

---

[55] A study of small mainline Protestant and evangelical Protestant colleges demonstrates that the sense of community is still strong in them and that there is generally an absence of this sense in the modern university. The author attributes the feelings of group welfare and belonging in these "congenial communities" to their small size. This characteristic, though true of the nineteenth-century colleges, does not penetrate the reasons for community in them. The author comes closer to the historical problem when he states: "Whether one sorts the colleges into mainline versus evangelical-fundamentalist groups or classifies them along some index of closeness of association with a denomination, regardless of which denomination, one finds that the more firmly and zealously a college is related to a church the more clearly it emerges as a distinctive college environment." C. Robert Pace, *Education and Evangelism: A Profile of Protestant Colleges* (New York, 1972), pp. 19, 25–28; quoted at pp. 36–37.

ERIC FONER

Thaddeus Stevens, Confiscation, and Reconstruction

IN THE HISTORY of American politics, Thaddeus Stevens is something of an anomaly. As a self-proclaimed radical, he seemed out of place at the center of a political system which—with the glaring exception of the Civil War—has perennially prided itself on its ability to resolve disputes without resort to extreme measures. Historians have found Stevens a baffling figure, whose unusual complexity of motivations and unique blend of idealism with political opportunism made him almost impossible to categorize. The most perceptive of his contemporaries described him simply as a revolutionary—or at least the closest thing to one imaginable in American politics. To a British observer, he was "the Robespierre, Danton, and Marat of America, all rolled into one." And a leading American newspaper attributed his influence in the 1860s to the nation's having undergone a political and social revolution which "demanded revolutionary qualities" of its leaders—qualities Stevens seemed to have in abundance.[1]

[1] "The American Constitution and the Impeachment of the President," *Blackwood's Edinburgh Magazine,* CIII (June 1868), 717; Springfield *Weekly Republican,* Au-

Only an unparalleled crisis like the Civil War could have brought a man like Stevens to the fore. His personal characteristics—cynicism, courage, imperviousness to criticism or flattery, brutal honesty, and willingness to use daring and even outrageous means to achieve his ends—were as necessary in wartime as they seemed inappropriate in peace.[2] And Stevens's combination of genuine idealism with a pragmatism learned in the school of Pennsylvania politics enabled him to recognize and articulate the policies which Union victory required. While Lincoln declared his conviction that the war must not degenerate into "a violent and remorseless revolutionary struggle," Stevens saw that this was precisely what it must become. From the outset he insisted that only the seemingly draconian measures of freeing and arming the slaves and seizing the property of the leading rebels could produce victory. In Congress, as chairman of the House Committee on Ways and Means, Stevens became "the master-spirit of every aggressive movement . . . to overthrow the Rebellion and slavery." By the end of the war he had acquired a national reputation as the radical of radicals, and at an age when most men have retired from active pursuits—he was

---

gust 15, 1868. Young Georges Clemenceau, reporting American events for a Paris newspaper, was much taken with Stevens, describing him as the "Robespierre" of one of the "most radical revolutions known to history." Clemenceau, *American Reconstruction 1865–1870*, ed. Fernand Baldensperger (New York, 1928), pp. 77, 79, 165, 227.

[2] For descriptions of Stevens's personality, see George Fort Milton, *The Age of Hate* (New York, 1930), pp. 263–264; J. W. Binckley, "The Leader of the House," *The Galaxy*, I (July 1866), 494; *The Reminiscences of Carl Schurz*, 3 vols. (New York, 1907–1908), III, 213–214; MS biographical sketch, probably by Edward McPherson, Thaddeus Stevens Papers, Library of Congress. For his prewar political career, see Richard N. Current, *Old Thad Stevens: A Story of Ambition* (Madison, 1942), chaps. 2–9; Fawn Brodie, *Thaddeus Stevens, Scourge of the South* (New York, 1959), chaps. 4–12.

seventy-three in 1865—Stevens embarked on the most important phase of his career.[3]

Any attempt to analyze Stevens's role in Reconstruction is immediately confronted with a paradox. Many historians of the period have depicted him as the dictator of the House and the major architect of Reconstruction. Even such hard-headed contemporary political leaders as James G. Blaine and Justin Morrill viewed him as "the animating spirit and unquestioned leader" of the House of Representatives. Stevens was certainly a master of parliamentary tactics. More than once he bullied the House into passing measures by choosing just the right moment to call the previous question, cutting off debate and forcing a vote. His quick tongue and sarcastic wit, moreover, made his colleagues of both parties consciously avoid tangling with him in debate. As one of them remarked, "I would sooner get into difficulty with a porcupine."[4]

And yet if Stevens was a political "dictator," his power was strangely limited. In Pennsylvania he was never able to challenge the Republican kingpins, Simon Cameron and Andrew Curtin, for control of the party machinery; and even in the House, as one puzzled newspaper observed, "no man was oftener outvoted." In addition, as recent research has made clear, the major Reconstruction legislation was

---

[3] Roy F. Basler, et al., eds., *The Collected Works of Abraham Lincoln,* 9 vols. (New Brunswick, N.J., 1953–1955), V, 49; J. A. Woodburn, "The Attitude of Thaddeus Stevens Toward the Conduct of the Civil War," *American Historical Review,* XII (April 1907), 567–568; *Congressional Globe,* 37th Cong., 1st sess., 414; 3d sess., 239; 38th Cong., 1st sess., 316; 2d sess., 126; Alexander K. McClure, *Abraham Lincoln and Men of War-Times* (Philadelphia, 1892), p. 265.

[4] William A. Dunning, *Reconstruction, Political and Economic, 1865–1877* (New York, 1907), p. 64; Justin S. Morrill, "Notable Letters from My Political Friends," *The Forum,* XXIV (1897–1898), 141; James G. Blaine, *Memorial Address on the Life and Character of James Abram Garfield* (Washington, D.C., 1882), pp. 10–11; W. R. Brock, *An American Crisis* (London, 1963), pp. 62–68; *Congressional Globe,* 37th Cong., 2d sess., 2054.

the work of no one man or faction but the result of a complex series of legislative compromises and maneuvers in which moderate senators and congressmen had as much influence as radicals like Stevens.[5]

Stevens was in fact not a dictator, but neither was he just another Republican politician. In a period of intense political and ideological crisis, his function was to outline a radical position toward which events would force the party to move, and to project the conditions under which change would occur. At a time when every Congress witnessed a high turnover of representatives, Stevens had a career of service stretching back into the 1850s. He could remind younger colleagues that he had been through the revolution from the beginning, and could speak of the times when southerners like "the mighty Toombs, with his shaggy locks, headed a gang who, with shouts of defiance, rendered this a hell of legislation." Throughout the Civil War, Stevens would stake out a position, confidently predicting that the nation would move leftward and adopt it within a year or two, and usually he was right. As a newspaper in his home district in Pennsylvania declared, "In all the leading questions of the late war, Mr. Stevens has been in advance of his compeers, but the Government has eventually seen the necessity of giving practical effect to his views of the national policy." [6]

Stevens, then, was "a man absolutely convinced, and

[5] Brooks M. Kelley, "Simon Cameron and the Senatorial Nomination of 1867," *Pennsylvania Magazine of History and Biography,* LXXXVII (Oct. 1963), 366–367, 388–389; Boston *Advertiser,* August 13, 1868; David Donald, *The Politics of Reconstruction, 1863–1867* (Baton Rouge, 1965), p. 81; Eric L. McKitrick, *Andrew Johnson and Reconstruction* (Chicago, 1960), 260–268, and *passim.*

[6] Cincinnati *Commercial,* January 1, 1866; *Congressional Globe,* 39th Cong., 1st sess., 2544; Woodburn, "Stevens and the Conduct of the War," pp. 571–572; Lancaster *Express,* September 8, 1865. Cf. the assessments of Stevens's leadership in New York *Tribune,* December 19, 1865; New York *Evening Post,* April 3, 1866; *Nation,* January 24, 1867.

in a sense rightly, that he and history were for the moment in perfect step." His record of having been proved right by events helps explain why, when Stevens rose to speak, the House fell uncommonly quiet, the galleries quickly filled, senators often dropped their work to attend, and, as a freshman congressman commented, "everyone expects something worth hearing." [7] And yet by the very nature of his leadership Stevens was most effective in providing his party with means, rather than ends. During the Civil War, Republicans eventually came to agree with Stevens that freeing and arming the slaves was the only way to achieve the unquestioned goal of Union victory. And during Reconstruction, Stevens would be most successful when his proposals seemed to provide ways of moving toward the party's commonly held goals of Republican ascendancy in the national government, protection of the basic rights of the freedmen, and reorganization of southern governments under the control of genuinely loyal men. Thus as events convinced Republicans that Stevens's proposals, including civil rights and suffrage for the freedmen, a period of military rule in the South, and even the impeachment of the President, were necessary for the achievement of their basic aims, they would follow Stevens—or at least move to the positions he had outlined. But Stevens failed completely in pressing for the confiscation and redistribution of the lands of the leading rebels, because he was unable to convince his party that such a policy was either an essential goal or an acceptable means to other ends.

The issue of confiscation had roots stretching back to the first years of the Civil War, when abolitionists and radical Republicans first linked the goal of landownership for southern blacks with that of emancipation. And as the war progressed, increasing numbers of Republicans were converted to the view that the confiscation of rebel prop-

---

[7] McKitrick, *Andrew Johnson and Reconstruction,* p. 268; Charles R. Williams, ed., *Diary and Letters of Rutherford Burchard Hayes,* 5 vols. (Columbus, 1922–1926), III, 9.

erty would be a legitimate war measure. The first Confiscation Act, of August 1861, was directed only against property used in aid of the rebellion, but in 1862 Congress enacted a far more sweeping measure, declaring all property of rebels liable to confiscation. President Lincoln, who strongly opposed widespread confiscation, forced Congress to pass an explanatory resolution, limiting the seizure of land to the lifetime of the owner. Only a handful of Republicans, Stevens among them, voted in opposition. The debates of 1862 indicated that while a majority of Republicans were willing to use confiscation as a war measure and a way of attacking slavery, far fewer envisioned a sweeping revolution of land tenure in the South.[8]

As the war progressed, however, the idea of permanent land confiscation gained wider support. In 1864 and 1865, Stevens and the veteran land reformer George W. Julian led a fight in Congress to repeal the joint resolution of 1862 and authorize the permanent seizure of rebel lands. By the end of the war both Houses, by narrow margins and in votes on different measures, had repealed the 1862 resolution. But no joint measure was ever enacted. The Freedmen's Bureau bill, passed in March 1865, did contain a provision assigning to freedmen and white refugees forty acres of confiscated or abandoned land, although the land was to be rented for three years and there was no promise of permanent ownership. Meanwhile, though the Lincoln administration had left the Confiscation Act of 1862 virtually unenforced, thousands of acres of abandoned land had fallen into government hands, and General Sherman's famous order settling freedmen on such land in South Carolina and Georgia seemed to some

---

[8] Walter L. Fleming, "'Forty Acres and a Mule,'" *North American Review,* CLXXXIII (May 1906), 721–737; T. Harry Williams, *Lincoln and the Radicals* (Madison, 1941), pp. 26–27; James G. Randall, *Constitutional Problems Under Lincoln,* rev. ed. (Urbana, 1964), pp. 276–280; Leonard P. Curry, *Blueprint for Modern America* (Nashville, 1968), pp. 85, 95–99; *Congressional Globe,* 37th Cong., 2d sess., 3400.

to presage a general policy of establishing the blacks on homesteads.[9]

At the outset of Reconstruction, therefore, the Republican party had taken some steps toward Stevens's goal of providing land to the freedmen from the estates of the planter aristocracy. But even in wartime the party had not overcome its inhibitions about such a policy, and once Union victory had been achieved, the notion to many Republicans became unthinkable. For confiscation flew in the face of too many basic tenets of the ideology which had carried the Republicans into the Civil War and which had emerged unchanged, even strengthened, by the war experience.[10] To a party whose outlook was thoroughly bourgeois—which believed that a free laborer, once accorded equality of opportunity, would rise or fall in the social scale on the strength of his own diligence, frugality, and hard work—confiscation seemed an unwarranted interference with the rights of property and an unacceptable example of special privilege and class legislation.

And yet there were values and aspirations, shared by most Republicans, to which Stevens could and did appeal in an attempt to build a pro-confiscation coalition. Republicans were committed to restricting the power of the planters, protecting the rights of the freedmen, and transforming the South into a democratic (and Republican) society. During the congressional debates of 1865–1867 most radical Republicans, and an increasing number of moderates, viewed black suffrage as the most effective

[9] *Congressional Globe,* 38th Cong., 1st sess., 19, 519; 2d sess., 1025–1026; LaWanda Cox, "The Promise of Land for the Freedmen," *Mississippi Valley Historical Review,* XLV (Dec. 1958), 413–419, 431–435; Patrick W. Riddleberger, "George Washington Julian: Abolitionist Land Reformer," *Agricultural History,* XXIX (July 1955), 109–110; Fleming, "'Forty Acres,'" pp. 722–725; Randall, *Constitutional Problems,* pp. 284–286, 316–317.

[10] Eric Foner, *Free Soil, Free Labor, Free Men: The Ideology of the Republican Party Before the Civil War* (New York, 1970).

means of achieving these goals and of obviating the need for massive federal intervention in the South. Stevens, however, challenged the idea that the impoverished and despised former slaves could immediately become independent voters. As he admitted to the House early in 1866, Stevens did not want Negro suffrage enacted for a few years. If the southern states were readmitted to the Union before the federal Constitution was altered to guarantee black rights and before the freedmen were given the economic wherewithal to establish their independence from economic coercion, the verdict of the Civil War would be undone. "They will give the suffrage to their menials, their house servants, those that they can control, and elect whom they please to make our laws. This is not the kind of suffrage I want." [11]

Stevens thus insisted that it was unrealistic to expect the freedmen to challenge effectively the political dominance of the South's traditional ruling class. John Andrew, the war governer of Massachusetts, who shared Stevens's perception, drew from it the inference that the only stable basis of reunion was an understanding between Republican leaders and "the natural leaders of opinion in the South"—a preview of the policy which would end Reconstruction in 1877. Stevens drew precisely the opposite conclusion. Realizing that emancipation had not destroyed the planter class, whose wealth rested not only on slaveholding but on control of prime black belt lands, he urged that such lands be confiscated.[12] The franchise by itself, he insisted, would not really touch the blacks' basic problems: "homesteads to them are far more valuable than the immediate right of suffrage, though both are their due." Most Republicans would reverse the prop-

[11] *Congressional Globe,* 39th Cong., 1st sess., 536.

[12] George S. Merriam, *The Life and Times of Samuel Bowles,* 2 vols. (New York, 1885), II, 125; Benjamin B. Kendrick, *The Journal of the Joint Committee of Fifteen on Reconstruction* (New York, 1914), pp. 92–105; *Congressional Globe,* 39th Cong., 1st sess., 2460, 2544.

osition, as did the radical congressman James Ashley of Ohio. "If I were a black man," Ashley declared, "with the chains just stricken from my limbs, without home to shelter me or mine, and you should offer me the ballot, or a cabin and forty acres of cotton land, I would take the ballot." Only George Julian, Wendell Phillips, and, occasionally, Benjamin F. Butler and Charles Sumner, stressed the land question, and none did so as consistently and forcefully as Stevens. Phillips, indeed, did not come around to this view until 1866, though when he did, he argued it much in the way Stevens had done:[13] "You cannot govern the South against its educated classes, with their social prestige. If they cannot be hung nor exiled, they must be flanked. . . . Four millions of uneducated negroes, with none of that character which results from position, with none of that weight which comes from one or two generations of recognized manhood, cannot outweigh that element at the South."

Confiscation, for Stevens, thus had two related goals. One was to destroy the power of the planter class; the other, to create a new class of black and white yeomen as the basis of future southern political and social power, and as allies of the Republican middle class of the North. Revolutionary as such a proposal may have been, it could be defended as the corollary of a traditional, widely shared value—the conviction that democratic institutions

[13] *Congressional Globe*, 39th Cong., 1st sess., 2459; 40th Cong., 1st sess., 205; Benjamin W. Arnett, ed., *Duplicate Copy of the Souvenir from the Afro-American League of Tennessee to Hon. James M. Ashley of Ohio* (Philadelphia, 1894), pp. 407–408; Riddleberger, "Julian," pp. 108–114; Benjamin F. Butler, *Butler's Book* (Boston, 1892), pp. 908–909, 961; *National Anti-Slavery Standard*, November 17, 1866. For Sumner's complex views on the relative importance of land and the suffrage, see David Donald, *Charles Sumner and the Rights of Man* (New York, 1970), 119–120, 201; Edward L. Pierce, *Memoir and Letters of Charles Sumner*, 4 vols. (Boston, 1877–1893), IV, 76, 229, 247–260; *The Works of Charles Sumner*, 10 vols. (Boston, 1870–1883), IV, 275; X, 220–225; XIII, 320–321.

must rest on an industrious middle class. Stevens had always paid homage to the ideal of the yeoman republic. As he declared in 1850, "the middling classes who own the soil, and work it with their own hands, are the main support of every free government." Stevens's complete lack of racial prejudice was evident in his assumption that distributing land to blacks would make them middle-class yeomen; that their social position, morals, and psychology were the outgrowth of slavery, not of racial inferiority, and could therefore be altered. But he also recognized that in view of the legacy of slavery and the hostility of southern whites, the traditional American ideal of success through thrift and hard work simply could not apply while the former slaves remained under their present disadvantages. But confiscation, he argued, could achieve a whole panoply of results central to the Republican ethos: [14]

> Nothing is so likely to make a man a good citizen as to make him a freeholder. Nothing will so mul-

[14] *Congressional Globe*, 31st Cong., 1st sess., Appendix, 141–143; 40th Cong., 1st sess., 205. A self-made man himself, Stevens once described his social ideals as those of "the honest farmer, mechanic or laborer," as opposed to both the aristocrat and the "vagabond, the idle and dissipated." The prosperous yeomen of Lancaster County, Pennsylvania, were the bedrock of his political strength. Stevens assumed that black yeoman farmers would act pretty much as white farmers did. He did not view the freedmen, just emerging from slavery, as members of a distinct culture who might react in unpredictable ways to economic stimuli. Where blacks were allowed the choice, there were already signs of a reluctance to cultivate the "slave crop" cotton for the market, and a tendency to retreat into self-sufficiency. Black farmers might, in other words, have turned out to be quite different from the market-oriented farmers of the North idealized by Stevens. *Proceedings and Debates of the Convention of the Commonwealth of Pennsylvania, to Propose Amendments to the Constitution . . .* , 14 vols. (Philadelphia, 1837–1838), III, 167; Lancaster *Express*, February 7, 1866; Joel Williamson, *After Slavery* (Chapel Hill, N.C., 1965), p. 44; Willie Lee Rose, *Rehearsal for Reconstruction* (Indianapolis, 1964), pp. 82, 170, 226.

> tiply the productions of the South as to divide it into small farms. Nothing will make men so industrious and moral as to let them feel that they are above want and are the owners of the soil which they till. . . . No people will ever be republican in spirit and practice where a few own immense manors and the masses are landless. Small independent landholders are the support and guardians of republican liberty.

There were other arguments as well for confiscation. For one thing, the seizure of planter lands would be a fitting punishment for the architects of the rebellion, those "who have murdered our brothers, our fathers, and our children." If the lands of the planter class, moreover, were seized and forty acres allotted to each freedman, there would still remain hundreds of millions of acres—90 percent of the land, in fact—which could be sold to help pay the national debt, reduce taxes, and provide pensions for Union soldiers and reimbursement for loyal citizens whose property had been destroyed during the war (of whom there were many in Stevens's home area of southern Pennsylvania). It would be, moreover, in Wendell Phillips's words, merely "naked justice to the former slave," whose uncompensated labor had cleared and cultivated the southern land and who was certainly entitled to "a share of his inheritance." But Stevens's basic appeal was to the remodeling of southern society: the transformation of an alien, undemocratic, severely stratified social order into a prosperous, democratic and loyal republic. "The whole fabric of southern society," he declared in 1865, "*must* be changed, and never can it be done if this opportunity is lost."[15]

Stevens seems to have assumed that such a desire was widely shared in the Republican party. And there was

[15] *Congressional Globe,* 39th Cong., 2d sess., 1317; *Reconstruction: Speech of the Hon. Thaddeus Stevens, Delivered in the City of Lancaster, September 7, 1865* (Lancaster, 1865), pp. 2–5; *National Anti-Slavery Standard,* June 15, 1867.

certainly some evidence for that assumption. Long before the Civil War, antislavery northerners had developed an extensive critique of the southern social order and had declared their wish that the South might be transformed into a society more akin to that of the North and West. And most Republicans in the early years of Reconstruction shared Carl Schurz's view that "a free labor society must be established and built up on the ruins of the slave labor society." But far fewer were prepared to accept confiscation as the means to this end, both because Stevens's plan conflicted with some basic Republican values and because the creation of a black yeoman middle class was not what important elements of the party had in mind for the economic future of the South. Republicans in Boston, New York, and Philadelphia (the ante-bellum centers of the cotton trade), as well as other northerners who hoped to invest in the postwar South, tended to favor the speedy revival of the cotton plantation system, with northern capital and migrants supplanting the former slaveholders. Blacks would remain an essentially propertyless plantation labor force, whose basic legal rights would be recognized but who would hardly be in a position to challenge propertied whites for political and economic dominance. When the New York *Times*, the leading spokesman for this view, spoke of the South's need for a "prosperous yeomanry," it was quick to add, "very many of them will be northerners." [16]

Another group of Republicans, more willing to grant

[16] Joseph Schafer, ed., *Intimate Letters of Carl Schurz, 1841–1869* (Madison, 1928), p. 341; William B. Hesseltine, "Economic Factors in the Abandonment of Reconstruction," *Mississippi Valley Historical Review,* XXII (Sept. 1935), 191–210; Philadelphia *Public Ledger,* January 23, 1866; Cincinnati *Gazette,* December 2, 1865; New York *Times,* August 18, November 2, 14, December 18, 1865; January 4, 15, 17, September 2, 1866. Cf. Thomas Wagstaff, "Call Your Old Master—'Master': Southern Political Leaders and Negro Labor During Presidential Reconstruction," *Labor History,* X (Summer 1969), 323–345.

complete legal and political equality to the freedmen, looked to a wider economic transformation of the South, including the creation of a diversified, industrializing economy. But again, the South was to be rebuilt under the auspices of northern capital and settlers. This was the view, for instance, of Horace Greeley's New York *Tribune*, the *Nation*, and spokesmen for Pennsylvania's iron industry. Greeley insisted that what the South needed most was not talk of confiscation, which would paralyze investment and economic development, but an influx of northern capital, settlers, and industrial skills. And Congressman William "Pig Iron" Kelley of Pennsylvania, after touring the South in 1867 and extolling the region's economic resources and latent wealth, concluded, "The South must be regenerated, and we of the North must do it." [17]

Stevens was never able to make confiscation palatable to such Republicans. He feared, indeed, that the quick economic reconstruction of the South under northern auspices was likely to leave the freedmen no better off than under continued planter domination. He may have been influenced by the arguments of George Julian, who in 1864 and 1865 repeatedly pointed to the danger that confiscated and abandoned lands would be swallowed up by northern speculators. In Louisiana, under the direction of General Nathaniel P. Banks, freedmen had been put to work on plantations controlled by such men in "a system of enforced and uncompensated labor." If this was any indication of the economic future of the South, it appeared that "in place of the slaveholding landowner . . .

---

[17] Earle D. Ross, "Horace Greeley and the South," *South Atlantic Quarterly*, XVI (Oct. 1917), 333–334; New York *Tribune*, September 12, 29, October 11, 1865; *Nation*, November 8, 1866; William D. Kelley, *Speeches, Addresses and Letters on Industrial and Financial Questions* (Philadelphia, 1872), pp. 182–183; Robert Sharkey, *Money, Class, and Party* (Baltimore, 1959), pp. 165–166.

we shall have the grasping monopolist of the North, whose dominion over the freedmen and poor whites will be more galling than slavery itself." [18]

That Stevens was less interested than other Republicans in speedy southern economic development under northern auspices was amply demonstrated during Reconstruction. He fought unsuccessfully in 1866 for a constitutional amendment authorizing an export tax on cotton —hardly the sort of measure investors in southern cotton plantations were likely to support. When Kelley pleaded for aid to a northern-owned railroad, on the ground that railroad development would aid the destitute freedmen of the region, Stevens scoffed: "May I ask my friend how many of these starving people he thinks are stockholders in this road?" And in 1868 he and Julian endorsed a measure, which passed the House but was killed in the Senate, declaring federal land grants to railroads in four Southern states forfeited and open to black and white settlers.[19]

Because he was an iron manufacturer and supporter of a protective tariff, many historians have pictured Stevens as a conscious agent of northern capitalism, bent on establishing the North's economic hegemony over the South. But northern business interests did not see it that way. As one Philadelphia businessman complained, after learning of Stevens's opposition to a federal bankruptcy

---

[18] *Congressional Globe,* 38th Cong., 1st sess., 1187–1188, 2251. When Stevens pressed the confiscation issue in 1867, his proposal included a prohibition of the sale of lands in plots exceeding 500 acres, an attempt to prevent the engrossment of large tracts of land by northern speculators. *Congressional Globe,* 40th Cong., 1st sess., 203.

[19] *Congressional Globe,* 39th Cong., 1st sess., 3240–3241, 3687–3688; 2d sess., 985; New York *Tribune,* March 23, 1867; John J. McCarthy, "Reconstruction Legislation and Voting Alignments in the House of Representatives, 1863–1869" (unpublished doctoral dissertation, Yale University, 1970), p. 263.

law to aid business in the South, "he seems to oppose any measure that will not benefit the *nigger*." [20]

The combination of ideological and economic obstacles to confiscation became fully apparent after Stevens, in September 1865, outlined his views on Reconstruction in a widely reprinted speech. Only a handful of Republicans endorsed his program, the most cordial reaction being that of an editor who told Stevens that the speech itself had been well received, "with the exception of your extreme views on confiscation. Some object to going as far in that measure as you purpose." Stevens, however, was not the sort to be disheartened by criticism. When Congress convened in December 1865, he introduced and the House quickly passed a resolution directing General O. O. Howard, superintendent of the Freedmen's Bureau, to report how much property under his jurisdiction had been returned to its owners, and "under what pretense of authority." Stevens's purpose was to make plain that President Johnson's lenient pardon and amnesty policies and his insistence that all land which had not been sold be returned to its pardoned owners were leading to wholesale evictions of blacks from abandoned lands on which they had been settled. Howard's reply, which was not ready until April, made the impact of Johnson's policies plain: virtually all the land under Bureau authority had been restored to the former rebels, while the amount in black hands was minuscule.[21]

---

[20] J. Williamson to Thomas A. Jenckes, February 16, 1866, Thomas A. Jenckes Papers, Library of Congress. For views of Stevens as an agent of northern capitalists, see Current, *Stevens,* and Williams, *Lincoln and the Radicals.* Of course, as Sharkey shows in *Money, Class and Party,* northern capitalists were hardly unanimous on political and economic questions.

[21] *Reconstruction—Lancaster Speech;* J. W. McClurg to Stevens, September 27, 1865; Joseph Bailey to Stevens, September 22, 1865, Stevens Papers; *Congressional Globe,* 39th Cong., 1st sess., 104; 39th Cong., 1st sess., House Executive Document No. 99; New York *Times,* May 5, 1866.

Even before Howard's report had been received, Stevens introduced a confiscation measure in the House. The occasion was the bill extending the life of the Freedmen's Bureau. Introduced by the moderate senator Lyman Trumbull, the bill had wide support among Republicans, and Johnson's eventual veto of it would be a decisive step in his break with the party. As drafted by Trumbull, the bill set aside three million acres of public land in the South for homesteading by freedmen and white refugees, affirmed for three years the title of freedmen to the lands set aside for them by General Sherman, and authorized the Bureau to buy lands for resale to blacks. In Stevens's view, none of these provisions was satisfactory. The public domain in the southern states consisted largely of hill and swamp lands, and the impoverished freedmen did not possess the capital necessary to establish homes and farms there, or to buy land from the Bureau. And there was no promise of permanent ownership of the Sherman lands. The bill did not touch the economic power of the planters, nor did it give freedmen access to the black belt land which was the key to the southern economy. When it came to the House, Stevens declared, "I say that this bill is a robbery."

When the Trumbull bill reached the House floor early in February 1866, Stevens proposed a substitute measure, adding "forfeited estates of the enemy" to the land open to settlement, making certain that the land could be purchased by blacks on easy terms, and making permanent their possession of the Sherman lands. When this substitute came to a vote it was overwhelmingly defeated, 126 to 37; Republicans divided 37 in favor, 86 opposed, with 10 abstentions, and many of the House's leading radicals, including Ashley of Ohio and Kelley of Pennsylvania, opposed it.

The tangled complexities of the land question were further illustrated two days after Stevens's substitute was rejected and the Freedmen's Bureau bill passed, when the House with virtually unanimous Republican support passed

Julian's Southern Homestead Act, opening all public land in the South to settlement and giving blacks and loyal whites preferential treatment until 1867. Republicans were thus quite willing to offer freedmen the same opportunity to acquire land which whites had received under the Homestead Act of 1862; they simply refused to take land from the planters to make farmers of blacks. As Stevens had foreseen, the Julian bill was a dismal failure. The land involved was so inferior, and the freedmen so lacking in capital, that by 1869 only four thousand black families had even attempted to take advantage of the Act, and many of these subsequently lost their land.[22]

These votes of February 1866 posed a dilemma for Stevens. He could have accepted them as defining for all practical purposes the limits to which Republicans were willing to move toward providing blacks with land and reorganizing southern society. As William McFeely has pointed out, the Freedmen's Bureau bill despite its limitations did hold out the possibility of a gradual but far-reaching change in the South's land system. It established federal responsibility for giving blacks access to land, and for assisting them in purchasing it on credit. Because the policy did not involve severe punishment of the planters, a complete upheaval of southern society, or special privilege for the blacks, it commanded wide support in Republican ranks. Had Stevens thrown his weight behind the measure as an acceptable alternative to massive confiscation, it might have become, in effect, official Republican policy on the land question. Yet Stevens's whole experience in the 1860s predisposed him not to accept these votes as a final verdict. The conservative New York *Herald*

[22] *Congressional Globe*, 39th Cong., 1st sess., 655, 658, 748, 1966; William S. McFeely, *Yankee Stepfather, General O. O. Howard and the Freedmen* (New Haven, 1968), pp. 213–220, 226–229; Christie Farnham Pope, "Southern Homesteads for Negroes," *Agricultural History*, XLIV (April 1970), 202–205; Warren Hofnagle, "The Southern Homestead Act: Its Origins and Operation," *Historian*, XXXII (Aug. 1970), 615–629.

could exult over his defeat ("thus we see. . . . the real strength of the Jacobins in the House"), but Stevens might have retorted that when he first proposed a measure for the use of black troops it had received only thirty votes. He had always been ahead of his party, he once remarked during the war, but "I have never been so far ahead. . . . but that the members of the party have overtaken me." [23]

Stevens's strategy was based on the judgment that a prolongation of the national crisis would push the Republican party to the left. The longer the crisis lasted, he thought, the more radical the final settlement was likely to be. Throughout 1866 and 1867, Stevens bided his time on the land question, devoting his energies to the Fourteenth Amendment and Negro suffrage, while trying to delay a final settlement. The leftward drift which Stevens counted on as the dynamic element of the political situation was explained by the *Nation* during the hectic debates of February 1867: "Six years ago, the North would have rejoiced to accept any mild restrictions upon the spread of slavery as a final settlement. Four years ago, it would have accepted peace upon the basis of gradual emancipation. Two years ago, it would have been content with emancipation and equal civil rights for the colored people without the extension of suffrage. One year ago, a slight extension of the suffrage would have satisfied it." [24] Now, in March 1867, the Republicans succeeded in passing the first Reconstruction Act, temporarily forcing the planter class from participation in politics and imposing Negro suffrage on the South. And, just as southern intransigence had swelled the ranks of the Republican party in the 1850s and forced it to embrace emancipation and the arming of the slaves during the Civil War, Stevens could hope that if southern whites again obstructed northern goals, the party would move to an even more radical

[23] McFeely, *Yankee Stepfather,* 229–231; New York *Herald,* February 8, 1866; *Congressional Globe,* 37th Cong., 2d sess., 243.
[24] *Nation,* February 21, 1867.

measure—confiscation. Yet the passage of the Act revealed the weakness of Stevens's strategy. As the New York *Times* had observed in 1866, Stevens's program "presupposes the continuance during peace of a public opinion which acquired force under the excitement and perils of war."[25] Inevitably, however, the impulse for a return to normal, for an end to the crisis, had grown in the Republican party—and Stevens, though unhappy with the new Reconstruction measure, had been powerless to block it. Now, the political initiative in effect passed to southern whites. If they accepted the new situation "in good faith," they could destroy whatever chance Stevens's more radical policies might have had.

Although most historians of Reconstruction have not emphasized the fact, confiscation was very much a live political issue in the spring and summer of 1867. But while the debate was very animated, it soon became clear that the fears aroused by Stevens's proposals far outweighed any attractions the plan contained. When Congress reconvened in March 1867, Stevens, ill and too weak to speak, had a colleague read a long speech and a bill providing forty acres to freedmen from confiscated land. "To this issue," he announced, "I desire to devote the small remnant of my life." At the same time, Charles Sumner pressed the issue in the Senate, and outside of Congress Benjamin Butler, Wendell Phillips, and the American Anti-Slavery Society endorsed Stevens's proposals.

The moderate majority of Republicans, however, were determined that Congress should embark upon no new Reconstruction experiments until the success or failure of the recently enacted measures had become clear. Stevens's bill was postponed to December, and Sumner's resolutions were handily defeated. William P. Fessenden, perhaps the most powerful Senate Republican, informed Sumner, "This is more than we do for white men." To which Sumner responded, "White men have never been in

[25] New York *Times*, February 2, 1866.

slavery." The furthest some Republicans would go was a warning to the South. If the recently adopted Reconstruction plan did not achieve satisfactory results, several highly respectable Republican journals declared, confiscation would be the logical next policy. Surprisingly, only the generally conservative Philadelphia *North American*, a self-proclaimed spokesman for the manufacturing interests of Pennsylvania, seemed genuinely sympathetic to confiscation. The key question of Reconstruction, the *North American* announced, was the fate of the "plantation oligarchy," and those who opposed Stevens's proposals "must find some other means of destroying this landed aristocracy." The journal also emphasized that the creation of a yeoman class in the South would greatly benefit northern industry (which in 1867 was suffering from the postwar recession). "Just in proportion as the freedmen rise in the social scale will they consume more of the fabrics we sell to the South. Just in proportion as the South refuses to let them rise . . . do we suffer in our trade." If small farms replaced plantations as the basis of southern agriculture, the South would "buy ten dollars of merchandise off us for every one it now takes." [26]

Despite the discouraging response, Stevens continued to press the land issue. In June, he made public a letter addressed to the county assessors of southern Pennsylvania, informing them of his intention to "prosecute the claims for confiscation at the next session of Congress," and requesting a detailed list of Civil War losses which might be reimbursed from the proceeds of confiscated

[26] *Congressional Globe*, 40th Cong., 1st sess., 49, 203; Springfield *Weekly Republican*, March 23, 1867; New York *Times*, March 13, June 7, 12, 1867; *Sumner Works*, XI, 124–129; *National Anti-Slavery Standard*, June 15, 22, 1867; James M. McPherson, *The Struggle for Equality* (Princeton, 1964), p. 411; Chicago *Tribune*, July 18, 1867; Philadelphia *Press*, March 21, May 8, 1867; Boston *Advertiser*, April 27, 1867; Philadelphia *North American and United States Gazette*, March 14, 16, May 1, 27, 1867.

lands. He specifically instructed the assessors to omit his own property from the list, since some opponents charged that his real aim was to secure compensation for his Caledonia Iron Works, destroyed by the Confederates in 1863. "Feeble as my own powers are," Stevens concluded, "if I had five years more added to my life, I should not doubt that this would become an accomplished fact." [27]

By the end of July, the influential Cincinnati *Commercial* could report the existence of "a considerable number of decided advocates of the confiscation of rebel property" in Republican ranks. By then, however, the opponents of confiscation were marshaling their forces. The sudden prominence of the confiscation question forced Republicans to take sides, and most made it clear that Stevens's proposals were incompatible with their basic beliefs. Respected radical journals like the *Nation* insisted that while possession of property would be eminently desirable for the freedmen, for the government to give them land would suggest that "there are other ways of securing comfort or riches than honest work." "No man in America," it added, "has any right to anything which he has not honestly earned, or which the lawful owner has not thought proper to give him." At the same time, more conservative Republicans denounced Stevens for adding to "the distrust which already deters capitalists from embarking in [the South's] enterprises." The New York *Times* printed dispatches from correspondents in the South, reporting that "*the fear of confiscation*" was paralyzing business. When investors in plantations went to southern banks for loans, declared a letter from South Carolina, they were met with the query, "How can you give security against Thaddeus Stevens?" From Georgia it was reported that gloom hung over the men of "intelligence, influence, and property," because they believed that as long as the confiscation

[27] New York *Times*, May 29, June 2, 1867. See New York *Herald*, May 2, 1866, attributing Stevens's confiscation proposals to his desire for compensation for the burning of his iron works.

question was agitated, "neither capital nor emigration will flow this way." [28]

Perhaps even more threatening, in the *Times*'s view, was the precedent which might be set by the confiscation of southern property. Others might also warn that the "process of division," once begun in the South, would not be confined there, but it was the *Times* that expressed most clearly the fears felt by northern men of property:

> If Congress is to take cognizance of the claims of labor against capital . . . there can be no decent pretense for confining the task to the slave-holder of the South. It is a question, not of humanity, not of loyalty, but of the fundamental relation of industry to capital; and sooner or later, if begun at the South, it will find its way into the cities of the North. . . . An attempt to justify the confiscation of Southern land under the pretense of doing justice to the freedmen, strikes at the root of all property rights in both sections. It concerns Massachusetts quite as much as Mississippi.[29]

These fears were exaggerated by confiscation's being only one of a series of what the *Nation* called "schemes for interference with property or business" which were agitating the public scene in the spring of 1867. Labor activity seemed to have reached a new peak, with "strikes among

---

[28] Cincinnati *Commercial*, July 25, 1867; *Nation*, March 21, May 9, 16, 1867; New York *Times*, February 19, March 10, April 10, June 27, 1867. Cf. Springfield *Weekly Republican*, April 27, June 15, 1867, and Gaillard Hunt, ed., "Letter of William Henry Trescott on Reconstruction in South Carolina, 1867," *American Historical Review*, XV (1910), 574–583, in which Trescott, a wealthy planter and moderate southern political leader, warned Senator Henry Wilson that agitation of the confiscation question was eroding "the natural influence of capital on labor, of employer on employed," which "must always exist" in a stable, prosperous society.

[29] New York *Times*, July 9, 1867. Cf. Boston *Advertiser*, June 13, 1867; "The Agrarians—Division of Property," *De Bow's Review*, n.s., IV (Dec. 1867), 586–588.

the workmen of every kind throughout the country," and demands for federal and state laws to enact the eight-hour day.[30] In June, the radical senator Ben Wade delivered a widely reported speech in Kansas, declaring that with the slavery issue settled, a new political question—the relations of capital and labor—was about to emerge. "Property," said Wade, "is not equally divided, and a more equal distribution of capital must be wrought out." Though Wade quickly backtracked when his speech aroused a furor in Republican circles, the *Times* insisted that it was now "perfectly clear that we are to have a political party based on the broadest and plainest doctrines of agrarianism. A war on property is to succeed the war on Slavery." [31]

Complicating the political scene—and the confiscation question—still further was the relation between the land issue and the development of the Republican party in the South. Despite black suffrage, most Republicans still envisioned their nascent southern coalition as an alliance of southern merchants, business interests, Whiggish planters, and black voters, with the white propertied elements in control. Republicans, of course, expected most of the newly enfranchised blacks to align with their party, but it was the southern whites who seemed to possess the attributes—"knowledge, character, intelligence, and ability"—necessary for political leadership. The confiscation

[30] *Nation,* June 27, 1867; Philadelphia *Press,* May 3, 16, 1867; Cincinnati *Commercial,* April 15, June 5, 1867; E. L. Godkin, "The Labor Crisis," *North American Review,* CV (July 1867), 199. In New York, the month of May witnessed strikes involving railroad workers, masons, hod carriers, stablemen, printers, carpenters, and shoemakers. New York *Tribune,* May 13, 14, 16, 18, 1867.

[31] William F. Zornow, " 'Bluff Ben' Wade in Lawrence, Kansas: The Issue of Class Conflict," *Ohio Historical Quarterly,* XIV (1956), 44–52; New York *Times,* June 12, 20, July 1, 1867; Felice A. Bonadio, *North of Reconstruction: Ohio Politics, 1865–1870* (New York, 1970), 148–149.

plan seemed certain to alienate the support of propertied whites, and would create instead a class-oriented party of poor blacks and whites in which a solid black vote would be the controlling element. This fear was succinctly expressed by the *Times:* "Mr. Stevens and General Butler are determined to build up a Southern Party called Republican, on the scheme of confiscation. They expect to get by that bribe the whole negro vote and enough of the white vote to control the Southern States." [32]

In a sense the *Times* was right, although Stevens would hardly have called confiscation a "bribe." He certainly knew, however, that as one newspaper reported in 1867, "these black voters are overwhelmingly in favor of confiscation," and that support for the plan had been growing among white southerners as well. As early as January 1866, Stevens had received letters from southern loyalists endorsing his plans as being the only way to break planter domination. By 1867, such prominent organs of southern Republicanism as the Raleigh *Standard* were speaking in favor of it, and the Philadelphia *Press* reported from Alabama that if confiscation were submitted to a vote in that state, "a majority both of blacks and whites would vote for it." Southern white Republicans seemed to be coming to the realization that if the planters' economic hegemony were not broken, they would eventually "be sure to control the policy of the community." In Stevens's view, moreover, the confiscation plan would allow southern Republicans to transcend the troublesome race issue by uniting freedmen and poor whites on an economic basis. As the Washington *Daily Morning Chronicle,* Stevens's leading newspaper supporter, explained,

[32] Springfield *Weekly Republican,* March 18, 1867; New York *Tribune,* March 21, 23, 1867; New York *Times,* June 10, 1867. Cf. Cincinnati *Commercial,* April 12, 1867; Springfield *Weekly Republican,* April 27, 1867; New York *Times,* April 30, May 13, 20, June 13, August 21, 1867.

"the great question of Reconstruction is not a question of race supremacy . . . but . . . is really and truly a question of the rights of labor." [33]

The prospect of the confiscation and redistribution of planter lands, the Boston *Advertiser* reported in June 1867, "has taken possession to a large extent of the mind of the loyal population of the South—the poor whites and landlack negroes." This was hardly to say, however, that there were not strong Republican elements in the South which opposed such a measure. As each southern state went through the process of organizing a Republican party in the spring of 1867, virtually every convention found itself divided between "confiscation radicals" and more moderate Whiggish elements. The results were not comforting to moderate and conservative northern Republicans. In Alabama the Union League resolved that if former rebels did not accept the new political situation "in good faith," Congress should confiscate their lands. In North Carolina a Republican mass meeting called on Congress to enact Stevens's latest measure. Most disturbing was the situation in Virginia, where black delegates at the state convention almost to a man demanded a confiscation plank. Most white Republicans, led by the venerable John Minor Botts and other one-time Whig Unionists, opposed the plan, but the blacks were supported by certain white radicals such as the Reverend James Hunnicutt, the editor of a Richmond newspaper. In the end, an uneasy compromise was

---

[33] Philadelphia *North American and United States Gazette*, July 1, 1867; J. H. Rea to Stevens, January 9, 1866; Henry W. McVay to Stevens, March 1, 1867; P. H. Whitehurst to Stevens, March 22, 1867, Stevens Papers; William Birthright to John Broomall, July 14, 1867, John Broomall Papers, Historical Society of Pennsylvania; Raleigh *Standard*, cited in New York *Times*, April 10, 1867; Philadelphia *Press*, cited in New York *Times*, May 30, 1867; Boston *Advertiser*, June 25, 1867; Washington *Daily Morning Chronicle*, December 13, 1867.

reached, in a resolution threatening confiscation if planters tried to intimidate black voters.[34]

Northern Republicans, including many radicals, were alarmed at the apparent influence of men like Hunnicutt among the freedmen. "Nothing could be more ominous of disaster," declared the Boston *Advertiser*, ". . . than such an array of class against class in the Southern States" as Hunnicutt and others sought. To counteract pro-confiscation influence, three Republican orators, all considered radical in the North, visited the South in the late spring, addressing gatherings of freedmen. Horace Greeley spoke at a large meeting at Richmond's African Church. "I beg you to believe," Greeley told the blacks, "that you are more likely to earn a home than get one by any form of confiscation. . . . Confiscation shrivels and paralyzes the industry of the whole community subjected to its influence." Senator Henry Wilson brought the same message to Virginia and South Carolina, and William D. Kelley also visited the South, praising its potential for economic development and informing the freedmen that "they can have homes of their own by working hard and saving what they earn—not otherwise." [35]

From Washington, Stevens looked on as the gospel of work was brought to the freedmen. Late in April, he denounced Wilson's Virginia speech and warned that "no man should make promises for the party. . . . Who authorized any orator to say that there would be no confiscation?" In May, he reiterated his criticism of the "Repub-

[34] Boston *Advertiser,* June 13, 1867; New York *Times,* April 8, 19, May 2, 18, 30, June 12, 1867; New York *Tribune,* April 20, 24, 1867; Hamilton J. Eckenrode, *The Political History of Virginia During the Reconstruction* (Baltimore, 1904), p. 67; Alrutheus A. Taylor, *The Negro in the Reconstruction of Virginia* (Washington, D.C., 1926), pp. 209–212.

[35] New York *Tribune,* April 25, May 6, 17, 27, June 10, 1867; New York *Times,* April 24, 1867; Chicago *Tribune,* July 17, 1867; Jack P. Maddex, *The Virginia Conservatives, 1867–1879* (Chapel Hill, N.C., 1970), p. 53.

lican meteors" pursuing their "erratic. . . . course" through the South, and in June he announced his intention of pushing the confiscation plan at the next session of Congress. But by the end of May it had become apparent that Greeley, Wilson, and Kelley were far closer to the mainstream of Republican opinion than was Thaddeus Stevens. Speaker of the House Schuyler Colfax and Senate leader Fessenden publicly supported Wilson against Stevens's criticisms, and a committee of congressmen charged by the Republican caucus with overseeing political developments in the South declared that the rights of property would not be infringed (although it did piously urge landholders to offer land for sale to blacks at reasonable rates). It was apparent, in short, that whatever southern Republicans desired, the party in the North was hardly prepared to embrace confiscation.[36] Consequently, as the summer progressed, talk of confiscation subsided in southern Republican conventions.[37]

By the end of 1867, the leftward drift which had characterized the Republican party since the beginning of the Civil War had definitely come to an end. The party suffered a series of reverses in the state elections of 1867, which many Republican leaders blamed squarely on Stevens, the radicals, and their "extreme theories." The election returns greatly strengthened the hand of Republicans like the Ohio banker Henry Cooke and Boston's liberal industrialist Edward Atkinson, who were determined to "put down" the "ultra infidelic radicals" and "prevent the creation of an exclusive black man's party [in the South] and also kill the scheme of confiscation." As the party turned toward respectability, conservatism and Grant, it

[36] New York *Times*, April 28, May 24, 29, June 22, 1867; New York *Herald*, July 8, 1867; New York *Tribune*, May 23, 1867; Boston *Advertiser*, May 25, 1867.

[37] New York *Tribune*, March 26, April 30, 1867; New York *Times*, June 22, July 31, September 9, 19, 27, 1867; *Nation*, August 8, 1867; J. G. de Roulhac Hamilton, *Reconstruction in North Carolina* (New York, 1914), pp. 245–247.

appeared certain that, as an Ohio politician observed, "the Negro will be less prominent for some time to come." [38]

By August 1868, when he died, Stevens's political influence was at low ebb. In his characteristically cynical way he had told an interviewer, "I have no history. My life-long regret is that I have lived so long and so uselessly." He died aware that planters were already beginning to use economic intimidation to counter black voting power and that sharecropping and the crop lien—a new "system of peonage," as he called it—were spreading in the black belts, threatening to keep the freedmen permanently dependent on the planters. Stevens was nonetheless still a formidable figure, venerated by the freedmen and by millions of other Republicans, and his death produced a public expression of grief second only to the funeral of Lincoln. It marked in some ways the end of an era, symbolizing the transition from ideology to political expediency as the guiding force of the Republican party. Though the Philadelphia *Press* declared, "He dies at the moment when the truths for which he fought a long and doubtful battle have permanently and almost universally triumphed," James G. Blaine, one of the rising politicos who would control the party's destinies in the 1870s, saw it differently. "The death of Stevens," Blaine observed, "is an emancipation for the Republican party." [39]

---

[38] Ellis P. Oberholtzer, *Jay Cooke, Financier of the Civil War*, 2 vols. (Philadelphia, 1907), II, 28; Sharkey, *Money, Class, and Party*, pp. 95, 119; Mary L. Hinsdale, ed., *Garfield-Hinsdale Letters* (Ann Arbor, 1949), p. 112. Cf. Springfield *Weekly Republican*, October 26, 1867; *Harper's Weekly*, October 26, 1867; Philadelphia *North American and United States Gazette*, October 11, 1867; Michael Les Benedict, "The Rout of Radicalism: Republicans and the Election of 1867," *Civil War History*, XVIII (Dec. 1972), 334–344.

[39] New York *Tribune*, August 14, 1868; *Independent*, August 27, 1868; Brock, *American Crisis*, p. 282; Philadelphia *Press*, August 12, 1868, George F. Hoar, *Autobiography of Seventy Years*, 2 vols. (New York, 1903), I, 239. Shortly before his death, Stevens predicted that in the future southern whites would bar black voting by

Between 1860 and 1868 revolutionary changes had taken place, changes for which contemporaries gave Stevens more than an average share of the credit. Slavery had been abolished, the freedmen granted civil and political equality, and democratic institutions established in all the southern states. But the final step of the Second American Revolution, the provision of an economic underpinning to the blacks' newly won freedom, had not been taken. The failure of Stevens's campaign for confiscation, his demand that society confront the basic economic questions which the abolition of slavery had entailed, exposed the limitations of the Republican party's middle-class ideology. At the same time, it exposed the vulnerability of Stevens's anomalous position as a radical in politics. Lacking a political base outside the Republican party, Stevens could be successful only so long as his proposals gave no fundamental challenge to the values and interests of the Republican mainstream. Possibly a more flexible man than Stevens, one willing to talk less flamboyantly of punishing traitors, revolutionizing southern society, and destroying social classes, one prepared to accept some form of limited, compensated expropriation of land and its sale on credit, might have achieved more for the cause of black landowning than did Stevens. Probably, however, the very idea of confiscation violated too many of the basic Republican verities for the party ever to become reconciled to it.[40]

---

adopting property qualifications "applicable to all classes alike, which would reach down to just about the black line," and he condemned the emerging sharecropping and crop lien systems. *Congressional Globe,* 40th Cong., 2d sess., 108, 1966, 2214.

[40] In *Beyond Equality* (New York, 1967), an important contribution to the historiography of Reconstruction, David Montgomery has argued that radical Republicanism broke up in the late 1860s under the impact of forces outside Reconstruction, particularly the emergence of a class-conscious labor movement whose demands challenged the radicals' vision of a harmonious social order founded on equality before the law. Mont-

Stevens's failure, indeed, revealed the limits to which a bourgeois capitalist culture, even in its most radical phase, will voluntarily yield to radicalism. What is actually most striking about the confiscation debate is the way it prefigured the disillusionment which would soon overtake radical Reconstruction. The same fears aroused by confiscation—special privilege, corruption, black domination, dramatic social upheaval by government fiat, a general undermining of the principles of good government—would shortly come to be associated with Reconstruction itself. The arguments used against Stevens between 1865 and 1867 would eventually justify the entire abandonment of Reconstruction.

---

gomery, however, ignores the fact that all the challenges he cites, from the danger of class legislation to the radicals' inability to move beyond "equality before the law," were present in an issue at the core of Reconstruction —confiscation. Cf. W. E. B. Du Bois, *Black Reconstruction* (New York, 1935), a frustrating, flawed, but monumental study which deserves careful reading by anyone interested in Reconstruction. Chapter 14 discusses the decline of radicalism.

JAMES MCLACHLAN

American Colleges and the Transmission of Culture: The Case of the Mugwumps

ACADEMIC INTELLECTUALS in America have always hoped to influence public affairs, either directly or—perhaps more realistically—by molding potential leaders through education. Such influence, however, has always been difficult to trace. American educators, therefore, were overjoyed when Franklin Roosevelt, in one of his most famous campaign statements of 1932, declared that "there is no safety valve in the form of a Western prairie to which those thrown out of work by the Eastern economic machines can go for a new start." It was known that in the spring of 1904 Roosevelt had been enrolled in History 10B, Frederick Jackson Turner's course on the "Development of the West" at Harvard. Here seemed to be a perfect example of the influence of education on public affairs: the future president's image of American society had been decisively and demonstrably molded by one of the most eminent of the Progressive historians. Subsequent examination, however, somewhat clouded the picture. It appeared that Roosevelt had spent the first six weeks of

Turner's course on a Caribbean cruise, and that the 1932 remark was probably the work of Adolf A. Berle, one of Roosevelt's speechwriters. Roosevelt left Harvard, most would agree, as intellectually unsullied as when he entered.[1]

Historians, in fact, have been inclined to treat a particular individual's three- or four-year stay in an American college as providing him with little more than a useful status indicator, a certificate that guaranteed him an income higher than that of the average grammar or high school graduate. Aside from direct training in immediately utilitarian skills, and perhaps in science, most historians would probably agree that football and other extracurricular activities have had more significance in shaping the mind of the undergraduate than the formal elements of the course of study. Is it, however, impossible to trace a line of influence between an individual's or a group's conscious intellectual experience during their college years and elements of their mature thought and expression? Can we discern with any assurance the actual traces of the process by which colleges transmit culture? The search for the frontier theory in Franklin Roosevelt's speeches assumes, perhaps, too simple and literal-minded a process. We might do well instead to examine the college years of a particular group for more subtle elements of culture—a style of thought, a mode of discourse, the emerging outlines of a particular social and intellectual world view. Once having located the cultural style acquired in youth, we might then try to demonstrate its expression in maturity.[2] The following pages attempt to do this with one

[1] Frank Freidel, *Franklin D. Roosevelt: The Apprenticeship* (Boston, 1952), p. 72.

[2] Apparently, only three serious historical attempts to connect undergraduate education with particular cultural style exist: Henry Steele Commager makes a glancing but persuasive reference to that theme in his "Leadership in Eighteenth-Century America and Today," *Daedalus*, XC (Fall 1961), 652–673; Allen F. Davis, in *Spearheads for Reform: The Social Settlements and the*

group of late-nineteenth-century Americans—the Mugwumps.

In every period of American life there are certain social types that come to symbolize for later generations the qualities most characteristic of the earlier age. Aside from Andrew Jackson himself, when one thinks of the pre-Civil War years the images of the mountain man, the pioneer, or the abolitionist come to mind, all conveniently symbolizing complex social movements. For the two or three decades after the Civil War three types in particular seem to have captured the popular historical imagination: the robber baron, the machine politician, and the civic reformer, or Mugwump. Visually, the first two images have been fixed by the cartoons of Thomas Nast. One is the bloated, curiously Shylock-like figure of Boss Tweed of New York, greedy, deceptive, and corrupt; the other is the monopolist, squatting on his moneybags like a great obscene chicken. The image of the Mugwump, however, is much less clear.

George Haven Putnam, the New York publisher, has told us how the Mugwumps viewed themselves. "Each generation of citizens," he wrote, "produces a group of men who are free from self-seeking and who, recognizing their obligation to the community, are prepared to give their work and their capacities for the service of their fellowmen." [3] Putnam was thinking of men like the liberal German émigré Carl Schurz, one-time Civil War general and Secretary of the Interior; of Edwin L. Godkin, editor of the New York *Nation;* of the reformer Thomas Wentworth Higginson; of George William Curtis, editor of *Harper's Weekly:* of the men who were the most prominent ad-

Progressive Movement, 1890–1914 (New York, 1967), pp. 23–39, argues convincingly that the first generation of social workers took up their careers in response to the summons of the Social Gospel educators, as does George R. Peterson in *The New England College in the Age of the University* (Amherst, 1964), pp. 172–195.

[3] *Memories of a Publisher: 1865–1915* (New York, 1916), p. 112.

vocates of one type or another of "reform" in the twenty or so years after the Civil War. Such men were among the instigators of the liberal Republican movement in 1872 and the mass defection (in which they acquired the name Mugwump) from the Republican party in 1884. They formed the core of the drive for civil service reform and the free trade and tariff reform movements. They typically called too for municipal, legal, and ballot reforms, and they supported a universal amnesty for the South, hard money, and the gold standard. At the turn of the century their favorite cause was anti-imperialism. Inheritors of certain aspects of a once widespread eighteenth-century Anglo-American political ideology that placed strong emphasis on the necessity of republican "virtue" (in the sense of an "unselfish devotion to the public good"[4]), they wanted a government run by an educated and responsible elite, or, in a favorite phrase of their preeminent historian, James Ford Rhodes, by men of "property and intelligence." Puzzled and disturbed by the growing industrialization of post-bellum America, they viewed the age of Grant with disdain and disgust. They sometimes found it difficult to decide which was the more pernicious, the "tyranny" of the professional politician, or the new businessman, with his vulgarity and his influence on politics.

The complaint of Charles Francis Adams, Jr., is familiar: "I have known, and known tolerably well," he wrote toward the end of his life, "a good many 'successful' men—'big' financially—men famous during the last half-century; and a less interesting crowd I do not care to encounter. Not one that I have ever known would I care to

[4] The definition of "virtue" is borrowed from Gordon Wood's "Introduction" to his anthology *The Rising Glory of America, 1760–1820* (New York, 1971), p. 6. For an introduction to American republican ideology, see Robert E. Shalhope, "Toward a Republican Synthesis: The Emergence of an Understanding of Republicanism in American Historiography," *William and Mary Quarterly*, 3d ser., XXXIX (Jan. 1972), 49–80. The study of this ideology has yet to be carried into the nineteenth century.

meet again, either in this world or the next; nor is one of them associated in my mind with the idea of humor, thought or refinement. A set of mere money-getters and traders, they were essentially unattractive and uninteresting."[5]

The Mugwumps' attitude toward most politicians was even less appreciative than their opinion of the new industrialists: "self-seeking political tricksters" was one of their milder epithets. In 1884 they said of James G. Blaine, presidential candidate of the Republican party: "We know what Blaine is, and always has been—a liar . . . we will expose him in all his naked ugliness." A politician might charitably be considered a "moral lunatic," but at best he remained a type that, as one Mugwump said, only a man "who had never been in prison or in politics might safely acknowledge as a friend."[6]

Historians have certainly been aware of the Mugwumps. They stalk through the pages of James Ford Rhodes's classic history of the United States, always ready to stage a bolt from the Republican party (though by no means all were Republicans) if they suspect that political morality is about to be compromised. Many historians have suggested that they represent a type, but Richard Hofstadter made what was perhaps the most provocative characterization of—in Eric Goldman's phrase—the "patrician reformer." In his *Age of Reform* (1955) and in *Anti-intellectualism in American Life* (1963) Hofstadter depicted the Mugwump type as the "old gentry," men or the sons of men who had been leaders in their communities before the Civil War—small merchants, manufacturers, and professionals. Well educated, accustomed to rule benevolently, they were pushed aside by the postwar *nouveaux riches* and the political bosses. While quantitatively

---

[5] Charles Francis Adams, Jr., *An Autobiography: With a Memorial Address by Henry Cabot Lodge* (Boston, 1916), p. 190.

[6] Henry Adams, *Democracy: An American Novel* (New York, 1952), p. 233.

they lost nothing, qualitatively they were dwarfed in both prestige—or status—and in wealth by men like Vanderbilt, Gould, or Morgan. No longer big fish in little ponds, they found themselves little fish in a great national ocean. Many of the reform movements of the 1870s and 1880s, Hofstadter suggested, could best be understood as the Mugwumps' reaction to their comparative loss of status, or to what he called the "status revolution" of the later nineteenth century.[7]

The concept of status revolution and the interpretation of politics as the acting out of status anxieties quickly came under attack. C. Vann Woodward and Norman Pollack, among others, severely challenged Hofstadter's interpretation of the Populist movement. And R. B. Sherman, comparing the leaders of the Massachusetts Progressive movement with leaders of the Massachusetts Republican party, found that they had "essentially similar class characteristics"—both Progressives and Republicans tended to be well-to-do native Americans, urban, Anglo-Saxon, Protestant, and college-educated.[8]

---

[7] Eric Goldman, *Rendezvous with Destiny: A History of Modern American Reform* (New York, 1956), pp. 10–28; Hofstadter, *The Age of Reform: From Bryan to F.D.R.* (New York, 1956), pp. 131–172; Hofstadter, *Anti-intellectualism in American Life* (New York, 1963), pp. 145–196.

[8] For a survey of applications of the status concept, see Robert W. Doherty, "Status Anxiety and Reform: Some Alternatives," *American Quarterly,* XIX (Summer 1967), 329–337. For negative criticism of applications of the concept, see Gerard A. Brandmeyer and R. S. Denisoff, "Status Politics: An Appraisal of the Application of the Concept," *Pacific Sociological Review,* XII (Spring 1969), 5–11. See also C. Vann Woodward, *The Burden of Southern History* (New York, 1960), pp. 141–166; Norman Pollack, "Hofstadter on Populism," *Journal of Southern History,* XXVI (Nov. 1960), 478–500; Richard B. Sherman, "The Status Revolution and Massachusetts Progressive Leadership," *Political Science Quarterly,* LXXVIII (March 1963), 59–65. The development of Hofstadter's historical thought—and that of his critics—is ably surveyed by Arthur M. Schlesinger's

Most criticism of the status interpretation tended to focus on its application to the Populist and Progressive movements. Little if any attention was devoted to rethinking its application to the group to which Hofstadter had first applied it, the Mugwumps. The most recent study of the Mugwumps, for instance, manages to avoid any mention whatsoever of the status concept.[9] This was understandable; there seemed to be few obvious groups with which to compare the Mugwumps. Less understandable was the neglect of an effort to account for the Mugwumps' unique political, social, and intellectual styles in terms more complex than a simple listing of the elements of their "social origin." [10]

The Mugwumps themselves, as we have seen, perceived two specific contemporary types, the industrialist and the machine politician, as their most obvious "negative reference groups," as exemplars of all the trends they deplored in contemporary America. And, in fact, an empirical survey of social variables in the backgrounds of all three groups does reveal important differences in fathers' occupations, in religious denomination, in occupation, and in other areas. For our immediate purposes, however, the most striking difference between Mugwumps, industrialists, and politicians lies in the educational experience of each group:

"Richard Hofstadter," in Marcus Cunliffe and Robin W. Winks, eds., *Pastmasters: Some Essays on American Historians* (New York, 1969), pp. 345–374.

[9] See John G. Sproat, *"The Best Men": Liberal Reformers in the Gilded Age* (New York, 1968).

[10] Gerald W. McFarland's insistence on the Mugwumps' "intense awareness of class attachments" to my mind severely distorts his otherwise admirable prosopographical investigation of 396 Mugwumps in his "The New York Mugwumps of 1884: A Profile," *Political Science Quarterly,* LXXVIII (March 1963), 40–58. Geoffrey Blodgett outlines the mind of the Massachusetts Mugwumps with considerable subtlety in *The Gentle Reformers: Massachusetts Democrats in the Cleveland Era* (Cambridge, Mass., 1966), pp. 19–47.

EDUCATION OF MUGWUMPS, NEW YORK CITY OFFICIALS, AND INDUSTRIAL ELITE [11]

	Mugwumps		Industrial Elite		NYC Officials	
	Total	%	Total	%	Total	%
l subjects	185	——	303.	——	129	——
cation known	181	97.8	183	60.0	44	34.1
nded college	149	82.3	——	37.0	9	20.5
not attend llege	32	17.7	——	63.0	35	79.5
rand total	181	100.0	183	100.0	44	100.0

[11] The figures on the "industrial elite"—leaders of the textile, steel, and railroad industries in the 1870s and 1880s—are drawn and recalculated from Francis W. Gregory and Irene D. Neu, "The American Industrial Elite in the 1870s: Their Social Origins," in William Miller, ed., *Men in Business: Essays in the History of Entrepreneurship* (Cambridge, Mass., 1952), p. 203, Table 7. Figures on the politicians are drawn and recalculated from Norman A. Dain, "The Social Composition of the Leadership of Tammany Hall in New York City, 1855–1865" (unpublished master's thesis, Columbia University, 1958), p. 157, Table 8.

The 185 Mugwumps comprise a random sample, drawn from lists of participants in four different reform movements: the Liberal Republican movement of 1872, the civil service reform movement, the free trade movement, and the Independent Republican (or Mugwump) movement of 1884. The final list of Mugwumps was compiled from a wide variety of sources. Citation of all works consulted would run to unnecessary length, but among the most useful were the following:

Liberal Republican Movement of 1872: Letters to the New York *Daily Tribune* for March 30, April 17, and June 22, 1872, supporting the Cincinnati Convention of Liberals; from Earle D. Ross, *The Liberal Republican Movement* (New York, 1919).

Free Trade Movement: the 1881 and 1882 membership lists of the New York Free Trade Club, now in

All three groups were, for their times, conspicuously well educated. The median number of years in school for Americans born in 1865 was only eight, while in 1880 only 2.72 percent of eighteen- to twenty-one-year-olds were registered in institutions of higher education.[12] The Mugwumps, however, did not define themselves with reference to the American population as a whole, but in contrast to two specific groups in the population. Compared to contemporary industrial leaders or to machine politicians they were a very well-educated group indeed. Not only were more than four-fifths of the Mugwumps college-educated, but more than half had gone to just two colleges—about 35 percent to Harvard and 16 percent to Yale. The rest went to a scattered group of institutions best described as the "New England college type"—Amherst, Dartmouth,

---

the New York Public Library's Ford Collection. Half the members of this organization did not live in New York; their names are included on its rolls.

Civil Service Reform Movement: the *Minutes* and *Proceedings* of the National Civil Service Reform League and its Executive Council for the years 1882–1884, also in the Ford Collection; also from Ari A. Hoogenboom, *Outlawing the Spoils: A History of the Civil Service Reform Movement, 1865–1883* (Urbana, Ill., 1961).

Independent Republican Movement of 1884: from Richard R. Bowker, Horace E. Deming, and George Walton Green, *Report of the National Committee of Republicans and Independents, Presidential Election of 1884* (New York, 1885).

A lengthy list of biographies, autobiographies, and memoirs provided the biographical data on the Mugwumps. More than fifty works were consulted in the search for such data: they included state, national, and regional biographical encyclopedias, college yearbooks, class reports and necrologies, and newspaper obituary notices. The following works were among the most useful: *Dictionary of American Biography* (New York, 1928–1958); the *National Cyclopedia of American Biography* (New York, 1892–); and *Who Was Who in America,* 3 vols. (Chicago, 1942–1959), Vol. I.

[12] U.S. Department of Commerce, *Historical Statistics of the United States from Colonial Times to 1957* (Washington, D.C., 1960), pp. 211, 214.

Williams, Union, Hamilton, Antioch, and others.[13] Moreover, a significant part of the Mugwumps' self-image rested on the fact that they were college-educated men. The editor George William Curtis's perennial address, "The Public Duty of Educated Men," expressed a widely shared vision of their role in American society.[14] The experience of their college years, obviously, had left a deep impress on the Mugwumps' image of themselves, of their role in social and political affairs, and of their cultural style. The Mugwumps' undergraduate experience, however, had been that of the American college at a specific time, in a particular period of institutional history.

In the 1880s the Mugwumps were men in early middle age; their mean age in 1884 was forty-eight. Assuming that most of them had graduated from college when they were about twenty-one years old, then, the vast majority would have attended college in a period extending from the mid-1840s to the early 1870s. They were, in other words, the last generation to be educated in what for want of a better term has been called the "old-time college" —the American college before it was decisively transformed by the emergence of the modern university.

In the history of American higher education these years are usually described as a period of decline for the paternalistic, authoritarian, dogmatic, old-time college. In the words of one historian, the pre-Civil War classroom

> was a dreary place. The students were subjected to a curriculum which rarely gave them any choice of courses, hardly ever a choice of teachers. They were submitted to a teaching routine consisting almost entirely of tedious daily recitations, and governed in detail by disciplinary rules that were excessively

[13] Mugwumps who attended colleges other than Harvard or Yale were scattered among 41 different institutions, as follows: Amherst, 7; Brown, 6; University of Pennsylvania, 5; Williams, 5; Columbia, 4; other U.S. institutions, 42; and foreign institutions, 4.

[14] Charles Eliot Norton, ed., *Orations and Addresses of George William Curtis,* 2 vols. (New York, 1894), I, 266.

> demanding. Since their instructors were set over them as policemen, outbursts of mutual hostility were a perennial motif. Term time was frequently punctuated by student riots, and putting the cow in the chapel was a standard college prank.

The curriculum of the period is usually described as consisting of little more than poorly taught classics, a bit of moral philosophy, a smattering of science, and obsolescent mathematics.[15] The picture is a gloomy one; it has been fixed by—among others—Henry Adams, who graduated from Harvard in 1858. "Harvard College," Adams wrote in his *Education,* "was probably less hurtful than any other university then in existence. It taught little, and that ill, but it left the mind open, free from bias, ignorant of facts, but docile. The graduate had few strong prejudices. He knew little, but his mind remained supple, ready to receive knowledge." [16]

Both the conventional historical picture and the image of the college conveyed by Adams contain a considerable amount of truth—but not all the truth. Consider, for instance, Adams's plaint about Harvard: "He could not afterwards remember the name of Karl Marx mentioned, or the title of 'Capital'. He was equally ignorant of Auguste Comte. These were the two writers of his time who most influenced its thought." [17] Actually, it was unlikely that *Capital* would have been discussed on any American campus between 1854 and 1858, since it was not published until 1867. As for Comte, the moral philosopher Francis Bowen, Adams's teacher at Harvard, went out of

---

[15] Richard Hofstadter, "The Revolution in Higher Education," in Arthur M. Schlesinger, Jr., and Morton White, eds., *Paths of American Thought* (Boston, 1963), p. 272. Much the same picture is conveyed by Frederick A. Rudolph in *The American College and University: A History* (New York, 1962).

[16] Henry Adams, *The Education of Henry Adams* (New York, 1931), p. 55.

[17] *Ibid.,* p. 60.

his way to denounce his pernicious views.[18] And if in his old age Adams remembered Harvard's effect on his education negatively, when he graduated in 1858 he had actually written: "I have had an infinitely pleasanter time than I ever had before . . . I do not believe that it would be possible to pass four pleasanter years. . . . My wishes are for a quiet and a literary life, as I believe that to be the happiest and in this country not the least useful." [19] After four years at Harvard Adams was settled in the main role of his long life—he would become a man of letters, an intellectual. His years in college must certainly have had some influence in determining his choice.

Satisfied or dissatisfied with their education, most Mugwumps spent four years in an old-time college. They had shared a common curriculum of classics, mathematics, and a little science. In these years every student took at least one other course, a course which I think had a major impact on the formation of the Mugwumps' cultural style. This was the course in Moral Philosophy, usually given in the senior year by the president of the college.[20] President Kirkland's course at Harvard was said to

---

[18] Ernest Samuels, *The Young Henry Adams* (Cambridge, Mass., 1948), pp. 26–27.

[19] Henry Brooks Adams, Autobiography, in MS Classbook, Class of 1858, Harvard University Archives, Widener Library, Cambridge.

[20] Satisfactory modern histories of neither American moral philosophy nor the college curriculum exist. A history of American moral philosophy can be pieced together from the following: Lawrence A. Cremin, *American Education: The Colonial Experience, 1607–1783* (New York, 1970), pp. 459–468; Douglas Milton Sloan, *The Scottish Enlightenment and the American College Ideal* (New York, 1971); Anna Haddow, *Political Science in American Colleges and Universities, 1636–1900* (New York, 1939); Gladys Bryson, "The Emergence of the Social Sciences from Moral Philosophy," *International Journal of Ethics,* XLII (April 1932), 304–323; Bryson, "The Comparable Interests of the Old Moral Philosophy and the Modern Social Sciences," *Social Forces,* XI (Oct. 1932), 19–27; Bryson, "Sociology Considered as Moral Philosophy," *The Socio-*

bring "the breath of intellectual life . . . into the dead body of the college." Francis Wayland at Brown, Timothy Dwight at Yale, and particularly Mark Hopkins at Williams were famous. "All Williams men have a family resemblance," a former student of Hopkins declared. "They all bear the mark of the same mind." [21] The mind in question was the mind of the American moral philosopher.

Almost forgotten today, moral philosophy was the preeminent American philosophy of the pre-Civil War era. Out of it have developed most of the contemporary social sciences—economics, anthropology, political sci-

---

logical Review, XXIV (Jan. 1932), 26–36; George P. Schmidt, *The Old Time College President* (New York, 1932), pp. 108–145; Donald Harvey Meyer, "The American Moralists: Academic Moral Philosophy in the United States, 1835–1880" (unpublished PhD dissertation, University of California, Berkeley, 1967); and Wilson Smith, *Professors and Public Ethics: Studies of Northern Moral Philosophers before the Civil War* (Ithaca, 1956). The best single study of American moral philosophy is Daniel Walker Hower, *The Unitarian Conscience: Harvard Moral Philosophy, 1805–1861* (Cambridge, Mass., 1970).

The standard history of the college curriculum, R. Freeman Butts, *The College Charts Its Course* (New York, 1939), is distorted by its progressive bias. Two older studies are still worth consulting: G. Stanley Hall, "On the History of American College Textbooks and Teaching in Logic, Ethics, Psychology and Allied Subjects," American Antiquarian Society *Proceedings,* n.s., IX (1893–1894), 137–174; and Louis F. Snow, *The College Curriculum in the United States* (New York, 1907). An excellent brief sketch of the old-time college curriculum can be found in George W. Pierson, *Yale College: An Educational History, 1871–1921* (New Haven, 1952), pp. 69–73.

If the implications of Norman S. Fiering's article on encyclopedics, "President Samuel Johnson and the Circle of Knowledge," *William and Mary Quarterly,* 3d ser., XXVII (April 1971), 199–236, are properly pursued it should be possible to rewrite completely the history of the formal curriculum.

[21] Franklin Carter, *Mark Hopkins* (Boston, 1892), p. 128; Alexander Young, *A Discourse on the Life and Character of the Rev. John Thornton Kirkland* (Boston, 1840), p. 51.

ence, sociology, and so forth.[22] Basically, it was the analysis and interpretation of the current mores, in form and content going back to Aristotle and the preoccupations of the Greek philosophers. The moral philosopher characteristically tried to establish new relationships that he thought would be more highly ethical and advantageous than current ones. The course in moral philosophy had been taught in American colleges at least since the mid-eighteenth century, though it was sometimes referred to as moral science, intellectual philosophy, science of mind and morals, or simply as metaphysics and ethics. The professor would treat in his course what we would now call psychology (then known as pneumatology, or the philosophy of mind); a section on economy, sections on government, jurisprudence, international law, taste, ethics, and religion. All these subjects were usually tied together by two controlling ideas: the starting point was human nature, and the object was to suggest improved ethical relationships between men. "You may plainly perceive both how extensive and how important moral philosophy is," John Witherspoon told his classes at Princeton in about 1770; ". . . its importance is manifest from this circumstance, that it not only points out personal duty, but is related to the whole business of active life. The languages, and even mathematical and natural knowledge, are but hand maids to this superior science."[23] Around 1800 at William and Mary the senior course would have been constructed like this:

> 1. Logic and the Philosophy of the Human Mind. On these subjects the works of Duncan, Reid, and Professor Stewart are studied.
>
> 2. Rhetoric and Belles Lettres. Here Dr. Blair's *Lectures* are chiefly used.
>
> 3. Moral Philosophy. In this department the author studied is Paley.

[22] Bryson, "Emergence of the Social Sciences."
[23] John Witherspoon, *Lectures on Moral Philosophy* (Princeton, 1912), p. 140.

4. Natural Law. Rutherford and Burlamaqui.
5. Law of Nations. Vattel and Martens.
6. Politics. Locke, Montesquieu, Rousseau.
7. Political Economy. Smith's *Wealth of Nations*.[24]

Five of the authors named are of the Scottish school of philosophy; as the nineteenth century wore on, the philosophy which was taught took on more and more the character of the Scottish "common sense" school. Before the Revolution, President Witherspoon of Princeton introduced the early group of Scottish philosophers to America —Hutcheson, Lord Kames, Adam Smith, Adam Ferguson. The American editions of their works and those of later Scottish philosophers often outnumbered the British. By the 1830s an American school of moral philosophers had arisen: among the most prominent were Francis Bowen of Harvard, John Bascom of Williams, and Francis Wayland of Brown. Wayland's *Elements of Moral Philosophy* (1835) became perhaps the most popular textbook in the field, with more than 100,000 copies sold by the turn of the century.[25]

Both the writers and the professors followed much the same arrangement of their subject. As Gladys Bryson has succinctly described the process, the philosopher or professor would first set forth his aims, his starting points, and his methods. Then he would establish his foundation stone, what he considered to be the "facts" of human nature. With this he would expound his definition of what every subject matter needed in order to be considered "scientific": a general principle capable of unifying and organizing the whole mass of material. On this foundation of the "facts" of human nature the moralist then built a generalized ethical teaching. The professor would then apply the generalized teaching to the various social insti-

[24] Samuel Miller, *A Brief Retrospect of the 18th Century*, II (New York, 1803), 503.
[25] Recently made available in a reprint ed. by Joseph L. Blau (Cambridge, Mass., 1963).

tutions, which were abstracted, and regarded as so many fields for the application of that law. In the course of describing the history and the function of the institutions, however, the moral teaching was often lost sight of or applied only loosely.[26] The result was often something like a contemporary introductory course in sociology or human relations. In any case, it gave the philosopher free rein to talk about his own interests and about current affairs.

One example will serve to give the flavor of the moral philosophy course at its loosest. In 1829 President Eliphalet Nott of Union College began his senior course by saying: "It has been my endeavor these twenty years, since I have had the care of youth, to make men rather than great scholars. I shall not give you long lessons, but shall lead you to exercise your own minds in much thought." After which, if a student's notes are to be trusted, Nott discussed the causes of early death among Methodist ministers, the evils of drunkenness, the uses of New England singing societies, the best way to handle mobs, and the existence of ghosts.[27] More than intellectual dilettantism was involved here. The ultimate effect of Nott's course (it was based on readings in Lord Kames's *The Elements of Criticism*) was apparently profound. One former student recalled:

> Lord Kames himself would have rubbed his eyes in astonishment, if he could have seen and heard the use that was made of his book. He would have found it so amplified and expanded that, instead of a compend of aesthetics, it had become a comprehensive study of human nature, ranging over the whole field of physical, moral, and intellectual philosophy, and applied to practical use in business, politics, and

---

[26] The preceding four sentences consist of paraphrase and direct quotation from Bryson, "Comparable Interests," pp. 19–20.

[27] Instructions delivered to the senior class in Union College, MS notes by W. Soul and H. Baldwin, 1829, as quoted in George P. Schmidt, "Intellectual Crosscurrents in American Colleges, 1825–1855," *American Historical Review*, XLII (Oct. 1936), 50.

> religion. . . . Many a clergyman, many an author, many a lawyer and statesman has found that Dr. Nott and "Kames" have given him the solution of some of the most perplexing problems of his life.[28]

Only one other element in the ante-bellum college seems to have aroused as much interest and involvement among the students as the moral philosophy course—the undergraduate literary and debating societies. All ante-bellum colleges had at least one, and often several more, such societies. The subjects debated in the societies mirrored not only the questions of the day but the ethical concerns raised by the moral philosophers. Yale's Brothers in Unity society, for example, early in the century debated such topics as these: "Are the abilities of the sexes equal?" and "Ought the immigration of foreigners into this country be encouraged?" (1816); and in 1817, "Are the blacks inferior to the whites in point of mental abilities?" There was remarkable continuity in the range of subjects considered in the debating societies over the course of the nineteenth century. In 1864, in the midst of the Civil War, Princeton's Cliosophic Society was debating such questions as "Ought the free negroes to be incorporated into the State by securing the right of Suffrage?" "Ought women to enjoy the rights of citizenship?" "Are the purely literary advantages of this college adequate to the wants of the Students?" [29] The debating societies, in effect, were student

---

[28] Frederick W. Seward, *Reminiscences of A War-Time Statesman and Diplomat* (New York, 1916), p. 65.

[29] David Potter, *Debating in the Colonial Chartered Colleges: An Historical Survey, 1642–1900* (New York, 1944), p. 85 and *passim;* and Thomas S. Harding, *College Literary Societies: Their Contribution to Higher Education in the United States, 1815–1876* (New York, 1971). The literary societies were far more than debating clubs: for a full discussion of their organization, activities, and goals, see James McLachlan, "The Choice of Hercules: American Student Societies in the Early Nineteenth Century," in Lawrence Stone, ed., *The University in Society* (Princeton, 1974), Vol. II.

workshops in the practical application of the moral philosophy they were learning in their classes.

Today, most of the subjects covered in the pre-1870 course in Moral Philosophy would be considered independently in separate courses in the political and social sciences. In fact, the modern college curriculum in these areas derives directly from the old courses in moral philosophy. Some of the subjects began to split off from the parent moral philosophy course quite early. At Yale, for instance, political economy was first taught as a separate subject in 1825, though still in the senior year and still by the college president, Jeremiah Day, who also taught ethics, theology, and metaphysics. The breaking of the circle of knowledge, however, was a slow process. As late as 1854, when Horace Mann became president of Antioch, he was expected also to be professor of political economy, intellectual and moral philosophy, constitutional law, and natural history. By the end of the 1850s moral philosophy was beginning to bulge at its seams with newly accumulated masses of knowledge. The collapse in moral philosophy's dominant role in the college curriculum can perhaps be dated 1872, when the Reverend William Graham Sumner was appointed professor of political and social science at Yale, with the avowed purpose of relieving President Noah Porter from the necessity of teaching the senior course in moral philosophy.

From the 1870s on, the splintering of the staple concerns of moral philosophy into such modern fields as economics, sociology, and anthropology proceeded quickly. Americans retained no overarching notion of a general field of inquiry into human affairs, such as the Germans would express in *Wissenschaft,* or the French by the phrase *les sciences humaines.*[30] American social scientists

[30] For an enlightening discussion of the organization of knowledge in Europe and the United States, see John Higham's "The Schism in American Scholarship," in his *Writing American History: Essays on Modern Scholarship* (Bloomington, 1970), pp. 3–24.

would claim to be guided only by positive information and the scientific method. In fact, of course, the ethical and moral concerns of moral philosophy informed many of the concerns of American social scientists—one can make a reasonable case for regarding the late C. Wright Mills as the last great American moral philosopher. Nor did the course in moral philosophy itself disappear completely from the American curriculum. Like so much else of the ante-bellum college, it survives in its purest form on the secondary level, where something much like it is often given as the senior course in "public affairs," or "social studies."

The ultimate aim of the academic moral philosopher was to train his students to an almost Renaissance notion of "virtue." A generous supply of virtuous men, hopefully, would form a responsible moral elite capable of guiding the nation wisely. "Every educated man," declared President Noah Porter of Yale, "who assumes the function of teaching or leading his fellow-men, finds that one of his principal functions is to discuss and enforce propositions of duty. Clergymen, jurists, publicists, political leaders, teachers, writers, and journalists are, by the virtue of their office, expounders of Moral Science."[31] With the Mugwumps, American educators had formed just such a generation of moral philosophers.

In *"The Best Men": Liberal Reformers in the Gilded Age*, the most recent full-scale historical study of the Mugwumps, John Sproat concludes on a note of positive loathing toward his subjects. "Viewing postwar America as a series of little morality plays, he [the Mugwump] instinctively stepped forward to play the role of Virtue. He possessed a wonderful confidence in his power to distinguish between right and wrong. . . . As guardian of the right, he proposed to broadcast his influence for decency throughout society. No economic, political, or social evil

[31] Noah Porter, *The Elements of Moral Science, Theoretical and Practical* (New York, 1885), p. 12.

would escape his attention."[32] Noah Porter and other American academic moral philosophers would have been pleased; this was precisely the group they had been trying to create for more than a hundred years. The American college had decisively shaped a generation's cultural style.

When the Mugwumps looked about them at what they considered the "corruption" of the United States in the 1870s and 1880s they typically prescribed two remedies for the nation's ills: the reform of the civil service and free trade. Civil service reform would restore the control of the government to educated, responsible men, while free trade would break the power of the new industrialists and the budding corporations. Man, they had learned in their colleges, was a rational being; it followed that if a citizen's own best interests were carefully explained to him, he would invariably choose the path leading to their gratification. The purification of politics, the destruction of the spoils system, and a government staffed by the educated and moral would lead to efficiency and economy. Were not these qualities which would serve the rational self-interest of everyone? High tariffs protected certain classes, raised prices, and led to wars: free trade, obviously, would serve Americans better. If these facts were presented clearly to them, the Mugwumps thought, they would surely choose the course leading to their greatest good. The Mugwumps, therefore, based their propaganda on an appeal to the reason and self-interest of the electorate. Both the American Free Trade League and the Civil Service Reform League were founded by them as avowedly educational organizations. Even more characteristic of the Mugwumps' style was the Society for Political Education, founded in 1880. If only the voters, George Haven Putnam wrote, could be exposed to "wise, wholesome, and educational treatises in regard to the obligations of citizens and the possibilities of action by citizens," if only they could be swayed by "reasonable argument,"

[32] Sproat, *"The Best Men,"* p. 275.

then what Edwin Godkin, editor of the New York *Nation*, called "fellows of the lewder and baser sort" might be driven out of public office.[33]

The Society for Political Education was meant to do just that. Indeed, the programs it designed were a public version of the old college course in moral philosophy, but now with all the American electorate as the senior class. The advisory board of the Society included such Mugwumps as Putnam, Charles Francis Adams, Jr., A. Sydney Biddle of Philadelphia, Franklin MacVeagh of Chicago, Horace Rublee of Milwaukee, and William Graham Sumner of New Haven. Its treasurer was a reform candidate for mayor of New York, Edward M. Shepard, and its secretary and guiding spirit was the tireless Richard L. Dugdale, author of the classic study in inherited original sin, *The Jukes*.

The members of the Society thus described their aims: "The Society was organized," they said, "by citizens who believe that the success of our government depends on the active political influence of educated intelligence, and that parties are means, not ends. It is entirely nonpartisan in its organization, and it is not to be used for any other purpose than the awakening of an intelligent interest in government methods and purposes tending to restrain the abuse of parties and to promote party morality." [34]

The Society constructed an elaborate plan to disseminate its principles, a sort of national correspondence course in moral philosophy. It sent out annual courses of reading for its members, supplied what it called "sound" books on economic, political, and social questions at low cost to its members, and tried to help in establishing reading and corresponding circles and clubs for discussing such questions. One of the Society's first publications was an ex-

[33] Putnam, *Memories of a Publisher*, p. 172.

[34] See "Society for Political Education," on the inside of the front cover of Edward Atkinson, *What Is a Bank?* (New York, Society for Political Education, 1880).

haustive critical bibliography of works on economic, political, and social questions, compiled by the economist David A. Wells, Sumner, Dugdale, and others. The book is divided into eleven sections, which correspond closely in subject matter to the major concerns of the old courses on moral philosophy. The bibliography was followed up by a pamphlet called *Subjects and Questions for Debate.* Here the provincial member of the Society was shown how to go about conducting his own course in moral philosophy. First, he was to try to make elementary definitions of terms such as government, labor, capital, law, politics, and so forth. Next, the member was supplied with a list of subjects on which to sharpen his ideas. Last, in the manner of the college debating societies, he was given a list, as the pamphlet put it, of "political and economic questions, already matters of controversy before the public, or which are likely to become such in the not distant future." Among the subjects for debate were questions such as these:

> —"Do the advantages of large corporations outweigh their defects?"
>
> —"Is the unlimited immigration of Chinese desirable or politic?"
>
> —"Are rich men under any moral obligation to give or bequeath a part of their wealth to the communities in which they live?" [35]

In a series of pamphlets published in the 1880s the Society directed the attention of its members to the problems of the city (the urban slum, municipal government, and the like), as well as to the problem of the Indian and that of the Negro. In other words, the Society in the 1880s, though still working within the framework of the traditional concerns of moral philosophy and with much of

[35] Society for Political Education, *Subjects and Questions Pertaining to Political Economy* (New York, 1881); Richard R. Bowker and George Iles, eds., *The Reader's Guide in Economic, Social and Political Science . . .* (New York, 1891). Several earlier editions of this work were published.

moral philosophy's ethical impetus, directed the attention of its members to those problems in American life which would become the characteristic concern of the Progressive generation. Progressivism, in fact, emerged full-blown in the Society's 1891 Bibliography, which contains a section on conservation contributed by Gifford Pinchot. Late in the 1890s the Society gave up its work, believing that new journals and magazines finally were directing the attention of the American public adequately to questions of national concern.[36] The educational work of one group of college-educated Americans was finished. In the next generation positivism, theories of evolution, and the persuasive model of inquiry of the physical sciences would shatter the ethical certainties of the moral philosophers—but the philosopher's typical objects of concern would remain a major focus of the college curriculum and of American social inquiry.

---

[36] *Ibid.*, i, 113–115.

DOROTHY ROSS

The "New History" and the "New Psychology": An Early Attempt at Psychohistory[1]

AT A TIME when a number of American historians are embarked on an attempt to join psychology and history, it is instructive to reexamine the first interdisciplinary effort of this kind in America. The historians of the Progressive Era, with their eagerness to shape history to the needs of social progress, might not strike us as the most likely proponents of psychological history. Though they were genuinely interested in enlarging their study beyond the limits of politics, their focus was on broad trends of development which they thought of as "social forces." In revolt against the idealistic and romantic styles of his-

[1] I would like to thank Carl Schorske and Jerrold Seigel for their suggestive criticisms of this essay while it was still in manuscript. I use the term "psychohistory" to denote the systematic use of systematic psychologies in the writing of history. I do not mean to suggest that such usage denotes a separate branch of history, nor that it ought to be limited to psychologies of the unconscious.

tory common in the nineteenth century, they believed that the business of history, like that of science, was to investigate the common and regular occurrences which composed basic patterns of historical development, and which lay hidden below the surface variety of events and the accidental imprints of exceptional personalities.[2] The kind of historical analysis which was most characteristic of this "New History" was economic interpretation. And yet for one leader of the movement, psychology and psychological forces played an equally important part. James Harvey Robinson (1863–1936), drawing on the "new psychology," made a systematic effort to order his historical inquiry along lines suggested by psychological science. Robinson used chiefly the functional, genetic psychology common in academic circles at the turn of the century, and then—very haltingly—early psychoanalysis. Both these strains of psychology helped to focus his analysis on the forces of "irrationality" operating beneath the surface of history. They helped him also to construct a model of historical change, but as we shall see, Robinson, and his students and colleagues in the "New History," found it difficult to translate the model into a coherent body of psychohistorical work.

Robinson became interested in joining psychology and history through his devotion to the theory of evolution and the hope of evolutionary progress. Robinson was part of that first wave of academic reformers whose evolutionary ideas and reformist zeal allowed them to ride some of the Darwinian crosscurrents which brought their own special field into touch with other disciplines.[3] Born in Bloomington, Illinois, to a cultured and well-to-do family,

---

[2] See John Higham, in Higham et al., *History* (Englewood Cliffs, N.J., 1965), pp. 92–116, 158–182.

[3] An account of this generation, which includes Robinson, is Morton G. White, *Social Thought in America: The Revolt Against Formalism* (New York, 1947). See also Dorothy Ross, *G. Stanley Hall: The Psychologist as Prophet* (Chicago, 1972), especially chap. 14.

Robinson early developed an interest in natural history.[4] With his younger brother Benjamin, who later became a distinguished botanist, Robinson examined nature in the field; at an Illinois normal school, and later at Harvard, he took more advanced work in biology. This laid the basis for his permanent and informed interest in science and enabled him, as he later wrote, "to consort without embarrassment with embryologists and biologists."[5] Robinson was also firmly set in a genetic orientation: any phenomenon could be understood, he believed, by explaining its origin and development over time. The exciting theories of evolution which animated the life sciences during his apprenticeship years remained the framework of all his thinking, and the "genetic method" seemed to him the preferred method of all branches of knowledge.[6]

Robinson's interest in biological and evolutionary science was directed to psychology while an undergraduate at Harvard, when he studied with William James. James was then applying Darwinian insights to the amalgam of British associationism and Continental physiology which comprised the new, scientific psychology. What personal concerns may have heightened Robinson's interest in psychology are unclear. Harry Elmer Barnes, Robinson's student and friend, noted that at Harvard and at times later

---

[4] The most illuminating biographical study of Robinson is Harry Elmer Barnes, "James Harvey Robinson," in Howard W. Odum, ed., *American Masters of Social Science* (New York, 1927), pp. 321–408. See also Rae Wahl Rohfeld, "James Harvey Robinson and the New History" (unpublished PhD dissertation, Western Reserve University, 1965); and Luther V. Hendricks, *James Harvey Robinson, Teacher of History* (New York, 1946). On Robinson as an intellectual historian, see Robert Allen Skotheim, *American Intellectual Histories and Historians* (Princeton, 1966), pp. 73–80; and John Higham, *Writing American History* (Bloomington, Ind., 1970), pp. 53–54.

[5] Barnes, "JHR," pp. 321–325.

[6] Robinson, "The Newer Ways of Historians," *American Historical Review,* XXV (Jan. 1930), 245–255.

in his life, he suffered from depression.[7] If Robinson felt a personal need for psychology, however, he concealed it; as we shall see, the most striking quality of Robinson's psychohistory was its impersonality.

Robinson took an extra year at Harvard to write an essay on "The Original and Derived Features of the Constitution of the United States," and then went on to study in Germany, under Hermann von Holst at Freiburg. He took his degree at Freiburg in 1890. Working in the most specialized form that evolutionary ideas had taken in historical study, the monographic investigation of the development of Western political institutions, Robinson found himself immersed in the painstaking study of sources and the detailed reconstruction of historical forms, work analogous in style to the studies in botany and zoology he knew and liked. The next year he began teaching at the University of Pennsylvania, and in 1895 moved on to Columbia University, continuing for several years thereafter to make detailed studies, translations, and compilations of source materials. He was then chiefly interested in the origins of the Reformation and of the French Revolution.

Throughout, however, Robinson maintained contact with men in other disciplines who took a broad evolutionary view: at Pennsylvania, these included Simon Patten, who was concerned with the evolution of economic ideas and institutions, and E. G. Conklin, student of the cultural implications of biological evolution. Later at Columbia, Robinson met Edward L. Thorndike, who was conducting genetic investigations in the psychology of learning, and John Dewey, who was extending James's Darwinian revolution in psychology and philosophy.[8] Robinson's interdisciplinary interests could no doubt develop more easily at a time of still-fluid institutional ties between history and the newly emerging social and behavioral sci-

---

[7] Barnes, "JHR," p. 326.

[8] Hendricks, *JHR*, p. 5; Barnes, "JHR," p. 330.

ences, but what brought them to the surface, apparently, was his increasing concern after 1903 for the presentist, reformist uses of history. Whether his friendship with Charles Beard, which goes back to that date, was the decisive factor, or whether Robinson was responding to the quickening meliorist temper of the culture at large, his desire to make the past serve the purposes of the future led him to ally himself more consciously with the progressive social sciences of his day and to find in the new psychology ammunition for his historical reformism.[9]

Robinson's turn toward psychology and reform took place within the framework of a rationalist view of history. According to Barnes, Robinson's study of the origins of the French Revolution and the Enlightenment enlarged his view of history. Like his hero Voltaire, he came to think of history as a struggle between reason and irrationality. Led backwards in time by his concern for origins, he found evidence of the recurring struggle in each prior age. He found it "difficult to tell where to start [and] where to stop." From "an intensive student of historical texts and methodology," he became "a cosmic interpreter of historical materials." He became a simplistic interpreter as well. While learned in the texts of the Enlightenment, he was also enthusiastic about the nineteenth-century historians who celebrated the triumph of science over superstition, John William Draper, W. E. H. Lecky, and Andrew D. White. For Robinson, evolutionism confirmed this view of progress. Among his colleagues at Columbia, Robinson maintained his scholarly reputation through his undisputed mastery of the primary sources of European history, but in his teaching and writing, he became a popular iconoclast: one of his students aptly called him "the last of the *philosophes*." [10]

Robinson therefore gave increasing attention to the

---

[9] The emergence of Robinson's presentism and the influence of Beard after 1903 are suggested by Rohfeld, "JHR and the New History," p. 171.

[10] Barnes, "JHR," pp. 352–354, 361, 376–387; Rohfeld, "JHR and the New History," pp. 12–18, 29–34.

history of ideas. As early as 1895, when he first came to Columbia, he introduced material on intellectual history to his students, and beginning in 1900 his course in European history was transformed into a history of the intellectual classes of Western Europe. He now wrote a number of textbooks which spanned all of medieval and modern Europe. Although these texts chronicled chiefly the advance of the forces of nationalism, democracy, and industrialism, they also called repeated attention to the seminal importance of advances in knowledge, science, and technological invention. Robinson expressed his theory of history as the progress of reason most clearly, however, in a collection of essays, *The New History* (1912) and *The Mind in the Making* (1921). After 1920, when he resigned from Columbia University to help establish the New School for Social Research and to devote his energies to adult education, his work lay entirely in these broader areas.[11] There is thus no major work of historical scholarship per se by which we may judge Robinson. But his essays and texts, as well as the work of the many historians who emerged from his seminar at Columbia, do give us the means for examining Robinson's early attempt at psychohistory.

[11] A bibliography of Robinson's works appears in Hendricks, *JHR*, pp. 114–117. His most notable historical monograph is the article on the Reformation in the eleventh edition of the *Encyclopaedia Britannica*. His chief theoretical statements are made in *The New History: Essays Illustrating the Modern Historical Outlook* (New York, 1912) and *The Mind in the Making: The Relation of Intelligence to Social Reform* (New York, 1921). His most important texts, on the college level, were *An Introduction to the History of Western Europe* (Boston, 1902–1903), 2 vols., rev. 1924–1926 and again in 1934; and, with Charles Beard, *The Development of Modern Europe: An Introduction to the Study of Current History* (Boston, 1907–1908), 2 vols., rev. 1929–1930. For the critical role of advances in knowledge in stimulating social, political, and economic progress, see *Mind in the Making*, pp. 164–165; *An Introduction* (1924), II, 506; *Development of Modern Europe* (1929), pp. 444–449, 522.

Psychology could enter Robinson's historical work at three different levels, and it is important to recognize the influence it exerted at each one. There was, to begin with, Robinson's theory of history, the base from which he explicitly and implicitly interpreted the movement of history. Then, following closely from this, was his conception of the purposes and problems of historiography. Lastly, there was the particular web of description and explanation, the finer analysis of particular events, by which Robinson constructed his historical monographs and narratives. Let us look first at his theory of history.

The struggle between reason and irrationality in Western history began, according to Robinson, in ancient Greece and Rome. Even before the formal collapse of the Roman Empire, however, the forces of unreason triumphed, persisting until the seventeenth century. Not even the Renaissance and Reformation, Robinson argued, truly broke the reliance on faith and authority which was characteristic of the medieval world. Against the "Protestant apologists," he stressed the intolerant and nationalistic character of the "Protestant revolt." It was only with the advent of critical thinking and science in the seventeenth century that modern history truly began. The pace of progress thereupon began to accelerate, and by his own day men had finally come to understand that through the use of scientific intelligence they could control their own progress and the further course of history.[12]

Robinson's rationalism was uneasily allied with two other strains of historical theory. True to his grounding in evolutionary science, he stressed the continuity of history, and hence the long slow movement of historical time. Recent discoveries in archaeology had impressed on him both the enormous span of man's prehistory and the relative closeness to modern man of the so-called primitive societies studied by anthropology. A favorite device of Robin-

[12] *Mind in the Making*, Parts I, II, IV, V, VI; *New History*, chap. 4; Barnes, "JHR," p. 372.

son was to liken all time since the species *Homo sapiens* first appeared on earth to the twelve hours on the face of a clock. Recorded history would have appeared at only twenty minutes before twelve, the flowering of Greece at only seven minutes before the hour, and modern industrial society, with its rapid rate of change, in the last thirty seconds of the world's history.[13]

True also to the positivism of the scientific history of his time, he argued that history ought to be concerned not with "heroic persons and romantic occurrences," not with "the doings of poisoners, adulterers, and lunatics," but with the "overwhelming significance of the small, the common, and the obscure." [14] In his texts, Robinson tended to eschew exceptional and dramatic events for the chains of basic political and social development which marked the path of progress.

But reason—by Robinson's own account—was itself an *un*common occurrence, a difficult achievement far more seminal to the course of history than any other. Its recent flowering in the form of science, moreover, suggested a sharp acceleration of historical time, to the extent that contemporary history constituted a radical disjunction with the past. In *The New History,* Robinson managed to hold these discordant elements in suspension. But after the First World War, goaded both by his impatience for reform and by his growing pessimism, Robinson tended to describe history as a past to be overcome. History came to represent not so much the gradual evolution of elements still alive in the present as a massive dead weight holding men back from their future. Robinson now glorified the role of his scientific innovators.[15] There was, he said, besides the great generals and statesmen, "another class of chieftains . . . in the world of thought, as bold

[13] *New History,* pp. 64, 89–92, 239; *An Introduction* (1902 ed.), I, chap. 1.
[14] *New History,* pp. 10–11, 15, 48.
[15] *Mind in the Making,* particularly Parts I, II, and VI.

as any general or explorer," men who "pursued new ideas and confronted them with knightly valor."[16] Robinson's rationalist faith, it seems, was far more potent than his evolutionary and positivist sense of history.

It is not surprising, then, that this faith also directed the use he made of the new psychology. Even more than the German psychologists, who first made their subject a laboratory science, the American psychologists emphasized the scientific character of their work. Science, they believed, was the highest product of the evolution of the race. As they moved to displace the older philosophical and introspectionist psychologists from their chairs in the universities and from their role as popular moral guides, the struggle lent credence to their view of history as the progressive triumph of scientific reason over the counterforces of religion and superstition. While Robinson need hardly have gone to the new psychology for his rationalism, he surely found in it substantial reinforcement.[17]

Where psychology exerted its most critical influence on Robinson, however, was in drawing his attention to the nonrational components of human behavior. Despite their high valuation of reason, the new psychologists held a hierarchical conception of mental function which stressed the importance in man of functions below the level of creative reason. Taking their cues from Darwin, Spencer, and William James, American psychologists were concerned with those elementary functional processes like attention and habit formation by which the individual adapted to his surroundings. Accepting the biological continuity between animals and man, they studied such basic psychological processes among lower forms of animals, as

---

[16] *An Introduction* (1924 ed.), II, 96.

[17] On the rationalism of Robinson's generation of social thinkers, see White, *Social Thought in America;* on the new psychologists, see Ross, *G. Stanley Hall,* chaps. 10, 11.

well as in children, in the hope of discovering the simpler forms of complex adult responses.[18]

The conclusions from this work which most attracted Robinson were those which appeared to emphasize the unreasoning elements in human experience. Robinson was particularly drawn to two new fields of psychology: the study of animals, and social psychology. What Robinson called "animal psychology" was exemplified by Edward L. Thorndike, whose experiments with animal subjects were an effort to discover the simple elements of the learning process. It was a commonplace of the functionalists that, as James had argued, most mental function was the product of that "region of intelligence which man possesses in common with the brutes." Constructing a genetic hierarchy of learning processes, Thorndike tried to show that the kind of trial-and-error learning typical of lower animals formed the basis of human learning as well.[19]

The second strain of functional psychology which impressed Robinson, social psychology, was then still—as he recognized—in a rudimentary state. A number of philosophers, psychologists, and sociologists, particularly the group associated with the University of Chicago, were working toward an understanding of what came to be

---

[18] The major histories of the new psychology in America are contained in larger histories of psychology; see especially Edwin G. Boring, *A History of Experimental Psychology* (New York, 1957), and Gardner Murphy, *An Historical Introduction to Modern Psychology* (London, 1929). William James's *The Principles of Psychology*, 2 vols. (New York, 1890), is the primary source for the state of the subject in its early, eclectic form; Robert S. Woodworth, *Dynamic Psychology* (New York, 1918), offers an excellent view of the directions in which the discipline evolved over the following decades.

[19] *New History*, pp. 96–97; William James, "Great Men and Their Environment," reprinted in *The Will to Believe, and Other Essays in Popular Philosophy* (New York, 1897), pp. 245–251. On Thorndike, see Robert S. Woodworth, "Edward Lee Thorndike, 1874–1949," in National Academy of Sciences, *Biographical Memoirs*, XXVII (1952).

generally understood only later—how both personality and culture were formed by creative interaction between the individual and society.[20] Robinson was impressed by their description of the individual's dependence on his social environment. He pointed to the processes of imitation and suggestion described by Gabriel Tardé as a key to how the individual absorbed his ideas from his culture in a kind of "dogmatic slumber." From anthropology, moreover, he drew assumptions about the "irrational" character of primitive thought processes and their survival in civilized societies.[21] These hierarchical analyses of learning and socialization thus appeared to be centrally concerned with those elements in human nature which acted as conservators or inhibitors of historical progress—those forces which held back the reign of science.

In seizing upon these aspects of the new psychology, Robinson was, in fact, drawing out only some of the more simplistic implications to be found there. James and Thorndike themselves came to stress the important ways in which human thinking advanced beyond the simpler kinds of learning found in lower forms of animals. While the psychologists believed that historically and biologically older and simpler kinds of thinking were still perpetuated through socialization or through hereditary mechanisms, they also saw that these processes were more intimately linked with those of creative reason than Robinson real-

---

[20] The history of the Chicago school of social psychology and its influence on the social and behavioral sciences in America has yet to be written. Hamilton Cravens and John C. Burnham, in "Psychology and Evolutionary Naturalism in American Thought, 1890–1940," *American Quarterly*, XXIII (Dec. 1971), 635–657, examine the transformation of these studies from a genetic to a psychosocial orientation. For an introduction to the history of social psychology, see Gordon W. Allport, "The Historical Background of Modern Social Psychology," in Gardner Lindzey and Elliot Aronson, eds., *The Handbook of Social Psychology*, 2d ed. (Reading, Mass., 1969), Vol. I.

[21] *New History*, pp. 89–92, 97–98; Tardé, *The Laws of Imitation* (New York, 1903), pp. 74 ff.

ized. John Dewey soon pronounced Tardé's conception of imitation a dead end for social psychology: the process of interaction between the individual and his social milieu was more complex. As James Mark Baldwin had shown, "In the individual invention is as natural as imitation. Indeed normal imitation is rarely free from invention." The result of the work of James and the new psychologists was to show how sentiments, needs, and common experience intertwined with human rationality.[22]

Robinson, however, used the new psychology to make his dichotomous view of history even more clear-cut. In *The New History* he argued that most ideas in history had been the product of "simian" or primitive ways of thought, perpetuated by imitation and habit beyond their usefulness. In the last prewar years of Progressive optimism, Robinson was confident that scientific reason would triumph.[23] But in the fuller statement of his psychological theory of history made after the war, *The Mind in the Making,* he was far less sanguine. Using the same model from the new psychologists, Robinson now added Wilfred Trotter's "herd instinct," together with the Freudian "unconscious," to emphasize the regressive tendencies of human nature. "Mankind," he lamented, was "lethargic, easily pledged to routine, timid, suspicious of innovation." [24] Robinson's bleak view now separated him sharply from those "progressive" historians who based their analysis on economic and class interests. "Our convictions on important matters are not . . . often dictated by sup-

---

[22] James, *Principles of Psychology,* I, chaps. 2, 4; Thorndike, *Educational Psychology* (New York, 1913), Vol. II; John Dewey, "The Need for Social Psychology," *Psychological Review,* XXIV (1917), 266–277; James Mark Baldwin, *The Individual and Society, or Psychology and Sociology* (Boston, 1911), pp. 22, 149–150.

[23] *New History,* pp. 97, 250–266.

[24] *Mind in the Making,* pp. 33–48, 81. Robinson referred to Trotter's "Herd Instinct and Its Bearing upon the Psychology of Civilised Man," *Sociological Review,* I (July 1908), 227–248.

posed self-interest. Most of them are *pure prejudices* in the proper sense of that word. . . . They are the whisperings of 'the voice of the herd.' "

While an elitist view of history was implicit in Robinson's theory from the start, it was now starkly expressed. Truly creative thought, he was more convinced than ever, was very rare and was mostly resisted by the masses of men. It was the product of what Thorstein Veblen called "idle curiosity," found only occasionally in exceptional individuals. "So History, namely change, has been mainly due to a small number of 'seers,'—really gropers and monkeyers—whose native curiosity outran that of their fellows and led them to escape here and there from the sanctified blindness of their time. The seer is simply an example of a *variation* biologically. . . ." These innovations were then passed on to the "innumerable inferior members of the species who could by no possibility have originated anything for themselves, but who can, nevertheless, suffer some modification as a result of the teaching of others." [25]

The roots of this elitist view were indeed embedded in the hierarchical theories of the new psychologists. James himself had left it unclear whether all minds were capable of creativity in any significant degree. James seemed at times to assume the creativity of individuals in general ("the Grants and Bismarcks, the Joneses and the Smiths"), while at others he tended to contrast "the highest order of minds," the "Great Men" of history, with more ordinary minds, perpetually enslaved to habit and suggestion.[26] Later psychologists tried to soften the disparity. Baldwin in particular argued that in the overall course of society's affairs, "It is, in fact, the slight variations which are more usually fruitful." Robinson, however, never paid much attention to Baldwin's work, and in the wake of the war, he fastened on evidence which would heighten the disparity

---

[25] *Mind in the Making,* pp. 48–62, 79–80.

[26] James, "Great Men and Their Environment," pp. 225–226. Cf. James, *Principles of Psychology,* II, chap. 22.

between his uncommon rationalist heroes and the common, subrational herd.[27]

Like his view of history, Robinson's conception of the purposes and problems of the historian was reinforced and given sharper focus by his reading in psychology. In line with his rationalist and reformist perspective, Robinson argued that the object of historical study was to help a person "catch up with his own times." [28] By exposing the irrational roots in the past of so many current ideas and practices, intellectual history would open men's minds to the scientific ideas needed in the present and future. In a nicely worked-out analogy, Robinson described history as an extension of memory, and defined memory as the new psychologists saw it, as an organization of past experience which functioned to orient the individual in the present. Accordingly the historian must stay on the cutting edge of knowledge, using the advancing discoveries of behavioral and social science constantly to extend and refine his understanding of the past. His conception of the past would then be usable in constructing an analysis of the present and a blueprint for the future. The historian could thus serve as "critic and guide of the social sciences, whose results he must synthesize and test by the actual life of mankind as it appears in the past." [29]

Among all the social sciences, it was psychology that

---

[27] James Mark Baldwin, *The Individual and Society,* p. 154. See also Woodworth, *Dynamic Psychology,* pp. 128–152. Robinson would have found Baldwin's premises basically uncongenial, for Baldwin never abandoned his philosophical and aesthetic values to scientism, and he believed that there was "no general antagonism of interests" between the individual and society. *The Individual and Society,* pp. 118, 151.

[28] *Development of Modern Europe* (1909 ed.), I, Preface.

[29] *New History,* chaps. 1 and 2. As Morton White points out (*Social Thought in America,* pp. 53, 64), the idea that history could aid reform by uncovering the atavistic elements of present culture was also present in the early work of John Dewey, Thorstein Veblen, and Oliver Wendell Holmes.

suggested to Robinson the central question the historian ought to ask: "the great and fundamental question of how mankind learns and disseminates his discoveries and misapprehensions. . . ." With the help of animal and social psychology, Robinson expected to find sharper and more liberating answers to the rationalist historian's chief problem, "the real nature of progress and retrogression."[30]

The ultimate test of any theoretical outlook, however, is how well it illumines the facts of history. How pertinent are its concepts and methods to historical analysis, and how skillful is the historian in applying them in the writing of history? In Robinson's case we have virtually nothing to go on: he made next to no use of his own psychohistorical theories.

In the theoretical portions of *The New History*, Robinson suggested some ways in which psychological concepts might be used in historical analysis, but in the book's few substantive historical essays—on the fall of Rome, on the rise of natural rights philosophy in France on the eve of the Revolution, or on the history of historical writing—not one psychological interpretation was offered. In his later essay, *The Mind in the Making*, Robinson did devote several chapters to a sketch of Western intellectual history from ancient to modern times which attempted a certain amount of psychological analysis. But even his disciple Harry Elmer Barnes admitted, "As an intellectual history of Europe the volume is pathetically inadequate. . . .": it was rather a presentation of "the leading generalizations" which might be drawn from such a history. Robinson never wrote the history itself.[31] In his textbooks, where some aspects of intellectual history are worked out in sufficient detail to offer the opportunity for psychohistorical analysis, no hint of such analysis appears. Why?

Robinson may have had tactical reasons for keeping his corrosive ideas out of high school and college text-

---

[30] *New History*, p. 93.
[31] Barnes, "JHR," p. 398.

books. He himself lamented: "We do not dare to be honest enough to tell boys and girls and young men and women what would be most useful to them in an age of imperative social reconstruction." [32] But Robinson surely had other opportunities to make the connections between psychology and history. Nor did he himself lack skill either in close historical analysis or in generalizing from it to larger historical categories.

What appears to have crippled Robinson's effort was a combination of factors pertaining to Robinson himself, the character of his psychohistorical theory, and the nature of the new psychology he wanted to use. Robinson's faith in progress and his conviction that history ought to serve the cause of reform directed the greater part of his energies into proselytizing and popularization rather than into actual historical investigation. It was the "lessons" of history, rather than history itself, that most captured his interest. Even in the section of *The New History* where he tried to show specifically how historians might use psychology, he kept slipping away from concrete examples to the promise that psychology would "invariably suggest new points of view and new interpretations." [33] As time went on, Robinson's faith stood less and less in need of confirmation by direct historical analysis.

Ironically enough, the character of Robinson's psychohistorical theory also led him away from a psychological analysis of historical phenomena. His developed theory, as we have seen, attributed historical change to the intellectual innovations of the great rationalist and scientific thinkers, innovations which were then absorbed by the primitive and suggestible masses. But he argued that geniuses were beyond the reach of psychohistorical explanation. He thought that the "seer," endowed with a superabundance of Veblen's "idle curiosity," was "simply an example of a *variation* biologically. . . ." Robinson

---

[32] *Mind in the Making*, p. 220.
[33] *New History*, p. 100.

was thus following William James, who in 1880 had argued that " the causes of production of great men lie in a sphere wholly inaccessible to the social philosopher. He must simply accept geniuses as data, just as Darwin accepts his spontaneous variations. . . . the relation of the visible environment to the great man is in the main exactly what it is to the 'variation' in the Darwinian philosophy. It chiefly adopts or rejects, preserves or destroys, in short *selects* him." [34] Thus genius could have little reference to individual psychological development or to the molding influences of family and culture.

One of Robinson's students who was most sensitive to the problems of personality, Preserved Smith, recognized this difficulty. The aim of the new history, Smith said, was to get below "the surface events of politics and the accidental action of personality," which in turn meant the study of economic forces, material conditions, and the psychology of historical groups—a psychology determined by "anthropological or racial factors." What room was there in this for individuality? "The tendency of the race to produce remarkable individuals must be assumed as a variable; the only problem that can be answered is the use made of such men, and the extent and nature of their influence." Yet Smith had "misgivings" about this: "Try as they may to jump out of their skins, men cannot write about other men as they write about bees and about atoms. . . . To lay stress on the personal is to make history unscientific; to omit it altogether is to make our study inhuman. The one fails to satisfy the intellect; the other to interest the emotions, which have their reasons the reason knows not of." In 1929 Smith could not see a way out of this "extremely awkward predicament." [35]

---

[34] James, "Great Men and Their Environment," pp. 225–226.

[35] Preserved Smith, "The Place of History Among the Sciences," in *Essays in Intellectual History, Dedicated to James Harvey Robinson by his Former Seminar Students* (Freeport, N.Y., 1929), pp. 212–218.

Despite such a theory of genius, one might still try to analyze the rational processes of history's great thinkers. But Edward L. Thorndike's psychology of learning was singularly inappropriate for use on Descartes or Newton. Thorndike's theory of "connectionism" offered no tools for dealing with the complex patterns of individual or group thinking the historian had to confront. Like most of the new psychologists who retained the atomism of their philosophical forebears, Thorndike focused on the most elementary psychic processes. Studying how simple learned connections were formed between stimulus and response, he assumed that units of such connections were the building blocks of the complex adult personality. The analysis of how such units formed particular patterns of thought, character, and temperament in the individual, however, remained for Thorndike a "task . . . for the future."[36]

In a more general way, the discussion of learning in the new psychology, with its emphasis on the joining and recombination of elements, might have suggested to a historian of ideas a way of analyzing the major strands of intellectual history. Arthur O. Lovejoy, for example, who learned his philosophy at Harvard, where the Jamesian tradition was still very much alive, may have been led by this tradition to view intellectual history as a kind of chemical analysis in which historical ideas are to be separated into their elements.[37] Such use of the new psychology would be impressionistic rather than technical, and would

---

[36] Thorndike, *Educational Psychology* II, 53, 55–56; III, 386. The one approach Robinson made to this kind of analysis was his statement that the argument for the existence of God made by Anselm and Descartes was "an illustration of the native operations of a mind that has made a wholly gratuitous hypothesis and is victimized by an orderly series of spontaneous associations." But Robinson is only using the terminology of scientific psychology to make a commonplace observation derived from logic.

[37] Lovejoy discusses this conception of intellectual history in his Introduction to *The Great Chain of Being* (Cambridge, Mass., 1936).

have had to be matched by independent facility in the analysis of ideas. But even on this level, Robinson's ideological focus kept him from applying the new psychology's atomistic style to a sustained analysis of the history of ideas.

The whole bias of Robinson's rationalist faith led him to seek psychological explanations not for his rationalist heroes, but for the irrationalism of the herd. In his sketch of European intellectual history in *The Mind in the Making*, nearly all his psychological "analysis" falls in this category. He began by arguing that the opposition in Greece to the skepticism of the great philosophers was traceable to the fact that "criticism is against nature, for it conflicts with the smooth working of our more primitive minds." The medieval world turned to faith rather than reason because "it was necessary only *to believe* to be saved, and believing is far easier than thinking." The reliance of that world on authority, its intolerance of deviation, and its self-important world view were all inveterate tendencies of man's primitive mind. While Robinson knew that historians of religion had already begun to use such concepts as animism and totemism in an exact and illuminating way, for him these concepts obviously performed only a pejorative function.[38] They were terms of dismissal rather than analysis.

Surely the most potentially useful of the available approaches to irrationalism was psychoanalysis, a type of psychology which was only beginning to be understood during the period of Robinson's active historical work. Popular and simplified expositions of Freudianism appeared in some number after 1909, and Robinson became interested in the subject during the teens.[39] However, in

[38] *Mind in the Making*, pp. 100, 108, 127, 131, 143.

[39] For the American reception of Freud before World War I, see Nathan Hale, *Freud and the Americans: The Beginnings of Psychoanalysis in the United States, 1876–1917* (London, 1971). On Robinson's interest in Freud, see Barnes, "JHR," p. 330.

The Mind in the Making, psychoanalysis was merely grafted onto his Darwinian theory, serving to augment his emphasis on older irrational types of thinking surviving in every adult and to embellish the argument with an occasional reference to "reaction-formation" or the "unconscious." Robinson added the child mind to the animal, savage, and traditional minds which he saw buried in every modern individual, but that was as far as it went; the child mind was the only one of the four he did not describe in detail. He explained the omission briefly in a footnote: although the relationship of the child to its parents must permanently affect adult ideas, particularly regarding attitudes toward authority figures, "It is impossible to discuss here the results which a really honest study of child psychology promises." The motives for such restraint can only be guessed.[40] Two of Robinson's students, however, tried to follow this new lead.

Preserved Smith made a cautious attempt to use psychoanalysis in history in a study of Martin Luther which he published in 1913. While Smith sensed that psychoanalysis was compatible with the unmasking urge of Darwinian and Progressive thought, he also saw that the psychoanalytic study of individuals violated certain assumptions of the "New History." He began his study, therefore, arguing that personality was indeed important in history. While William James was right to say that the originality of great men cannot be entirely explained, "very much can be ascertained by careful study of the materials at hand and by the comparative method." [41] Smith then found in Luther's excessive preoccupation with the devil, and with his own "concupiscence" and sense of unworthiness, evidence of a pathologically severe Oedipus complex. It was really Luther's sense of defeat in these oedipal and sexual struggles, his desperate conclusion that he could not

[40] *Mind in the Making,* pp. 35–36, 65–66, 142.

[41] Preserved Smith, "Luther's Early Development in the Light of Psycho-Analysis," *American Journal of Psychology,* XXIV (July 1913), 360–361.

himself conquer his sexual temptations but must rely solely on his faith in God, that resulted in his famous Protestant revelation.[42]

Although Smith promised that another study would follow, further developing this thesis, none ever appeared. He may have felt uneasy with the reductionism of his analysis. Or, presented with evidence that Luther's preoccupations were also prevalent in the culture at large, he may not have known how to reconcile this evidence with his sense of Luther's individual pathology. Smith returned, as we have seen, to the limitations of the "New History" and the wistful hope that they could somehow be surmounted.

Harry Elmer Barnes, however, who studied Freudian psychology under Stanley Hall at Clark University, found it an exciting method for exposing the hidden forces of irrationality beneath the surface of events. Although conceding on the one hand how difficult it was to apply psychoanalysis to historical figures and past ages, Barnes proceeded on the other to provide facile, capsule analyses of dozens of historical figures and cultural institutions. The substance of these "analyses" was that things were seldom what they seemed: that an underlying motive or character trait could explain a wide variety of surface behavior, even while operating in a way quite contrary to what showed on the surface. This might appear in Jefferson's antipathy to authority, Augustine's transformation of libertinism into hatred of fleshly desire, or "Mr. Coolidge's compensation for faithful services to the grasping and unscrupulous

[42] *Ibid.*, pp. 361–377. Smith suggested that Luther's sexual temptation may have been chiefly that of masturbation, an interpretation which Erik Erikson, in *Young Man Luther* (New York, 1958), pp. 28–29, finds a flagrant misreading of the sources. Smith's emphasis on masturbation, the publication of his essay in G. Stanley Hall's *American Journal of Psychology,* and his referring to the founder of psychoanalysis as "Sigismund Freud," an early usage of Hall, all suggest that Smith, then teaching at Amherst, may have come under Hall's influence.

American plutocracy in a philosophy of frugality, piety, candor, sincerity and uprightness."[43] This last jibe accorded in spirit with that side of the New History which emphasized economic interpretation. As Perry Miller and humanistic historians were later to complain, men's ideas "have been officially decided by modern psychologists to be generally just so many rationalizations constructed by the subconscious to disguise the pursuit of more tangible ends."[44]

It was actually the popularizers, however, not the psychologists themselves, who linked hidden motives of material self-interest to the unconscious feelings analyzed by Freud. Clearly neither Barnes nor Smith had more than a superficial knowledge of psychoanalysis, and with Barnes, that knowledge was tailored to his debunking spirit. Still, it must be admitted that Freudian theory was at this period dominated by a concern for the instinctual development of early childhood and its pathological consequences. Even the more knowledgeable of its exponents who attempted analyses of historical figures were intent on uncovering pathology and its infantile sources. It would require the development of psychoanalytic ego psychology and the maturation of personality theory and social psychology before historians would have available theories which took into account the constructive aims of the ego and their connections with instinctual development.[45] It would also require the emergence among historians of a feeling for complexity to replace the simplicities of the

---

[43] Barnes, *The New History and the Social Studies* (New York, 1925), pp. 221–267, particularly 232.

[44] In his introduction to *The New England Mind* in 1933; quoted in Skotheim, *American Intellectual Histories and Historians,* p. 189.

[45] For brief introductions to these developments, see David Rapaport, "A Historical Survey of Psychoanalytic Ego Psychology," in Erik H. Erikson, *Identity and the Life Cycle* (New York, 1959), Psychological Issues, Monograph 1; Murphy, *Historical Introduction to Psychology,* 3d ed. (New York, 1972), chaps. 25, 26.

"New History" before they would be able to use such a psychology.[46]

There was still another kind of psychology emerging during this period which Robinson and his students failed to appreciate. This was the social psychology growing out of the Chicago school. Baldwin, for example, added perceptive shadings to the model of individual intellectual innovators and social imitation. He distinguished between types of socialization, pointing out that individuals can absorb social elements on the level either of judgment or of the imagination. The response of people to the novelty of a social reformer, moreover, was not the same when they were part of a crowd as it would be when they were members of a "reflective group" such as a committee or a legislature. These categories provided, of course, little for the historian to go on. They anticipated analyses in psychology and sociology which would not be elaborated until later decades. Still, they might have offered Robinson, had he been attuned to them, a more variegated approach to his central historical question.[47]

Perhaps the most interesting of the Chicago work for the historian was that of William I. Thomas.[48] Thomas came to sociology and social psychology through reading in anthropology, and his first essay on social psychology was rooted in a genetic framework of psychic function and

---

[46] Higham, *History*, pp. 117–144, 198–232. See also Richard Hofstadter's discussion of the values of complexity in *The Progressive Historians* (New York, 1968), pp. 437–466.

[47] Baldwin, *Individual and Society*, pp. 47, 73–74. For a discussion of the development of the concept of the "crowd" in sociology, see Leon Bramson, *The Political Context of Sociology* (Princeton, 1961).

[48] On Thomas's work, see Edmund H. Volkart, ed., *Social Behavior and Personality; Contributions of W. I. Thomas to Theory and Social Research* (New York, 1951); Herbert Blumer, *An Appraisal of Thomas and Znaniecki's The Polish Peasant in Europe and America* (New York, 1939), and Morris Janowitz, ed., *W. I. Thomas on Social Organization and Social Personality* (Chicago, 1966).

social comparison. In his early collection of sources on "social origins," Thomas quoted Robinson at length, and approved his device of foreshortening historical time and his claim that the study of primitive societies and their modes of thinking were highly relevant to the study of history.[49] Robinson, in turn quoted Thomas as authority for the importance of anthropology to history and the use of the evolutionary point of view in all the sciences.[50] In the course of Thomas's later study of Polish immigrants, however, he cut loose from his genetic moorings entirely and based social psychology as well as sociology on the interaction of culture and personality, a framework appropriate to the study of historical cultures. Thomas published his new ideas in five large volumes between 1918 and 1920.[51] From that point onward Robinson ignored his work. Only Thomas's older ideas reappear briefly in Robinson's *The Mind in the Making* of 1921, and indeed Thomas is mentioned only in passing in Barnes's far longer survey of the social and behavioral sciences in 1925.[52]

Thomas may have alienated the historians by his desire to differentiate sociology and social psychology from history, the whole tendency of his work being precisely to disentangle these new studies from their attachments to

---

[49] Thomas, "The Province of Social Psychology," *American Journal of Sociology,* X (Jan. 1905), 445–455; *Source Book for Social Origins* (Chicago, 1909), pp. 5–12. As Burnham and Cravens have pointed out, Thomas in the latter work was already using the modern concept of culture ("Psychology and Evolutionary Naturalism," *loc. cit.*). It is also clear that he was beginning to see in the psychological model based on habit, attention, and the problem-solving situation fundamentally sociological phenomena—what he later called the "social situation," the "definition of the situation," and social norms. (Cf. Volkart, *Social Behavior and Personality,* pp. 6, 12, 232.)

[50] *New History,* pp. 76–77, 89.

[51] Thomas and Florian Znaniecki, *The Polish Peasant in Europe and America,* 5 vols. (Chicago and Boston, 1918–1920).

[52] *Mind in the Making,* p. 64; Barnes, *The New History.*

historical evolutionism. Sociologists, he urged, ought to study contemporary peoples by comparative methods. Reversing the Darwinian order, he now argued that historians would be able to understand past societies only on the basis of their understanding of contemporary ones.[53] This altered viewpoint was actually far more relevant to the historian's close analysis of historical cultures than the earlier genetic scheme had been. Instead of diverting the analysis into categories appropriate to animals and primitive societies, it emphasized factors internal to the culture itself. Ironically, while Robinson was urging his fellow historians to read about experiments in animal psychology, Thomas was urging his fellow social scientists to analyze "human documents": the letters, life histories, newspapers, court records, and archives of social agencies long familiar to the historian.[54]

Thomas was moving away not only from geneticism but from the whole complex of psychohistorical problems that interested Robinson. Thomas's analysis in *The Polish Peasant* revolved around the phenomena of social organization, disorganization, and reorganization. Thomas believed the key to these phenomena to be the relative persistence of social rules or norms, and he analyzed the effects of social organization and disorganization on personalities oriented in different ways toward these social rules. He drew his conclusions from a close empirical analysis of the cultural milieu of the peasantry in Poland, including its recent historical development, and the nature of its response to transplantation in America, including the development of Polish-American communal ties and the conflicts in cultural norms which arose throughout

[53] Thomas and Znaniecki, *The Polish Peasant*, I, 17–18.
[54] Robinson, "Newer Ways of Historians," pp. 245–249; on Thomas's method, see Blumer, *An Appraisal*, pp. 28–53. It should be noted that Thomas's peers, too, were not altogether receptive to his approach; many hoped to eliminate subjective evidence entirely from their studies and to work instead with quantitative data.

the process. Thomas's study was at once an excellent historical account of the Polish-American experience and an important theoretical work. Indeed, it was unequaled in social vision by an American historian until Oscar Handlin's *Boston Immigrants* was published twenty years later, or in psychological insight until Handlin's *Uprooted* appeared still another decade beyond.[55]

One "new historian" who might have gained from Thomas's perspective was Frederick Jackson Turner. Turner regularly included psychology among the list of social and behavioral sciences historians ought to consult, and he was, as David Potter has pointed out, centrally concerned with a problem in social psychology, the formation of the individualistic, democratic frontier character. There is no evidence, however, that Turner ever actually consulted the psychologists himself.[56] If he had, *The Polish Peasant* could have suggested to him the terms of a far more direct attack than he was able to make on the problem of how different peoples and new conditions converged on the frontier to form the American character. Even then, Turner might not have recognized the value of the book, for his own historical attitudes might well have led him to resist casting the frontier experience in terms of "disorganization."

To ask Turner to have appreciated the importance of Thomas's work, as we asked Robinson and his students to

[55] Oscar Handlin, *Boston's Immigrants: A Study in Acculturation* (Cambridge, Mass., 1941; rev. and enl., 1959); *The Uprooted: The Epic Story of the Great Migrations That Made the American People* (Boston, 1951).

[56] David M. Potter, *People of Plenty: Economic Abundance and the American Character* (Chicago, 1954), pp. 7, 22–23, 142–160. Turner referred to psychology in his address to the St. Louis Congress of Arts and Sciences in 1904, "Problems in American History," reprinted in *The Significance of Sections in American History* (New York, 1932), pp. 20–21; and in his AHA presidential address of 1910, "Social Forces in American History," reprinted in *The Frontier in American History* (New York, 1920), pp. 330–334.

understand the subtler implications of functional psychology and of psychoanalysis, is to ask them to have participated in the long and difficult development of essentially new points of view in psychology and sociology, a task requiring them to follow in depth the perceptions and logic internal to these fields of study. Equally important, it is to ask them to do this even when the ideological implications of psychology ran counter to their own historical attitudes and values, and hence to abandon or rework their historical attitudes as a result. This is too much to expect from a historian like Robinson, whose rigid ideological commitments kept him from using even the few ready concepts of the functional psychologists for historical analysis. Nor did he inspire his students to this task.[57] To my knowledge, only two of his many students ever tried to carry on his psychohistorical program: Preserved Smith, whose psychohistorical attempt aborted, and Harry Elmer Barnes, who shared his mentor's speculative bent and went over largely into the field of sociology.[58] Many of Robinson's students nonetheless became distinguished historians in the fields of intellectual history, the history of science and technology, and the history of social and political

---

[57] Barnes, "JHR," p. 338, lists among Robinson's students James T. Shotwell, Charles Beard, Carl Becker, Carlton J. H. Hayes, Lynn Thorndike, Arthur M. Schlesinger, Harold U. Faulkner, Dixon Ryan Fox, Louise R. Loomis, and John Herman Randall, Jr.

[58] Barnes's principal historical works were a massive text, *An Intellectual and Cultural History of the Western World* (New York, 1937), in which psychological motivation appears only rarely, as in discussing the sexual repressiveness of medieval Christianity and the "abnormal personal experiences of Paul and Augustine" (p. 293); and *The Genesis of the World War: An Introduction to the Problem of War Guilt* (New York, 1929), in which there is a brief introductory section on the basic psychological causes of the war, revolving around the "cult of war" and "savage patriotism" (pp. 9–14). On Barnes, see Arthur Goddard, ed., *Harry Elmer Barnes, Learned Crusader* (Colorado Springs, Ralph Myles, 1968), particularly the chapter by Stanton Ling Davis, pp. 176–232.

movements. Beneath the ahistorical mold in which Robinson cast his psychological history, he apparently maintained a large residuum of historical curiosity and skill which stimulated his students.

Robinson envisioned, however, a different role for the historian. He wanted him to be the "critic and guide" of the social scientist, a collaborator who made the past usable in the conception of the present and projection of the future. But he was too willing himself to abandon historical analysis for prophetic rhetoric and too committed to his rhetorical program to recognize the depth of either psychological or historical understanding that would be required before a body of psychohistorical work could actually be created.

One need hardly add that this task remains formidable today. If the experience of Robinson and the New Historians is any guide, it will require on the part of historians not simply a borrowing of usable methods and modes of analysis, but self-critical attention to the way in which their historical attitudes interlock with the ideological implications of psychological theories, and close examination of the implications of those theories for actual historical analysis.

DAVID BURNER
and THOMAS R. WEST

A Technocrat's Morality: Conservatism and Hoover the Engineer

THE TERM "conservative" in politics and social thought offers the benefits not of precision but of ambiguity. If we cannot define such words so that they will stay put, neither can we do without them; they have gathered to them whole clusters of conflicting meanings, and indicate for us important cores of experience having all the contradictions of experience. "Conservative," which in its typical American usage stands for a fairly small-spirited economics and politics, also puts these into a larger context, the nostalgically remembered small towns, the plain old virtues and Fourth of July rhetorics in which, many American conservatives suppose, their individualist economics are rooted. The doctrine of competitive selfishness and the richer feeling for a neighborly American past have got firmly associated, whether by accident or by a logic the doctrinaires cannot describe; and the historian is left with something more interesting than logic alone would have given him.

The more common American notion of political conservatism, however, is not the most inviting one to work with: it is too immediate and polemical, and it has never acquired doctrinal solidity. What we propose is to take the very American figure of Herbert Hoover, who by American terminology was a Progressive and later a conservative, and see what he looks like against a background of philosophically stronger conservative and traditionalist concerns elaborated in Western thought in the face of the modern political and technological revolutions. Hoover's own career, we think, contains hints of a broad and generous society somewhat on the lines drawn by philosophical traditionalists; but they are no more than hints. We want to clarify and extend them.

Philosophical conservatives since the French Revolution have insisted upon a thing that their American political namesakes reveal little conception of—the density and sacredness of community. Community as the conservative understands it is not the numerical majority but a more mysterious and substantive event. Edmund Burke contrasted the pale rationalisms of the French revolutionaries to the massiveness of the British social system, its splendid bulky architecture of institutions, cemented with loyalty and love. When in the late nineteenth century an element in the traditionalist sensibility went paradoxically leftward, as with the socialist visions of men like William Morris with their society of good craftsmen working by hand rather than machine, it offered a community lighter and more spontaneous than the Burkean but more directly communal. The England of Burke's imagining was a compressed mass of men, objects, traditions; Morris's anarchy springs to communal life in the shared joy of workmanship. And Hoover, if he is to earn the title to a larger conservatism than that of catchword politics, is going to have to say something about the nature of community.

The individual whom the conservative ushers into the

community is, again, of deeper substantiality than the being whom liberals have tended to define politically as a voting unit, economically as a unit of energy and consumption, and spiritually as Man possessed of Rights. Some conservatives, Alexis de Tocqueville among them, have argued that the individual owns his greatest freedom and dignity when he is firmly established at some definite place in the social system, having its varied tangible connections with the rest of society. The ante-bellum southerner, according to Allen Tate, had public identity only in his material property. In either case we are presented with an individual whose mind and character are founded in grainy fact, social or physical. The craft socialists, on the other hand, defined the individual as a worker; but rather than constituting a working unit of production, he is a being of skill and creative urge. Or conservative man may have his fullness in his contradictions, or in a capacity for evil that many secularist and environmentalist liberals tend to deny him; or in good manners and a cool, disciplined reason, or a cold, burning asceticism that liberal psychology dislikes.

The commerce, within the sorts of societies traditionalists have prescribed, between community and the individual has been more precarious than they have recognized. The collective system may dominate the private person. Believing that a man's identity is provided by his exact and unchanging placement in a social order, some traditionalist philosophies give no sense of what it might be for him to win his selfhood from an environment that will not go out of its way to define him. When our conservatives offer us, as an antidote to mass society, the severe disciplined individual who can keep himself clear and whole in the face of what they consider the modern thrust toward license and personal degeneration, the balance of person and collectivity is threatened once more, for this stern aristocrat may turn fastidiously away from the common life. In any event, we shall need from Hoover some idea, however implicit, of the individual in community.

The kind of American experience that Hoover reflected at his best does suggest a limited yet going relationship between the workman and his community that is based, loosely and incompletely, in the American facts of technology and a fluid social system.

Hoover spoke for the principle of order in social and economic life. The orderings he championed were of two sorts, which just barely avoided contradicting each other. There were, on the one side, the broader sorts of structure and efficiency that he imposed, as technician and administrator, upon sizable parts of the economy; and on the other, there was the voluntary collectivity of a more democratic and even neighborly variety, the cooperatives and service organizations from which he hoped for much. Possibly Hoover did not consider in any comparative way the chilly technocratic systems and the voluntaristic popular associations he worked to achieve, the clash in tone or the similarities in design and objective. Together, however, Hoover's programs reflect a belief in the susceptibility of things to get themselves into order, and give us an image of an America fluid in its social and economic existence, freely grouping itself into little collective projects as need demands, then breaking again into its primal flowing energies. Hoover, then, did trace the possibilities for a more generous and collective life in America, the collectivist methods grounded upon American technology. Beyond that, he attempted no definite conception of community: we shall not discover in his works a society thickly textured and variously colored like that of Edmund Burke, or simple and almost eucharistic like the community some romanticists have depicted.

Technology provides also the special brand of individual autonomy that Hoover embodied. He had nothing very extensive to say about the bearing of the modern technological process upon the individuality he wished might survive in America. So we shall have to make the connections. It is important, though, that Hoover's cooperative republic of workers would consist not of the handcraftsmen whom romanticists and some socialists have looked for, but rather of workmen in the cool metallic facts of Hoover's machine civilization; for that civilization has about it an austerity, an emphasis upon a schooled private competence, a way of spreading its citizens out thinly, at its separate points of operation, that play nicely against the forces of mass democracy. When Hoover described his fellow citizens, he seemed to be thinking of them as being somewhat like himself: educated, active, professional in business, even perhaps just a little bit well-to-do. We do not find, in the life or writings of Hoover, the sense philosophical conservatives give us of individual man in his rich inexplicable substance any more than we find a community as plenteously endowed as traditionalists envision; but we do have a sober and strong individuality.

Hoover's ideas and programs for society were shaped by his experience in engineering and business. His world was aggressively modern; and as his career acquired a larger and more public scope, and he turned from arranging a mining project to ordering the affairs of vast enterprises and then of society as a whole, he looked the image of a technocrat, as the social philosophers have been called who wanted a civilization perfected by its experts. The point is important for an understanding of the Hoover whom we are relating here to spokesmen for a more philosophically elaborate conservatism. For modern technology can expect a difficult hearing among people of conservative instinct. They will give their assent more easily to the land in its continuity, in the rhythms of nature that repeat themselves upon it, than to machinery with its artificial rhythms and its disruptive, innovating powers; and their taste will approve the substantial and tangible quality of the soil as opposed to the abstract properties of science and mechanical technique. Yet machine technology has its offering to make to the kinds of philosophically grounded social commentators we are considering. Its relentless precisions imply an ascetic morality—the early twentieth-century British poet and critic T. E. Hulme, in his opposition to liberal humanism, found the hard lines and surfaces of a mechanical civilization admirably suggestive of religious absolutes; while an advanced technology has also given us architectures, such as that of Frank Lloyd Wright, that are light and supple, flexibly responsive to varieties of human need, organic to their surroundings: architectures that breathe as pliantly with the human community they are to order and express as conservatives expected inherited institutions to do. Hoover the technician-moralist did not explore the ascetic symbolism of his technology, nor did Hoover the man of order and collectivity talk of anything so abstruse as functionalist architecture. The effect of his industrialist career upon his social thinking was more subterranean: it caused the growth within him, by practical experience, of a feeling for the efficient orderings of people and things. Our story, therefore, will center on Hoover's largely unexamined earlier years, and observe him as an engineer and industrialist thinking about problems that are simultaneously professional and social—sketching out, for the most part unconsciously, a few rough shapes for a just society operative within the private corporation.

Some of Hoover's early pronouncements on labor are unpromising. In 1897 he became mine manager for the London firm of Bewick, Moreing at the remote Sons of Gwalia in Western Australia. Of a labor incident there he wrote:

> During the week I have had two strikes. In the first instance I asked the men to change shifts at point of employment instead of on the surface—each man by this means cut twenty minutes per diem from his time underground. The men met and determined to strike and I therefore promptly posted a notice that we would not grant the usual hour off on the Saturday shift, but the men would have to work the full forty-eight hours [raised by Hoover a few weeks previously from forty-four], and intimated we were prepared for any strike by importing Italians. The

> men sent a delegation then asking for a Meeting, at which I agreed to compromise allowing them the Saturday hour as before, if they would change at point of employment.
>
> Again the Truckers in the lower Level struck for a rise in pay owing to the wet ground. We discharged the entire crew at that level, and replaced them with men at the old rate.
>
> Again it had formerly been the custom to pay double pay for Sunday work, which we stopped, and six men working on Sunday refused to proceed. We discharged them and replaced them with new men.
>
> I have a bunch of Italians coming up this week and will put them in the mine on contract work. If they are satisfactory I will secure enough of them to hold the property in case of a general strike, and with your permission will reduce wages. We now pay 5/—per day more than any other mine on the field. . . .[1]

During the years 1899 to 1901, Hoover was in China for Bewick, Moreing. He began by underrating the effectiveness of Chinese labor; but he decided that since the Chinese were paid only one twenty-fifth as much as Western workmen and "their tendencies to dishonesty are probably no greater than those of other human beings under the same conditions," their cheap labor was an asset.[2]

While Hoover was thinking like this, he was also revealing another side. One of his first recommendations on

---

[1] Mine Manager's Letterbook, Sons of Gwalia, May 23, 1898, Herbert Hoover Presidential Library, West Branch, Iowa.

[2] On Hoover and China, see his articles "Present Situation of the Mining Industry in China," *Engineering and Mining Journal,* LXIX (May 26, 1900), 619–620; "The Kaiping Coal Mines and Coal Field, Chihle Province, North China," *Transactions of the Institution of Mining and Metallurgy,* X (1901–1902, Meeting of June 19, 1902), 426, 427; and "Metal Mining in the Provinces of Chi-Li and Shantung, China," a paper read before the Institution of Mining and Metallurgy on March 28, 1900, *Abstract of Proceedings,* VIII (London, 1900), 330.

his arrival in Tientsin in 1899 was to abolish the contract system of labor—a slave system, he called it—and replace it with one rewarding individual merit.[3] Tong Sha-li of the Chinese Engineering and Mining Company believed that Hoover's interest in relief work originated during the Boxer siege of Tientsin. Tong, who lost his wife and young daughter in the bombings, was forever grateful to Hoover for saving another daughter and carrying from Tong's burning house a number of the dead and injured. For nearly twenty days, Tong recalled, Hoover led men to deserted shops from which they carried food and water to two large groups of refugees.[4] Hoover was not only doing the acts of private conscience and kindness a good man might perform for others: he was revealing possibilities for public leadership.

After transferring a Chinese company to Moreing, Hoover became a full partner in London and worked as a technical consultant and publicist. Here he seems to have learned a broader view of relations between labor and management. "My firm," he was quoted as saying in 1905, "since I joined it [as a partner] four years ago . . . has never been an advocate of cheap labor or reduced wages." [5] He could let go a large number of inefficient workers, but by paying high wages for the best he built up the most efficient labor force in Australian mining.

Hoover's attitude toward labor continued to refine itself. A mark of his growth is his change of attitude toward

---

[3] "Present Situation of the Mining Industry in China," p. 619.

[4] Tong Shao-yi to Arthur Train, June 5, 1932, Hoover Collection, Bodleian Library, Oxford University; see also Loo Etong to Hoover, February 18, 1921; George E. Sokolsky to Hoover, January 17, 1920, "Chinese Affair," Pre-commerce Early Years, Herbert Hoover Presidential Library; New York *Herald Tribune*, April 20, 1928.

[5] "Ethics of West Australian Mining," *West Australia Mining, Building, and Engineering Journal*, December 2, 1905; John McCarty, "British Investment in Western Australian Mining, 1880–1914," *University Studies in History and Economics* (Perth, 1961–1962), p. 21.

Western Australia's compulsory arbitration law. Hoover rejoiced in March 1906 that Western Australia had recently "freed itself from a Labor government," and might now revoke the law.[6] The new government left it unchanged. But in 1909 Hoover wrote, "Some years of experience with compulsory arbitration in Australia and New Zealand are convincing that although the law there has many defects, still it is a step in the right direction, and the result has been of almost unmixed good to both sides. One of its minor, yet really great, benefits," he added, "has been a considerable extinction of the parasite who lives by creating violence."[7]

That dedication appeared in a matured and fully humane statement of the labor issue. *Principles of Mining* was based on previously published articles and on lectures delivered at the Columbia School of Mines and at Stanford. In "the design and selection of mining machines," Hoover wrote, "the safety of human life, the preservation of the health of workmen under conditions of limited space and ventilation, together with reliability and convenience in installing and working large mechanical tools, all dominate mechanical efficiency." He recommended that management pay higher wages to able workers and take "a friendly interest in the welfare of the men," offering them "justifiable hopes of promotion." Always a lover of efficiency, he endorsed piecework and cash bonuses. In a passage toward the end of the book, Hoover undertook to lecture reactionary capitalists. Noting that engineers in executive positions should guide employers in their relationship with labor, he described unions as "normal and proper antidotes for unlimited capitalistic organization." After a period of demagoguery and violence, unions seek harmony. They are "entitled to greater recognition. The time when the employer could ride roughshod

[6] *West Australia Mining, Building, and Engineering Journal,* March 31, 1906.
[7] Herbert Hoover, *Principles of Mining* (New York, 1909), p. 168 n.

over his labor is disappearing with the doctrine of 'laissez faire' on which it was founded. The sooner the fact is recognized, the better for the employer." Strikes hurt business, Hoover realized, and good relations between union and employer reduce their number and duration. Part of the blame for reactionary ideas lay with the academic economists: "When the latter abandon the theory that wages are the result of supply and demand, and recognize that in these days of international flow of labor commodities and capital, the real controlling factor in wages is efficiency, then . . . an educational campaign may become possible." [8]

Hoover's position on labor is typical of him as he moved into an explicit progressivism. The insistence on efficiency, the tone of reasonableness with which he mixes justice and self-interest—"Now isn't this the sensible thing all around?" he seems to be saying—suggests the successful engineer who has thought about how, with decency, to get good performance out of his people, and who wants to put everything, even justice, upon a sound working basis. Here will be Hoover's principle of order, or one of them. The book pleases with its humanity; it is also frustrating. The claim that generous treatment of the workers is necessitated by economic facts not only flattens the moral tone; it is not even especially convincing. Can we believe that efficiency, profit, and justice march so closely together—does the world usually work so tidily? It is really, we are certain, the moralist who is speaking here, wistfully sure, as we would all like to be, that the moral imperative can enlist even self-interest in its aid; and the reader regrets that the moralist did not pay himself the honor of revealing himself more positively and standing on his own terms.

Hoover's statement of a labor policy is an instance of his commitment to justice and welfare within the particular collectivity. Even as he became in American terms

---

[8] *Ibid.*, pp. 125, 163, 165, 167–168.

a progressive, his career was acquiring that larger implication that would bring him about as close as he would come to philosophical conservatism—the revelation that in the pursuit of justice you need not deal with Society at a single swoop but can work to perfect the smaller societies composing it. The Right knows the concept in the form of corporatism, and the Left possesses it in ideas of communes and of workers' councils. But Hoover, without really seizing and articulating it—hence we must use the word "implication"—gave it another distinctive character by emphasizing the element of cold technical analysis and planning that is to bring justice to the collective unit. This he did with special clarity in his consideration of fair treatment for the investor.

It troubled Hoover that London promoters and even company directors often distorted the reports of trained engineers. The remoteness of the Australian mines encouraged disingenuousness; promises that knowledgeable investment circles of Melbourne would laugh at could provoke euphoria on London Wall. Hoover's early writing in professional journals stressed the need for greater uniformity in gold mine accounting. Since so much mining stock, he wrote in 1903, was held by public companies, uniformity was essential for the protection of the small investor. Easily corrupted government inspectors, whose work was wasteful and whose jobs were tempting political plums, solved nothing, Hoover insisted; he advised simply forbidding mine managers and engineers from holding any financial interest in the firms that employed them. Hoover set a reasonable return on mining investment at 6 percent, a figure considerably below what most stockholders considered fair.[9]

Hoover's scholarly articles on mining show a sharp intellectual interest in business and technical problems at hand. He rejected the careless technique of mine valua-

[9] "Gold Mine Accounts," *Engineering and Mining Journal,* July 11, 1903; May 24, 1904; August 4, 1904; *Principles of Mining,* pp. 167–168.

tion that added 50 percent to the value of the mineral in sight; he urged a subtle taking into account of adjoining mines, bores, continuities. The ordering of mine finance, he argued, would benefit the investor without sacrificing "the very necessary position of the vendor or promoter." At the same time he wanted "to adjust the engineer's view-point to the ultimate purpose of the valuation of mines for sale purposes." [10]

In the *Mining Magazine* for 1912, Hoover advanced a careful scheme for reform of mining speculation. He began by listing eight factors for arriving at the assured profit on a mine; prospective value was something else, arrived at by a mixture of intuition and knowledge of psychology and geology. Patterning his argument on "the great railway system," Hoover proposed that the assured profit be represented by safe debentures capital, redeemable out of such profit; and all of the share capital should be assigned to prospective value. The share capital, then, is wholly speculative. Offering to the public the whole of the debentures, the promoter is justified in retaining for himself much of the share capital, which is pure risk. Having observed that the general public suffers its largest investment loss in new issues, Hoover writes: "If the promoter or vendor underestimates the capital necessary to bring the mine to production, he will have to pay the penalty in the loss of his entire share-interest through foreclosure of the debentures, or, alternatively, to supply the money to prevent such an event." Hoover looked for a time when investment trusts would hold the less speculative securities in mining enterprises; this too would rationalize the industry, placing in the hands of engineers the decision as to where capital was deserved and needed.[11]

Hoover despaired at the more foolish speculator. "From an economic point of view . . . ," he wrote, "capi-

[10] "The Valuation of Gold Mines," *Engineering and Mining Journal*, May 19, 1904.
[11] "Mine Valuation and Mine Finance," *Mining Magazine*, VII (Oct. 1912), 275–277.

tal in the hands of the Insiders [promoters, vendors, brokers, and so forth] is often invested to more reproductive purpose than if it had remained in the hands of the idiots who parted with it."[12] Hoover had angry words, however, for promoters who become "drones on the community, or establish families of drones, or squander [their money] on riotous living. . . . The most hopeful view is that they will reinvest their takings in reproductive work and continue to devote their experience and abilities to the augmentation of the national wealth."[13]

In the first decade of the twentieth century, the Australian mines under Bewick, Moreing's technical management summed into a near-monopoly. The firm's prosperity came about in part through the influence of Hoover, whose generally optimistic but careful reports inspired great confidence among mining investors. His rise to directorship over a number of mining companies was itself a triumph of rationality, for these positions had often been held by retired military gentlemen picked for the honor the appointment would do them and the enterprise rather than for their technical or financial knowledge. By 1904 Hoover could claim great credit for a number of enlightened policies on the part of Bewick, Moreing: reporting mine developments in Western Australia simultaneously with their publication in London; compelling mine managers to file copies of the assay plans with the West Australia Department of Mines; giving the press free access to the mines; estimating and publishing the value of ore exposed at mines through continuing audits at regular periods; publishing the working costs of mines and yet paying the highest wages on the gold fields.[14] Even when profits declined, Hoover's intimate friend Francis Govette insisted on maintaining wages against a proposal by other firms to

[12] "The Economics of a Boom," *Mining Magazine*, VI (May 1912), 371.
[13] *Ibid.*, p. 372.
[14] *West Australia Mining, Building, and Engineering Journal*, December 3, 1904.

reduce them. (Hoover wrote many of Govette's reports and statements.) Bewick, Moreing moved its men about to productive mines, striving to prevent needless unemployment.[15] All this was publicized by the *West Australia Mining, Building, and Engineering Journal*—surely some kind of mouthpiece for the firm, with its consciousness of public relations. Hoover urged further reforms for the protection of the mining investor: each month "full details" of the working costs should be submitted by the mine managers and published in the *Government Gazette*.[16] Near the end of the decade W. J. Loring described the firm's labor policy: "for dealing through unions (where necessary) amicably my advice would be first of all to maintain a high standard of pay . . . select the best overseers . . . furnish the workmen with the best tools that can be purchased, making the working conditions as nearly perfect as is practicable." [17] We have an admirable example of welfare capitalism, the well-composed private collectivity.

The distinguishing thing about Hoover in this period, again, is his workmanlike absorption in the details and the larger character of his calling. If we have made too sharp a contrast between the craft socialists, those radical democratic reactionaries, and the representatives of the machine age that they protested, here is the chance to correct ourselves. In Hoover's thinking there is a spirit as of one who is a master of the guild.

Hoover believed in comprehensive training for a mining engineer. Each of the thirty-two mines under Bewick, Moreing's direction as of 1904 was headed by an engineer who was also its commercial and administrative director. Technical training, Hoover claimed, would evoke a professional sense, instilling honesty in an industry that rewarded dishonesty. Coming after thorough work in the humanities, the training should emphasize "the purely

[15] *Ibid.*, August 27, 1906.
[16] *Ibid.*, September 3, 1906.
[17] *Ibid.*, January 5, 1910; *Mining Magazine*, November 1909, pp. 199–200.

theoretical groundwork of the engineering profession," especially scientific studies; for Hoover argued that the schools, instead of trying to reproduce practical working conditions, should encourage students to take jobs during the summers. Hoover took pride in Bewick, Moreing's policy of offering young mining school graduates a two-year apprenticeship—a training in all departments of their main interest. Here the young "can get an adequate balance of what constitutes commercial vs. theoretical conditions." Hoover thought that in the education of mining engineers, America did a better job of combining administration and purely technical skills; the British were too conscious of class to allow their young men to be trained in both.[18]

Reflective also of Hoover's identity with his profession are his writings about the history and condition of mining. In Australia he wrote of the future of gold production; in China of ancient and modern coal deposits. In 1912 he and his wife published a translation of *De Re Metallica,* a sixteenth-century work by Georg Bauer, who used the pen name Agricola. The purpose of the task was to "strengthen the traditions of one of the most important and least recognized of the world's professions." [19] The book is not only a compendium of medieval mining practices but an apology for the harsh conditions under which miners labored. Yet in this book are found many of the hallmarks of modern mining: the eight-hour day, various forms of insurance and charity, guilds for the interchange of knowledge.

Hoover had a promotional strain that clashes with the technical workmanship. His biggest venture in the manipulation of public sentiment came in his efforts to secure British participation in the Panama Pacific Exposition of 1914, a trade conference designed to publicize the rich resources and markets of the American west coast. Here an unobtrusive approach was essential, given the require-

[18] "The Training of the Mining Engineer," *Science,* XX (Nov. 25, 1904), 716–719.

[19] Authors' introduction, p. 8.

ments of English politics. But Hoover formulated grandiose plans, including a scheme to bring King George V through the Panama Canal to San Francisco, the site of the exposition, and Sir Arthur Conan Doyle presented the Prime Minister a petition of British authors asking for participation. Controversy over the collection of canal tolls thwarted Hoover, but he tried one approach after another, fervently holding to a trust in the power of public opinion.[20] Still, Hoover's efforts over the years to elicit public support for his various schemes, whether entrepreneurial or altruistic, had typically an unobtrusiveness that sat well with his character of sober workman and suited his shy personality. He gave secluded interviews or issued press releases. Hoover's liking for the silent exercise of influence recalls his college days at Stanford, where from the modest office of student treasurer he rewrote the school constitution.

Some eighteen months before the war broke out and Hoover entered Belgian relief work, he granted a very pessimistic interview to the New York *Sun*. The discovery of great new mining districts was unlikely, he said, and "new, isolated mines will not replace the frail and dying members." No industry had had such a generous supply of capital for every promising enterprise, and the increase in percentage recovery of ore from 60 to 90 left little space for further technical improvement.[21] Hoover, moreover, had become a multimillionaire. What room, he may have asked himself, was left in the mining industry for achievement? As a businessman with interests on five continents he had naturally acquired a broad grasp of international politics. Appalled by unproductive economies, bureaucratic waste, and the failure to realize the potential of social and economic resources, Hoover increasingly looked toward a career of public service, in which he would later work so

[20] "Pre-Commerce Panama Pacific International Exposition—Miscellaneous," Herbert Hoover Presidential Library.
[21] September 8, 1912.

earnestly at building clean-lined new social architectures.

Hoover admired Theodore Roosevelt and supported his Bull Moose campaign. Hoover's own progressivism at this time fits the definition that Robert Wiebe has offered for the reformist ideas of the early twentieth century, the belief that the way to social progress is through advanced technical expertise applied to society by continuing administration. More especially Hoover was near to embodying the virtues proposed by the radical sociologist Thorstein Veblen, whose work Hoover read.[22] Veblen praised the clean impersonal workmanship of the machine era, compelled to exactness and honesty by the intricately resistant materials it deals with; and Hoover, despite the streak of promotionalism that Veblen would have disliked, was a devoted and articulate practitioner of his technical profession. Veblen would be calling upon the engineers and technicians to take from the hands of the promoters, who had no concern for efficiency, the management of the entire technical plant, and of modern society; Hoover had already become an engineer-manager on a great scale, and was soon to transfer his talents to the public realm.

That part of his career is well known. As administrator in the government during the First World War, as organizer of vast humanitarian relief, as Secretary of Commerce under Harding and Coolidge, when Hoover labored for the standardization of industrial equipment, and as president, he had opportunities to bring his enlightened management to society as a whole. He also gave expression to softer and more emotional elements in his thought that balance against the pure technician: a liking for voluntary cooperation, for example. Hoover had always been talking about cooperation of a sort, imposed by corporate management upon the components of the enterprise and willingly assented to by the varied beneficiaries.

---

[22] At a New York dinner Hoover complained that mining engineers had to take a position below the "parasitic" professions of theology, law, and war. *Engineering and Mining Journal,* March 14, 1914.

But Hoover during the twenties spoke of a more spontaneous and democratic organization—sprung, to be sure, from rational self-interest as well as altruism. He proposed, for instance, that the government support voluntary cooperatives among farmers formed for the more orderly growing and marketing of produce. He was revealing as well a view of human nature differing from the economic conception of man that Hoover's technological rationalism might have inclined him to. The individual represented in *American Individualism* (1922) and *The Challenge to Liberty* (1934)—the second book being Hoover's protest against the New Deal—comes out to be not a mechanism motored by wants and profits but the imaginative, creative source of civilization and its varied achievements, among them economic inventiveness.

We are reminded here of Richard Hofstadter's distinction between the "hard" side of farming, its self-interested and businesslike quality, and its "soft" side, its exalting of the virtuous yeoman. We would propose for Hoover as a technician something similar, though more favorable to him: the "hard" side of him was his urge to efficiency; the "soft" technician thought that man's imagination, his cooperative abilities, his kindlier instincts, all fit well with his productive drives. And it is when Hoover's rationalist principles of order are touched with emotion, and with an idea of the voluntary community, that his presentation of the ordered collectivity most nearly suggests the classical conservative sensibility.

A larger extension of these things might have given Hoover's career a different turn. Why did he come down so angrily upon the New Deal, a movement committed to rationalizing a chaotic economy he himself had labored to order; an administration eager to save and extend family ownership of homes and land; a President who practiced through government a humanitarianism much like his own? It was perhaps in good part a matter of political polarization. After so scarring an end to his presidency, after being brutally characterized as an arrogant, socially indifferent man of wealth, after the "Hoovervilles" and the "Hoover depression," Hoover had to believe that something fundamental separated him from his enemies, and he had to submit some argument proving how much better his policies would have worked. But if Hoover's recoil from the New Deal has causes that fall short of pure ideology, it implies nevertheless the differences between his temperament and the temper of a fully developed conservatism.

A clue lies in the familiar contrast between the nonpolitical Hoover and Roosevelt the consummate politician. Skilled politicians are by the nature of things endemic to liberal and democratic states. Yet successful politics, or Roosevelt's kind at any rate, can also imply the particular virtues of conservative society. They operate by intuition and a delicate tact, qualities that the conservative exalts and the rationalist liberal suspects; and these gifts join the statesman and his constituency in a community of feeling. The community is also the object of the good politician's craft, for his strength lies in his ability to recognize the varieties of groups and conditions there and compose them into some sort of tenuous harmony, to detect the sources of social morale and know how to reinforce it, to be the keeper of the community's traditions or to articulate its newer ideas. Surely there was much integrity in Hoover's failure to practice this kind of politics. He could not easily have violated the correct aloofness that was built into his character, a cast of mind suggesting the impersonal milieu and the austere virtues of the technician. Besides, he had proceeded upon the unspoken principle that communities maintain themselves not by emotion and fine adjustment but by purposefulness infused with plain decency and guided by an engineering sort of rationality. But in lacking the political sense, however honorable the lack, Hoover missed an important element in conservatism.

An example of Hoover's distance from the public mood is supplied by the banking crisis of 1933. It can be argued, to be sure, that Hoover, in hesitating to close the banks without Roosevelt's concurrence, was a good conservative, distrusting any rupture in the community's delicately continuous activities and knowing the demoralization that could result from closure. But Roosevelt's bank holiday, whatever may have been his reasons for it, probably spoke better to the public temper. The community needed at the moment the sight of some dramatic and positive act on the part of the government, and the bank holiday—essential in any case for the economy—provided it.

Unpossessed of a politician's feeling for his community, Hoover also made some very specifically unconservative judgments about the relationship of community to its inhabitants. When Hoover condemned the New Deal for its threat to the autonomous individual, he seemed implicitly to be describing personal autonomy as though it is a product of self-generating will. Philosophical conservatism has thought differently, concerning itself with the complexity of the social context in which strong individual character flourishes. Hoover could recognize that in the most desperate circumstances—war-broken Belgium, or America at the worst moments of the depression—the individual is helpless and must have relief, and Hoover is to be honored for his compassionate response; but he did not fully grasp the more subtle ways in which, a sensitive and well-founded conservatism might decide, the New Deal was buttressing personal independence and enterprise: its efforts for small private property and for social insurance, its disciplining of corporate power, its support of industrial unionism, its psychology of hope—though he did commend some of these elements in the New Deal.

A specific instance would be the administration's approach to the problem of relief. It knew—and Hoover, given more time, could surely have come to know—that relief could be so designed as not only to fill empty pockets but also to restore dignity and self-esteem; and so it made its rescue measures into something larger and more affirmative. WPA and its sister programs turned reliefers into workers, sharing in grandly visionary projects for building the nation and regenerating its spirit.

All this points up what might be called the aesthetic distance between Hoover's thinking and that of a classical conservatism. While conservatism revels in the variousness of existence, the crazy tangled substance of society (which it will sometimes preserve at the expense of social justice), Hoover's vision was spare and got much of its dignity from the spareness. His paucity of political skill represented an unwillingness to perceive, in a tactile way, the differences among political groups and among leaders; the absence from his writing of any large investigation into the social setting of independent individuality meant that he gave us no extensive sense of the rich variations in character the social condition can spawn. Yet a love for diverse coloration of personality does suggest itself in Hoover's eulogies, often eloquent, to an open individualism. The decade of the New Deal was a welter of democratic assemblages, governmental programs at cross-purposes, and through it all an image—a bit romantic, and popular among intellectuals—of the American people as various, folkish, potent with collective energy. If it was not an image to please an aristocratic traditionalist of European background, it meant an American version of the Burkean taste for a concrete living social order. Hoover the conservative, truly conservative in his commitment to association and to a national heritage, should have been at home with it. He could at least have been able, as a voluntarist and as a masterly administrator, to do something toward instructing it away from the total bureaucratization that threatened its more democratic impulse.

We have chosen to be arbitrary with Hoover, to impose on him a label that history has only accidentally given him, and to see how he fitted it, and how he did not. Hoover would not have to apologize for failing to be our perfect philosophical conservative: the term that in *The Challenge to Liberty* he favored for his philosophy was "Liberalism." No more arbitrarily he could be called a progressive, a libertarian, or a technocrat, and then we would have some new set of questions to ask and contradictions to discover. Hoover spoke on his own for social values as lean and stately as the engineering principles they resemble, fortifying them with a generous social commitment. Though he did not possess the political touch that would have enabled him to capture his America, his mind was formidably American in its conviction that a society can will itself into order out of sheer determination and a sober workmanlike address to the task.

OTIS L. GRAHAM, JR.

The Planning Ideal and American Reality: The 1930s[1]

I

HERBERT HOOVER, whatever his failings, was a very prescient man. In the midst of the political campaign of 1932 he peered into the future and divined that the meddlers were coming. His insight was sound—that the conscious management of society was about to be expanded in countless ways. Whatever may have been the governing ideal of the New Deal, its daily work load was the expansion of social management. In this it accelerated a process long under way, one which has since transformed both the private and the public sectors of American life.

By the 1930s a trend toward social management, based upon bureaucratization and centralization of decisionmaking, had gathered momentum through fifty years and more of modern history. In both public and private

[1] The author is grateful to James M. Banner, W. Elliott Brownlee, David Burner, Hugh D. Graham, Carroll Pursell, John E. Talbott, Robert Kelley, John T. McAlister, and William Leuchtenburg for critical readings of this essay.

life, zones of control encroached upon the uncharted areas where "nature took its course." This had been the central dynamic of the Progressive Era, and the World War had further stimulated the trend toward consolidation and bureaucratic control. During the 1920s, when federal power slowed its expansion, state and local governments, corporations, universities, churches, and other private institutions continued to centralize their activities, to add research and operating agencies specialized by function, and to move toward standardized procedures, all designed to extend control over unpredictable environments. Clearly, history aimed at enhanced coordination and management, and moved away from the haphazard social flux of the nineteenth century, when social direction had somehow derived from the sum of individual choices.

Hoover's own career in government had contributed to the trend toward a more rationalized and interdependent society, but by 1932 he feared that the future threatened a too rapid reduction of individualism. His sensitive antennae had detected the planning instinct, the social engineer, in the words of his evasive rival. Many thought Hoover's instincts faulty, since Roosevelt appeared to be an amiable but not a bold individual, one whose opinions oscillated gently about a shifting but moderate political center. Yet Hoover's premonition, if a bit hysterically felt, was accurate enough. Roosevelt, too, had been shaped by progressivism and the war mobilization, and his tutors in the 1920s had been leading figures in the drive for expanded government intervention in the areas of relief, public power, and resource conservation. In his Jefferson Day speech, April 18, 1932, Roosevelt had expressed admiration for a Jefferson somewhat unfamiliar to many of the Virginian's admirers, a man who stressed the primacy of the national interest and who concentrated men's thoughts upon "the shared common life" rather than the predicament of individuals. In that address Roosevelt spoke for "a true concert of interests" which could be realized only by an expansion of planning—"not for this period alone, but for our needs for a long time to come." He was to express similar collectivist views on other occasions in 1932, especially in the speech at Oglethorpe, Georgia, in May, and in the Commonwealth Club speech in September.

It was never entirely clear, on these occasions when the candidate's words rang with managerial overtones, whether he expressed deep convictions or merely the rhetorical representations of an experimental temperament. Yet the impulse to social planning, as Hoover must have known, had already taken hold of other and better minds than Roosevelt's. That humanity could and must manipulate its social as well as its natural environment, and do so rationally and collectively, had been the central message of leading social theorists since the late nineteenth century—Lester Ward, Richard Ely, E. A. Ross, Herbert Croly, Thorstein Veblen, Simon Patten, Charles Van Hise, John Dewey. When Hoover's own team of social scientists reported on *Recent Social Trends* in 1932, they found planning and centralization on the increase everywhere in American life, and recommended more of it. George Soule, always timely, brought together both the achievements and the prospects of social planners in *A Planned Society* in 1932. When Roosevelt selected three academics to advise him in the 1932 campaign, he found Adolf Berle, Raymond Moley, and Rexford Tugwell all to be advocates of more extensive social intervention by government.

Tugwell was especially committed to replacing drift with mastery, in Walter Lippmann's earlier phrase, and was the most articulate spokesman of the managerial impulse in the Roosevelt circle. As early as 1927 he had believed American social development to be out of control: "It is a ghostly Flying Dutchman which carries us all, from which there is no escape, yet which we cannot define because we cannot see it whole, which we cannot guide because we have not yet invented compass, sextant, or rudder, and whose crew we cannot control because we lack the idea of discipline."[2] In that predepression year Tugwell was perhaps one of a very few who had decisively abandoned the traditional faith that individual pursuit of wealth would somehow add up to social progress. By 1932, the argument for management had gained strength from the collapse of an essentially unregulated economic system. "The cat is out of the bag," Tugwell wrote in June 1933. "There is no invisible hand. There never was. We must now supply a real and visible guiding hand to do the task which that mythical, nonexistent, invisible agency was supposed to perform, but never did."[3]

Yet it was one thing to predict an accelerated trend toward social intervention under the new administration, and another to forecast its forms. As one might expect of any complex undertaking by thousands of individuals reflecting diverse backgrounds and interests, contradictions nestled comfortably against one another in Roosevelt's Washington, and no single theory bestrode the whole. People in and out of government called for "planning," but differed widely in their definition of the term, or in the depth of their commitment to the departures from tradition which might be required. And most of the enthusiastic and reform-oriented new arrivals to the capital never used the word "planning" to describe what they intended to do with the corrective power of government. But with all the diversity, intervention was the common thread. New Dealers were managers by nature, hoping to extend rationality and control to areas of confusion. "What!" exclaimed Sherwood Anderson, after hearing the talk of the younger officials in the Department of Agriculture and the CCC in 1933. "You dream of a physical America controlled, plowing of the land controlled—this or that section of America to be permanently in forest—river flow control, floods con-

[2] *Industry's Coming of Age* (New York, 1927), p. 208.
[3] Tugwell, "Design for Government," Address, Federation of Bar Associations of Western New York, June 24, 1935, in Tugwell, *The Battle for Democracy* (New York, 1935), p. 14.

trolled at the flood source?"[4] Indeed they did, even though they differed on means, on timing, on priorities. "Our economic life today," said Roosevelt, "is a seamless web. We cannot have independence . . . unless we take full account of our interdependence."[5] The people who came to Washington with him, like their enlightened contemporaries in the worlds of business, journalism, medicine, public health, academia, and elsewhere, saw a society crippled because its mechanisms had spun off balance and assumed that the solution lay in some form of continuous adjustment by trained intelligence. In the new government, whether among career civil servants or newcomers, the language was that of managers: they talked about the importance of reliable data, of interrelationships, of constant surveillance, adjustment, balance, planning, control. Roosevelt articulated the managerial impulse on frequent occasions. "There was a time," he told the Young Democratic Clubs in 1935, "when the formula for success was the simple admonition to have a stout heart and willing hands. . . . But . . . today we can no longer escape into virgin territory; we must master our environment."[6] When sending the TVA proposal to Congress, he said: "Many hard lessons have taught us the human waste that results from lack of planning. Here and there a few wise cities and counties have looked ahead and planned. But our nation has 'just grown.' It is time to extend planning to a wider field."[7] And when asked by a reporter to account for the relative health of the economy in 1936, Roosevelt bluntly claimed: "Because we planned it so."

[4] Sherwood Anderson, *Puzzled America* (New York, 1935), p. 71.

[5] Samuel Rosenman, ed., *The Public Papers and Addresses of Franklin D. Roosevelt*, I (New York, 1938), 697.

[6] *Public Papers*, IV, 338.

[7] *Public Papers*, II, 122–123.

II

At the end of the 1930s, before war intervened, how stood the dreams of the social engineers, the advocates of public planning and control?

On the surface, America appeared to have come a long way, in the years from 1932 to Pearl Harbor, toward a society whose principal affairs were now managed, and in some ways perhaps even "planned," by public officials. Public authority had made extensive inroads into zones where behavior had formerly been uncontrolled by any coordinating influence. The central government had increased in size from 605,496 employees and a $4.6 billion budget in 1932 to 1,042,420 employees and a $9.1 billion budget in 1940; it had recently taken on new regulatory responsibilities in the areas of agriculture, banking, labor-management relations, resource use, radio broadcasting, food and drug quality, aviation, the wages and hours of labor in interstate commerce; it was lending money to farmers and homeowners, railroads and banks; was producing and selling electricity, dispensing pensions to the aged, relief to the unemployed, and devising employment for destitute artists, architects, city planners, and novelists. The Constitution had been reinterpreted to permit these and other managerial activities in a line of decisions stretching from the Social Security cases (1937) to the validation of the wage and hour law in *U.S.* v. *Darby* (1941). Constitutional barriers to federal economic regulation were effectively eliminated.

This sizable and only partial list of interventions, added to the already substantial public functions of the government when the decade opened, amounted in the minds of many contemporaries to an impressive advance toward the broad social management aimed at by the visionaries of 1932. The central task of the modern State, the manipulation of the economy to produce growth and full employment, had been shouldered. America still did not have social planning according to any blueprint, since few had aimed at so alien a concept, but it had a vigorously intervening government. Journalist James Burnham was widely thought to have written the most prophetic book of the year when, in 1941, he brought out *The Managerial Revolution,* extrapolating current trends to project a society run by trained experts in the public service.

In reality, as a few contemporaries realized, the end of the 1930s found the society still substantially out of the control of those who had assumed the job of guiding it. Economic policy on the eve of war continued to be formulated in the uncoordinated, dispersed ways of the predepression years, by men who were, like their predecessors, ignorant, confused, and guessing. When the economic writer George Soule visited Washington in 1933, he had expected to find a headquarters of some kind, with charts covering the walls showing payrolls, employment, production, prices, bank credit, new capital issues, foreign trade balances, public expenditures—and a set of planners pondering the figures. He found no such "war room," and there would never be one. After 1935 even the NRA's dispirited staff was disbanded, and economic policy for the balance of Roosevelt's presidency was shaped out of the sporadic interaction of a President with essentially no economic training or staff, a Secretary of the Treasury whose experience had been in farming and business, the director of the Bureau of the Budget with his tiny staff (the entire Bureau housed forty-five people in 1937), and the Finance and Ways and Means committees of Senate and House chaired by a Mississippi planter in the Senate and a series of ex-lawyers in the House, none with any economic staff to draw upon or the will to do so.

While some of these gentlemen, particularly a handful of Treasury economists who tried with little success to influence Secretary Morgenthau, saw fiscal policy as a means to manipulate the economy, most, including the President, perceived taxing and spending as chiefly political exercises in which the guiding considerations were a rescue level of humanitarian relief and a balanced budget. As a result, the fiscal impact of government operations was strongly expansionary during only two years of the entire decade (1931 and 1936, when veterans' bonuses were passed over executive objections). The government's fiscal policies were particularly irrational in 1937–1938, when social security taxes began to siphon off more than a billion dollars a year (excess of taxes over payments) into a reserve fund, and Roosevelt cut back the WPA and other programs to achieve a balanced budget. Never during the 1930s was fiscal policy either coherent or rational, and even if Roosevelt had adopted some overriding fiscal direction, state and local governments acted independently. Since most of them were retiring debt and contracting expenditures during the 1930s, they counteracted the central government's expansionary intentions—as weak and qualified as they were.

Monetary policy during the 1930s was similarly a story of inept management. The Federal Reserve Board entered the decade with rudimentary but nonetheless substantial powers over the supply and availability of money, but pursued almost exactly the wrong course from 1929 through 1932. The Board remained virtually passive amid the speculative fever of 1929 and then quashed what appears to have been a revival of economic activity in 1931 by raising the discount rate and sharply restricting open market purchases—in order to protect the international gold standard. Federal Reserve officials, along with American economists as a whole, were no closer to an adequate understanding of the proper countercyclical monetary policy under FDR than under Hoover, but some improvements both in monetary institutions and in management were made after 1933. FDR was an innocent in monetary theory, but he instinctively understood that America could not begin recovery while tied to the gold standard, and he assumed that some monetary expansion was indicated after the contraction of 1929–1933. (Almost a quarter of the money supply had vanished in that short period.) The administration went off the gold standard and, aided by angry inflationists with a strong congressional following, pressed the Federal Reserve into a passive phase from 1933 to 1937, during which an influx of foreign gold gradually expanded the money supply. Our silver policy was an insane interlude, with everybody losing but the mining companies. The Treasury itself kept the policy from producing much monetary inflation, although inflation would have been the only thing to justify this resurrection of Bryan's ghost. In any event, there was no operable consensus on what a correct monetary policy should look like. Still, the Federal Reserve, though missing the opportunity to pursue vigorous open-market purchases, at least did very little until 1937 and thereby allowed some monetary expansion to occur. Some economists link this accidental expansion to the degree of recovery which did take place.

In 1937 the Board's instinctive fear of inflation overcame the good sense even of chairman Marriner Eccles, and the Federal Reserve helped kill the small boom of early 1937 by raising interest rates and restricting open-market operations. In the end, the management of the money supply under Roosevelt was a mixture of bizarre experimentation, international irresponsibility, baffled passivity, and sudden activism to protect the dollar against imaginary runaway inflation, the whole unguided by any consistent principles. The result, by sheer chance, was actually a better monetary policy than under Hoover, but it would have been quite a feat to have done worse. It can at least be said that important steps were taken under the Glass-Steagall Act, the Emergency Banking Act, and the Banking Act of 1935 to strengthen the powers of the monetary authorities, and the banking system itself. These institutional reforms would prove useful later on, when the experts began to achieve that rudimentary understanding of monetary policy which was denied the men of the 1930s.

The managerial hand of the federal government was unsteady in other areas. The tax system amounted to a complicated mass of levies that accumulated according to political feasibility, accomplishing none of the goals announced for it such as prevention of monopoly or redistribution of income or wealth. This had been true prior to 1933, of course, but no scholar to my knowledge has ever made a strong defense of New Deal tax changes on any grounds, ethical or economic. As for the regulatory agencies, these were substantially free not only of presidential control or direction but of any firm policy goals of their own, and they drifted aimlessly along lines of their own choosing. In agriculture, heroic efforts had brought some production control to basic commodities, a step of great historic significance which was taken in the teeth of stubborn rural resistance to "scarcity economics." Yet the cumbersome apparatus of controls had not curbed overproduction even by 1940, and had contributed to the painful side effect of tenant displacement. The government's agricultural policies combined with market pressures to force some 40,000 families from the land each year; their wretched search for jobs and living facilities brought them to urban areas which could provide neither, and a belated tenant resettlement program brought only minimal relief.

The federal grant programs were another area of aimlessness. They increased haphazardly from the $5 million of 1915 to nearly $500 million by 1940, and included funds for highways, vocational education, agricultural extension, and public assistance under the Social Security Act. Federal grants were a policy instrument of enormous potential, but they were enacted piecemeal, with no thought of their effect in distorting state programs. When states matched federal funds, they diverted funds which might well have found other uses; monies spent on federal-state highway programs made it that much harder to spend on parks, schools, or public health. Further, federal grants were almost never offered on more favorable terms to the poorer states, which meant the loss of a prime opportunity to ensure a more uniform national performance in areas such as education, health, or public assistance.

In the use of resources, the dream of order had been

most vivid, the guidance of the marketplace most antisocial. Perhaps more than any other policy area, the matter of the natural environment and man's relationship to it requires an organic view and coordinated activities. With water, soil, and plant and animal life locked in an interrelated cycle, manipulation is never the sum of its parts. To be sure, there was more appreciation of this interrelatedness in the 1930s than ever before, and more strenuous efforts to shape effective conservation policy to mesh individual use with social good. Compared to past efforts, the advances of the 1930s earned the admiration of all friends of the American land. Partially owing to Franklin Roosevelt's strong personal interest in conservation, the government took steps toward improved land management. One thinks especially of the Soil Conservation Service, but also of programs inaugurated under the Taylor Grazing Act of 1934, the TVA, the removal of farmers from submarginal land, the reforestation activities of the Civilian Conservation Corps, and the "Shelterbelt" project of the Forest Service. At the end of the 1930s the waters of the Tennessee River and its tributaries were controlled by nine dams with twelve more under construction, the Boulder and Grand Coulee dams held back the waters of the Colorado and Columbia rivers, and the flood control acts of 1936 and 1938 seemed to commit the government to comprehensive prevention of floods, working from dam to watershed divides.

So praiseworthy were such efforts, and so well did the government tell the story of its conservation achievements, that the serious flaws of scale and organization have escaped general notice. The soil conservation effort, though vital and long overdue, was blunted from the start, and never reached its full potential. The early dream of Hugh H. Bennett and Henry A. Wallace of having all the Department of Agriculture's conservation programs channeled through seventy-six drainage districts had not survived the realities of federalism and interagency rivalries. The Soil Conservation Service finally arranged to work through tiny districts not much larger than counties (2,300 of them by 1952), governed by committees of local farmers with minimal national direction. The districts operated under forty-eight different state laws with authority to advise farmers on more enlightened land use, but less than 1 percent of the districts had the power to coerce them.

The government's management of water resources was plagued with similar irresolution and fragmentation. Some twenty-four federal agencies were involved in the development or the protection of water resources at the end of the 1930s. Their efforts were uncoordinated and had been undertaken in isolation. Single-purpose development remained the rule throughout, despite years of exhortation toward multiple-purpose planning at all the development sites. Only the TVA, of all the federal agencies involved in water resources, took the drainage basin as a conceptual framework and ecological unit. The great barrier to coordinated water management was the Army Corps of Engineers, which over the years had evolved wonderfully harmonious relations with Congress and local commercial groups interested in water transportation. It took its projects from the shopping list compiled by the Rivers and Harbors Congress, a private organization which had worked its way to a quasi-official position in governmental planning. The Corps of Engineers carried this list of pork-barrel requests to Congress without consulting any other federal agency or the White House, and reported back to Congress upon completion of its work. On three separate occasions during the 1930s the President attempted to break the Corps-Congress nexus, to force the Corps to clear its requests with the Bureau of the Budget, and to convert it from piecemeal operations to long-range, basin-wide planning. The Corps refused to be coordinated, seeing no need to be part of a wider framework. When Senator Norris proposed a central planning agency for conservation, Secretary of War George Dern, defending the Corps's independent role in flood control and navigational work, said that "each of these activities [flood control, erosion, pollution, wildlife preservation] is a separate problem, to be handled by a special group of experts. . . . Too much coordination . . . might prove harmful."[8] Congress agreed with Dern. To preserve the independence of the Corps the "rivers and harbors bloc" in Congress prevented the establishment of seven other TVA-type river authorities in 1938, deleted the request for a national resource conservation planning agency from the reorganization act of 1939, and in that act specifically prohibited the President from transferring the CE or altering any of its duties.

Since national coordination in conservation was so bitterly distrusted by all private groups involved in resource use, as well as by most federal agencies in the field, the government had to accept greatly expanded piecemeal efforts without coordination: a decentralized soil conservation effort, a decentralized program to protect public grazing lands, a TVA which would never reproduce itself, expanded appropriations for tree planting and purchase of additional public lands, and some flood control work at the points of greatest downstream hazard. A nation has been properly grateful for these advances, but close scholarly scrutiny has always revealed their shortcomings.[9]

---

[8] Arthur Maass, *Muddy Waters* (Cambridge, Mass., 1951), p. 74.

[9] "The National soil conservation program is permeated with duplication, overlap, conflict, and lack of coordination," wrote Charles Hardin in *The Politics of Agriculture* (Cambridge, Mass., 1952), p. 18; Arthur Maass concluded that "despite some five years of attempted policy coordination, the nation in 1939 had no program which could be dignified by the name 'national water policy,'" in *Muddy Waters,* p. 102; "The niggardly appropriations for grazing activity over the years," wrote Philip Foss of the administrative history of the Taylor Grazing Act of 1934, "have prevented any really significant conservation activities" (from *Politics and*

In retrospect, conservatives' fears of regimentation seem at best ludicrous. In the principal areas where the New Deal had attempted to exert managerial control, in the stabilization of economic activity and the conservation of natural resources, its efforts were uncoordinated, contradictory, and extremely solicitous of established local interests.[10] And while something less than masterful at economic and resource management, the central government after eight years of reform exerted little influence upon the education and health care of the people, and did not dare propose that it be granted even minimal influence over other basic social processes which blindly shaped the national future—urban and industrial land-use planning, the disposal of animal and industrial wastes, the procreation of humankind.

Grass [Seattle, 1960], p. 103); Wesley Calef concurred, writing: "The managerial staff is too small. Most range inspection is superficial, haphazard, and inadequate" (*Private Grazing and Public Lands* [Chicago, 1960], p. 88). After reviewing the performance of the more than twenty agencies involved in forestry management, Luther Gulick wrote: "There is no clean-cut, formally spelled-out forest policy" (*American Forest Policy* [New York, 1951], p. 27). Norman Wengert summarized in 1955: "There is no single all-embracing resource policy, and . . . to hope for it is futile" (*Natural Resources and the Political Struggle* [New York, 1955], p. 13).

[10] If one surveys the experience of other industrial nations in moving toward rational public management of economic life, one would find many examples of ineptitude to match the American record. In Britain, Derek Aldcroft found no conscious attempt at expansionary fiscal policy during the depression, no countercyclical theory guiding the actions of public officials, no relief policy; merely aimless, piecemeal planning by a conservative government to accomplish the rescue of faltering industries. Of all the European nations, excepting the U.S.S.R., Eric Lundberg has written of economic policy in the 1930s that "the measures taken were more inappropriate, more badly timed, more obviously wrong than most of the measures of similar importance adopted in the post-war (1945–) period." *Instability and Economic Growth* (New Haven, 1968), p. 69.

III

There are many reasons why the thrust toward social management, which the catastrophe of depression appeared to facilitate, made so much less headway across the 1930s than many had hoped. The national administration lacked the institutions and the mandate for the comprehensive surveillance and manipulation of a complicated $80 billion to $100 billion economy. The President's staff included several secretaries, a doctor, and two southern politicians (until 1939, when the Reorganization Act gave him six assistants; one of them, Lauchlin Currie, was an economist). The tiny National Resources Planning Board by 1940 had an energetic staff and was producing useful studies of resource policy, relief, national income, and the like, but the agency had few friends anywhere in government or outside of it, and feared to frame legislative recommendations or to lobby for them.

Roosevelt was painfully aware that there was no machinery through which he could gather reliable economic data, make forecasts, establish goals, issue orders, and analyze results. He made resourceful efforts to adapt or invent some central agency suitable to the task of overall management. An Executive Council of Cabinet officers met with decreasing frequency and effectiveness between June and December 1933. It was replaced by the National Emergency Council, a larger and more unwieldy discussion group which went so far as to send out state directors and agents to gather information in the field and try to explain federal programs. This agency never had legal status or a strong director, and Roosevelt soon stopped attending meetings. But the administrative confusion and programmatic disorder of the New Deal continued to trouble the President (he expressed surprise that the Republicans did not make this a larger issue in 1936), and in March 1936, FDR appointed a Committee on Administrative Management. Reporting in 1937 that "the time has come to set our house in order," the committee recommended the consolidation of all ninety-seven government agencies under twelve Cabinet departments, the strengthening of the presidency by the addition of six administrative assistants and a permanent planning board, and other minor centralizing and streamlining reforms. Their report was "not a request for more power," the three committee members wrote, "but for the tools of management. . . . To bring many little bureaucracies under broad coordinated democratic authority."[11] These modest changes would not have ensured the Executive's control of far-flung agencies that had powerful constituencies and strong congressional ties, but they would have been important first steps toward a more coordinated federal machinery. In the poisonous climate of the Court struggle, the reorganization was soundly defeated by a coalition of doctrinaire conservatives and some of Roosevelt's own agency heads who preferred the loose rein of the past. In 1939, Roosevelt was granted his six assistants, but little else the committee asked for. The structure of government remained as incoherent and unadapted to coordination as before. By 1940, the President's efforts to attain central legislative clearance through the Bureau of the Budget had been only partially successful. The Bureau under Executive Order 8248 in 1937 managed to channel the budgets of most federal agencies through its own fourteen-person division of Legislative Reference to filter out proposals which were contradictory to the President's program where he happened to have one. Yet some agencies, most notably the Corps of Engineers and the ICC, simply refused to inform the Executive of their budgets and plans, preferring to go directly to Congress as in the past.

But this lack of machinery, data, and trained personnel, together with the internal disorder of nearly a hundred government agencies, did not exhaust the difficulties. The

---

[11] President's Committee on Administrative Management, *Report with Special Studies* (Washington, D.C., 1937), p. v.

liberal mentality was deeply divided on the matter of state intervention. All liberals were advocates of a vigorous intervening government, but those whose education had been in the Wilson-Brandeis tradition were hostile to interventions which looked toward a permanent administrative bureaucracy. For reformers of this New Freedom persuasion, the marketplace should manage the economy, and it would do so once a vigilant government had eradicated special privilege and laid down inescapable rules of fair competition. Yet there was another tradition descended from Herbert Croly and TR, one which welcomed a continuous managerial role for public officials. Roosevelt brought to Washington people who were pure types of both of these social philosophies, and many more who were influenced by both and tended to move back and forth between centralization and decentralization, continuous bureaucratic management and self-enforcing legal restraints, planning and the marketplace. The 1930s never saw anything like a liberal consensus on the role of the state. Reformers who were emotionally ready for national planning remained a minority, surrounded by colleagues who had profound reservations. FDR himself mirrored the conflicts in the collective mind of liberals, although he appeared to lean, so far as we can tell, toward Tugwell rather than toward Brandeis. If he did not talk publicly of "national planning" after the debacle of NRA, he always believed that more intervention was necessary, pressed for it in a dozen areas, and fretted at the incoherence of the government's activities.

Actually, most New Dealers joined him in this. They were not Tugwellians with a crusading vision of a disciplined society, but they valued a higher administrative coherence than time and pressure had permitted. Nevertheless it seemed that each time the government edged toward the ideal of more comprehensive and more effectively interrelated management, there abutted the national individualism, the suspicion of coercion from political sources, the labyrinthine entrapments of the federal system, the deep localism of the people. Against these centrifugal forces the nationalizing institutions, most notably the political party, were no match. This, at least, was the way it looked to those in the Executive Branch who suffered so many reverses at the hand of a hostile Congress and a refractory, fragmented, unruly society.

IV

Yet if we merely review the frustration of the New Deal's managerial efforts we court a very great distortion of our perspective on the 1930s. The political rhetoric of the period suggests that the culture was still fundamentally hostile to the collectivist impulse, despite the economic emergency. On the one hand there stood a handful of New Dealers who were strong for various kinds of intervention and control; on the other a vast multitude of businessmen, professionals (with the single exception of university social scientists in the Northeast), publishers, some governmental officials, indeed the great bulk of the public, unalterably opposed to planning and public controls, horrified by the sudden appearance in freedom-loving America of this band of collectivists and meddlers. But this dichotomy between the New Deal and the basic national culture is profoundly misleading. The times were actually quite propitious for further encroachments upon unplanned sectors by the managerial imperative. Indeed, the private sector saw steady advances toward rationalization, consolidaton, centralization, bureaucratic order, and control, and it resembles the public sector in the 1930s in important ways.

In all instances, shifts toward bureaucratic control in the 1930s are extensions of institutional and intellectual developments which began much earlier. A full survey of this would show the advance of modernism in voluntary associations, religion, education, entertainment, recreation, in every aspect of organized social life. But it would surely begin with the corporation. If we look for dramatic increases in business consolidation we will not find it in the 1930s, for the merger wave that commenced about 1926 had ended by 1930 and the consolidations of the 1930s were statistically unimportant.[12] But in other ways the corporation continued its drive toward mastery of an unruly social environment. The larger and more farsighted corporations, especially those that had diversified their product lines, had begun in the 1920s to see the need for more effective control of production processes and marketing, and for adapting more flexibly to sudden changes in demand. Alfred Chandler has described the structural changes devised by Alfred P. Sloan for General Motors after 1923, changes which Chandler, Sloan, and everybody else have called "decentralization." The word is a misnomer. Faced with a diversified industrial enterprise too large to manage effectively from the traditional boardroom, the leaders of GM did establish semiautonomous product divisions, delegating to them many decisions such as purchasing and budgeting which had formerly been made at the top. But "decentralization" on the GM model meant more effective central control by top management, which could escape from production details to appraise overall performance and to anticipate future trends in consumer demand, financial conditions, and technology. Many large diversified corporations turned to the GM model: Standard Oil in the late 1920s, Hercules, Monsanto, and other chemical firms in the early 1930s, Westinghouse in 1934, and General Electric in 1939, to name only a few firms that shifted to the new structure. The method was to decentralize some functions in order to centralize the crucial decisions, and at all levels one finds the enlargement of bureaucracies to provide staff and line departments with specialized services.

This development touched only the larger corpora-

---

[12] See Ralph Nelson, *Merger Movements in American Industry: 1895–1956* (Princeton, 1959).

tions, and only the more farsighted among them. (Ford was a conspicuous holdout for the older ways, running his own firm as he always had out of his own erratic impulses, and falling behind GM and Chrysler every year.) But many corporations moved along other paths toward modernization. Leading businessmen began to see the need for more specialized knowledge long before the 1930s—not only for research into products and their manufacture, but for knowledge of the motivations as well as the physical and psychological limits of the work force, and of the shifting tastes of the consuming public. This meant adding new research bureaucracies to corporate structures: efficiency experts in the Frederick W. Taylor tradition, psychological testing bureaus to preselect the right employees for specialized tasks, and economic and market research offices to estimate the shape and size of demand. The beginnings of industrial research, in the forms of both scientific laboratories to improve products and bureaus of social scientists to assist with personnel handling and economic forecasting, reach back in some cases before World War I. Product research had its greatest expansion in the 1920s, stagnating somewhat in the early years of the depression. Yet by 1938 research budgets of corporations had surpassed the 1930 total of $166 million annually, and by 1940 had reached $200 million.

Industrial psychology went back to the pioneering work of Hugo Munsterberg and Walter Dill Scott just prior to World War I, and usually took the form of personnel testing. The 1920s was a decade of considerable skepticism about testing, but in the 1930s the growth of unionism drove employers to commit more of their resources to research and control programs in worker psychology. Standardized testing was used somewhat more in the 1930s than in the 1920s, and many firms added industrial and personnel relations departments. The famous experiments in worker psychology undertaken by Elton Mayo and others at the Hawthorne works of the Westinghouse Corporation from 1927 into the 1930s drew wide attention from employers interested in increasing productivity and reducing employee discontent. Sears, Roebuck added personnel relations departments in 1927, Bethlehem Steel in 1930, General Motors in 1931, the B&O Railroad in 1934, International Harvester in 1937, and so on. Public relations work was also enlarged during the 1930s, especially through trade associations formed not only to coordinate the activities of companies but to allow industries to speak with one voice to a public whose attitudes had not so long ago been left to chance. The PR budget of the National Association of Manufacturers, for example, was 7 percent of the total budget in 1933, but had jumped to 55 percent by 1937, to a total of $793 million. As for economic market research, the 1930s was really the germinal decade. A symposium at Harvard Business School in 1943 revealed that the attending executives, from companies like Westinghouse and Hercules Powder, had typically inaugurated economic research bureaus in the mid-1930s if they had taken the step at all. Just as Franklin Roosevelt was finding useful work for trained scientists and social scientists —economists, statisticians, city planners, soil chemists, botanists, engineers, and many lawyers—so was American industry employing more experts to help establish control over the disorderly, unmanaged areas of scientific invention, consumer tastes, and worker psychology.

Association is a prerequisite for control, and this indicator, too, signals the 1930s as a decade of continued collectivization. Lloyd Warner and his associates, in *The Emergent American Society: Large Scale Organizations* (1967), have established that of the more than 200,000 voluntary associations in the United States (12,000 of them national associations), 70 percent were established after 1900—30 percent from 1900 to 1920, 20 percent from 1920 to 1940, the rest after 1941. Of these, the "sociability" associations account for most of those founded prior to World War I, while groups interested in economic issues, government policy, recreation, and science dominated the list of those founded in the 1920s and 1930s. The trade association movement experienced especially rapid growth in the interwar years. There was a flurry of business association in the period 1925–1929, and then, after the stagnant years of the early depression, a dramatic increase during the NRA period when a quarter (23 percent) of the trade associations extant in 1938 had their genesis. At the end of the 1930s, a TNEC study counted 1,505 national or regional trade associations of commercial competitors engaged in lobbying, promotional activities, the dissemination of statistics, and making agreements on sales territories and prices, gradually extending collective controls over the ruthless and unpredictable workings of the marketplace.

Overshadowing the associational activities of businessmen in the 1930s was the growth of another type of organization engaged in collectivizing formerly unorganized individuals and activities—the labor union. Students of the 1930s are most familiar with the organizational drives of the auto and steel unions of the CIO, but a recent study of the unionization of air pilots, George E. Hopkins's *The Airline Pilots: A Study in Elite Unionization* (1971), captures the essence of the organizational process in an admirable way. Just prior to the depression, air pilots were an unorganized, highly individualistic set of men, a growing interest group with a strong collective identity as romantic and daring technicians, each a little Lindbergh pitted alone against dark space. Yet they had no control over wages, working conditions, aircraft safety, or entry into the field when the depression brought scarcity. Organization was hastened by wage cuts and layoffs, and was encouraged at crucial points by the sympathetic administration in Washington. By the eve of the war, there had taken place what Hopkins calls "the metamorphosis of the pilots from outspoken rugged individualists into close-lipped advocates of union solidarity." The Air Line Pilots Association now acted in the name of all pilots to replace the random whims of twenty-one airline owners and the free play of a chaotic marketplace with the central, industry-wide determination of wages, working conditions, and certification. This transformation from loose-knit individualism to a self-conscious, united interest group had commenced much earlier in other occupations, and had worked bureaucratic values deep into the culture by the time of the Great Depression.

For organizations already established by the 1930s, the advance of modernization took the form of structural shifts toward more elaborate bureaucracies and a more tightly coordinated operation. If one measures the growth of administrative staff relative to local units, using religious denominations as an example, one perceives the steady advance through the twentieth century of—to use Kenneth Boulding's phrase—the organizational revolution. The central staff of the Disciples of Christ, for example, increased ten times from 1900 to 1960, while the organized church doubled the sums spent on national administration and cut by 5 percent the budget of local churches. The 1930s did not interrupt this process, but continued it, despite the overall shrinkage of funds. Most American organizations, whether business, educational, professional, religious, or otherwise, were forced by the depression to cut budgets and staff from 1930 to about 1935. By the late 1930s, the tide ran again toward consolidation and the enlargement of central staff. In 1939, three Methodist denominations merged, to secure the advantages of central control of fund raising and other economies of scale. In 1936 all the Jewish groups raising funds for Palestine joined in the United Palestine Appeal, and in 1938 the United Jewish Appeal absorbed all fund-raising efforts on behalf of Jews at home and abroad.

And one might easily multiply examples of the evolution of the private sector toward new modes of social control, an evolution which preceded the New Deal, and then paralleled it.

V

This current of development in the private sector was, of course, modernization: a gradual evolution from multiplicity toward integration, from haphazard development toward planning, from the supremacy of entrepreneurs toward the supremacy of managers and bureaucrats, from chance toward prediction and foresight. No decade of evolution, however rapid, moves a large and complex society more than a modest distance toward modernity, for the old patterns are deeply ingrained. But the 1930s was a decade of accelerated modernization, after the paralyzing years 1930–1932 when few institutional changes were made anywhere in American life.

And it had important consequences for public policy under Franklin Roosevelt. The collectivist, interventionist cast of policy was virtually inevitable. Some rural congressmen and backward newspaper publishers kept the rhetoric of individualism in the forefront of public life, but the leading men in business and the professions were modernists, their own careers caught up in the search for more effective social intervention through enlarged and functionally specialized bureaucracies, research and planning staffs, and, where necessary, state intervention. It was therefore predictable that the federal government (and to a lesser extent state and local governments) should catch up, in a few dramatic strides, with the advanced private institutions in a common search for the instruments of expanded social control. Individuals made a difference, surely. Expanded government activities under Garner, or even Hoover, would have differed in style and also in many places in substance from the record Franklin Roosevelt made. But in the broadest sense, the New Deal was not thrust upon the country because Roosevelt had a weakness for liberal professors, social workers, and social experimentation. It was the natural embodiment of a broad and irresistible development toward enhanced social control and bureaucratization. Propelled by history, and given irresistible impetus by the depression, the New Deal could not have been long deferred even had the assassin's bullet found Roosevelt instead of Mayor Cermak in the Miami motorcade in December 1932. The cries of outraged individualists against that striking personality, Franklin D. Roosevelt, should not be allowed to obscure the extent to which public policy in its broad outlines was congenial to leading citizens and at one with the society's fundamental direction.

Yet if the advancing modernization of private institutions helped draw public policy itself toward adventures in control, it also set limits upon how far public planners could go. While other factors were at work, it was in part because the society had moved so far toward modernization that the government was blocked from attainment of the comprehensive national planning to which some public figures, including FDR, were basically attracted. As Alfred Chandler and Louis Galambos have perceptively written, the "high degree of bureaucratization in the American private sector in the 1930s" shaped and constrained New Deal policy "more than the oft-cited resistance to governmental interference. Each new policy, each new measure of control had to be pushed through an incredibly dense organizational environment." [13] In short, the thrust toward comprehensive social management was not parried by the fanatics, the "individualist" opponents of government intervention; it was captured, subdivided, and subdued by the very ones who shared the collectivist urge but who wanted control of a very different scope and accountability.

The perversion of the national planning ideal stemmed from no direct decision of New Dealers. In the beginning, especially, the administration seemed com-

[13] Alfred D. Chandler and Louis Galambos, "The Development of Large-Scale Economic Organizations in Modern America," *Journal of Economic History*, XXX (March 1970), 216.

mitted to coordinated national planning (albeit of a loose, cooperative, typically "American" type). But the rush of events smothered even these inclinations. Both Congress and the administration, responding to clamorous demands for public intervention by various groups, multiplied new agencies to cope with problems as they arose. Hopefully, there would be time to rationalize the government's impact, to mesh its many programs in a harmonious whole. Toward this end a harried President supported a small planning board, established two Cabinet-level coordinating committees which collapsed by 1935, and appointed in 1938 a Fiscal and Monetary Advisory Board of appropriate agency heads which became at once deadlocked in intergovernmental rivalries and failed to last out the year. These institutions, like the grander NRA, did not evolve into coordinating machinery suitable to the need. The NRA experiment, in particular, wasted time and shattered enthusiasm for central direction. While the President in his second term groped for control of his party and the Court, and for the right to reorganize the executive branch and the independent regulatory commissions, events made the decision about the nature and extent of management. Alliances were struck between private interests, bureaucrats, and interested politicians; the legislative mill ground forward, giving old agencies broader mandates or creating new agencies for specialized tasks. Control expanded by sectors. The advance toward social management went on, but by a hundred separate paths.

The enlargement of intervention followed a pattern. The hazards of a shifting, unstable economy increasingly prepared more minds to accept some degree of control as enterprises became larger and the stakes more sizable. The depression heightened the awareness of waste and caprice, and brought dissatisfaction with random social change to a critical mass in many economic sectors. Shrinking markets, dust storms, bread lines, collapsing banks—all spoke to many minds a message of excessive freedom, of insufficient forethought and control. When government bureaucrats or politicians finally moved to impose the order of law, it was almost invariably with the eager endorsement of the principle if not the details of intervention by all the immediately affected parties. An agency was established to pursue order, or a new mandate was given to an established agency. The governmental unit found private groups organized, fully ready to escape economic storms in the haven of public law. The agency entered upon its complicated duties without clear guidance from Congress, adopted a cooperative spirit, consulted with affected groups of private citizens with economic stake and expertise, and sought public support by decentralizing some of its decisionmaking processes and speaking the language of local participation. If regulation was not always in its initial phases completely satisfactory to the regulated interests, the passage of time enhanced the influence of organized groups and reduced the abstract zeal of the regulators. Those who might have expressed different evaluations and goals were screened from the process by bureaucratic walls, or by their own lack of organization and expertise. Thus the drive for control had been stopped short of *national* control; the framework was smaller, limited to a geographic locality or a cluster of interest groups. To those who had shaped this system the old order had provided insufficient predictability, but centralized national decisionmaking introduced unpredictabilities of its own. They therefore guided the political economy toward a middle ground where the context of control was restricted to the perspectives and interests of vitally affected groups.

By the end of the 1930s the State, which planners had intended to use to establish sufficient control over the fundamental affairs of the nation, was thoroughly Balkanized, its sovereignty compromised by the invasion along the edges of public policy by private groups with regular and often legalized roles in policymaking. As a result its many programs were not only internally contradictory, they were at odds with the universally desired goal of recovery; virtually every program worked toward the restriction of production in the midst of scarcity. Hundreds of groups had secured the haven of public protection from the marketplace, and there they could wait out the economic storms, fighting off occasional efforts to mesh and coordinate all State interventions into a coherent apparatus which the President, with his national constituency, might control. "Government by whirlpools," Ernest Griffith described Washington in the late 1930s.[14] Was America planned? George B. Galloway of the American Planning Association offered this summary in 1941: "Much of the so-called planning is scattered, partial, piecemeal, pluralistic, interventionist, uncoordinated, and dispersive . . . It lacks a clearly defined underlying rationale, a common direction. . . . From the viewpoint of national planning, the New Deal has been like Don Quixote who mounted his horse and rode off in all directions at once."[15] All through the 1930s, Roosevelt's words had pointed toward interrelated social management on a national scale, yet events had marched toward a type of planning which made the job of broad and comprehensive management every day more difficult and its realization more unlikely.

VI

As the 1930s wore on and central planning failed to materialize, many liberals found this not altogether a bad turn of events. The European planning experience, especially in its German, Italian, and Russian forms, gave rise to doubt that a State with planning powers could also permit political democracy. To be sure, a core of American liberal planners never relinquished the hope for a mechanism of coordination which would be democratic in form

---

[14] Griffith in George Galloway, ed., *Planning for America* (New York, 1941), p. 11.
[15] *Ibid.*, p. 46.

and spirit, and in the late 1930s Mordekai Ezekiel, Jerry Voorhis, Jerome Frank, and Ernest Griffith, among others, were still constructing blueprints. But liberals in general were not as sanguine about planning as they had been in 1932. Experience had given them an appreciation of the staggering difficulties involved in the management of an industrial society. In retrospect, the task faced by aspiring planners did dwarf contemporary human capacities, as the Brandeisians always insisted. The country was 3,000 miles across, and held 135 million people who in 1929 produced $104 billion worth of goods and services through a set of interactions which no social scientist understood except in broadest outline. This vast population responded to unmeasured hopes and fears, the availability of credit, the haphazard appearance of new technologies and products, shifting rates of interest, and daily calculations of advantage. The decisions of private citizens were a dark continent of unpredictability, and this was only to a slightly lesser degree true of public officials. There were 116,000 separate governmental units in America in the 1930s, taxing, spending, subsidizing, promoting, and penalizing in a whirl of uncoordinated motions.

In light of such realities, the compromise political economy that emerged helter-skelter out of the 1930s took on a certain appropriateness. John Chamberlain in his *The American Stakes* (1941) saw great merit in the post-New Deal "broker state" which admitted all organized interest groups to a share of power, exercising its light, prudent, consensual managerial role within the confines of what those groups would accept. John Kenneth Galbraith would make a similar defense of the system in *American Capitalism* (1952). To Galbraith, a rational public policy could be arrived at very satisfactorily by the interplay of organized interest groups. If the government found some important group unorganized, such as labor had been in the early 1930s, it could simply assist that group toward organization so that it might join the other bargainers in the marketplace of political power. To set policy through such mechanisms may have been "muddling through," but in the eyes of political scientists such as Robert A. Dahl and Charles Lindblom, it encouraged a vigorous democracy of contending citizens' associations, and was wiser in the end than the five-year plans handed down by remote experts. It was also argued that the post-New Deal political economy reduced the level of conflict by decentralizing and obscuring the sites of power and decisionmaking, and that the American civil service had an approachable, responsive style quite refreshing by comparison with the commissars or venal incompetents of more centralized regimes both left and right.

For a long time after the New Deal there was little opposition to these impressive arguments and the assumptions behind them. During the war the nation reluctantly accepted a vast and clumsy economic planning apparatus. When the war was over, a few men talked again of permanent national planning, but there was little resonance in the power centers of the country—less, probably, than in 1932. The New Deal system would do nicely. Advocates of a firmer governmental hand had to be content with the establishment of a Council of Economic Advisers to provide the President with economic advice. In the postwar era, America operated within the confines of the system of the late 1930s: a massive, busy collection of federal agencies, moving from year to year and from problem to problem without central guidance; a Congress too large and understaffed for initiative and without a national outlook; and a presidency with the appearance of great power but actually half-paralyzed by slack party discipline, congressional jealousies and delaying procedures, and the multiple divisions of federalism. But except for a residue of unreconciled individualists, intelligent people saw incalculable virtues in the system. It was responsive to (group) citizen pressures, flexible in programs, and sensitive to established interests; it presented to the public an approachable and cooperative civil service and well-run agencies free of graft; and it preserved a broad zone of freedoms for those who would pursue enterprise. And there was no return of the economic instability that had haunted the country since the 1870s.

The passage of time, however, has brought us around to a fundamental realignment of perspective. An environmental crisis has pushed to the front of the public agenda, and will remain there, most probably, until the end of humanity's occupation of this planet. We are on our beam ends; economic growth is now suspect, has been dethroned, will not pull us through. Both international and national welfare, as well as individual freedom in a very important sense, will in the future require enormously more effective and interrelated social controls. The fearful hazards of this social direction may be guessed from the experience of modern totalitarianism, even from part of the record of well-meaning bureaucracies in Sweden, Great Britain, and elsewhere. They include a threat to civil liberties, the stifling of the human imagination, and, worse, an ineptitude at management which rivals that of less comprehensive systems. For more than thirty years these clear hazards have given us caution, and led us to prefer our system of loose and poorly articulated controls to arrangements of greater rationality and coerciveness. But we have consumed our way, expanded and penetrated and interlocked our way to the obsolescence of that system of sector-sufficient, reactive management which took form in the lifetime of Franklin Roosevelt. A reasonable solution for the 1930s appears less reasonable every year, with every disclosure of the irrational behavior of American popular government.

Particularly telling, in an avalanche of criticism, have been the appraisals of our political economy by Tugwell and Banfield (1950), Henry Kariel (1961), Michael D. Reagan (1963), Grant McConnell (1965), and Theodore Lowi (1969). These writers argue that policymaking by the interplay of organized pressure groups has been a deeply conservative arrangement, ensuring the impotence of the unorganized—the consumer, the poor, the amorphous public, the unborn. In the 1970s, other objections have pressed forward. Given an increasingly competitive world market, some sacrifices and redistributions appear inevitable: that some prices must go down and some profits narrow, and that some groups must lose protection in order that the bracing winds of competition may invigorate their search for new technologies and improved productivity. Yet this route is substantially blocked by—among other things—the government's own commitment, expressed in a massive network of laws and agencies, to the isolated well-being of hundreds of powerful interest groups who for years have occupied special places in the fragmented machinery of a broker state. The maturing of this system took place by the end of the 1930s. By the eve of war virtually all important organized interests had edged into a protected zone of law, their affairs administered by a public-private mix of regulators and citizens' advisory groups in which private purposes ultimately dominated. The economy was a series of fortresses, private interests behind legal walls, dedicated to planning and control within the walls and invulnerable, or very nearly so, to outside influence.

Tugwell liked to describe those who, like himself, worked for a collectivist social management as "the middlemen of modernity." He knew they had been defeated, knew it as early as 1934 when he had a conversation about planning with FDR as the NRA staggered toward its demise. The President made it clear that he was through with central planning, that henceforth the government would either accept regulatory roles piecemeal, as the situation might dictate, or fall back upon New Freedom progressivism and work for an end to monopoly. Tugwell realized that the clumsy effort at coordinated planning had failed, and the collectivists would not soon get another chance: "I was asking for too much. It was not only NRA, it was the whole organic conception of a living nation, equipped with institutions for foresight, conjecture, and balance. It was not yet time for it. . . ." [16]

---

[16] R. G. Tugwell, "The Experimental Roosevelt," *Political Quarterly,* LXIX (July–Sept. 1950), 265.

A Selective Bibliography

This essay builds upon many sources, and only the most important ones may be mentioned here. The planning impulse was given voice at the beginning of the 1930s by George Soule, *A Planned Society* (New York: Macmillan, 1932), by Stewart Chase, *The Economy of Abundance* (New York: Macmillan, 1934), in Franklin Roosevelt's speeches and public papers, in Rexford G. Tugwell's prolific writings (for a complete listing of these, with analysis, see Bernard Sternsher, *Rexford G. Tugwell and the New Deal* [New Brunswick: Rutgers University Press, 1964]). By mid-decade the administration had backed away from the idea of planning, which had in any event never dominated its counsels entirely. Yet the idea of more extensive and better-coordinated management found classic voice in the *Report with Special Studies* of the President's Committee on Administrative Management (Washington, D.C.: Government Printing Office, 1937), and the ideal of national planning itself found continuing expression among intellectuals: see Jerome Frank, *Save America First* (New York: Harper and Brothers, 1938); Gerald W. Johnson, *The Wasted Land* (New York: Macmillan, 1938); Ernest S. Griffith, *The Impasse of Democracy* (New York: Harrison-Hilton, 1939); Mordekai Ezekiel, *Jobs for All Through Industrial Expansion* (New York: Alfred A. Knopf, 1939); and George B. Galloway et al., *Planning for America* (New York: Henry Holt, 1941). The New Deal's closest approximation to a planning agency was the National Resources Planning Board (which appeared first as the National Planning Board, then the National Resources Board, then the National Resources Committee); the agency's story is told in Charles E. Merriam, "The National Resources Planning

Board: A Chapter in American Planning Experience," *American Political Science Review,* XXXVIII (Dec. 1944), 1075–1088, and in John D. Millett, *The Process and Organization of Government Planning* (New York: Columbia University Press, 1947). The journal *Plan Age* was founded in 1934 by a group of planning-oriented citizens led by Lewis Lorwin. This journal, until its demise in 1941, is a prime source of information on the planning movement.

New Deal fiscal policies are summarized in Lewis H. Kimmel, *Federal Budget and Fiscal Policy: 1789–1958* (Washington, D.C.: The Brookings Institution, 1959), and somewhat more critically in E. Cary Brown, "Fiscal Policy in the 1930s: A Reappraisal," *American Economic Review,* XLVI (Dec. 1956), 857–879. Herbert Stein, *The Fiscal Revolution in America* (Chicago: University of Chicago Press, 1969), finds Roosevelt's policies less rational than Hoover's, but describes the 1930s as an important educational era for economists in the public service. Secretary of the Treasury Henry Morgenthau's intellectual shortcomings and budget-balancing influence are apparent in John M. Blum, *From the Morgenthau Diaries: Years of Crisis, 1928–1938* (Boston: Houghton Mifflin, 1959), and *From the Morgenthau Diaries: Years of Urgency, 1938–1941* (Boston: Houghton Mifflin, 1965). New Deal tax measures are analyzed in Gerhard Colm and Fritz Lehmann, *Economic Consequences of Recent American Tax Policy* (New York: New School for Social Research, 1938), and in Sidney Ratner, *Taxation and American Democracy* (New York: W. W. Norton, 1942). In his *Beckoning Frontiers* (New York: Alfred A. Knopf, 1951), we see that Roosevelt's chairman of the Federal Reserve Board, Marriner Eccles, had an advanced understanding of fiscal policy, but in his book, as in Lauchlin Currie's unpublished recollections, one sees the frustrations faced by the best New Deal economists who had to operate in the midst of an economically illiterate political elite.

The government's monetary policies have been given

relatively favorable evaluation in Arthur W. Crawford, *Monetary Management Under the New Deal* (Washington: American Council on Public Affairs, 1940). Milton Friedman and Anna J. Schwartz, *A Monetary History of the United States, 1867–1960* (Princeton: Princeton University Press, 1963), is more critical, as is the well-balanced new synthesis, Lester V. Chandler, *American Monetary Policy: 1928–1941* (New York: Harper and Row, 1971). G. Griffith Johnson's detailed review, *The Treasury and Monetary Policy, 1933–1938* (New York: Russell and Russell, 1939), complains about the President's efforts to bring monetary policy under executive control, but Johnson considerably exaggerates Roosevelt's long-range success. The best general view of New Deal agricultural policy is Murray Benedict, *Farm Policies of the United States, 1790–1950* (New York: Twentieth Century Fund, 1953); Rainier Schickele, *Agricultural Policy* (Lincoln: University of Nebraska, 1954), is also valuable. Grant McConnell, *The Decline of Agrarian Democracy* (Berkeley: University of California, 1953), is critical of the influence given to organized large farmers in New Deal policymaking, and David E. Conrad, *The Forgotten Farmers* (Carbondale: University of Illinois, 1965), and Arthur F. Raper and Ira Reid, *Sharecroppers All* (Chapel Hill: University of North Carolina, 1941), tell what happened to tenants. An indispensable study of overall economic thinking in the 1930s, and especially valuable on NRA, is Ellis Hawley, *The New Deal and the Problem of Monopoly* (Princeton: Princeton University Press, 1965).

The best comparative studies in economic policy are Andrew Shonfield, *Modern Capitalism* (New York: Oxford University Press, 1965); Erik Lundberg, *Instability and Economic Growth* (New Haven: Yale University Press, 1968); Derek H. Aldcroft, *The Interwar Economy: Britain, 1919–1939* (London: B. T. Batsford, 1970); Alfred Sauvy, "The Economic Crisis of the 1930s in France," *Journal of Contemporary History*, IV (Oct. 1969), 21–35; Derek Aldcroft, "The Development of the Managed Economy Before 1939," *ibid.*, 117–137; and William E. Leuchtenburg, "The Great Depression" in C. Vann Woodward, ed., *The Comparative Approach to American History* (New York: Basic Books, 1968).

There is as yet no single adequate survey of conservation under FDR. Edgar B. Nixon, ed., *Franklin D. Roosevelt and Conservation, 1911–1945*, 2 vols. (Hyde Park, N.Y.: General Services Administration, 1957), is an indispensable source. Anna L. Reisch, "Conservation Under Franklin D. Roosevelt," is an unpublished PhD dissertation (University of Wisconsin, 1952). The soil conservation program, explained with understandable affection in Hugh H. Bennett, *Soil Conservation* (New York: McGraw-Hill, 1939), is critically appraised in Charles M. Hardin, *The Politics of Agriculture: Soil Conservation and the Struggle for Power in Rural America* (Glencoe, Ill.: The Free Press, 1952). Somewhat more favorable are the essays in Henry Jarrett, ed., *Perspectives on Conservation* (Baltimore: Johns Hopkins University Press, 1958), and R. Burnell Held and Marion Clawson, *Soil Conservation in Perspective* (Baltimore: Johns Hopkins University Press, 1965). Robert Morgan, *Governing Soil Conservation: Thirty Years of the New Decentralization* (Baltimore: Johns Hopkins University Press, 1965), is a hard-headed study of great value. Advances in the management of water resources, as well as much overlap and confusion, may be surveyed in the essays by Gilbert White, Carter Goodrich, Albert Lepawsky, and Arthur Maass, in James W. Fesler, ed., "Government and Water Resources: A Symposium," *American Political Science Review*, XLIV (Sept. 1950), 575–649; see also Fesler, "National Water Resource Administration," *Law and Contemporary Problems*, XXII (Summer 1957), 447–471. Roosevelt's vacillations on the issue of water policy are traced in William E. Leuchtenburg, "Roosevelt, Norris and the Seven 'Little TVAs,'" *Journal of Politics*, XIV (Aug. 1952), 418–424. Some of the difficulties in attaining a more rational water policy are revealed in Jean Christie, "The Mississippi Valley Committee: Conservation and Planning in the Early New Deal," *The Historian*, XXXII (May 1970), 449–469, and Donald Swain, "The Bureau of Reclamation and the New Deal," *Pacific Northwest Quarterly*, LXI (July 1970), 137–146. The indispensable study of the Corps of Engineers is Arthur Maass, *Muddy Waters: The Army Engineers and the Nation's Rivers* (Cambridge: Harvard University Press, 1951). On forestry in the 1930s, see Samuel T. Dana, *Forest and Range Policy* (New York: McGraw-Hill, 1956), Luther H. Gulick, *American Forest Policy* (New York: Duell, Sloan and Pearce, 1951), and Charles A. Reich, *Bureaucracy and the Forests* (Santa Barbara: Center for the Study of Democratic Institutions, 1962). On the management of public range under the 1934 Taylor Act, see Wesley Calef, *Private Grazing and Public Lands* (Chicago: University of Chicago Press, 1960), and Philip O. Foss, *Politics and Grass* (Seattle: University of Washington Press, 1960).

The literature on the record of the regulatory commissions is increasingly critical. Marver Bernstein, *Regulating Business by Independent Commission* (Princeton: Princeton University Press, 1955), describes the loss of zeal characteristic of the agencies as they mature. Louis Kohlmeier, *The Regulators* (New York: Harper and Row, 1969), calls for the abandonment of the entire regulatory structure, and James Q. Wilson, "The Dead Hand of Regulation," *The Public Interest*, XXV (Fall 1971), 39–58, summarizes the critics' case more succinctly. But the capture of regulatory agencies by regulated business enterprise, while it has become a wide concern in the 1960s and 1970s, was a phenomenon of the 1930s as well. Earl Latham, *The Politics of Railroad Coordination, 1933–1936* (Cambridge: Harvard University Press, 1959), is an arresting case study of how an industry kept regulation within limits which did not threaten its interests. Particularly interesting for the evolution of cordial relations between the government and an industry which was not sure it desired federal regulation is Vincent P. Carosso, "Washington and Wall Street: The New Deal and Investment Bankers, 1933–1940," *Business History Review,* XLIV (Winter 1970), 425–445, and Michael E. Parrish, *Securities Regulation and the New Deal* (New Haven: Yale University Press, 1970). Another useful case study is Gerald D. Nash, *United States Oil Policy, 1890–1965* (Pittsburgh: University of Pittsburgh Press, 1968).

The tangle of governmental units in the U.S. and their complicated interrelations are described in William Anderson, *The Nation and the States* (Minneapolis: University of Minnesota Press, 1955); John C. Bollens, *Special District Governments in the United States* (Berkeley: University of California Press, 1957); and Clyde F. Snider, "American County Government: A Mid-Century Review," *American Political Science Review,* XLVI (May 1952), 66–80. State and local government in the 1930s seemed to be a consistent hindrance to federal efficiency and effectiveness in the eyes of Alvin Hansen and Harvey Perloff, in *State and Local Finance in the National Economy* (New York: W. W. Norton, 1944). For a supplementary account with a political emphasis, see James T. Patterson, *The New Deal and the States* (Princeton: Princeton University Press, 1969). Joseph P. Harris, "The Future of the Federal Grants in Aid," *Annals of the American Academy of Political and Social Science,* CCVII (Jan. 1940), 14–26, describes the haphazard growth of the federal grant programs. John Delafons, *Land-Use Controls in the United States* (Cambridge: Massachusetts Institute of Technology Press, 1969), is a British scholar's study of an important area of economic management. A generation after the New Deal, federalism, the reality of intergovernmental overlap in a nation of semisovereign states united in a federation, was described as a workable and resourceful system in Jane Perry Clark, *The Rise of a New Federalism* (New York: Columbia University Press, 1938), and Morton Grodzins, *The American System* (Chicago: Rand McNally, 1966; ed. by Daniel J. Elazar). James L. Sundquist and David W. Davis, in *Making Federalism Work* (Washington: Brookings, 1969), and William H. Riker, *Federalism* (Boston: Little, Brown, 1964), offer more critical perspectives. A perceptive overview is Rexford G. Tugwell and Edward C. Banfield, "Governmental Planning at Mid-Century," *Journal of Politics*, XIII (May 1951).

The New Dealers, of course, were not alone in attempting to manage American society through bureaucratic institutions and applied science. Scholars are increasingly aware that the study of public policy requires a broad social framework. Of the many books on organizational development and theory, an education begins with Roberto Michels, *Political Parties* (New York: Hearst's International Library Co., 1915); Ferdinand Tönnies, *Community and Society* (East Lansing: Michigan State University Press, 1957); and Max Weber, *Essays in Sociology* (New York: Oxford University Press, 1946; ed. by H. H. Gerth and C. Wright Mills); see also Bertram Gross, *The Managing of Organizations*, 2 vols. (New York: Free Press, 1964), a survey of theory and experience in organizational behavior, with a good bibliography; and Marion J. Levy, *Modernization and the Structure of Societies*, 2 vols. (Princeton: Princeton University Press, 1966), a theoretical and comparative introduction to modernization. Kenneth Boulding, *The Organizational Revolution* (New York: Harper and Brothers, 1956), is a long essay which analyzes the thrust of organization in recent years. Pioneering efforts by historians to utilize some of the insights from the literature on modernization include Robert Wiebe's *The Search for Order, 1877–1920* (New York: Hill and Wang, 1967); Alfred D. Chandler and Louis Galambos, "The Development of Large-Scale Economic Organizations in Modern America," *Journal of Economic History*, XXX (March 1970), 201–217; and Louis Galambos, "The Emerging Organizational Synthesis in Modern American History," *Business History Review*, XLIV (Autumn 1970), 279–290. An exceptionally valuable analysis with supporting data is W. Lloyd Warner et al., *The Emergent Ameri-*

can Society: Large Scale Organizations (New Haven: Yale University Press, 1967). Organizational developments in the business community are surveyed in Alfred D. Chandler, "The Large Industrial Corporation and the Making of the Modern American Economy," in Stephen E. Ambrose, ed., *Institutions in Modern America* (Baltimore: Johns Hopkins University Press, 1967); in U.S. Temporary National Economic Committee Monograph 18, *Trade Association Survey* (Washington, D.C.: Government Printing Office, 1941); and in Peter F. Drucker, *The Concept of the Corporation* (New York: John Day, 1946), a short and panegyric description of General Motors' innovations in corporate organization. The expansion of the use of social science research in industry is the subject of Loren Baritz, *Servants of Power* (Middletown, Conn.: Wesleyan University Press, 1960); Kendall Birr, *Pioneering Industrial Research* (Washington, D.C.: Public Affairs Press, 1957); and Matthew Radom, *The Social Scientist in American Industry* (New Brunswick: Rutgers University Press, 1970).

The reorganization of the executive branch for more effective management has been a major political and administrative issue since the days of Theodore Roosevelt, and the 1930s were particularly fertile in both ideas and action. Herbert Emmerich, *Essays on Federal Reorganization* (Huntsville: University of Alabama Press, 1950), and *Federal Organization and Administrative Management* (Huntsville: University of Alabama Press, 1971), are broad surveys of the issue by a leading student of public administration. Roosevelt's own problems are discussed in A. J. Wann, *The President as Chief Administrator* (Washington: Public Affairs Press, 1968). The story of the reorganization controversy of 1937–1939 is told in Richard Polenberg, *Reorganizing Roosevelt's Government* (Cambridge: Harvard University Press, 1966) and Barry D. Karl, *Executive Reorganization and Reform in the New Deal* (Cambridge: Harvard University Press, 1963). Fritz M. Marx, ed., *Public Management in the New Democ-*

racy (New York: Harper and Brothers, 1940), reflects the optimism of the new class of civil servants brought to influence during the 1930s. An important Rooseveltian contribution to management was the invigoration of the Bureau of the Budget and its assignment of coordinating tasks, which may be followed in John H. Reese, "The Role of the Bureau of the Budget in the Legislative Process," *Journal of Public Law*, XV (1966), 63–93. By the 1950s the inadequacies of the government's organization were glaringly apparent, and the executive reorganization issue stretched out through numerous commission studies and legislative battles. The major landmarks are the Hoover Commissions of 1949 and 1955, the Rockefeller Commission of 1953–1960, the Heineman Commission of 1966, and the Ashe Commission of 1969. For a review, see Harvey C. Mansfield, "Federal Executive Reorganization: Thirty Years of Experience," *Public Administration Review*, XXIX (July–Aug. 1969), 332–345. Despite occasional reforms, McGeorge Bundy, after his service under John F. Kennedy and Lyndon B. Johnson, was compelled to write a book about the weakness of the federal government, which he called, oddly enough, *The Strength of Government* (Cambridge: Harvard University Press, 1968).

Since the modern American political economy took on its mature outlines in the 1930s, the attempts to describe it have been divided into two general schools, which one might call the Favorable and the other the Critical. In praise of the American pluralist pattern, in which organized interest groups share power and contend for policy advantages in a setting of fragmented agencies, federalism, substantial decentralization of decisionmaking, and incremental rather than long-range planning, the following are the leading studies: John Chamberlain, *The American Stakes* (New York: Carrick and Evans, 1940); John Kenneth Galbraith, *American Capitalism* (New York: Houghton Mifflin, 1956); Morton Grodzins (cited above); Robert A. Dahl and Charles Lindblom, *Politics, Economics and Welfare* (New York: Harper and Brothers, 1953);

Charles Lindblom, "The Science of Muddling Through," *Public Administration Review*, XIX (Spring 1959), 79–88; Charles Lindblom and David Braybrooke, *A Strategy of Decision* (New York: Free Press, 1963); Charles Lindblom, *The Intelligence of Democracy* (New York: Free Press, 1966); and Aaron Wildavsky, *The Politics of the Budgetary Process* (Boston: Little, Brown, 1964).

Among the critics, there is a group who mistook the political economy of the 1930s as a dangerously centralized planning state, most notably Walter Lippmann, *The Good Society* (Boston: Little, Brown, 1937), and F. A. Hayek, *The Road to Serfdom* (Chicago: University of Chicago Press, 1944). This proved to be poor analysis and worse prophecy, and there subsequently developed a strong critical group with quite the opposite viewpoint, one which argued that the existing pluralist interest-group system was too fragmented and weak to protect the public interest. The classic studies here are E. Pendleton Herring, *Public Administration and the Public Interest* (New York: McGraw-Hill, 1936); Stuart Chase, *Democracy Under Pressure* (New York: Twentieth Century Fund, 1945); Rexford G. Tugwell and E. C. Banfield, "Grass Roots Democracy—Myth and Reality," *Public Administration Review*, X (Winter 1950), 47–55; Henry S. Kariel, *The Decline of American Pluralism* (Palo Alto: Stanford University Press, 1961); Michael D. Reagan, *The Managed Economy* (New York: Oxford University Press, 1963); Andrew Shonfield (cited above); Grant McConnell, *Private Power and American Democracy* (New York: Alfred A. Knopf, 1966); Charles L. Schultze, *The Politics and Economics of Public Spending* (Washington, D.C.: Brookings, 1968); Theodore J. Lowi, *The End of Liberalism* (New York: W. W. Norton, 1969); and the essays in William E. Connolly, ed., *The Bias of Pluralism* (New York: Atherton Press, 1969).

STANLEY ELKINS
and ERIC MC KITRICK

Richard Hofstadter: A Progress

I

THE PROCESS WHEREBY a truly innovative mind disengages itself from the web of its early surroundings can constitute a vastly absorbing subject. Conceivably such a disengagement may occur in more than one way. It may be effected convulsively, in a plenary act of repudiation—a conversion through which one mode of thought is replaced by another, frequently a kind of mirror image of its former self. But another way is not so much one of conversion as of subversion. A mind may simply grow away from the setting in which it was formed, one set of intellectual habits being steadily and persistently undermined by new ones. Occurring over time, rather than suddenly, the process is more intricate and less dramatic, yet it may be less wasteful and more thorough. A mind thus involved keeps many anomalies and divergences in balance, and sets up tensions that may be vivifying and regenerative. It is with such a mind that we are concerned here.[1]

The study of American history, when Richard Hofstadter first became attracted to it in the mid-1930s, was dominated by what might be called the "Progressive" mode. A governing assumption of that mode was that the movement of history exhibited an essentially adversarial quality: its dynamic element was conflict—conflict of an ongoing kind among the various basic interests the society contains. Ideas, to the extent that ideas mattered at all, were conceived in an instrumental character. Their value was measured mainly by the utility they might have in the achievement of worthy social, economic, and political ends, generally in the face of entrenched resistance. This

---

[1] We are not the first to undertake one or another aspect of this subject. Arthur Schlesinger, Jr.'s thoughtful essay, "Richard Hofstadter," in Marcus Cunliffe and Robin Winks, eds., *Pastmasters: Some Essays on American Historians* (New York, 1969), pp. 278–315, is one such effort, the most systematic to date, though written at a time when it could still be assumed of Hofstadter's work that many years of it remained before him. Christopher Lasch, "On Richard Hofstadter," *New York Review of Books*, XX (March 8, 1973), 7–13, designed as the Introduction to a new edition of *The American Political Tradition*, contains insights that apply well beyond that single work. Lawrence Cremin's brief pamphlet, *Richard Hofstadter (1916–1970): A Biographical Memoir* (Syracuse, 1972), is among other things an appreciation of Hofstadter's contribution to the literature on education in America. Tributes from close personal friends are Alfred Kazin, "Richard Hofstadter, 1916–1970," in *American Scholar*, XL (Summer 1971), 397–401; C. Vann Woodward, "Richard Hofstadter, 1916–1970," *New York Review of Books*, XV (Dec. 3, 1970), 10; J. R. Pole, "Richard Hofstadter, 1916–1970," *Journal of American Studies*, IV (Feb. 1971), 215–216; and Fritz Stern, "In Memoriam: Richard Hofstadter, 1916–1970," Columbia *Daily Spectator*, Oct. 29, 1970. The obituary in the New York *Times* (Oct. 25, 1970) was based in part on information which those closest to Hofstadter regarded as questionable, and it prompted a letter to the editor by Lionel Trilling which appeared in the *Times* on November 5.

way of dealing with ideas in American history emerged in the early years of the twentieth century—the so-called Progressive Era—and its most notable exponents were Charles A. Beard and Vernon L. Parrington.

Viewing the entire corpus of Richard Hofstadter's work, now that it has been completed and his career closed, one can think of reasons for concluding that the Progressive mode never did exercise much of a hold over him. He could not seriously conceive of means and ends in so mechanistic a way; he could not treat ideas as "tools" or "weapons." Nor, on the other hand, did he regard ideas as entities in themselves, though few took greater pleasure than he in analyzing them, and few were more skilled at doing so. But ideas are one thing, while mind in motion, with all its stratagems, advances, and reverses, can be quite another. It was this that came to preoccupy him: the varying conditions under which mind itself has been obliged to function in this culture, a problem with which Beard and Parrington were but little concerned. It hardly excluded a sensitivity on Hofstadter's part to what was desirable in the way of social policy. But it did mean that his attention was forever being drawn to the way in which people who professed given ideas actually behaved, and to the circumstances which may have rendered such ideas attractive to them. To Beard and most other Progressives this had largely been a matter of utility, of self- and group interest. But for Hofstadter the category of "interest" came to be so widened and diversified—extending to such complex items as status, personality, and career—that it added up to something of a qualitatively different order from anything he could have taken from the intellectual environment of his early maturity. His province was the entire landscape of mind in its specific American historical setting.

And yet to begin any discussion of Hofstadter's work in this vein is to miss some of the dialectic—indeed, the drama—of his own mind. There is little sign of his having been, when he wrote his first book, in anything like a state of rebellion against the "Progressive" mentality that still conditioned the teaching and writing of American history in the late 1930s and early forties. For that matter, his *Social Darwinism in American Thought*—written between 1940 and 1942 and published in 1944—would not have been what it was had it not been for the strong infusion of Progressivism which in fact went into it.

It is not difficult, on the other hand, to imagine that Richard Hofstadter, though his choices were to lead him elsewhere, might well have made a distinguished career for himself as a historian of ideas. *Social Darwinism* describes the impact that Charles Darwin's scientific discoveries had in America upon ways of thinking outside scientific circles. Darwin's authority, mediated in large part through the immensely popular writings of Herbert Spencer and through such arresting tag-formulas as "struggle for existence" and "survival of the fittest," seemed to impart the same impersonal sanctions to the workings of human society as those which presumably governed the brute realm of nature. "Darwinism" in the Gilded Age could be invoked as a "scientific" warrant for laissez-faire orthodoxy in business enterprise—the "naturalness" of tooth-and-claw competition—and for a conservative outlook on all schemes of "artificially" legislated social reform. Darwinian ideas were put to these very uses by such otherwise disparate personalities as the Yale social scientist William Graham Sumner and the industrialist Andrew Carnegie. It was only after sustained assaults by social theorists, philosophers, and reformers—beginning in the nineties and continuing into the early twentieth century—that Darwinism came to be discredited once and for all as a serious theoretical basis for the understanding of social processes. Among the earliest of these critics was the pioneering sociologist Lester Ward, who saw no meaningful continuity between the anarchic wastefulness of nature and the purposive collective planning of which human society was capable. Edward A. Ross, a thoroughly Progressive thinker, declared that the specious analogy between natural selection and the economic process was "a caricature of Darwinism, invented to justify the ruthless practices of business men." [2]

Hofstadter's book was a spirited account of the life, movement, and interpenetration of ideas; it also showed an extraordinary adeptness at setting forth lucid and compact expositions of ponderous bodies of thought. In this respect there is something virtuoso-like in his rendering of Herbert Spencer's "cosmic philosophy," a grand synthesis of the laws of the natural and human universe, replete with a moral system and joined together by all the latest findings in physics and biology.

But Hofstadter's *Social Darwinism,* for all its dexterity, was still an exercise in the Progressive mode. Not that this operated as an obvious restriction; it may even have contributed to the book's vivacity. And the book's terminal point lies, appropriately enough, in the Progressive Era itself: the final eclipse of Social Darwinism exactly corresponds in time with the emergence of a style of social thought which became one of the distinguishing marks of Progressivism. Nevertheless, this correspondence may have served to lower Hofstadter's guard against certain questionable inferences he would not have been guilty of later on, when he would no longer be constrained by the exigencies of an adversarial framework which required that the forces of conservatism and orthodoxy be ranged in order of battle against those of enlightenment and innovation. For example, though a "vogue of Spencer" [3] certainly occurred, the fascinations of Spencer probably owed a

[2] *Social Darwinism in American Thought* (Philadelphia, 1944), p. 137. It should probably be underlined that the Progressives repudiated not Darwinism but this particular perversion of Darwinian ideas—a distinction Hofstadter sometimes allowed to blur. Like most critics of Social Darwinism, Ward and Ross were themselves convinced evolutionists; they even perceived, as did Dewey and Veblen, that Darwinian theory might be applied to social problems in a positive as well as a negative way.

[3] "The Vogue of Spencer" was one of his chapter titles.

good deal more to the "cosmic philosophy" side of his work than to its explicitly Darwinian furnishings. Nor is there much evidence that the business world itself—aside from Andrew Carnegie, who was in every way exceptional—ever took up Darwinism in any systematic way, or would have known what to do with it if it had. The academician William Graham Sumner of course did, but Sumner too was an exception. He was the only American intellectual of the first rank to expound a truly Social Darwinist system, and even he never regarded himself as a spokesman for the plutocracy. If he had, few captains of industry would have been very comfortable with him anyway, in the light of his perverse views on the protective tariff.[4]

It may well be, in short, that the enemy—"Social Darwinism"—was to some degree created by the Progressives themselves, or at least imagined as bigger than it was, that they might take the greater satisfaction in cutting it down. This would not be the first issue in American history ("monarchy," universal suffrage, and imprisonment for debt are others that come to mind) to which such things had happened.

Yet after all this is duly noted, one still detects more than just a few signs scattered throughout Richard Hofstadter's first book to hint that the Progressive mode could never finally contain a spirit of his sort. His sense of irony, his appreciation of the complexities and contrarieties in human affairs, were already at work. He seemed already—to a degree that Parrington, for one, never achieved—to sense the inconsistencies of American "conservatism," and the paradox that men politically of the "right" could so often be daring innovators in other realms. Nor could he in full seriousness line up his good troops and bad in disciplined opposition and make them behave, even for a

---

[4] A view of Darwinism which makes a number of these points is R. Jackson Wilson, "Darwinism and Social Ethics: Introduction," in Wilson, ed., *Darwinism and the American Intellectual* (Homewood, Ill., 1967), pp. 93–106.

short segment of American history—as Parrington was determined to do for the whole span of it. William Graham Sumner, for example, his most obvious champion of the wrong, would not stay in his pigeonhole, and the young author's efforts to keep him there were almost indulgently half-hearted. He was only too aware that for all Sumner's reactionary ravings, his influence in the field of education "was always progressive," [5] and that with his free-trade convictions and detestation of imperialism, Sumner as general-in-chief for the forces of political orthodoxy and business Darwinism would have been quite hopeless. Moreover, the underside of Progressivism itself—with its racist themes of Anglo-Saxonism which Hofstadter despised—was exposed by him for what it was. And finally, his concluding observation on the role of ideas in history reads rather more like a statement from Mannheim on ideology than one from Beard, or from any other Progressive, on ideas as instruments of utility or convenience: "In determining whether such ideas are accepted, truth and logic are less important than their suitability to the intellectual needs and preconceptions of social interests. This is one of the great difficulties that must be faced by rational strategists of social change." [6]

II

Hofstadter actually started out (as he himself recalled a number of years later) with two broad lines of interest in

---

[5] *Social Darwinism,* p. 47.

[6] *Ibid.*, p. 176. On the face of it, this phrase might seem not unlike some of those to be found, say, in Beard's *Economic Interpretation of the Constitution.* Yet it represents in our opinion a transitional formulation, the key term being "*intellectual* needs and perceptions" (our emphasis): a question which never fully engaged Beard's attention.

history. One was the history of ideas, and the other "what might be called orthodox political history." [7] Yet he felt no great urgency about seeing them brought together, or even in considering whether they could or should be. He realized retrospectively that his keenest interests lay in neither of these categories, precisely speaking, but in a marginal realm that lay somewhere in between. He wanted to explore the conditions under which men think, and the values that set bounds to what and how they think, and to him one of the most fascinating fields in which this might be observed was politics.

Between no two of his books was there a sharper break, a transition more truly dramatic, than that between *Social Darwinism* and *The American Political Tradition*. In Hofstadter's second book, which appeared in 1948, the essay form emerged as the vehicle in which his powers would be at their freest. In twelve portraits of individuals and (in two cases) groups of individuals, he offered reassessments of leading political figures from the Founding Fathers to Franklin D. Roosevelt, and of the ideas, aspirations, and values they had lived by. "These portraits," he wrote, "are not painted in roseate colors. I am here analyzing men of action in their capacity as leaders of popular thought, which is not their most impressive function." But neither a new subject matter nor a newly perfected vehicle can fully account for the energy that characterized this work, an energy that had direct consequences for style. His prose had acquired both economy and a new velocity; it now crackled with confidence, wit, and a sense of mastery. Meeting Richard Hofstadter face to face at that period, after reading his book, one was astonished. The absence of personal contentiousness or of self-assertiveness in the man accorded not at all with the most striking quality in the writing: the assurance of a mind that is on

[7] "History and the Social Sciences," in Fritz Stern, ed., *The Varieties of History: From Voltaire to the Present* (New York, 1956), p. 359.

top of its subject and that delights in itself.[8] *Social Darwinism,* whatever its virtues, had been built on an inherently finite idea. *The American Political Tradition* seemed built on an inspiration, one that might be indefinitely expanded, and this showed on nearly every page.[9]

Hofstadter's new style was the product of—among other things—two major changes in his way of handling ideas. One was that Mannheim's sociology of knowledge, which had appeared as no more than a hint at the very end of *Social Darwinism,* had by now been fully internalized. The other was that a significant item of Progressive baggage, the "conflict" formula for dealing with movements of change in American life, had been all but dropped. Hofstadter had become convinced "of the need for a reinterpretation of our political traditions which emphasizes the common climate of American opinion," the existence of which had been "much obscured by the tend-

[8] *The American Political Tradition and the Men Who Made It* (New York, 1948), p. x. An important factor in accounting for the full emergence of Hofstadter's talent at this time, in addition to those discussed in the paragraphs that follow, was his marriage to Beatrice Kevitt in 1947. Mrs. Hofstadter's own sensitivity to style and her exceptional editorial gifts were of immeasurable assistance to him for the remainder of his life. The phrase about mind "delighting in itself" is borrowed—with thanks—from Lionel Trilling, who has used it several times in his own writings, most recently in *Mind in the Modern World: The 1972 Jefferson Lecture in the Humanities* (New York, 1973), p. 41. A number of those who heard this lecture in the spring of 1972 were struck by the extent to which it seemed to characterize the values by which Richard Hofstadter had lived—a coincidence, it appears, which was by no means unintended.

[9] It appears that Hofstadter had at the outset no grand design for his book; he had already done two or three essays when a Knopf editor encouraged him to write some more, so that in a way the book simply grew. But it grew logically and cumulatively, and, in a more basic sense purposefully, out of certain convictions he had reached about the intellectual coercions which the values of a bourgeois capitalist society can place upon the society's political leaders.

ency to place political conflict in the foreground. . . ."[10]

The significance of these two changes—what the connection between them was, and why they should have made such a difference—should be underlined. The Progressives did have at least the rudiments of a sociology of knowledge; they certainly perceived some relationship between ideas and interests. But the relationship was almost always rationalistic and reductionist, amounting to little more than the pleasure-pain calculus of classical political economy. Mannheim's conception was vastly broader and richer, embracing a whole range of elements, irrational as well as rational, matters of style and status as well as "interests" narrowly construed, which derived from a man's "position in time and society." Mannheim thought it useless to abstract for analysis arbitrarily selected items from that "position": one must try first to see it whole. The Progressives, moreover, generally did not even apply their own relatively crude scheme symmetrically. That is, one side in a conflict of ideas (the approved side) they tended to exempt from any rigorous scrutiny, evidently on the ground that the holding of ideas intrinsically meritorious requires no explanation. It was the other side that was presumed to think and behave only in accordance with its "interests." Needless to say, the impression of something pejorative about such behavior was difficult to avoid. Mannheim's categories, on the other hand, offered no such difficulty. They represented something not only greatly extended but impartially applied.[11]

It was then but a step to the discovery that when such criteria were extended to the disputes of American political life, the "combatants" would be found more often than not to be occupying much the same ground, their contentions

---

[10] *American Political Tradition*, p. vii.

[11] Karl Mannheim, *Ideology and Utopia: An Introduction to the Sociology of Knowledge*, trans. by Louis Wirth and Edward Shils (New York, 1968), especially pp. 264 ff. Hofstadter's debt to Mannheim is acknowledged in "History and the Social Sciences," pp. 361–362.

generally limited within the same fund of basic ideas and assumptions. This "common climate," which was made the master concept of *The American Political Tradition*, would come to be stigmatized many years later as "consensus history," a new and pernicious form of conservatism. But it was received in no such way at the time. Some did find the book shocking, but not on those grounds. Indeed, it was in certain ways a radical venture, owing more than a little to Marxist influences [12] as well as to Mannheim. And any analysis of American society in the combined spirit of Marx and Mannheim could hardly fail to disclose a bourgeois culture informed by bourgeois assumptions—the rights of property and the values of opportunity, self-interest, and self-assertion "within broad legal limits."

> Almost the entire span of American history under the present Constitution has coincided with the rise and spread of modern industrial capitalism. In material power and productivity the United States has been a flourishing success. Societies that are in such good working order have a kind of mute organic consistency. They do not foster ideas that are hostile to their fundamental working arrangements. Such ideas may appear, but they are slowly and persistently insulated, as an oyster deposits nacre around an irritant.[13]

Hofstadter found the "common climate" theme profoundly liberating in more than one way. Paradoxically, rather than "homogenizing" the subjects of his portraits

---

[12] Hofstadter had been well exposed to Marx's writings in the late 1930s and early 1940s. But as with anything else he allowed to "influence" him, Marxist ideas were admitted selectively—and here one may suspect that it almost required Mannheim to activate Marx, and to make Marx usable for him. Compare, e.g., the "Almost the entire span" passage quoted above with Karl Marx, "The Eighteenth Brumaire of Louis Bonaparte," in Emile Burns, ed., *A Handbook of Marxism* (New York, 1935), p. 128.

[13] *American Political Tradition*, pp. viii–ix.

it left him free to take account of their idiosyncrasies and their individuality. He was not constrained to find places for them in one or the other of opposing camps. By the same token he was not inhibited by the impulse to take sides himself, the need to be indulgent with one side and to blast away at the other. He could now, with impartial relish, take shots at everyone, and this—together with the tone of skeptical raillery—was what seemed a bit shocking. With the pieties laid aside, a diverse gallery of personages was exposed, and they found themselves nicked in unexpected places.

The variety of personalities and cases, the not wholly familiar essay form in which they were considered, and the deftness with which a great deal of material could somehow be accommodated in very brief compass gave to the book a deceptive air of both lightness and diffuseness. The impression was misleading, for there was a consistent line of demonstration and argument throughout. One saw, with fascinating variations from one essay to the next, the enveloping character of the values of a capitalist society: the intricate relatedness of those values, their enormous coerciveness, the limited extent to which individuals—whatever their point of departure—can achieve any distance from them (and the deceptions to which they are subject when they imagine that they have), and the ingenious quarantines which the society can devise—as in the cases of Calhoun and Wendell Phillips—for anyone who does reach, however contortedly, a posture of deviance.

It all made for a series of observations fresh and new for the times, sharply suggestive and in some cases brilliantly original. The Jacksonian movement was seen not simply as the "rise of the common man," where previous analysis had typically stopped, but also as something closely connected—as "a phase in the expansion of liberated capitalism." John C. Calhoun, perceiving the encroachments of aggressive industrial capitalism upon the world of slavery, becomes by a kind of curious inversion the "Marx of the Master Class." Abraham Lincoln is still a tragic figure, but on very different grounds from those of the Lincoln legend. He fell victim to that very self-made myth of the society that produced him and by which he lived: his driving ambition ("a little engine," as Herndon had put it, "that knew no rest") brought him at last to its pinnacle, the White House, where he found only "ashes and blood." The New Deal was the triumph of no articulated liberal theory and no scheme of systematic planning. Its leader was a man of no profound convictions, no prior suspicion that there were any basic defects in the capitalist system, and no economic knowledge whatever. Yet FDR was by the same token a man both amiable and receptive, willing to try anything, confident that "he could do no wrong," and able to say "my old friend" in "eleven languages."

"It is," one reviewer mildly observed, "a book without a hero." True enough, and though few of the author's darts were really poisoned, he did manage to toss them with a certain glee. Nobody of Thomas Jefferson's social status "could be quite the democrat Jefferson imagined himself." "A man like Jackson who had been on the conservative side of economic issues in Tennessee could become the leader of a national democratic movement without feeling guilty of any inconsistency." Calhoun was something of a self-exile from the main currents of American thought. He was "a minority spokesman in a democracy, a particularist in an age of nationalism, a slaveholder in an age of advancing liberties, and an agrarian in a furiously capitalistic country. Quite understandably he developed a certain perversity of mind." Grover Cleveland (whose career had recently been called by a distinguished historian "a study in courage") was "a taxpayer's dream, the ideal bourgeois statesman for his time: out of heartfelt conviction he gave to the interests what many a lesser politician might have sold them for a price." And so into the twentieth century. William Jennings Bryan "in an important psychological sense . . . was never a rebel at all—and this is a clue to the torpor of his mind." After the First World War

Bryan "became a publicity agent for the real estate interests, in which capacity his incurable vulgarity stood him in good stead." The speeches of Woodrow Wilson, urging a return to the competitive past, "sound like the collective wail of the American middle class." [14]

When the theme was tragedy, on the other hand, Hofstadter could rise to it with controlled dignity, as in the case of Lincoln's presidency: "As the months passed, a deathly weariness settled over him. Once when Noah Brooks suggested that he rest, he replied: 'I suppose it is good for the body. But the tired part of me is *inside* and out of reach.' There had always been a part of him, inside and out of reach, that had looked upon his ambition with detachment and wondered if the game was worth the candle." [15]

A final point, however, must be that while the key element of the Progressive mode—the "conflict" formula—was now virtually abandoned, this did not quite mean that Progressive influences had been entirely banished from Hofstadter's conceptual habits. Occasional traces remain, such as the faintly gratuitous "it has been a democracy in cupidity rather than a democracy of fraternity"—two qualities which are hardly bound to exclude each other. Another is the opening essay on the Founding Fathers ("An Age of Realism") and their conviction that man "was a creature of rapacious self-interest"—to which Charles A. Beard himself could hardly have objected.[16] Indeed, here we see Beard still being quoted with approval; here was one point at which Beard's spirit and Hofstadter's overall purposes still showed a semblance of congruity. It was not until the writing of Hofstadter's next major book on popular political culture, *The Age of Reform*, that the

---

[14] Quotations, in order, from C. Vann Woodward, in *Mississippi Valley Historical Review*, XXXV (March 1949), 682; *American Political Tradition*, pp. 19, 47, 90, 182, 190, 199, 251.

[15] *Ibid.*, p. 134.

[16] *Ibid.*, pp. viii, 16.

last vestiges of Beard's influence—at one time so considerable and so coercive—would be fully dissipated.

III

If the "common climate" device could serve as a release in the effort to examine individuals across the span of the American political past, the same device, or perhaps variations upon it, might be just as liberating when applied not only to individuals but also to whole groups and movements within a given segment of the past. Such proved to be the case with *The Age of Reform.* This book, which came out in 1955 and won a Pulitzer prize the following year, established Richard Hofstadter as a leading historian of his generation. Its appearance may also have done more than any comparable event of its decade to furnish for an emerging generation of historians not so much new knowledge as a new example. "To those of us who encountered *The Age of Reform* in graduate school," recalls Robert Wiebe, "he, more than any other writer, framed the problems, explored the techniques, and established the model of literate inquiry that would condition our study of the American past."[17]

There was a certain logic and appropriateness in both the subject and the period. The scope included the years 1890–1940, though the main attention was given to Populism and Progressivism, with a final chapter contrasting the latter movement to the New Deal. This was also the period that had produced the major eminences of modern historical writing—Beard, Parrington, and Turner, whose work had once so engaged Hofstadter's imagination. Reform was one of the great preoccupations of that era, and the patterns of thought within which historians had written about reform movements were inherited from that same era. To think of reform as the direct outcome of

[17] "Views But No Vista," *The Progressive,* XXXIII (Feb. 1969), 47.

"conflict" politics still seemed the common sense of the matter. The struggle may have been between one self-conscious interest group and another, or between regions, or between the forces of democracy and those of vested property, but the primary fact was always that of struggle.

This would seem especially to have been the case with the agrarian uprisings of the nineties. Progressive writers and others following in their spirit, for the most part sympathetic to the Populist movement, had pictured it in just such an adversarial way. But Hofstadter's skepticism had already warned him that an approach of this sort had its limits. He could no longer be satisfied with any simple linear version of what he knew to be an extremely complex social and economic process. Simply to see the Populists as responding to economic injustice in a posture of embattled virtue, armed with a reasoned, comprehensive program of remedies and reforms only to be overborne by the powers of industrial and moneyed capital, would be to rehearse old formulas and make few new discoveries. Hofstadter suspected that there were better ways of going about it, and that there were things still to be learned about popular movements in general and this one in particular.

Besides, he was still fascinated, as always, by ideas. He wanted to examine the mental picture the participants had of themselves and of what they were doing, and how they visualized the forces that were resisting them. His study of Mannheim had persuaded him that ideas are by no means a direct and uncomplicated reflection of "interest." They may also reflect for individuals and groups—perhaps through habit or historical inheritance—an ideal version of the world and of their own rightful place in it, complicated by the dissonances between that world and the world as it is. Hofstadter, turning to the Populist movement, was thus prepared for a whole series of incongruities, and prepared also for the effort that would be required to make sense out of them.

He saw a number of gross disjunctions. The Populist

self-image drew heavily upon the Jeffersonian vision of the worthy husbandman and the family farm, but in fact the American farmer was more a bedeviled rural businessman than an independent yeoman struggling to ward off the hostile forces of capitalism. In the Populists' rhetorical gestures, moreover, there was a narrowness and bigotry that accorded neither with their own self-image nor with the benign accounts that had subsequently been written of them. Nor did the Populists really measure up as representatives of a general reforming system. In their crabbed parochialism they had little sympathy with industrial labor, little use for the immigrant, little understanding of the problems of the city; and when they did get control of a state government or two they failed to do anything important. Finally, there was the disjunction between the political battles they fought and subsequent events. The total defeat of the People's party in 1896 did not have the kind of economic consequences one would expect from the repression and summary expulsion of a major class interest. The steady upturn in rural prosperity, beginning in 1896, reached in the years 1909–1914 a plateau which put American agriculture in the best position vis-à-vis other elements in the nation's economy that it had known since the Civil War, or would know again before World War II.

To fashion a device for managing these disjunctions —between perception and actuality, words and behavior, actions and consequences—Hofstadter postulated a "hard" and a "soft" side to the American farmer's mentality, and showed him as being activated not solely by one side or the other, but by both. It was the "soft" side that was so vulnerable to the Jeffersonian myth, the ideal of the "non-commercial, non-pecuniary, self-sufficient" yeoman dwelling in a rural arcadia of unspoiled virtue, honest toil, and rude plenty. It was this side, too, that could harbor all manner of anxieties, self-delusions, ignorance, xenophobia, sadistic fantasies, and wild visions of international conspiracy which pictured cabals of Jewish bankers about to take charge of the world. But from the "hard" side of his outlook the farmer saw the pecuniary character of his interests, and learned to act on them effectively. This meant business methods and, in time, pressure politics. On this side the farmer was neither a passive victim nor an embattled opponent but an integral part of the very system, the very complex of forces he otherwise imagined himself as combating: he was an active entrepreneur faced with a falling market. Had he truly been a Jeffersonian yeoman, he would neither have suffered so greatly nor afterward benefited so much. That is, it was his entrepreneurial, his "hard," side that had contributed most to the predicament he found himself in during the middle nineties, with the heavy investments he had made in land and machinery for increasing his productivity—but it was that same side that enabled him to cash in later, when the market improved. Many elements of the Populist program eventually found their way into law. The leading one, however, which was free silver, did not. It was also the "softest." The "hardest," the subtreasury plan, became a key feature of the New Deal's "Ever-Normal Granary" system. By that time a powerful agricultural lobby had long since come into being, as "hard" as could be, to show among other things what real "interest" politics could accomplish.

Before turning to his treatment of Progressivism, we should take some account of another influence. This was the example set, in the analysis of social structure and process, by one of Hofstadter's Columbia colleagues, Robert K. Merton.

Karl Mannheim had done much to redefine the "field" in which ideas and action occur, and to indicate with enhanced precision the relationships these bear to one another. But it was Merton, with the system now so closely associated with his name and which he called "functional analysis," who proved immensely suggestive with regard to ways of expressing and accounting for movement and change. Merton insisted that the "functional approach" was "neither new nor confined to the social sciences," [18] that it had been forced by cumulative experience upon every aspect of the study of man, and that his own interest was not so much in inventing new methods as in codifying what was already there—though "there" in considerable disarray—in the way of theory, method, and data. He was concerned with the procedures of qualitative analysis in sociology, social psychology, and social anthropology. And "codification," for all Merton's deprecatory modesty, proved to be a major creative act.

Perhaps no single concept among those so codified had a more pervasive effect in the border regions between the humanities and social sciences than the idea of "manifest and latent functions." Merton observed that in any "system," or patterned sequence of social action, may be discerned a variety of objective consequences, or "functions," by no means all of which are intended or even recognized. It is necessary on the one hand to make a conceptual distinction between the "manifest functions"—those consequences more or less consciously intended—and the "latent functions," those which are not. The heuristic benefit of such a distinction is that it can clarify the analysis of seemingly irrational social patterns. On the other hand, no discriminations of value are to be made between any functions, manifest or latent, at least for purposes of analysis: analytically all are value-neutral. Merton's most arresting example—since become something of a classic—was the latent functions performed by the urban political machine.[19]

---

[18] Robert K. Merton, *Social Theory and Social Structure: Toward the Codification of Theory and Research* (Glencoe, Ill., 1949), p. 47.

[19] Such functions included personalized welfare services, mobility for otherwise excluded social groups, and the umpiring and regulation of both legitimate and illegitimate business. *Ibid.*, pp. 73–81. On the other hand, an important voice from the social sciences to which Hofstadter did *not* respond until later on, as Robert Cross has reminded us, was that of Emile Durkheim. This

What functional analysis did for receptive historians was not so much to provide a specific methodology as to encourage and ratify an altered style of thought, a reordered intellectual economy. It made room for complexity and paradox, and put a high premium on subtlety. At the same time it suggested a mode of informal bookkeeping for the management of otherwise refractory, elusive, and unwieldy data. Hofstadter, for one, never adopted functional analysis in any self-conscious way as a formal theoretical system; he simply absorbed it into his literary habits. The absorption was well advanced by the time *The Age of Reform* was under way. The manifest functions of reform movements were well enough known. But their latent functions—some of which may well have been the products of unannounced, even unsuspected motivations—would bear exploring.

As he turned to Progressivism and the diverse activities associated with the Progressive movement, Hofstadter was struck by a series of paradoxes that did not lend themselves to simple explanations. One was the strong impulse for reform in a period of prosperity; another was the seeming absence, in many of the spokesmen for Progressivism, of clear class or interest motivations. Still another was the striking disproportion between emotions and objectives, and between professed aims and actual accomplishments. The general problem was to locate the varied sources of reform energy, to consider the devices used, and to analyze the style in which reform was addressed. Why, over and beyond their professed motives, did so many go about it with such intensity? What kinds of satisfactions did they experience, what kinds of strains might they have been seeking to alleviate?

Hofstadter made his account multidimensional rather

omission, Professor Cross says, "seems to me important for his early heavy-handed treatment of religious behavior and belief from which he had been at some point in his life too easily liberated." Letter to editors, Aug. 13, 1973.

than linear; the explanation he offered for the special character of the Progressive impulse was a constellation of both subjective and objective forces. One set of these may be grouped under the general heading of status.[20] In the two or three decades prior to the opening of the twentieth century profound alterations had been effected in individual, group, professional, and civic relationships from what they had been, or were imagined to have been, in the past. This "status upheaval," as Hofstadter called it, had brought with it a revised perception of society and one's own role in it; it had created new tensions and a new sense of urgency respecting ills to correct, adjustments to make, balances to restore. It had issued from a variety of causes and had a variety of consequences. There had been a vast expansion of the salaried and professional middle class; in prestige and deference some statuses (such as the academic) had risen; others (lawyers and clergy) had relatively declined; and what all this meant, if it had no other consequence, was a great broadening as well as transforming of the old civic-minded "mugwump" constituency. The accelerated trustification of industry in the nineties had meanwhile helped create new powers in the land and a new contingent of multimillionaires, nourishing the suspicions of all classes, not excluding that suspicion which old wealth perennially has of new. All of which made for an immense reservoir of undifferentiated but nonetheless real anxiety and resentment—and of potential reforming zeal—generally aimed at new bigness, new power, and new money. Nor could status tensions, especially among a somewhat hard-pressed middle class, have been much helped after the traumas of the nineties by the steady price inflation which began with the turn of the century. (The following decade, with its agitations over tariff and pure food and drug laws, saw the first appearance of "consumer politics.") And finally, the high tide of

[20] For further discussion of the "status" idea, see below, pp. 339–343.

immigration, directly connected—or so it seemed—with an aggravation of urban disorder, corruption, and bossism, placed a variety of psychic pressures on the old-stock native American element. Civic reform in the Progressive Era had a noticeable tinge of nativism.

A second explanatory device Hofstadter used, in addition to that of status, had to do with the functions of responsibility and guilt. The great civic enemy, it was widely believed, that must somehow be overcome and subdued was "the interests," which was quite in line with the adversarial mentality of Progressivism. And yet there was also to be perceived in popular literature a theme that may have gone even deeper: the real enemy was ourselves. Intellectuals of the period might want to picture social change as a matter of battling classes and interests (though even they would have occasional difficulty sustaining this line), but the popular image of American society at this same period seems to have been that of a body which, though basically sound, was plagued by corruptions and in need of purgation. Thus the trusts, the bosses, the "interests," while certainly real enough in their way, were also symbolic. They symbolized *our* failures, *our* lapses, the evils we in our sloth had allowed to grow up in our midst. So the call to reform was not so much a matter of one group accusing another as of a whole society accusing itself—appealing to its own Protestant conscience, its sense of responsibility, its own capacity for guilt.

A final, and closely related, category of explanation involved the psychology of exposure and the Progressive concept of "reality." Lionel Trilling, in a discussion of Parrington and literary realism, had recently observed that to this type of mind "reality" tended generally to mean something "hard" and "unpleasant." Hofstadter pounced on this insight, extended its implications, and applied it to the entire popular metaphysic of Progressivism. "Reality" was not only unpleasant; it tended also to be *hidden*—and this seemed further to hint that it would turn out, as often as not, to be bad. "Reality," indeed, "was the bribe, the rebate, the bought franchise, the sale of adulterated food. It was what one found in *The Jungle, The Octopus, Wealth against Commonwealth,* or *The Shame of the Cities.* . . . Reality was a series of unspeakable plots, personal iniquities, moral failures, which, in their totality, had come to govern American society only because the citizen had relaxed his moral vigilance."[21] Here, then, was the functional link to the phenomenon of muckraking, as well as an important key to its significance. The indispensable first step toward the reforming of an evil (since evils were always hidden) was to expose it. An extraordinary proportion of reformist energy did in fact go into this aspect of reform—the literature of exposure, getting the "inside story"—and it is perhaps not too much to say, in view of the comparative modesty of the objective results, that a disproportionate share of the satisfactions came from the same source. When Lincoln Steffens began muckraking American cities in *McClure's,* he received hundreds of enthusiastic letters from citizens in other places: "Come and show us up; we're worse than they are." Muckraking, of course, was a laying out of the facts, in order that the object might be seen and understood. But it was something else as well; it had a latent function. It was *self*-exposure, a vicarious form of confession and relief, a purgation in its own right.

The Age of Reform had an effect which might best be described as seismic. Most of the shocks—certainly the initial ones—were salutary and inspiriting, the reception being generally one of excited welcome. But there were delayed tremors that were not so salutary. Hofstadter had by now detached himself all but completely from the Progressive mode, and those for whom he served as a monitor were just as glad to close the accounts on it once and for

[21] *The Age of Reform: From Bryan to F.D.R.* (New York, 1955), p. 200; cf. Lionel Trilling, "Reality in America," in *The Liberal Imagination: Essays on Literature and Society* (New York, 1950), pp. 3–21.

all. But things would prove to be not quite that simple; that mode had struck its roots very deep. (It may represent, even now, something fundamental in the American historical consciousness.) At the very least it was not to be undermined without some aftermath of resentment.

One of the reviews, by William Appleman Williams, gave a foretaste of what was to come a few years later on when this resentment had had time to collect itself. *The Age of Reform,* Williams said, was "not History" but rather a present-minded neoconservative argument, "delivered in a stage whisper," which "amounts to an extensive criticism of radicals." Williams was also offended by Hofstadter's use of social science concepts—especially with regard to status—at the expense of research in "the primary sources." These complaints prefigured most of the subsequent criticism.[22]

---

[22] William A. Williams, "The Age of Re-Forming History," *Nation,* CLXXXII (June 30, 1956), 554. Some have also taken exception to Hofstadter's handling of the New Deal in *The Age of Reform.* The same analysis which he applied to the Progressive reform impulse might have been applied to the New Deal as well; instead, he chose to represent the New Deal as a break with the past, to emphasize interest politics, and to concede a primary role to the expert and technician rather than to the Progressive-type reformer.

There may be a case for questioning such an approach (the present authors recall having questioned it themselves when the book was in manuscript): sufficiently similar reformist elements are discernible in both periods to warrant stressing a strong line of continuity between them. Hofstadter, however, believed that the conditions of the 1930s were sufficiently unprecedented—the overwhelming economic pressures created by the depression, together with the willingness to accept major intervention by government in matters of economic and social policy—to justify treating the New Deal as a unique phase in the American experience.

But however one may come down on the question, the fact remains that this section of *The Age of Reform,* being something of an afterthought with many elements of obiter dictum, did not represent a level of analysis in any way comparable to what went into the sections

The criticism began to accumulate in the early 1960s. Other works had by then appeared, also emphasizing the unities rather than the divisions of American life, and critics had devised the pejorative category "consensus history" in which to group them. They had postulated a "school," and installed Hofstadter himself in it. The "consensus" attitude in *The Age of Reform,* they were now saying, had led Hofstadter to minimize the sharpness of the issues which the Populists and Progressives confronted and the seriousness of the struggles in which they engaged.[23] Another line of attack was directed at Hofstadter's "status" concept as a factor in the Progressive impulse. The critics believed that recruitment into Progressive politics was more or less random—perhaps not wholly so with regard to class, but certainly with regard to status—and one of them showed that in the state leadership rosters of the three party organizations (Republican, Democratic,

---

on Populism and Progressivism. It was certainly not what made the book: it was less noticed and less discussed than the rest, and it might even have been left off altogether without much altering the general impression which *The Age of Reform* made on those who read it.

[23] Norman Pollack, "Hofstadter on Populism: A Critique of the Age of Reform," *Journal of Southern History,* XXVI (Nov. 1960), 478–500; *The Populist Response to Industrial America* (Cambridge, Mass., 1962), *passim;* "Fear of Man: Populism, Authoritarianism, and the Historian," *Agricultural History,* XXXIX (April 1965), 59–67 (with comments by Oscar Handlin, Irwin Unger, and J. Rogers Hollingsworth, *ibid.,* 68–85); *The Populist Mind* (Indianapolis, 1967), pp. xix–xlviii. A theme consistently stressed in these writings is the historian's duty to work in the "primary materials." On the emergence of a "consensus" school, the earliest—and by far the most judicious—statement is John Higham, "The Cult of the 'American Consensus': Homogenizing Our History," *Commentary,* XXVII (Feb. 1959), 93–100. With regard to Hofstadter himself, however, Higham has stated categorically: "He is, in my opinion, the finest and also the most humane historical intelligence of our generation." Letter to E. L. McKitrick, September 13, 1970.

and Progressive) in the campaign of 1912, the same status groupings, in about the same proportions, were to be found in all three. Another questioned the status argument by pointing out that none of the social sciences—least of all social psychology—had bodies of theory for dealing with problems of status that were sufficiently dependable, or sufficiently agreed upon, for historians to use with any assurance, and that an understanding of Progressivism was much more quickly arrived at by beginning with the issues themselves than by examining the backgrounds of the reformers.[24]

Taking account of the criticism and then going back to the text can be rather baffling. One is not quite prepared for how little the book's persuasiveness has diminished, and that in itself is something of a problem. One exasperated critic ascribed this to Hofstadter's literary virtuosity. ("Individuals are hung, drawn and quartered but in such an innocent and disarming way that no unfriendliness seems intended.")[25] It is true that Hofstadter's skill as a writer was of a very high order, and also that as a target he is very elusive. But this is scarcely an explanation for anything; "literary skill" is not one of those superficial attributes that can easily be detached from what one achieves with it. What still needs to be traced, certainly in Hofstadter's case, are the movements not of a pen but of a mind. None denied his reasonableness. How was it, then,

---

[24] Richard B. Sherman, "The Status Revolution and Massachusetts Leadership," *Political Science Quarterly*, LXXVIII (March 1963), 59–65; Andrew M. Scott, "The Progressive Era in Perspective," *Journal of Politics*, XXI (Nov. 1959), 685–701; David P. Thelen, "Social Tensions and the Origins of Progressivism," *Journal of American History*, LVI (Sept. 1969), 323–341. Certain more peripheral aspects of Hofstadter's argument are questioned in J. Joseph Huthmacher, "Urban Liberalism and the Age of Reform," *Mississippi Valley Historical Review*, XLIX (Sept. 1962), 231–241; and John Braeman, "Seven Progressives," *Business History Review*, XXXV (Winter 1961), 581–592.

[25] Scott, "Progressive Era in Perspective," p. 688 n.

that to some this very reasonableness could be so maddening? What was it that could make his procedure so deeply disturbing?

The key would seem to lie not in literary mystification but in the procedure itself. Hofstadter covered himself at every turn; for all his interest in the psychic components of reform activity, he specifically allowed for an objective validity in each of the aims the reformers pursued. Moreover, an avoidance of dogmatism was built into his very language. He insisted that he wanted his formulations to be taken as tentative, "and not as an attempt to render a final judgment." [26] Yet Hofstadter's scheme, while "tentative," was not exactly amorphous. Being multidimensional and functional, it was so constructed that it could serve as an agenda for what might be looked for in any reform situation; at the same time it was devised in such a way that almost any item in it could be modified or corrected without substantive effect on the argument as a whole—which was, essentially, that reform movements have both manifest and latent functions, and that each kind requires attention.

Even the problem of status and the relation of status changes to reform energy—that aspect of Hofstadter's argument most often attacked—itself remains far from settled. The enormous expansion—eightfold between 1870 and 1910—of the "new middle class" of specialized professional, white-collar, and public service personnel is a matter of record. That this had consequences—that connections are to be found between the emergence of such a constituency, the status dislocations which accompanied it, and a new sensitivity to civic issues—still seems highly probable.[27]

[26] *Age of Reform,* p. 22; David Hawke, "Interview: Richard Hofstadter," *History* (a Meridian periodical), III (Sept. 1960), 136.

[27] For example, Richard Sherman's sampling study (referred to above, and cited in note 24) seems to show no significant status differences among the leadership of any of the three parties in 1912, the "Progressive"

To view the problem in another way: beginning with the issues themselves instead of with the backgrounds of the reformers is perfectly defensible as a tactical procedure. But no procedure should inflate itself into a self-denying ordinance—not if it insists on staying clear of social psychology or of anything else that might help, or renouncing the effort to find a status connection at all. To do that is to narrow the scope of understanding, and to reduce the field arbitrarily to familiar manifest functions. In that spirit it would be hard not to read Hofstadter as saying of the reformers' work that it was "merely" a matter of status tensions (or "only" of guilt), "instead of" an acute perception of objective needs. But "merely" and "instead of" were no part of Hofstadter's scheme, and are nowhere to be found in it. His categories are not mutually exclusive. He was adding an entirely new dimension to the problem of reform, though unavoidably violating a good many settled habits of thought. The complaints about "consensus," moreover, are misleading. Hofstadter's alternative to "conflict" politics was not really "consensus" politics; it was the more complex politics of latent functions.

To pretend, on the other hand, that Hofstadter's work was free from animus would be pushing things too far. Those who took particular offense at his treatment of the

included. One might therefore, with some justification, conclude that status differentiation cannot be taken as the mark of the Progressive type. But if the sampling were done in a different way it might bring results that would themselves read quite differently. That is, if an analogous sample were taken for the year 1890 and another, say, for 1910 (or 1912), they might show a marked shift in the types of men being recruited *into politics generally:* a movement of certain status categories from private to public life. One would then certainly be entitled to say that the consequences of such a movement included, among other things, "progressive" politics and a "progressive" public temper. On the expansion of middle-class professional groups (in addition to Hofstadter's own discussion of it), Robert H. Wiebe, *The Search for Order, 1877–1920* (New York, 1967), especially pp. 111–132, is excellent.

Populists did so with cause. He certainly overdrew the anti-Semitism he imputed to them; whatever anti-Semitism there was among the Populists probably had few or no practical consequences, and was no more pronounced than that to be found in various other social groups. It was also obvious that he had neglected the southern Populists —who faced special problems, who made some real efforts to cope with the dilemma of race, and who did not benefit as did the northerners from the upturn of prices.[28]

Nevertheless, an idealized version of the Populist crusade, even with the efforts that have since been made to correct Hofstadter's, is not likely to be restored. The parochialism, the self-righteous bigotry, the zany elements Hofstadter discerned in it will remain as part of the equation, too circumstantial and too real to be exorcised. Nor was his emphasis on these aspects a matter of caprice. For all his detachment, Hofstadter did have something normative in mind. In making a special effort to redress an older view he wanted to embody some of his own convictions about how intellectuals in general and historians in particular should and should not write about reform movements, there being things about which they, as intellectuals, ought to know better. "Liberal intellectuals," he wrote,

---

[28] C. Vann Woodward, "The Populist Heritage and the Intellectual," *American Scholar,* XXVIII (Winter 1959–1960), 55–72 (also in *The Burden of Southern History,* enl. ed. [Baton Rouge, 1968], pp. 141–166); "The Ghost of Populism Walks Again," *New York Times Magazine,* June 4, 1972, pp. 16–17, 60, 63–64, 66–69; Walter T. K. Nugent, *The Tolerant Populists: Kansas Populism and Nativism* (Chicago, 1963), especially chaps. 1–2; Norman Pollack, "The Myth of Populist Anti-Semitism," *American Historical Review,* LXVIII (Oct. 1962), 76–80; John Higham, "Anti-Semitism in the Gilded Age: A Reinterpretation," *Mississippi Valley Historical Review,* XLIII (March 1957), 559–578. Populist anti-Semitism did, however, play enough of a part in the 1896 campaign that Bryan felt obliged on at least one occasion to repudiate it. See Samuel McSeveney, *The Politics of Depression: Political Behavior in the Northeast, 1893–1896* (New York, 1972), pp. 186–187.

> . . . suffer from a sense of isolation which they usually seek to surmount by finding ways of getting into rapport with the people, and they readily succumb to a tendency to sentimentalize the folk. Hence they periodically exaggerate the measure of agreement that exists between movements of popular reform and the considered principles of political liberalism. They remake the image of popular rebellion closer to their heart's desire. They choose to ignore not only the elements of illiberalism that frequently seem to be an indissoluble part of popular movements but also the very complexity of the historical process itself.[29]

Such movements, whatever else may be said of them, provide a setting and an atmosphere anything but congenial for the life of ideas, except at a distance. This point was for Hofstadter part of a broader and in many ways more fundamental preoccupation, well antedating *The Age of Reform.* It concerned the conditions under which mind itself must function, and historically has functioned, in American society.

IV

The master criterion that had guided Vernon L. Parrington throughout *Main Currents in American Thought* was not essentially intellectual, but political. Parrington's organizing principle had been to group men and ideas in one of two fundamental—and almost primordially antagonistic—categories; "radical" or "conservative" represented both a means of classification and a measure of merit. For Richard Hofstadter such categories could have no direct pertinence. He found it no guarantee of merit that ideas should originate from either "left" or "right"; they might, conversely, flourish in either setting. Popular movements of any kind, however ("leftist" or "rightist"), aroused his

[29] *Age of Reform,* pp. 18–19.

suspicion, for which he thought he had good reason. The McCarthyite frenzy of the early 1950s he saw as just such a popular movement, similar in a good many ways to the Populism of the nineties. He said so, and was attacked for it, of which more shortly.

Hofstadter could conceive a wide variety of circumstances in which mind might be coarsened, perverted, or stupefied, and he made this clear very early. (His working over of Calhoun and Bryan in *The American Political Tradition*, for doing just that, came at a time when he still saw himself as attached to the political left.) There was never a time when he did not have a hard eye for the yahoo, the bigot, the philistine, and the bonehead. He detested anti-intellectualism in all shapes, sizes, colors, and persuasions.

At about the time of Columbia's bicentennial in the 1950s, Hofstadter and his colleague Walter Metzger were asked to prepare a book on the history of academic freedom in American higher education. They agreed, Hofstadter to cover the "age of the college" up to about 1860 and Metzger to deal with that of the university for the modern period. In the reigning atmosphere and in view of their own sentiments, they might have been powerfully tempted to produce a tract for the times. The temptation was resisted, and the resulting volume, despite its title, was not in any direct sense even "about" academic freedom. As historians they saw clearly that, since academic freedom as an idea had been codified only in relatively recent times, it would be a somewhat sterile effort to go looking through the past for violations of a "principle" that did not yet exist. To Hofstadter, responsible as he was for the earlier period, this consideration weighed with a special force.

He also had reason to suspect that "repression," exerted in a direct official way, was only part of the problem of intellectual life in America, even in the supervised setting of academic institutions. It was rather a question of conditions that operated not so much to "repress" mind as simply to discourage and stultify it, only some of which might be "official" and intended—and, conversely, of conditions that might serve to release mind, even at a time when no formal principle of academic freedom was recognized. He would seek to "shed new light on the history of the academic man and the complex circumstances under which he has done his work," and he would do it functionally. As a result, the interludes of relative freedom, as well as the stultifications of the mid-nineteenth-century college, were discovered to be largely the latent functions, the unanticipated consequences, of other processes.

For example, the relatively easy atmosphere at Harvard in the early eighteenth century was hardly the product of any official conviction that either tutors or students had a right to deviant opinions. Rather, a split in the dominant Congregationalist front had the practical effect of bringing a fair measure of toleration; on the other hand it was not regarded as very seemly anyway for gentlemen to squabble with gentlemen over each other's values and behavior. Or, at a somewhat later period, it was not principle alone but a strong competition for students that encouraged the colleges to make a point of religious toleration and liberty of conscience. (But this was not academic freedom: selective recruitment of "sound" professors meant that such toleration was not extended to teaching.) Religious heterogeneity encouraged freedom, at least indirectly. Homogeneity—in places where denominational lines could be held—had the opposite effect; the most stultifying period of all, the first half of the nineteenth century, was that in which small denominational colleges multiplied out of all proportion to need and support. They were governed by boards of control whose concerns, sectarian and other, frequently had little or no room for what might be remotely recognized as intellectual effectiveness. The only guarantee of freedom for a faculty (for whom a true professional category did not yet exist) was often a strong and "authoritarian" president who could, as an academic himself, stand between them and a bigoted board or an ignorant local public. He could sometimes be very good at it. Yet a college functioning in this way was very unlike the traditional European institution, where academic freedom was typically related to the strengths not of chancellors and rectors but of a self-governing faculty.[30]

Academic Freedom was published in 1955. By the time Hofstadter's next book on the life of ideas appeared in

[30] For a book written with such vigor, *Academic Freedom* has over the years received surprisingly little criticism, and only recently has any of this reached print. Douglas Sloan, in "Harmony, Chaos, and Consensus: The American College Curriculum," *Teachers College Record,* LXXIII (1971–1972), 221–251, has entered a demurrer to Hofstadter's bleak picture of the "old-time college," suggesting that when other community resources are taken into account—as in cases where auxiliary forms of edification and instruction were locally accessible, though not formally attached to the institution—these colleges look somewhat less impoverished. Another sort of criticism comes from James Axtell, who charges Hofstadter with a "Whig," or onward-and-upward, view of American higher education which represents everything that came before the age of the university as backward and benighted: "The Death of the Liberal Arts College," *History of Education Quarterly,* XI (Winter 1971), 339–352. This appears, however, to be largely a polemical misrepresentation of Hofstadter's actual argument. It seems especially so when *Academic Freedom* is read in conjunction with an earlier and much lesser known book Hofstadter wrote with C. DeWitt Hardy, *The Development and Scope of Higher Education in the United States* (New York, 1952). In it, he has some very hard things to say about the diffusion of purpose which the universities introduced into the educational process with their indiscriminate proliferation of "practical" subject matter, widespread electives, and extracurricular life. "Indeed, the elective system seemed like an academic transcription of liberal capitalist thinking" (p. 50). And it was in this same connection that Hofstadter remarked, in a very un-Whiggish tone: "One of the most conspicuous things about American writing and speaking on education is a strange and pervasive reluctance . . . to admit that enjoyment of the life of the mind is a legitimate and important consummation in itself . . ." (p. 104). Wilson Smith, though not directly challenging Hofstadter, offers a new and more charitable assessment of the old-time college in the present volume.

1963, a new epithet had been shaped to characterize the tendency of his work. It was related to the charge of neo-conservatism but was even more sweeping. The new book, *Anti-intellectualism in American Life*, together with the body of criticism that had accumulated following *The Age of Reform*, now revealed him as an "elitist."

The charge of "elitism," of course, hits at the exposed flank of anyone who is making claims for the primacy of intellect. The subject itself, especially when conceived in categories of "pro" and "anti," has elitist (though not necessarily "conservative") implications which are difficult to avoid. Whether this is a proper point for criticism is thus somewhat problematical.[31]

On quite other grounds, however, even Hofstadter's partisans may well be restrained from pronouncing *Anti-intellectualism* an unqualified success. It would certainly have been a very different book if Hofstadter had gone about it in the same way he did with *Academic Freedom.* That is, if he had once again refrained—as he consciously had in the previous inquiry—from searching through a many-contoured history for a single element that received its definition only in relatively recent times, and that had seldom gone under the name he gave it, the result would have looked less like a pathology and more like on objective historical commentary on the fortunes of mind in America. Nor would history itself have emerged in quite so oddly flattened a state as it did here.

On the face of it, and in view of Hofstadter's own interests, "anti-intellectualism" would seem a not unreasonable subject for historical treatment. Intellectuals by the 1950s had come to see anti-intellectualism both as a problem and as one of the conditions of life. But Hofstadter was understandably concerned that it not be thought about in an unduly present-minded way; anti-intellectualism (or whatever else it might be called) was

---

[31] See Kenneth S. Lynn, "Elitism on the Left," *The Reporter*, XXIX (July 4, 1963), 37–40.

surely not new. It ought to be placed in the perspective of time. Here was another problem in the sociology of mind, to be examined in a historical context; he had done this sort of thing before, and successfully. Why not again? Besides, he would be breaking new ground. There might be traps, but such is the risk with any exploratory reconnaissance where few others have ventured.

Hofstadter's procedure was to run a line through American history in each of four general realms of endeavor—religion, politics, business, and education—and to see what conditions in each most made for anti-intellectualism. In religion, viewed from the base line of a highly intellectual Puritan clergy, things appear to go steadily downward from the Great Awakening on, while contempt for mind, in an ascending scale, is no better exemplified throughout the nineteenth century than in the succession of popular revivalists from Charles Finney to Dwight Moody to the ineffable Billy Sunday. The generation of the Founding Fathers represented an age of intellect in politics. Not so with the generations that followed, and there were correlations at any number of points between the rise of mass politics and a kind of chronic anti-intellectualism. The fortunes of intellectuals in government are to be traced, if not by a steady descent, certainly in fluctuations and cycles: they had, to say the least, their ups and downs. The colonial merchant, with his cosmopolitan outlook, represented in certain ways the ideal type of the cultivated man. The ideal broke down with the nineteenth-century businessman, "practical" becoming a key value determinant whenever it was a question of anything connected with mind, and so business assumed its place "in the vanguard of anti-intellectualism in our culture." [32] As for popular education, the status of teacher was distressingly low from the beginning, and in the recent past the very conception of what the aims of education

---

[32] *Anti-intellectualism in American Life* (New York, 1963), p. 237.

ought to be had taken a perversely anti-intellectual form with the "life adjustment" movement that followed World War II.

The book was characteristically full of choice bits and flashes of insight. The shenanigans, for example, of Billy Sunday: "There is a hell and when the Bible says so don't you be so black-hearted, low-down, and degenerate as to say you don't believe it, you big fool!" Or Hofstadter's picture of the Mugwump reformer of the 1880s, finicky about power and more concerned with propriety than with success. Or Teddy Roosevelt making intellect "masculine," or the withdrawal-and-return cycle of intellectuals in government under Wilson, FDR, and Kennedy.[33] As expected, there was much here that was sharp, bright, and new.

But however suggestive the insights, they fail to be cumulative. The book is something of a catalog, growing more by solemn repetition than by actual development; it is uncharacteristically short on irony, and once the main idea has been announced, there are few surprises thereafter. This is perhaps only to be expected when one finds what one is bound to find, not so much because of what is "out there" as because all the safeguards against *not* finding it have been built into the subject's very definition. If "intellectualism" is to represent the rational and reflective side of virtually any occasion (as it comes close to doing here), then it is hard to see how anti-intellectualism will not be with us always, even in a community populated only by "intellectuals."

To put it another way, Hofstadter's approach in *Anti-intellectualism* is not truly functional: his plan of organization would not allow it. Stopping at each of a series of complex social processes (religious practice, democratic politics, mass education) to look only for their *dys*functions—and only one general kind at that, those involving anti-intellectualism—is a very different thing from examining one, or each, of these processes to see how they

---

[33] *Ibid.*, pp. 122, 172–229.

work. There were certainly other functions, as well as other dysfunctions, unfolding themselves with consequences quite other than those exhibited here. For example, with the disintegration of formal church polity that occurred in the eighteenth century there was certainly a functional link to anti-intellectual revivalism, but there was another link—and a very direct one—to toleration and enhanced intellectual freedom. Or, while the democratization of political life had anti-intellectual consequences, including the vastly reduced importance of ideology in political discourse, another consequence was the most highly sophisticated informal institution—parties—hitherto devised anywhere for preserving civility in political contention and making it less than a life-and-death struggle. Presenting such examples to Hofstadter, moreover, would have been carrying coals to Newcastle. No one was more aware of these very items than he; on other occasions, not preoccupied with anti-intellectualism, he wrote about them himself with both penetration and detachment.

The McCarthyite agitation, as Hofstadter said at various times, had had much to do with the growth of his own perceptions. But *Anti-intellectualism* should probably be counted as one of the less fortunate by-products, locked as it is in the very present-mindedness Hofstadter thought he was warning against. When he postulated a great American heartland "filled with people who are often fundamentalist in religion, nativist in prejudice, isolationist in foreign policy, and conservative in economics" as a standing menace to intellectuals and intellectualism, he was victimized by the "Progressive" fallacy which he himself, in other ways, had done so much to expose. History may indeed be, among other things, a series of chronic struggles. But whether the "struggle" aspect is the most illuminating one at any given point—in cases of anti-intellectualism or of anything else—cannot be judged in advance. *Anti-intellectualism in American Life* won its author another Pulitzer prize. But prizes aside, we may conjecture

Richard Hofstadter at Columbia University, 1968.

that the very subject might have looked quite different to him had he written the book five years later, at a "worse" time,[34] perhaps, but a time much richer in ironies for the intellectual life than the earlier part of that decade.

A more salutary side of what McCarthyism did for Hofstadter's understanding may be variously seen in *The Paranoid Style in American Politics, and Other Essays*, published in 1965. This was a collected series of pieces, written between 1951 and 1965, whose leading motif was the politics of the irrational. The essays were concerned with political movements whose participants' behavior seemed all out of proportion to the actual issues. Such behavior ranged from the "paranoid"—an obsession with plots and conspiracies, like those that haunted the Anti-Masons, the nativist movements of the 1840s and 1850s, the Populists, and the McCarthyites—to the extravagantly pugnacious, as with the jingoists who howled for war with Spain in 1898, or the Goldwaterites who wanted, almost above all else, to punish the liberal Republicans.

There were two aspects of these movements that particularly drew Hofstadter's interest. One was the political style they generated: tense, dogmatic, extremely bellicose, and encouraging a special kind of emotional radicalism ("left" or "right" made little difference) which he distrusted almost by instinct. He saw the anti-intellectual and potentially undemocratic character of this "radicalism" and recognized it as a threat to calculability in political life. The other aspect was the impossibility of explaining such movements solely with reference to the objective issues.

Most of the essays dealt with more or less specific questions within a relatively manageable scope, and this allowed Hofstadter to be clinical, curious, detached, and ironic in looking at them. For all his detestation of the "paranoid style," he could actually treat his grass-roots "paranoids" with a certain wry indulgence. This shows,

[34] On the campus events of 1968, see below, pp. 348–353.

for example, in his handling of William ("Coin") Harvey, whose schemes of monetary reform made such a stir in the nineties. Already somewhat chastened by the sharp response to his rather strained treatment of Populist anti-Semitism in *The Age of Reform* (which he specifically acknowledged here), he deals with that same theme in Harvey's writings in accents that are almost benign.[35]

One of Hofstadter's ideas—that of "status politics," as applied to the "pseudo-conservatives" of the 1950s as well as to the Goldwaterites and John Birchers of the 1960s—had already had a career of more than a decade, and had produced, and would continue to produce, some very intriguing intellectual consequences. "We have, at all times," he wrote, "two kinds of processes going on in inextricable connection with each other: *interest politics,* the clash of material aims and needs among various groups and blocs; and *status politics,* the clash of various projective rationalizations arising from status aspirations and other personal motives." In times of prosperity, status politics tends to be most prominent; in depressions, "politics is more clearly a matter of interests." [36]

This concept, worked out in conjunction with Seymour Lipset and used in the work of both, was first presented in Hofstadter's 1954 essay, "The Pseudo-Conservative Revolt," which appeared the following year in the much-discussed *New American Right,* a collection of pieces on the McCarthyite phenomenon by him, Lipset, and a number of others.[37] The "status politics" idea, which Hofstadter extended and developed in *The Age of Reform,*

---

[35] "Free Silver and the Mind of 'Coin' Harvey," in *The Paranoid Style in American Politics, And Other Essays* (New York, 1965), pp. 238–315, an essay which first appeared as the Introduction to the 1963 John Harvard Library edition of William H. Harvey's *Coin's Financial School.*

[36] *Paranoid Style,* p. 53.

[37] Daniel Bell, ed., *The New American Right* (New York, 1955). Essays by Bell, Nathan Glazer, Richard Hofstadter, Seymour Lipset, Talcott Parsons, David Riesman, and Peter Viereck.

began drawing fire in the late fifties and early sixties. He thereupon tried twice, in "Pseudo-Conservatism Revisited: A Postscript—1962" and "Pseudo-Conservatism Revisited—1965,"[38] to amend, qualify, and refine it. The criticism had made him a bit defensive. Whatever should happen to his idea (whether it went under the name "status politics" or some other), he strongly believed that room should be preserved for *some* analytical category in which to take account of political behavior not directly oriented to the satisfaction of specific rational interests—and meanwhile he did not want this one too hastily thrown out.

The aggregate effect of the criticism was not to destroy the concept itself, though many historians seem to have taken for granted that it has. "Status politics" has acquired a place in political sociology, together with the explicit recognition of Hofstadter's and Lipset's part in putting it there. Actually the criticism has been of two quite different kinds, exhibiting two divergent sets of objectives. The tendency of the one has been to refine and discriminate, to suggest new possibilities, and thus to advance the concept even while criticizing it.[39] The other tendency has been not so much to widen, but to constrict, our understanding of this or any alternative analytical mode.[40]

---

[38] The first of these essays—little more than a note—appeared in a new and enlarged edition of the above-cited work, renamed *The Radical Right* (Garden City, 1963), pp. 81–86; the other is in *Paranoid Style*, pp. 66–92.

[39] See, e.g., Joseph R. Gusfield, *Symbolic Crusade: Status Politics and the American Temperance Movement* (Urbana: University of Illinois Press, 1963), especially pp. 17 ff. (discussed in the following paragraph); Gerard A. Brandmeyer and R. Serge Denisoff, "Status Politics: An Appraisal of the Application of a Concept," *Pacific Sociological Review*, XII (Spring 1969), 5–11; and Robert W. Doherty, "Status Anxiety and American Reform: Some Alternatives," *American Quarterly*, XIX (Summer 1967), 329–337.

[40] Among social science writings which tend generally to dismiss "status politics" as a concept not worth de-

The expansive tendency is best exemplified in the work of Joseph R. Gusfield. In *Symbolic Crusade: Status Politics and the American Temperance Movement* Gusfield criticized Hofstadter's too-ready imputation of "irrationality" to all forms of political action which fell outside a "class" or "interest" model. He himself, however, fully shared Hofstadter's commitment to finding a satisfactory procedure whereby such behavior might be explored and understood; he accepted Hofstadter's terminology and proceeded to invest it with considerably greater precision. For him, status politics consisted of relatively purposeful "political conflict over the allocation of prestige," in which the goals were "symbolic," though not for that reason any less "real."

Gusfield worked out a highly suggestive "dramatistic" theory to account for the periodic struggles, often "bitter and fateful," of status groups over control of the symbolic acts by which government confers or withholds ("acts out") respect. "Status" itself, moreover, is rather more fluid in Gusfield's terminology than it would be if it remained in its more familiar "occupational" connotation. Status groups define themselves with reference not simply to occupations but to styles of life, values, beliefs, habits of consumption—to a whole range of "characterological" and "cultural" matters. (And the "cosmopolitans-versus-locals" polarity suggested by Merton as an index of social and moral orientation has probably been a good deal more

---

veloping are: Nelson W. Polsby, "Toward an Explanation of McCarthyism," in Polsby and others, eds., *Politics and Social Life: An Introduction to Political Behavior* (Boston, 1963), pp. 809–824; Martin Trow, "Small Businessmen, Political Tolerance, and Support for McCarthy," *American Journal of Sociology*, LXIV (Nov. 1958), 270–281; Raymond E. Wolfinger and others, "America's Radical Right: Politics and Ideology," in David E. Apter, ed., *Ideology and Discontent* (London, 1964), 262–293; and Michael P. Rogin, *The Intellectuals and McCarthy: The Radical Specter* (Cambridge, Mass., 1967), *passim*. The last-named is discussed below.

important, especially for so-called right-wing movements, than specific geographical location.) This "dramatistic" approach (which, following Kenneth Burke, treats language and thought as modes of action) applies to acts of legislation, court decisions, official pronouncements, and rituals of state, and may embrace questions ranging from the fluoridation of water and the control of domestic Communism to the censorship of pornography and the recognition of foreign governments. Compromise in such a struggle is exceedingly difficult. "The language of status issues, essential to their symbolic import, is the language of moral condemnation. . . . The sources of conflict are not quantitative ones of the distribution of resources. Instead they are differences between right and wrong, the ugly and the beautiful, the sinful and the virtuous." [41]

A quite different handling of Hofstadter's "status politics" concept is seen in Michael P. Rogin's *The Intellectuals and McCarthy,* whose tendency is to push it out of the way by what almost amounts to a change of subject. The legitimacy of Rogin's doing this need not be questioned; he had his own concerns, not at all similar to Hofstadter's. But since his book has been cited [42] as evidence of the concept's having been disposed of through due process, a note may still be in order. Rogin's own subject, to which the phenomenon of McCarthyism itself is in many respects quite secondary, is an entire philosophical point of view on American history and politics whose errors he wished to expose and which he defined as "pluralism." The "pluralists," who are very numerous and of whom Hofstadter is one, have been led by their profoundly conservative preferences to see American political life as a matter of broker elites mediating and managing the plural interests of society, their own ultimate interest being stability above all. This commitment to stability has induced in the pluralists

[41] *Symbolic Crusade,* p. 184.

[42] E.g., Schlesinger, "Richard Hofstadter," in Cunliffe and Winks, eds., *Pastmasters,* pp. 310–311; Woodward, "Ghost of Populism," p. 66.

a deep fear of popular ("mass") movements. They see Populism as such a movement, but mistakenly see McCarthyism as another. Both Populism and McCarthyism, Rogin argued, were animated by clear, logical, and rational interests, though of quite different kinds, the McCarthy movement having in fact been manipulated by the very sort of elites the pluralists see as legitimate mediators of *all* interests.

Rogin makes an interesting, and in our opinion quite valid, point in stressing the part played in the 1950s by the articulate intellectual class itself in inflating through its own lamentations McCarthy's reputation and power. The share Hofstadter himself may or may not have had in this is a suitable point for debate. But to homogenize him with a whole collectivity of pluralist intellectuals, and thus to "explain" his writing what he did, is to take less than seriously the extent to which his concerns were analytical and not ideological. Hofstadter's very specific concern with non-interest politics has in effect been defined as not really consequential, Rogin's procedure being one which allows for no pursuit of that problem at all. McCarthyism, Rogin says, *was* interest politics: the interest of Republican leaders in exploiting the issues of the Cold War and Korean War for party purposes. He discredits the similarity Hofstadter and other pluralists thought they saw between the pathologies of Populism and McCarthyism by showing that the localities supporting agrarian radicalism in the 1890s were not the same ones that supported McCarthy sixty years later. The characterological features of McCarthy's following, the kind of question crucial to Hofstadter and Gusfield, are not of primary interest anyway, because *all* American political movements can be characterized as "moralistic." Rogin's position may be arguable on its own merits. But whether his and Hofstadter's have been, or can be, debated under a common set of ground rules is itself debatable. One does not need to be a "pluralist" (or to abhor rational mass movements as a way of changing society, or to look with favor on elites manipulating institutions) to be nonetheless keenly interested in what is for the moment being called status politics. And whether McCarthyism does or does not qualify as a "mass" movement, Rogin's approach would not be much help in understanding Anti-Masonry, Know-Nothingism, the Ku Klux Klan, or for that matter Populism, which do.

"Historians and social critics of the present generation," Hofstadter insisted, "have a particularly urgent need for such an analytical instrument as status politics: it serves to keep their conception of political conflict from being imbued with the excessive rationalism that infused the work of the two preceding generations. . . ." He was here referring to the Progressives, and among those he specifically mentioned were Charles A. Beard, Frederick Jackson Turner, and Vernon Louis Parrington.[43] These, as it also happened, would be the subjects of his next book.

V

For Richard Hofstadter the year 1968 was a point of resolution and synthesis for a long train of accumulated observations regarding the life of the mind in America. The year was marked by two pivotal events. One was the completion and publication of another major book; the other was the crisis at Columbia, a crisis not of ideas but of the environment itself from which ideas issue. The entire life of Hofstadter's own mind up to that point had been a special course of preparation for both these events.

The Progressive Historians: Turner, Beard, Parrington was a book about the three figures who had dominated the current tradition of American historical writing at the moment Hofstadter himself first became acquainted with it. A full examination of their major writings, their influence, and the governing assumptions under which they wrote, this was by far the most sensitive and complete

[43] *Paranoid Style,* p. 90.

study of these men and their work that had yet been done. But for all Hofstadter's judicious solicitude for the achievements of the past, it was apparent early in the course of the book that he did not believe he was writing about a living tradition. The influence—certainly the direct influence—of all three had dwindled to virtually nothing, and Hofstadter in the very act of preparing his study was in his way confirming this. The book was a monument and an epitaph to its subjects.

Some wondered, indeed, why he had gone to the trouble. There was something idiosyncratic here; it seemed a peculiarly personal thing to do. Why? Back of the question lay certain ironies. Hofstadter himself had done more than any one writer to form the tradition—whatever it should finally be called—that had taken the place of the one the Progressives represented, which meant that he could feel himself least able to take theirs for granted. He had probably never been aware of the precise moment when he had ceased to be, as it were, a Progressive himself. So there must have been a special urgency about seeing whole, once and for all, what it was that had seemed at one time so important, and that had now been left behind forever. The time had come, in short, for a final settlement of accounts.

Turner, Beard, and Parrington had each in his way tried to impose sense and meaning upon the whole of American history through an act of thought, almost an act of will. For this alone they were due a certain homage. But there were deep difficulties in a conception of American history whose secrets were held to be decipherable by so simple a formula as the conflict each saw between East and West, or rich and poor, or farmer and businessman. The setting thus offered was one in which the historical imagination was almost bound, sooner or later, to run out of nourishment.

Hofstadter had got Turner and Parrington out of his system fairly early, and could deal with them with fewer afterthoughts than he could with Beard. Though Turner's frontier idea would retain an unexpected vitality, which was all to the good, the primitivism of Turner's own celebration of the frontier virtues had profoundly anti-intellectual overtones. Nor was Turner himself in the usual sense a man of ideas. He had one good one of his own; he had another—that of "sections" as an organizing device for political history—which never came to much. As a teacher he could suggest and inspire, but as a writer he produced little, and for this there could be in the end but one explanation. What he had to say could be traversed in fairly short order.[44] Parrington was a good deal more prolific. Yet his work, too, was essentially animated by a single principle. It was the first successful effort to embrace in survey form the entire history of literary endeavor in America, and it had been written with learning and verve. Yet once the formula was mastered, which was easy enough, every next step became all too predictable. The forces of aristocracy and democracy, and the exigencies of the struggle between them, left to no man's ideas the room for—even the right to—a life of their own. Parrington thought the Puritans could be understood without bothering with their theology, and his Anglophobia ran so deep that he could convince himself, contrary to all fact, "that American democratic thought was basically French in origin." Hawthorne lacked imagination in preferring the unwholesome "shadowy world" he conjured up for *The Scarlet Letter* to the "hurrying ships seeking strange markets" that he saw at the port of Salem. Parrington did not

[44] Ray A. Billington, while generally conceding the limited scope of Turner's ideas, has nevertheless described in fascinating detail an aspect of the man's influence —in addition to his success as a teacher—which is perhaps less appreciated than it ought to be. This was the enormous impact Turner's example at Wisconsin had on the historical profession (with his very modern concern over library resources, documents collections, graduate fellowships, and staff) at precisely the moment when academic history was in the initial phase of professionalizing itself. *Frederick Jackson Turner: Historian, Scholar, Teacher* (New York, 1973).

know where to put Poe at all, except "quite outside the main current," as he himself expressed it, along with "the psychologist and the belletrist." [45]

With Beard, Hofstadter's feelings were rather more complex, and he came to his eventual conclusions by easy stages, somewhat as it must have happened in his actual experience. It was Beard, he had categorically stated on another occasion, "who got me excited about American history." Traces of his first enthusiasm were still discernible in *The American Political Tradition*, fourteen years after he first read *The Rise of American Civilization*, as well as in his 1950 essay "Beard and the Constitution." [46]

The attractions of Charles Beard's example are once more made credible. Beard was able to persuade others to study historical problems in "an eminently critical way," and his efforts to locate ideas sociologically was at least a step along the path Hofstadter himself would take. And Beard's acts in the interest of intellectual freedom—his resignation from Columbia over just such an issue in 1917, or his public scourging of William Randolph Hearst's efforts to get the National Education Association to support his Red-hunting campaign of 1935—must have been deeply satisfying for a young aspirant to contemplate. These things still could be, and were, reviewed with relish. Moreover, some of the most striking instances of disingenuousness in Beard's writings—his uses of evidence in *An Economic Interpretation of the Constitution*, or in *President Roosevelt and the Coming of the War*—were discussed, though candidly, with a leniency that had not characterized prior criticism of these same works. Much could be forgiven Beard, considering the breadth and generosity of view so often evident in his life and work.

And yet the incorrigible vice in Beard was his in-

---

[45] *The Progressive Historians: Turner, Beard, Parrington* (New York, 1968), pp. 420–423, 387, 393.

[46] Hawke, "Interview," p. 141; see above, p. 313: "Beard and the Constitution: The History of an Idea," *American Quarterly*, II (Fall 1950), 195–213.

capacity, when all was said and done, to take ideas seriously. Those, for instance, of the Founding Fathers: "In 1913 Beard found nothing in the ideas of the Founding Fathers that made him feel so close to basic realities as the old Treasury records he had enterprisingly turned up."[47] Connecting ideas with interests was in principle well and good, but it is doubtful whether in the end Beard —for all his professions—really came very close to doing this. For Hofstadter, on the other hand, ideas *were* interests.

Ideas—interests—"reality": these remained oceans apart for all three of the Progressive historians. With such phrases as "fled from reality" and "removed from the odors of the shop," Parrington and Beard could both refer to Henry James, "a major writer in whom their interest was relatively casual," with all the perspicacity of small-town Rotarians. For them and for Turner "reality" did, after all, amount to something *other* than the use men made of their minds and sensibilities. What remained, then, when the accounts were justly settled, was a residue of philistinism. They lacked the sense of complexity.[48]

Still, Hofstadter concluded, in something of an afterthought, "I suppose we may expect that the very idea of complexity will itself come under fire once again, and that it will become important for a whole generation to argue that most things in life and in history are not complex but

[47] *Ibid.*, p. 246. "For all the amplitude and moral intensity of political thought in the Revolutionary era, he seems to have believed its residue was not fundamentally important for the Constitution. Whereas his chapter on the economic interests of the members of the Convention runs to almost eighty pages and puts its conclusions in a highly particularized form, his chapter on their 'political doctrines' (a revealing choice of terms, since it suggests fixed commitments, academicism, and sterility rather than vital ideas) is a rather perfunctory pastiche of quotations drawn very selectively and sometimes rather out of context from the records of the Convention, and it takes up only one third as much space." *Ibid.*, pp. 246–247.

[48] *Ibid.*, pp. 393–394.

really quite simple. This demand I do not think the study of history can gratify."[49]

At some early point in the planning of *Anti-intellectualism* back in the 1950s Hofstadter had got himself stuck with the assumption that mind's major battles in American culture were those fought between "intellectuals" on the one side and the rest of society on the other. That is, the most serious menaces to mind were those coming from outside the intellectual community, however such a community might be defined; it was somehow very difficult to picture the philistines, or at any rate the Goths and Vandals, as dwelling within the walls. Of course he knew otherwise, but mainly as a kind of qualification. For him or anyone else to conceive a major *formal* modification in the overall scheme of *Anti-intellectualism in American Life* would have required a strong cue from the opposite direction. No better cue can now be imagined than the Columbia campus upheaval of 1968. And, as it now appears, no one was actually quicker to sense this when it happened than Hofstadter himself. Anti-intellectualism could take its most vicious form in the very setting most specifically designed for the fostering and protection of intellect.

We conjectured above, with this in mind, that *Anti-intellectualism* would not have been the same book had it been written five years later. Two specific issues, among the many the book dealt with, suggest themselves as examples. One is Hofstadter's assault on the "life-adjustment" movement in public education, whose bland inanities he saw as having done much to deny a generation of high school students the bracing discipline of academic challenge and intellectual effort. He may well have been right, yet the students who rampaged across the Columbia campus and so many others in the late sixties were not of the life-adjustment generation at all, but of a successor

[49] *Ibid.*, p. 466.

cohort that had been raised on the new math, new science, "excellence," "enrichment," Advanced Placement, and the most ferocious kind of academic competition. Pressed to the screeching point in high school, many of them found college—where the work was not that much newer or more challenging—a colossal letdown. A conversion to the contemplative, the reflective, the speculative aspects of mind was perhaps not to be expected as the most logical consequence of what they had just been through.

Another example is the quasi-debate carried on in the closing pages of *Anti-intellectualism* over the proper relation between intellect and power. Resisting the contention that the intellectual's duty is to hold himself aloof from the corrupting influences of power, Hofstadter maintained that the participation of intellectuals in government worked to the advantage of both intellect and the public service.[50] (The ideal, of course, was the example of the Founding Fathers.) By 1968 it might seem to have been "proven"—with such examples as McGeorge Bundy, Dean Rusk, and a host of lesser lights—that government service *was* in fact corrupting. Yet the rhetoric of the campuses—the insistence that *any* dealings with government, especially those of even the vaguest military character, amounted to traffic with the enemy—had now given the question a form in which it was scarcely debatable at all. The previous argument, which had assumed at least some kind of balance between involvement and independence, was obsolete. Old opponents now found themselves as often as not on the same side with regard to a whole set of new issues in which the right to make discriminations about anything was being challenged by root-and-branch remedies for everything.

For all Hofstadter's dismay at seeing his university threatened not by outsiders (as might have been assumed from the viewpoint of either *Anti-intellectualism* or *Aca-*

---

[50] *Anti-intellectualism*, pp. 395 ff.; see also "A Note on Intellect and Power," *American Scholar*, XXX (Autumn 1961), 588–598.

demic Freedom) but by its own population, the effect on him was nonetheless not one of shell shock. He retained a kind of poise and reasonableness that no one who saw him during that period could fail to notice. Though keenly concerned and anything but passive, he took no prominent forensic role, as a number of his colleagues did; he was visible, but in no self-assertive way. Yet he was always somewhere at hand, and seemed to have a peculiarly nice sense of just what was taking place. It was as though everything he saw was in some way recognizable, that there were prepared places in his mind where most of it could be put, and that given some rearranging, there was surprisingly little here that he had not, somehow, already thought about.

There was, for one thing, the atmosphere of revivalism: the deep emotion, instant conversions, brotherhood, joy of salvation, apocalyptic imagery of a sinful world, and a revivalist oratory as crude, coercive, and innocent of ratiocination as anything in the repertory of Billy Sunday. Then there was the gross disproportion between issues and behavior. There were actually few significant divisions of principle in any part of the university on either the war in Vietnam or the imperatives of racial justice. On the other hand, there were status tensions everywhere: not only between such bloc elements as faculty, students, and administration but also within various subgroups—graduate students, blacks, "jocks," junior faculty, and very obviously the chapel clergy, for whom a revivified moral role was positively galvanizing. Moreover, the sharpest axes tended not to be ground by the "best" students. There was much talk and considerable confusion about "elitism," and no wonder: the very meaning of "elite" had vastly altered within the previous decade. Ivy League graduates were no longer quite the elite they could once see themselves as being. The very atmosphere which a national culture furnishes, and in which expectations are normally formed with regard to status, recognition, and respect, *had* been poisoned by a callous and abominable war. What people did, then, during this interlude was all tied up with the picture they had of themselves, of how they counted and where they fit, at a critical point in the process of self-realization. And finally, there was the political style, and its absorption with symbolic rather than "objective" issues. The language was that of moral condemnation ("right and wrong, the ugly and the beautiful"), of conspiracy (connivance at selling the university's brains to the powers in Washington), and of "reality" (defense contracts). Throughout it all, undeniably, there was no end of idealism.

It was, of course, new and appalling to nearly everyone. Nevertheless the constellation was one Hofstadter seemed to find less astonishing than did most others. There was nothing very flashy about his demeanor or his comings and goings during that period. But everything he did, mostly small things, was done with the precision of one who understood. He turned up at meetings. He kept in touch with his students; all knew he was accessible. He was not immobilized, either by outrage, or by mock humility, or by guilt. He sometimes wondered, to be sure, "whether the game was worth the candle." But the students had not suddenly turned into monsters; nor had they acquired special truth or sudden illumination. He respected their sincerity, but was not prepared to believe that the state they were in was exactly a normal one. During those few weeks he came to acquire a quiet authority that somehow penetrated and was recognized for what it was throughout the university. For the first time in Columbia's history, the commencement address that June was delivered by a member of the faculty rather than the university's president. The one chosen was Richard Hofstadter, and he was chosen not simply as the man of character, but as the man who knew.

Any statement in the form of a public address ought to be read "in context." But sometimes there is more than one context. This particular statement, seen against its immediate background, has an air almost of detachment.

It does not dwell on the mournful state of the world or of the current academic scene, though these are mentioned. Read in another context, however, and seen as a single example of a general principle, Hofstadter's address is yet another synthesis of concerns that had occupied him for at least the previous twenty-five years: the conditions—here it was again—required for the functioning of mind. The language is not that of ceremony but of analysis. Its subject is both the value and the fragility of the only institution, the modern university, that can provide those conditions in their freest and most ample form.

It can do this because of certain "remarkable commitments." One is the idea that "somewhere in society there must be an organization in which anything can be studied or questioned." Another is that of academic freedom, "applicable both to faculty and students," which rests "upon the willingness of people to consider that they may be mistaken." These are ideas of great sophistication, involving extraordinary demands, requiring immense restraint, and requiring also that the restraints "normally be self-imposed, and not forced from the outside." No persons, no groups, should consider themselves exempt from them. The university's character as a center of free inquiry and free criticism is "a thing not to be sacrificed for anything else."

But the university, being "the only great organization in modern society which considers itself obliged not just to tolerate but even to give facilities and protection to the very persons who are challenging its own rules, procedures, and policies," makes itself by the same token so fragile that to subvert it "is all too easy, as we now know." The "forcible occupation and closure of a university's buildings with the intention of bringing its activities to a halt is no ordinary bargaining device—it is a thrust at the vitals of university life." The university may well stand in need of reform. But reform is an undertaking that "cannot be carried out under duress."

The closest he came to the hortatory mode, which

was not very close, was to deal with the essentially rhetorical question of how the university could go on after what had just happened. "I can only answer: How can it not go on? . . . What kind of people would we be if we allowed this center of our culture and our hope to languish and fail? That is the question I must leave with you." [51]

VI

For some reason it does not occur naturally to anyone familiar with Hofstadter's books to ask which one might have been his "best." We tend rather to think of their consequences. For instance, to the generation that entered graduate school in the late forties, when Beard's influence still lay heavily upon the historical imagination, *The American Political Tradition* was a liberating sanction whereby some of the more cumbersome conceptual habits of Progressivism could be abandoned. A comparable impact was made upon those coming up in the mid-fifties, as we have already seen, by *The Age of Reform.* Amid such consequences—the very setting free of the speculative energies, which occurred with so many—the notion of "best" becomes somewhat fluid and relative. Perhaps so, and yet it might still be argued that of all Hofstadter's books *The Idea of a Party System,* published in 1969, presented the least disparity between intention and achievement, and thus in its way approached a special kind of perfection.

Here, in relatively brief course, Hofstadter invests with a certain deceptive obviousness what may be the most important occurrence in the history of American political culture. This was the emergence and public acceptance of a system of political partisanship that recognized the right of an opposition not simply to express itself

[51] "The 214th Columbia University Commencement Address," *American Scholar,* XXXVII (Autumn 1968), 583–589.

within the legislature but to organize and agitate outside of it as well, doing all it could to displace an incumbent administration so that it might itself assume the powers of government. That modern American politics does in fact have this character has been understood for some time; it has also been understood—more or less—that there was once a time when parties were *not* regarded as legitimate. What Hofstadter did was to account for the transition, and to make it credible. His book is a model analysis of the relationship between a given political environment and the intrusion of a radically novel conception of politics.

Hofstadter's problem, a peculiarly complex and subtle one, was that of dealing simultaneously with change on two quite different levels, one being that of attitude and theory, the other, of political practice. The two were of course related, but not so closely that shifts on one plane might not occur more or less independently of what was going on at the other. Men felt they must denounce parties even while building them, and this in turn set up strains which could only be resolved either by amending the theory—which proved surprisingly difficult—or, more commonly, by heroic efforts to make changing practice square with received doctrines. Certain leading members of the Founding Fathers' generation managed, virtually in spite of themselves, to build a major opposition party. At the same time they could never quite bring themselves to recognize in theory the legitimacy of party politics.

In the Anglo-American world of the eighteenth century, political discussion, as Hofstadter points out, "was pervaded by a kind of anti-party cant." There were variations on this. One was the Bolingbroke-Hamilton view that parties created chronic strife, were subversive of good government, and should therefore be suppressed. Another was the Hume-Madison position, according to which parties must be regarded as necessary evils, an inevitable by-product of free government, and thus probably not to be destroyed without destructive consequences for freedom itself. They were best endured through efforts to check and limit the damage they might do. The only major voice to argue that parties were not only inevitable, but useful as well, was that of Edmund Burke, but Burke's views had little influence in America.

The Founding Fathers not only made no provision in the Federal Constitution for parties, they assumed they were making provisions against them. In erecting the eighteenth-century penchant for "balanced government" into a formal system of separated powers and of checks and balances, they would thereby control the evils that might otherwise ensue should any element of society become a majority force and try to usurp the powers of the state. The greatest of evils were those created by parties and factions, whose tendency if left unchecked would be to disrupt the constitutional balance. James Madison, arguing for acceptance of this constitution in *The Federalist,* was not making a positive case for parties, though some authorities have thought otherwise. He was assuming, rather, that although parties were probably inevitable, the very multiplicity of interests in society would bring forth a corresponding multiplicity of factions, thus neutralizing the mischief they might otherwise do and preventing any one of them from becoming a tyrannous majority. "With the Madisonian formulation," Hofstadter says, "thinking on the role of party had thus reached a stage of profound but fertile ambiguity. To unravel the ambiguity would require an entire additional generation of political experience." [52]

With the political crises of the 1790s, during which he himself became the leader of a "faction," Madison was forced to make certain alterations in his view of parties and their place in public life. Whereas what he had formerly most feared was a powerful and thus potentially despotic majority, he argued in 1792 that what justified the "Republican interest" (as his and Jefferson's party

[52] *The Idea of a Party System: The Rise of Legitimate Opposition in the United States, 1780–1840* (Berkeley, 1969), pp. 67–68.

styled itself) was precisely that it commanded *majority* support: that it represented the great body of the people, defending true republican principles in the face of a Federalist faction which spoke only for the interests of a powerful few and was in fact plotting to replace republicanism with monarchy.

But this was still not to justify a *system* of parties: it did not mean that an opposition as such was necessarily legitimate. The Republicans were, to be sure, an "opposition," endeavoring to check the evil and monarchical influence of the entrenched Federalists. But what justified them was that they constituted a natural majority which would in time triumph and either absorb the Federalists or scatter their remnants forever. Parties might thereupon be rendered negligible. Nor did Madison's views alter very much after the so-called Revolution of 1800, with its peaceful transfer of power to his own party. The Federalists, being essentially a subversive force whether as the party in power or as an opposition, could never be regarded as legitimate as long as they remained in existence. Needless to say, the Federalists took the same view of the Republicans. James Madison lived another forty-four years after making his 1792 statement, but neither he nor any of the Founding Fathers' generation ever quite took the final theoretical step, even though they had in certain ways acted as if they were already members of modern political parties. They could never quite imagine their opponents legitimately in power, nor conceive that parties might some day require no higher justification than simply their own existence.

But a new generation did take that step, not only in practice but to a considerable extent in theory as well, and Hofstadter uses the career of Martin Van Buren to exemplify how it was done. Van Buren, rising from humble beginnings by way of the law in upstate New York, represented a type admirably suited to the new politics which the incipient democratization of public careers seemed more and more to call for in the decade or so following the War of 1812. Adversary dealings constituted the medium in which he worked—but with a difference. Gregarious and amiable, Van Buren had the county courthouse lawyer's instinct for drawing a nice line between his professional associations and his personal friendships or enmities, and for keeping the one from influencing the other. He carried much the same attitude into politics. The Albany Regency, in the organization of which Van Buren was the leading spirit, was built up at a time when the ideological rancors that had characterized the politics of the Founding Fathers were losing most of their old sharpness. The Regency, whose resources would eventually be placed at the service of the emergent Jacksonian movement, was held together not by "proud and jealous notables" but by professionals like himself, men whose claims to advancement were based not on social eminence or ideological purity but on hard work, faithful service, and willingness to subordinate individual interest to party unity. "Party unity," as Hofstadter puts it, "was the democrat's answer to the aristocrat's wealth, prestige, and connections," and exhortations to keep the organizational faith became, in effect, "an anti-ideological force." [53]

The time had come, moreover, when Van Buren and his associates could see that there was yet another element, beyond organizational loyalty, indispensable to party unity. This was the existence of a stable opposition, which stood as a kind of guarantee of stability and predictability for the system as a whole, and the implications were enormous. One could prepare oneself to lose from time to time as part of the game, and do it with a minimum of hard feelings. This acceptance, this actual welcoming, of a permanent opposition "in turn marked the longest single step toward the idea of a party system." [54]

The Idea of a Party System affords the occasion for some other observations—thus far deferred—on the character

[53] *Ibid.*, p. 246.
[54] *Ibid.*, p. 226.

of Hofstadter's work. This book in particular raises some intriguing questions (as indeed do most of the others) about the idea of "originality" and what that quality consists of. There is no one item in the book that appears to be strikingly novel (though a number in fact are), and the end-product has a familiarity and a logic that another combination of these same items might not have given it. But it may well be that the genius here is that of having made it all look so easy, which is something other than a mere matter of rearranging elements already on hand, of reordering a series of previous insights, some fragmentary and others more highly developed, into a tidy and harmonious composite. It is rather a process of rethinking it all through that is itself profoundly creative. Part of the essence of creativity is exhibiting things as though they ought to have looked that way all along, and allowing us to persuade ourselves that they have. And anyone with such a talent may have to forgo at least some of the rewards of "originality."

Yet synthesis of this sort does not occur automatically; it is not achieved without a strong self-conscious purpose and without strong governing ideas. The "idea of a party system" may be a deceptively obvious one, yet Richard Hofstadter was the first to expound it effectively in its historical setting. Why so effectively, yet somehow so unobtrusively? His techniques themselves are sophisticated enough. His sense of the functional, already considered, is at work throughout. The book is full of typologies, imparting a marvelous clarity to the clusters of ideas thus organized, and a precision of outline to be found in no other discussion of the subject. Nor had this aspect of lucidity, this gift for creative synthesis, been seen for the first time in *The Idea of a Party System.* It had shown on many a prior occasion; it had been imposed upon materials widely disparate in nature and in some cases previously unfamiliar to Hofstadter himself.[55]

[55] For example, a distinguished medievalist has remarked that Hofstadter's handling of the medieval uni-

But again, why? How could these syntheses have been so diverse and yet so successful? The answer, in part, may be that at least one of the roles Hofstadter set for himself was that of *mediator* in the life of ideas, which is not a role most historians either consciously or instinctively assume. Nor is this simply a matter of bringing the news of ideas from realms of specialization in a form which other persons of intelligence may apprehend. The true mediator is not only sensitive to all the currents around him; he is acutely aware that there is not an underlying harmony in the life of ideas at all, but a kind of natural anarchy. Things are not automatically related; they do not "speak for themselves"; they are not ipso facto visible to any who may be inclined to look. They must pass through the mediator, and are transformed; the genuine mediator of ideas, as Henry James once said of the novelist, is the "large, lucid reflector," and the talents required are not dissimilar.

The mediator's gift, that is, may be seen as peculiarly a literary one. "I read a good deal of literary criticism," Hofstadter once remarked, "and a lot of the cues I've taken come from it." [56] This had not always been the case, but a choice of sorts seems to have been made at a critical stage in the writing of *The Age of Reform*, early in the 1950s. His closest social science friends—prominent among whom was the late C. Wright Mills—responded to his preliminary drafts with a multitude of suggestions that applied more to their own special interests than to his broader ones, and had he followed them he would have

versities is the best single thing in print on the subject; an authority on post-Civil War monetary history has said the same of his piece on "Coin" Harvey and free silver; and a leading colonialist has made the very same point with regard to his section on the colonial churches in *America at 1750*. The key point here is not whether these specialists (John Mundy, Allen Weinstein, Jack Greene) are "correct" in their appraisals, but that for none of them was Hofstadter's work "derivative." They were judging him as a peer in their own fields.

[56] Hawke, "Interview," p. 139.

had to write another sort of book entirely. Social science formed a part, but only a part, of his intellectual personality. It was at about this very time, on the other hand, that he began fully to appreciate what his Columbia colleague Lionel Trilling could offer him, not so much in the way of criticism but as a literary example. Trilling was not one of the "New Critics"; rather he fulfilled as a man of letters many of the functions philosophers once performed before they, too, became technicians: his interests and concerns ranged over the entire province of life, society, and morals. There would prove in time, inasmuch as Hofstadter subsequently read everything Trilling published, something reassuringly inexhaustible about such an example.[57]

One item—among a great many—to which he must have responded with a special relish, and which revealed various affinities of temperament between the two, was a little piece called "On Not Talking." In it, Trilling, recalling that there was a time when Baudelaire the poet could be the best critic of painting of his day, deplores the reluctance nowadays of the artistic and intellectual professions to ask each other any more serious questions, to venture across one another's "boundaries." This comes from the inhibitions generated by pedantry, from a loss of innocence, "a fear of being wrong, an aspiration to *expertise*." (Neither Trilling nor Hofstadter ever set much store by that sort of *expertise*.) There is a stunning sub-essay here on Delacroix, a man of genius who talked to everyone about everything, and Trilling must have taken the same kind of delight in doing it as Hofstadter did whenever he took up any new subject he was not "sup-

[57] He must have been struck, e.g., on coming across this: "The literary mind, more precisely the historical-literary mind, seems to me the best kind of critical mind that we have. . . ." Lionel Trilling, "The Situation of the American Intellectual at the Present Time," in *A Gathering of Fugitives* (Boston, 1956), p. 73. Other information in this paragraph comes from conversations with Beatrice K. Hofstadter.

posed" to know about or talk about. The essay closes on a note of praise for the "divine amateur" in William James, who was always rushing in where angels feared to tread, and who "wanted to dispel the air of secrecy that attends all established professions." It was, among other things, a large conferral of legitimacy upon the role of mediator.[58]

Hofstadter in 1956 wrote a curious and somewhat difficult essay, with an elusive argument full of ambiguous transitions, which he called "History and the Social Sciences." Ostensibly it is in praise of the benefits social science has brought to the study of history. The author ends up predicting, however, that the most effective benefits will prove not to be methodological or "scientific" ones at all: the best thing social science can do for history is to enhance its literary properties. This is because on the one hand "it is the achievement of those forms of literature that are most like history that they deal significantly with problems of human character," while on the other, the social sciences can bring the historian "a fresh store of ideas" with which to do this. They can offer "a sort of literary anthropology," assisting him in achieving "a kind of portraiture of the life of nations and individuals, classes and groups." At the same time there is one aspect of the "scientific" ideal in which the historian can take no refuge. He cannot count on cumulative progress through small forward steps in the form of microscopic scholarly monographs. Monographs do not in themselves quite "add up"; true synthesis does not occur in that way; the historian hoping to achieve important work must, unlike the scientist, ultimately take on the large questions all over again for himself. Eventually he must address such categories as the Reformation, the Renaissance, the Industrial Revo-

[58] *Ibid.*, pp. 143–152. An earlier kind of literary "influence" was the writings of H. L. Mencken, with their bubble pricking and buffoonery, which so delighted Hofstadter in his youth. The essay on Bryan in *The American Political Tradition*, for example, is highly reminiscent of the spirit in which Mencken dealt with the same subject.

lution, the wars and social upheavals, the great transitions of corporate life. When he does this, he is persuaded "to think of history as being not only the analysis but the expression of human experience." His search is "for clues not simply as to how life may be controlled but as to how it may be felt, and he realizes more fully than before how much history is indeed akin to literature." [59]

VII

It was in such a spirit as this that Richard Hofstadter turned at last to what he envisioned as being the consummatory effort of his own life. In the spring of 1969 he had announced to his publisher that he planned to spend the next eighteen years writing a history of the United States which would consist of three substantial volumes of about a half-million words each. Its chronological span would extend "from mid-18th century to the recent past." The organizing themes would be primarily political, but there would be generous room for whatever might be appropriate and necessary in the way of economic, biographical, and cultural analysis. All of which meant that his own guess of more than a dozen years before—that the historian who hoped somehow to count could not rest content with small things, that he would eventually feel called upon to deal with "the great turning points in human experience"—had become a self-fulfilling prophecy. It may well have occurred to him that the most recent major effort in any way analogous to what he had in mind was still Charles and Mary Beard's *Rise of American Civilization,* which had made so singular an impression on him in his youth.

Hofstadter's ambivalence toward close monographic work remained, and if anything went deeper than ever.

---

[59] "History and the Social Sciences," pp. 363 ff., especially 369–370.

He still believed that a monograph could deal with no more than "an extremely narrow segment of reality," and that even when added together monographs could not in themselves "yield comprehensive answers to comprehensive questions." Nevertheless he held an immense respect for them, and the very proliferation of such work over the previous two decades had made for enormous, unsettled problems in the way of "a general interpretive synthesis." He himself now intended to confront those problems. He would play the role, on the largest scale yet, of mediator.[60]

He was able to devote scarcely one year of the projected eighteen to this new work, and at the time of his death had completed no more than a fraction of it. The fraction itself, however, had already reached the proportions of a modest-sized book. Its unit of accumulation had been the familiar and long-perfected essay form, and the manuscript had acquired sufficient structure and substance not only to warrant publication but to justify a projection or two as to what might have been the character of the completed work. It appeared posthumously in 1971 under the title *America at 1750: A Social Portrait.*

It is a safe guess that no general work purporting to be a history of early America ever opened upon so somber a tableau as that which emerges from the initial chapters of this one. This is because, for once, the author chooses to begin by showing the modes whereby the country was being peopled. "Men would not come unless they were gulled into great expectations, stirred by some searing resentment or compelling ideal, or traduced or forced." While the practice of white servitude would all but disappear by the end of the eighteenth century, at least half the incoming whites at mid-century—indentured servants, redemptioners, convicts—would begin their new life in an unfree condition. Nor could they ever, it seems, hope for very much. Poor in spirit as well as in goods, no more

---

[60] *Ibid.*, p. 369; *America at 1750: A Social Portrait* (New York, 1971), pp. viii–ix.

than one or two in ten would end up living productive lives or achieving a decent measure of comfort after their terms were over. "But with white servants," the author warns in turning to the slave trade and black slavery, "we have only begun to taste the anguish of the early American experience." [61]

Hofstadter's picture of these elements of the American population occupies nearly half his book, and it made a palpable impression on those who read and commented upon it. He must have acquired either a new sense of social engagement—keeping up with the times, as his younger eulogists insisted—or else simply a tendency with advancing age and declining health to look more and more on the darker side of everything. But whatever there may have been in such conjectures, they seem less and less pertinent as the book proceeds. One finishes it, indeed, with an impression of recovery: a recovery in considerable part of that curious buoyancy—whether the subject matter were dark *or* bright—which had characterized his earliest work. This is glimpsed in "The Middle-Class World," which follows the first part. That world, still largely rural, held most of the keys to the common life of the colonies, and was already imposing itself from both below and above upon the assumptions, aspirations, and values of an entire society. The final section is splendidly realized. It is on the state of the churches and the advent of the Great Awakening—"the first major intercolonial crisis of the mind and spirit," [62] a milder second counterpart in America of the Reformation—and it has about it the zest of understanding, the lightness of mastery.

There had been long stretches, to be sure, in Hofstadter's recent writings, preoccupied as he was with the present and with so many contemporary concerns, that echoed with a certain pessimism.[63] But a return to the

[61] *Ibid.*, pp. 16, 65.
[62] *Ibid.*, p. 216.
[63] E.g., "America as a Gun Culture," *American Heritage*, XXXI (Oct. 1970), 4–10; "Reflections on Violence in the

distant past, so it would seem, had now brought a new freedom and detachment, a kind of rejuvenation. The old playfulness is loose once again (the revivalist James Davenport "launched himself upon New London in July, where he left a good portion of his listeners in hysteria and went off singing through the streets"), as well as the impish connoisseurship of odd quotations ("The planters," said Henry Laurens in 1750, "are full of money").[64] And finally, his revisitation of the past brought him once more to the threshold of what amounted to a new interpretive idea. This was his emerging conception, hitherto largely undeveloped by anyone, of the functions of religion in shaping political practice in provincial America.

In dealing with the churches and the revivals of the mid-eighteenth century Hofstadter was on ground he had already reconnoitered in previous work. But he was no longer concerned with drawing special inferences regarding, say, academic freedom or anti-intellectualism (though the latter is mentioned); he was interested now, in a broader and more detached way, in seeing how the whole thing worked, and in viewing the range of consequences which these agitations had for an emerging society. Though the several churches came out of it deeply split from the bitter quarrels they had undergone, another result, paradoxically, was their reinvigoration: not so much in doctrine as in style. The style of worship had become far more popular than before, and "enthusiasm," moderate or extravagant, pointed a challenge everywhere to established creeds and professional ministries. And America

---

United States," in RH and Michael Wallace, eds., *American Violence: A Documentary History* (New York, 1970), pp. 3–43; to which should perhaps be added an interview, printed as "The Age of Rubbish," *Newsweek*, LXXVI (July 6, 1970), 20–23.

[64] *America at 1750*, pp. 262, 163. "Charles [II] was much more a libertine than a libertarian; but he was almost as intelligent as he was self-indulgent, and he was afflicted by fits of open-mindedness as well as rage." *Ibid.*, p. 192.

was not only a competitive forum for a multiplicity of sects, themselves full of inner strains, but also one "in which the religious impulse had to battle with other intense and countervailing impulses," such as those of making money. Considering the "fierce persecutory tyranny of religious fanatics" that had been only too familiar throughout Christendom in the previous century, it was a condition that could be lived with, even though the consequences had been intended by virtually nobody. The plurality of forces converging here could only make toleration, and eventually full religious liberty, "the most amenable solution for civic life." [65]

These contradictory influences—the contentions of a revitalized religious constituency, as well as that comity which was the only principle left whereby they might be peaceably contained—could hardly have failed to impress themselves on quite another realm, the formation of Americans' political habits. The elements of a new theory on this are all present in *America at 1750*, and its full unfolding, had the work been allowed to proceed, may be seen as a certainty. One such element—having to do with the spirit in which Americans broached revolution—was that although too determined a search for direct doctrinal connections can lead to misplaced effort, nevertheless few at the time could think and speak of revolution in a wholly secular language. Their religious experience gave them an idiom in which rebellion and resistance could be pictured "as an incident in some providential scheme." Moreover, the colonials had already had a great deal of political experience before rebellion occurred to any of them, and the community schisms of the Great Awakening era—in which they found themselves with choices, and consequently influence, to which they had not previously been accustomed—had done much to enlarge it. Further, there was a direct line between faction in religion and faction in politics, and the logic of pluralism emerged, with a

[65] *Ibid.*, pp. 188–189, 292.

kind of inevitability, for the management of both. And finally, politics itself in the colonial era was given much of its content by matters of sectarian concern. A whole catalog of religious issues having nothing to do with faith and doctrine—but involving taxation, the chartering of educational institutions, the rights of jurors, and the holding of public office—regularly functioned as items and counters in the life of politics throughout the colonies.

It was all there, and Hofstadter's conversation was full of it as he warmed to the work. But it was at this point, with the Great Awakening and its implications, that the work was interrupted. On October 24, 1970, he departed, as he himself had written of one of his favorite politicians many years before, "in the midst of things."[66]

[66] On FDR: *American Political Tradition,* p. 347.

PAULA S. FASS

The Writings of Richard Hofstadter: A Bibliography

I · *Books*

Social Darwinism in American Thought, 1860–1915. Philadelphia: University of Pennsylvania Press, 1944. 2d rev. ed., *Social Darwinism in American Thought.* Boston: Beacon Press, 1955.

The American Political Tradition and the Men Who Made It. New York: Alfred A. Knopf, 1948. 2d ed., with Introduction by Christopher Lasch. Knopf, 1973.

The Development and Scope of Higher Education in the United States, with C. DeWitt Hardy. New York: Columbia University Press, 1952.

The Development of Academic Freedom in the United States, with Walter P. Metzger. New York: Columbia University Press, 1955. Reissued as *Academic Freedom in the Age of the College.* New York: Columbia University Press, 1961.

The Age of Reform: From Bryan to F.D.R. New York: Alfred A. Knopf, 1955.

Anti-intellectualism in American Life. New York: Alfred A. Knopf, 1963.

The Paranoid Style in American Politics and Other Essays. New York: Alfred A. Knopf, 1965.

The Progressive Historians: Turner, Beard, Parrington. New York: Alfred A. Knopf, 1968.

The Idea of a Party System: The Rise of Legitimate Opposition in the United States, 1780–1840. Berkeley, California: University of California Press, 1969.

America at 1750: A Social Portrait. New York: Alfred A. Knopf, 1971.

II • *Textbooks, Readers, Collections of Documents, and Other Volumes*

The Great Issues in American Politics. The Fund for Adult Education, 1956. Republished as *Ten Major Issues in American Politics.* New York: Oxford University Press, 1968.

The Constitution, by Joseph N. Welch, with Richard Hofstadter and the Staff of Omnibus. Boston: Houghton Mifflin, 1956.

The United States: The History of a Republic, with Daniel Aaron and William Miller. Englewood Cliffs, N.J.: Prentice Hall, 1957. 2d ed., 1967.

Great Issues in American History: A Documentary Record. 2 vols. New York: Vintage, 1958.

The American Republic, with Daniel Aaron and William Miller, 2 vols. Englewood Cliffs, N.J.: Prentice-Hall, 1959, 1970.

American Higher Education: A Documentary History, with Wilson Smith, 2 vols. Chicago: University of Chicago Press, 1961.

The Progressive Movement, 1900–1915. Englewood Cliffs, N.J.: Prentice-Hall, 1963.

Coin's Financial School by W. H. Harvey, ed. with an introduction by Richard Hofstadter. Cambridge, Mass.: The John Harvard Library, Belknap Press, 1963.

The Structure of American History, with William Miller and Daniel Aaron. Englewood Cliffs, N.J.: Prentice-Hall, 1964.

Sociology and History: Methods, with Seymour Martin Lipset. Sociology of American History Series. New York: Basic Books, 1968.

Turner and the Sociology of the Frontier, with Seymour Martin Lipset. New York: Basic Books, 1968.

Great Issues in American History. 3 vols. I. *From Settlement to Revolution, 1584–1776,* with Clarence L. Ver Steeg; II. *From the Revolution to the Civil War, 1765–1865;* III. *From Reconstruction to the Present Day, 1864–1969.* New York: Vintage, 1969.

American Violence: A Documentary History, with Michael Wallace. New York: Alfred A. Knopf, 1970.

A People and A Nation, with Clarence L. Ver Steeg. New York: Harper & Row, 1971.

III · *Foreign Editions*

The American Political Tradition: Great Britain, Jonathan Cape; Israel, Yachdav, United Publishers Co., Ltd.; Japan, Iwanami Shoten Publishers; France, Seghers; Italy, Il Mulino; Spain, Seix Barral.

The Age of Reform: Great Britain, Jonathan Cape; Italy, Il Mulino; Japan, Tushindo Kounsha Publishers.

Anti-intellectualism in American Life: Great Britain, Jonathan Cape; Italy, Giulio Einaudi; Japan, Ogawa Publishers; Brazil, Civilização Brasileira; Spain, Tecnos.

The Paranoid Style in American Politics: Great Britain, Jonathan Cape; Japan, The Simul Press.

The Progressive Historians: Great Britain, Jonathan Cape; Argentina, Paidós.

America at 1750: Great Britain, Jonathan Cape; Italy, Giulio Einaudi.

Great Issues in American History, 2 vols.: Italy, Opere Nuove.

IV · *Articles in Journals*

"The Tariff Issue on the Eve of the Civil War," *American Historical Review,* XLIV (Oct. 1938), 50–55.

"William Graham Sumner, Social Darwinist," *New England Quarterly,* XIV (Sept. 1941), 457–477.

"Parrington and the Jeffersonian Tradition," *Journal of the History of Ideas,* II (Oct. 1941), 391–400.

"William Leggett, Spokesman of Jacksonian Democracy," *Political Science Quarterly,* LVIII (Dec. 1943), 581–594.

"U. B. Phillips and the Plantation Legend," *Journal of Negro History,* XXIX (April 1944), 109–124.

"The Roosevelt Reputation," *The Progressive,* XII (Nov. 1948), 9–12.

"From Calhoun to the Dixiecrats," *Social Research,* XVI (June 1949), 135–150.

"Turner and the Frontier Myth," *American Scholar,* XVIII (Oct. 1949), 433–443.

"Farewell to Political Criticism," *The Progressive,* XIII (Dec. 1949), 33–35.

"American Power: The Domestic Sources," *American Perspective,* IV (Winter 1950), 32–36.

"Winston Churchill: A Study in the Popular Novel," with Beatrice K. Hofstadter, *American Quarterly,* II (Spring 1950), 12–28.

"He Speaks for Dixie," *New Leader,* XXXIII (July 8, 1950), 19–20.

"Beard and the Constitution: The History of an Idea," *American Quarterly,* II (Fall 1950), 195–213.

"The Salzburg Seminar, Fourth Year," *Nation,* CLXXI (Oct. 28, 1950), 391–392.

"The Fitzgerald Revival," *The Progressive,* XV (April 1951), 33–35.
"Democracy and Anti-intellectualism in America," *Michigan Alumnus Quarterly Review,* LIX (Summer 1953), 281–295.
"The Pseudo-conservative Revolt," *American Scholar,* XXIV (Winter 1954–55), 9–27; also in *Perspectives USA,* XII (1955), 10–29.
"The Myth of the Happy Yeoman," *American Heritage,* VII (April 1956), 42–53.
"Could a Protestant Have Beaten Hoover in 1928?" *Reporter,* XXII (March 17, 1960), 31–33.
"The Right Man for the Big Job," *New York Times Magazine,* April 3, 1960, pp. 121–122.
"A Note on Intellect and Power," *American Scholar,* XXX (Autumn 1961), 588–598.
"Idealists and Professors and Sore Heads, The Genteel Reformers," *Columbia University Forum,* V (Spring 1962), 4–11.
"The Child and the World," *Daedalus,* XCI (Summer 1962), 501–525.
"Some Comments on Senator Goldwater," *Partisan Review,* XXXI (Fall 1964), 590–592.
"A Long View: Goldwater in History," *New York Review of Books,* III (Oct. 8, 1964), 17–20.
"The Paranoid Style in American Politics," *Harper's Magazine,* CCXXIX (Nov. 1964), 77–86.
"Antitrust in America," *Commentary,* XXXVIII (Aug. 1964), 47–53.
"Goldwater and His Party: The True Believer and the Radical Right," *Encounter,* XXIII (Oct. 1964), 3–13.
"The Goldwater Debacle," *Encounter,* XXIV (Jan. 1965), 66–70.
"Fundamentalism and Status Politics on the Right," *Columbia University Forum,* VIII (Fall 1965), 18–24.
"Spontaneous, Sporadic and Disorganized," *New York Times Magazine,* April 28, 1968, p. 112.

"The 214th Columbia University Commencement Address," *American Scholar,* XXXVII (Autumn 1968), 583–589.
"Uncle Sam Has Cried 'Uncle!' Before," *New York Times Magazine,* May 19, 1968, pp. 30–31, 121.
"A Constitution Against Parties: Madisonian Pluralism and the Anti-party Tradition," *Government and Opposition,* IV (Summer 1969), 345–366.
"The Future of American Violence," *Harper's Magazine,* CCXL (April 1970), 47–53.
"America as a Gun Culture," *American Heritage,* XXI (Oct. 1970), 4–11, 82–85.
"The Importance of Comity in American History," *Columbia University Forum,* XIII (Winter 1970), 9–13.
"The Coming of the Americans," *American History Illustrated,* VI (Oct. 1971), 4–11, 43–47.

V · *Articles in Collections*

"The Impact of Darwinism," in Columbia University, Contemporary Civilization Committee, *Chapters in Western Civilization,* II (New York: Columbia University Press, 1948), 123–143.
"Preface," to Frederick Lewis Allen, *The Big Change* (New York: Harper, 1952), pp. vii–viii.
"Manifest Destiny and the Philippines," in Daniel Aaron, ed., *America in Crisis* (New York: Knopf, 1952), pp. 173–200.
"Charles Beard and the Constitution," in Howard K. Beale, ed., *Charles A. Beard: An Appraisal* (Lexington: University of Kentucky Press, 1954), pp. 75–92.
"Department of History," in R. Gordon Hoxie et al., eds., *A History of the Faculty of Political Science, Columbia University* (New York: Columbia University Press, 1955), pp. 207–249.
"The Pseudo-conservative Revolt," in Daniel Bell, ed., *The New American Right* (New York: Criterion Books,

1955), pp. 33–55. (Also in Bell, ed., *The Radical Right* [Garden City, New York: Doubleday Anchor, 1963], pp. 75–95.)

"History and the Social Sciences," in Fritz Stern, ed., *The Varieties of History* (New York: Meridian Books, 1956), pp. 359–370.

"American Higher Education," in College Entrance Examination Board, *College Admissions: The Interaction of School and College* (Princeton, N.J.: 1956), pp. 15–24.

"The Political Philosophy of the Founders of the Constitution," in American Studies Conference, *America in the 20th Century* (Bad Godesberg, Germany: 1959).

"Darwinism and Western Thought," in Henry L. Plaine, ed., *Darwin, Marx, and Wagner: A Symposium* (Columbus: Ohio State University Press, 1962), pp. 47–70.

"Preface," to Andrew Sinclair, *Prohibition: The Era of Excess* (Boston: Little, Brown, 1962), pp. vii–viii.

"The Revolution in Higher Education," in Arthur M. Schlesinger, Jr., and Morton White, eds., *Paths of American Thought* (Boston: Houghton Mifflin, 1963), pp. 269–290.

"Pseudo-Conservatism Revisited: A Postscript," in Daniel Bell, ed., *The Radical Right* (Garden City, New York: Doubleday Anchor, 1963), pp. 97–103.

"What Happened to the Antitrust Movement? Notes on the Evolution of an American Creed," in Earl Cheit, ed., *The Business Establishment* (New York: Wiley, 1964), pp. 113–151.

"Alexis de Tocqueville," in Louis Kronenberger, ed., *Atlantic Brief Lives: A Biographical Companion to the Arts* (Boston: Little, Brown, 1965), pp. 795–798.

"History and Sociology in the United States," in Seymour M. Lipset and R. Hofstadter, eds., *Sociology and History: Methods* (New York: Basic Books, 1968), pp. 3–19.

"Political Parties," in C. Vann Woodward, ed., *The Com-*

parative Approach to American History (New York: Basic Books, 1968), pp. 206–219.

"North America," in Ghita Ionescu and Ernest Gellner, eds., *Populism: Its Meaning and National Characteristics* (New York: Macmillan, 1969), pp. 9–27.

VI · *Book Reviews (Chronologically)*

E. Merton Coulter, ed., *Georgia's Disputed Ruins. New York Herald Tribune Books,* April 18, 1937, p. 14.

Vida D. Scudder, *On Journey. New York Herald Tribune Books,* April 18, 1937, p. 3.

Isaac Goldberg, *Major Noah, American-Jewish Pioneer. New York Herald Tribune Books,* April 25, 1937, p. 19.

Georgia Harkness, *The Recovery of Ideals. New York Herald Tribune Books,* June 6, 1937, p. 13.

A. H. Murray, *The Philosophy of James Ward. New York Herald Tribune Books,* July 11, 1937, p. 10.

Everett E. Edwards, comp., *The Early Writings of Frederick Jackson Turner. Political Science Quarterly,* LIV (Dec. 1939), 638–639.

Dwight L. Dumond, *Anti-slavery Origins of the Civil War in the United States. Pennsylvania Magazine of History and Biography,* LXIV (April 1940), 284–285.

Max Lerner, *Ideas Are Weapons. Political Science Quarterly,* LV (Dec. 1940), 621.

Richard W. Leopold, *Robert Dale Owen. Mississippi Valley Historical Review,* XXVII (March 1941), 638–639.

Maurice R. Davie, *Sumner Today: Selected Essays by William Graham Sumner, with Comments by American Leaders. New England Quarterly,* XIV (Dec. 1941), 774–775.

Clement Eaton, *Freedom of Thought in the Old South. Pennsylvania Magazine of History and Biography,* LXV (Jan. 1941), 107–109.

Wood Gray, *The Hidden Civil War.* George Fort Milton,

Abraham Lincoln and the Fifth Column. New Republic, CVII (Oct. 19, 1942), 517–519.

Charles and Mary Beard, *The American Spirit. New Republic*, CVIII (Jan. 4, 1943), 27–28.

Bernard De Voto, *The Year of Decision: 1846. New Republic*, CVIII (May 3, 1943), 610–611.

Charles A. Beard, *The Republic: Conversations on Fundamentals. New Republic*, CIX (Oct. 25, 1943), 591–593.

David Loth, *The Story of Woodrow Wilson.* Thomas A. Bailey, *Woodrow Wilson and the Lost Peace.* William Diamond, *The Economic Thought of Woodrow Wilson.* Gerald W. Johnson, *Woodrow Wilson. New Republic*, CXI (Aug. 28, 1944), 251–252.

Arthur E. Morgan, *Edward Bellamy.* Mary Earhart, *Frances Willard. New Republic*, CXII (Jan. 8, 1945), 58–60.

Adrienne Koch and William Peden, eds., *The Life and Selected Writings of Thomas Jefferson. Briarcliff Quarterly*, I (Jan. 1945), 227–231.

Claude G. Bowers, *The Young Jefferson: 1743–1789. New Republic*, CXII (March 19, 1945), 394–396.

L. L. and Jessie Bernard, *Origins of American Sociology. Journal of Economic History*, V (May 1945), 93–94.

Jay Monaghan, *Diplomat in Carpet Slippers. New Republic*, CXII (June 4, 1945), 797–798.

David F. Bowers, *Foreign Influences in American Life. Political Science Quarterly*, LX (June 1945), 319.

Jerome Frank, *Fate and Freedom. New York Times Book Review*, July 8, 1945, p. 5.

Linnie Marsh Wolfe, *Son of the Wilderness: The Life of John Muir, New York Times Book Review*, July 29, 1945, p. 7.

H. C. F. Bell, *Woodrow Wilson and the People.* Thomas A. Bailey, *Woodrow Wilson and the Great Betrayal. New Republic*, CXIII (Aug. 6, 1945), 164–165.

J. Bartlet Brebner, *North American Triangle. New York Times Book Review*, August 26, 1945, p. 4.

William F. Quillian, *The Moral Theory of Evolutionary Naturalism. Annals of the American Academy of Political and Social Science,* CCXLI (Sept. 1945), 180.

Carl Van Doren, ed., *Benjamin Franklin's Autobiographical Writings. New York Times Book Review,* October 21, 1945, p. 4.

Arthur M. Schlesinger, Jr., *The Age of Jackson. New Republic,* CXIII (Oct. 22, 1945), 541–542.

George F. Willison, *Saints and Strangers. New Republic,* CXIII (Dec. 10, 1945), 805–806.

Samuel W. Tait, Jr., *Wildcatters: An Informal History of Oil Hunting in America. New York Times Book Review,* March 31, 1946, p. 32.

Nathan G. Goodman, ed., *A Benjamin Franklin Reader. New York Times Book Review,* April 7, 1946, p. 34.

Merle Curti, *The Roots of American Loyalty. New Republic,* CXIV (May 27, 1946), 779–780.

Frank Graham, *Al Smith, American. Political Science Quarterly,* LXII (March 1947), 159.

Joseph L. Blau, ed., *American Philosophic Addresses, 1700–1900. William and Mary Quarterly,* 3d ser., IV (July 1947), 377–379.

Roy F. Nichols, *The Disruption of American Democracy.* William B. Hesseltine, *Lincoln and the War Governors. Nation,* CLXVII (Aug. 14, 1948), 190–191.

John Tebbel, *George Horace Lorimer and the Saturday Evening Post. The Progressive,* XII (Aug. 1948), 34.

Geoffrey Gorer, *The American People: A Study in National Character. Political Science Quarterly,* LXIII (Sept. 1948), 440–442.

John C. Miller, *Triumph of Freedom, 1775–1783. Nation,* CLXVII (Sept. 4, 1948), 269–270.

Frank McNaughton and Walter Hehmeyer, *Harry Truman, President. Political Science Quarterly,* LXIII (Sept. 1948), 479.

Keith Sward, *The Legend of Henry Ford. The Progressive.* XII (Oct. 1948), 32–33.

J. C. Long, *The Liberal Presidents*. James Hart, *The American Presidency in Action: 1789*. *New Republic*, CXIX (Dec. 6, 1948), 25–26.

Dixon Wecter, *The Age of the Great Depression*. Broadus Mitchell, *Depression Decade*. *Commentary*, VII (Jan. 1949), 99–101.

Arthur M. Schlesinger, *Paths to the Present*. *Nation*, CLXVII (March 26, 1949), 363–364.

Daniel J. Boorstin, *The Lost World of Thomas Jefferson*. *South Atlantic Quarterly*, XLVIII (April 1949), 288–290.

Thomas H. Greer, *American Social Reform Movements*. *Annals of the American Academy of Political and Social Science*, CCLXIII (May 1949), 240–241.

Ernest Samuels, *The Young Henry Adams*. *Mississippi Valley Historical Review*, XXXVI (June 1949), 160–161.

James Playsted Wood, *Magazines in the United States: Their Social and Economic Influence*. *Annals of the American Academy of Political and Social Science*, CCLXIV (July 1949), 163–164.

Edward Nicholas, *The Hours and the Ages*. *Saturday Review of Literature*, XXXII (Sept. 10, 1949), 22.

Oscar Handlin, ed., *This Was America*. *New England Quarterly*, XXII (Sept. 1949), 413–415.

Morton G. White, *Social Thought in America*. *New York Times Book Review*, December 18, 1949, pp. 3, 13.

V. O. Key, Jr., *Southern Politics*. *Commentary*, IX (April 1950), 388–390.

Jonathan Daniels, *The Man of Independence*. *Nation*, CLXXI (Oct. 14, 1950), 344–345.

William Harlan Hale, *Horace Greeley: Voice of the People*. *New Republic*, CXXIII (Nov. 13, 1950), 19–20.

Julian P. Boyd, ed., *The Papers of Thomas Jefferson*, Vols. I and II. *Political Science Quarterly*, LXVI (March 1951), 152–154.

F. O. Matthiessen, *Theodore Drieser*. *Nation*, CLXXII (April 28, 1951), 398.

Donald Fleming, *John William Draper and the Religion of Science. Journal of Southern History*, XVII (May 1951), 282–283.
Arthur M. Schlesinger, *The American as Reformer. Mississippi Valley Historical Review*, XXXVIII (June 1951), 93–94.
Russel B. Nye, *Midwestern Progressive Politics. New York Times Book Review*, July 15, 1951, p. 3.
Elting E. Morison, ed., *The Letters of Theodore Roosevelt*, Vols. I and II. *Commentary*, XII (Aug. 1951), 195–197.
Elting E. Morison, ed., *The Letters of Theodore Roosevelt*, Vols. III and IV. *New York Times Book Review*, October 28, 1951, p. 3.
Thornton Anderson, *Brooks Adams: Constructive Conservative. Nation*, CLXXIV (Feb. 23, 1952), 184–185.
George Dangerfield, *The Era of Good Feelings. New Republic*, CXXVI (March 10, 1952), 18–19.
Oscar Handlin, *The Uprooted. Partisan Review*, XIX (March–April 1952), 252–256.
Robert Green McCloskey, *American Conservatism in the Age of Enterprise: A Study of William Graham Sumner. Political Science Quarterly*, LXVII (March 1952), 129–130.
Van Wyck Brooks, *The Confident Years, 1885–1915. The Progressive*, XVI (April 1952), 37.
Samuel Lubell, *The Future of American Politics. The Progressive*, XVI (July 1952), 27–28.
Elting E. Morison, ed., *The Letters of Theodore Roosevelt*, Vols. V and VI. *New York Times Book Review*, August 17, 1952, p. 7.
Donald Drew Egbert and Stow Persons, eds., *Socialism and American Life. Nation*, CLXXV (Sept. 6, 1952), 196–197.
Mary R. Dearing, *Veterans in Politics: The Story of the G.A.R. New York Times Book Review*, February 8, 1953, p. 16.
Elting E. Morison, ed., *The Letters of Theodore Roosevelt*,

Vols. VII and VIII. *New York Times Book Review,* February 28, 1954, p. 7.

Elting E. Morison, ed., *Cowboys and Kings: Three Great Letters by Theodore Roosevelt. New York Times Book Review,* October 31, 1954, p. 26.

Richard W. Leopold, *Elihu Root and the Conservative Tradition. Yale Law Journal,* LXIV (Nov. 1954), 149–152.

Reinhard H. Luthin, *American Demagogues: Twentieth Century. The Progressive,* XVIII (Dec. 1954), 35–36.

Louis Hartz, *The Liberal Tradition in America. New York Times Book Review,* February 27, 1955, pp. 7, 34.

Robert E. Brown, *Charles Beard and the Constitution.* Robert Allen Rutland, *The Birth of the Bill of Rights, 1776–1794. Commentary,* XXII (Sept. 1956), 270–274.

Arthur M. Schlesinger, Jr., *The Age of Roosevelt: The Crisis of the Old Order, 1919–1933. Encounter,* IX (July 1957), 74–77.

Rexford G. Tugwell, *The Democratic Roosevelt. The Progressive,* XXI (Dec. 1957), 38, 40.

"Of Politics and Politicians." *New York Herald Tribune Books,* Paperback Section, January 15, 1961, pp. 4, 13.

John P. Roche, *The Quest for the Dream. New York Review of Books,* I (Jan. 23, 1964), 12.

Richard Lowitt, *George W. Norris. New York Review of Books,* I (Feb. 6, 1964), 7.

George Dangerfield, *The Awakening of American Nationalism. Book Week,* January 17, 1965, p. 5.

Andrew Sinclair, *The Available Man: Warren Gamaliel Harding. New York Review of Books,* IV (June 3, 1965), 12–13.

Sigmund Freud and William C. Bullitt, *Thomas Woodrow Wilson, Twenty-eighth President of the United States: A Psychological Study. New York Review of Books,* VIII (Feb. 9, 1967), 6–8.

Martin Green, *The Problem of Boston: Some Readings in*

Cultural History. The Public Interest, No. 6 (Winter 1967), 68–74.

VII • *Miscellaneous: Interviews, Letters, Comments*

"Communication," *Journal of the History of Ideas,* XV (April 1954), 328–329.

"Historian's View of the Mass Media," interview by P. D. Hazard, *Senior Scholastic* (Teacher's Edition), LXX Feb. 1, 1957), 5.

"Interview: Richard Hofstadter," by David Hawke, *History,* III (New York: Meridian Books, 1960), 135–141.

"Eisenhower's Views Asked," letter to the editor, *New York Times,* June 16, 1964, p. 38.

Comment on Erik Erikson, "Psychoanalysis and Ongoing History: Problems of Identity, Hatred and Nonviolence," *American Journal of Psychiatry,* CXXII (Sept. 1965), 250–253.

"Conversation," in A. Alvarez, *Under Pressure: The Writer in Society* (Baltimore: Penguin Books, 1965), pp. 111–114, 139–140.

"Thrift and Sin," an exchange, *Columbia University Forum,* IX (Winter 1966), 49.

"To Define Populism," remarks summarized in *Government and Opposition,* III (Spring 1968), 142–144.

"Letter to the Editor," *William and Mary Quarterly,* 3d ser., XXVII (Jan. 1970), 183.

"The Age of Rubbish," interview, *Newsweek,* LXXVI (July 6, 1970), 20–23.

"Richard Hofstadter," interview in John A. Garraty, ed., *Interpreting American History: Conversations with Historians* (New York: Macmillan, 1970), pp. 143–160.

THE CONTRIBUTORS

MARVIN MEYERS is Harry S. Truman Professor of History at Brandeis University. He is the author of *The Jacksonian Persuasion* and co-editor of *Sources of the American Republic.* He received the Dunning Prize from the American Historical Association in 1958.

LINDA K. KERBER is associate professor of history at the University of Iowa. She is the author of *Federalists in Dissent: Imagery and Ideology in Jeffersonian America.*

JAMES M. BANNER, JR., is associate professor of history at Princeton University. He is the author of *To the Hartford Convention: The Federalists and the Origins of Party Politics in Massachusetts, 1789–1815,* and, with others, of *Blacks in America: Bibliographical Essays.*

LAWRENCE W. LEVINE is professor of history at the University of California, Berkeley. He is the author of *Defender of the Faith: William Jennings Bryan, The Last Decade, 1915–1925.*

WILSON SMITH is professor of history at the University of California, Davis. With Richard Hofstadter, he edited *American Higher Education: A Documentary History.*

ERIC FONER is associate professor of history at City College, The City University of New York. He is the author of *Free Soil Labor, Free Men: The Ideology of the Republican Party Before the Civil War; America's Black Past;* and *Nat Turner.*

JAMES MCLACHLAN is editor of *The Biographical Dictionary of Princetonians, 1746–1776,* and is associated with the Shelby Cullom Davis Center for Historical Studies at Princeton University. He is the author of *American Boarding Schools: A Historical Study.*

DOROTHY ROSS is assistant professor of history and Philip and Beulah Rollins Bicentennial Preceptor at Princeton University. She is the author of *G. Stanley Hall: The Psychologist as Prophet.*

DAVID BURNER is associate professor of history at the State University of New York, Stony Brook. He is the author of *The Politics of Provincialism: The Democratic Party in Transition, 1918–1932,* co-author of *America Since Nineteen Forty-Five,* and editor of *The Diversity of Modern America.*

THOMAS R. WEST is associate professor of history at The Catholic University of America. He is the author of *Flesh and Steel: Literature and the Machine in American Culture.*

OTIS L. GRAHAM, JR., is professor of history at the University of California, Santa Barbara. He is the author of *An Encore for Reform: The Old Progressives and the New Deal; The Great Campaigns: Reform and War in America, 1900–1928;* and editor of three textbooks.

STANLEY ELKINS is professor of history at Smith College. He is the author of *Slavery: A Problem in American Institutional and Intellectual Life.*

ERIC MCKITRICK is professor of history at Columbia University. He is the author of *Andrew Johnson and Reconstruction* and editor of *Andrew Johnson: A Profile* and of *Slavery Defended: Views of the Old South.*

PAULA S. FASS is assistant professor of history at Rutgers University. Her dissertation was *The Fruits of Transition: American Youth in the 1920's.*

INDEX OF NAMES

Abbot, W. W., 60 *n.*
Abernethy, Thomas P., 70 *n.*
Adams, Abigail, 42 *n.*, 43 *n.*
Adams, Charles Francis, Jr., 187–8, 204
Adams, Henry, 139, 188, 194–5
Adams, Jasper, 130
Adams, John, 54
Agricola, 249
Aldcroft, Derek, 270 *n.*, 292–3
Alexander, James W., 141 *n.*
Allmendinger, David, xiii
Allport, Gordon W., 217 *n.*
Anderson, Nicholas Longworth, 139
Anderson, Sherwood, 260–1
Anderson, William, 295
Andrew, John, 161
Andrews, Columbus, 79 *n.*
Angell, James Burrill, 139 *n.*
Anselm, St., 224 *n.*
Apter, David E., 85 *n.*
Arewa, Erastus Ojo, 95 *n.*
Aristotle, 197
Ashley, James, 162, 169
Atkinson, Edward, 180, 204
Augustine, St., 227, 233 *n.*
Averitt, Robert, xiii
Axtell, James, 332 *n.*

Backus, Emma M., 106, 109, 117 *n.*, 119, 120, 122
Bacon, A. M., 107 *n.*, 108 *n.*, 110 *n.*, 111 *n.*, 119, 122
Bacon, Leonard, 142–4, 149
Bailey, Joseph, 168 *n.*
Bailyn, Bernard, 134 *n.*
Baldwin, James Mark, 218, 219, 220 *n.*, 229
Banfield, Edward C., 287, 296, 299
Banks, Nathaniel P., 166
Banner, James M., Jr., ix, 85 *n.*, 257 *n.*
Baritz, Loren, 297
Barnard, Henry, 140 *n.*
Barnes, Harry Elmer, 209, 210 *n.*, 211, 213 *n.*, 221, 225 *n.*, 227–8, 230, 233
Barzun, Jacques, xiii
Bascom, John, 198
Bascom, William R., 99 *n.*
Baskin, Prince, 113
Baudelaire, Charles, 360
Bauer, Georg, 249
Beard, Charles A., 211, 212 *n.*, 233 *n.*, 302, 306, 313–14, 343–4, 346–7, 362
Beard, Mary, 362
Beatty, R. C., 141 *n.*
Becker, Carl, 233 *n.*
Beecher, Catharine, 58
Beecher, Lyman, 132 *n.*
Bell, Daniel, 338 *n.*
Benedict, Michael Les, 181 *n.*
Benedict, Murray, 292
Bennett, Hugh H., 267, 293
Berle, Adolf A., 185, 259
Bernstein, Marver, 294
Biddle, A. Sidney, 204
Bier, Jesse, 100 *n.*

Index of Names

Billington, Ray A., 345 *n.*
Binckley, J. W., 155 *n.*
Birr, Kendall, 297
Birthright, William, 178 *n.*
Blaine, James G., 156, 181, 188
Blair, Hugh, 197
Blau, Joseph L., 127
Blodgett, Geoffrey, 190 *n.*
Blum, John M., 291
Blumer, Herbert, 229 *n.*, 231 *n.*
Bolingbroke, Viscount, 354
Bollens, John C., 295
Bonadio, Felice A., 176 *n.*
Boring, Edwin G., 216 *n.*
Botkin, B. A., 117 *n.*, 122
Botts, John Minor, 178
Boucher, Chauncey S., 64 *n.*, 72 *n.*, 77 *n.*, 78 *n.*
Boulding, Kenneth, 279, 296
Bowen, Francis, 194, 198
Bowker, Richard R., 192 *n.*
Bowles, Samuel, 161 *n.*
Brady, Patrick S., 80 *n.*
Braeman, John, 325 *n.*
Bramson, Leon, 229 *n.*
Brandeis, Louis D., 273
Brandmeyer, Gerard A., 189 *n.*, 339
Braybrooke, David, 299
Brewer, J. Mason, 114
Bridenbaugh, Carl, 66 *n.*, 69 *n.*
Brock, W. R., 156 *n.*, 181 *n.*
Brodie, Fawn, 155 *n.*
Brooks, Noah, 313
Broomall, John, 178 *n.*
Brown, Charles Brockden, 37–8, 41–3, 53, 59
Brown, E. Cary, 291
Brown, Richard Maxwell, 66 *n.*, 81 *n.*
Brownlee, W. Elliott, 257 *n.*
Brubacher, John S., 145 *n.*, 146 *n.*, 147 *n.*, 149 *n.*
Bryan, William Jennings, 312–13, 328 *n.*, 361 *n.*
Bryson, Gladys, 195 *n.*, 197–9
Buchanan, James, 84 *n.*, 93
Bundy, McGeorge, 298, 349
Burke, Edmund, 236, 238, 355
Burke, Kenneth, 341
Burlamaqui, Jean, 198
Burner, David, xi, 257 *n.*
Burnham, James, 263
Burnham, John C., 217 *n.*, 230 *n.*
Burton, O. Vernon, 60 *n.*
Butler, Benjamin F., 162, 172, 177
Butts, R. Freeman, 145 *n.*, 196 *n.*

Calef, Wesley, 270 *n.*, 294
Calhoun, John C., 60, 64 *n.*, 69, 77, 89–92 *passim*, 311–12, 330
Cameron, Simon, 156, 157 *n.*
Carnegie, Andrew, 303, 305
Carosso, Vincent P., 295
Carroll, E. Malcolm, 90 *n.*
Carson, James Petigru, 64 *n.*, 89 *n.*
Carstensen, Vernon, 150 *n.*
Carter, Elizabeth, 42
Carter, Franklin, 196 *n.*
Cash, W. J., 68
Catherine, Empress of Russia, 42
Cermak, Anton, 281
Chamberlain, John, 285, 298
Chambers, William N., 62 *n.*
Chandler, Alfred, 275, 281, 296–7
Chandler, Lester V., 292
Channing, Steven A., 61 *n.*
Charles II, King of England, 365 *n.*
Chase, Salmon P., 77
Chase, Stewart, 290
Chase, Stuart, 299
Christensen, A. M. H., 103 *n.*, 107 *n.*, 109, 112, 113 *n.*, 117 *n.*, 119, 122 *n.*
Christie, Jean, 294
Clark, Jane Perry, 295
Clark, Kenneth Wendell, 95 *n.*
Clawson, Marion, 293
Clay, Henry, 89–90
Clemenceau, Georges, 155 *n.*
Cleveland, Grover, 312
Cole, Arthur C., 64 *n.*, 90 *n.*
Colm, Gerhard, 291

Index of Names

Come, Donald R., 134 *n.*
Cometti, Elizabeth, 63 *n.*
Commager, Henry Steele, 185 *n.*
Comte, Auguste, 194
Conklin, E. G., 210
Conrad, David E., 292
Cooke, Henry, 180
Cooke, Jay, 181 *n.*
Coolidge, Calvin, 227, 251
Cooper, Thomas, 43–4, 140 *n.*
Cornelia, mother of Gracchi, 42
Cox, LaWanda, 160 *n.*
Craven, Avery O., 64 *n.*
Cravens, Hamilton, 217 *n.*, 230 *n.*
Crawford, Arthur W., 292
Cremin, Lawrence A., 195 *n.*, 301 *n.*
Croly, Herbert, 259, 273
Cross, Robert D., xiii, 318–19 *n.*
Culbertson, Anne Virginia, 109 *n.*
Cunningham, Charles E., 45 *n.*
Cunningham, Noble E., Jr., 62 *n.*
Current, Richard N., 155 *n.*, 168 *n.*
Currie, Lauchlin, 271, 291
Curry, Leonard P., 159 *n.*
Curti, Merle, 136 *n.*, 150 *n.*
Curtin, Andrew G., 156
Curtis, George William, 186, 193

Dacier, Anne Lefèvre, Mme., 42
Dahl, Robert A., 286, 298
Dain, Norman A., 191 *n.*
Dana, Samuel T., 294
Danton, Georges Jacques, 154
Darwin, Charles, 215, 223, 303
Dauner, Louise, 113 *n.*, 123
Davenport, James, 365
Davis, Allen F., 185 *n.*
Davis, David W., 296
Davis, Stanton Ling, 233 *n.*
Day, Jeremiah, 201
Delacroix, Eugène, 360
Delafons, John, 295
Deming, Horace E., 192 *n.*
Denisoff, R. Serge, 189 *n.*, 339 *n.*
Dennie, Joseph, 37
Dern, George, 268–9
Descartes, René, 224 and *n.*
Dewey, John, 210, 218, 220 *n.*, 259, 304 *n.*
Dod, Albert B., 140 *n.*
Doherty, Robert W., 189 *n.*, 339 *n.*
Donald, David, 157 *n.*, 162 *n.*
Dorr, Thomas Wilson, 149
Dorson, Richard M., 100 *n.*, 101–2
Douglas, Stephen A., 93
Doyle, Arthur Conan, 250
Draper, John William, 211
Drinker, Elizabeth, 51
Drucker, Peter F., 297
DuBois, W. E. B., 183 *n.*
Dugdale, Richard L., 204–5
Dundes, Alan, 94 *n.*, 99 *n.*
Dunning, William A., 156 *n.*
Durkheim, Emile, 318 *n.*
Duverger, Maurice, 62 *n.*
Dwight, Timothy, 45, 52–3, 196

Eaton, Peggy, 92
Eccles, Marriner, 265, 291
Eckenrode, Hamilton J., 179 *n.*
Edwards, Lee R., 53 *n.*
Eggleston, Edward, 134 *n.*
Elazar, Daniel J., 84–5 *n.*
Elizabeth I, Queen of England, 42
Ellis, A. B., 99 *n.*
Ely, Richard, 259
Emmerich, Herbert, 297
Erikson, Erik, 227 *n.*, 228 *n.*
Ervin, Kingsley, xiii
Ezekiel, Mordekai, 285, 290

Fairchild, James Harris, 131, 142 *n.*
Fass, Paula, xii
Faulkner, Harold U., 233 *n.*
Ferguson, Adam, 198
Fesler, James W., 293

Index of Names

Fessenden, William P., 172, 180
Fiering, Norman S., 196 *n.*
Finnegan, Ruth, 99 *n.*
Finney, Charles G., 140 *n.*, 334
Fish, Carl Russell, 90 *n.*
Fishwick, Marshall, 113 *n.*
Fleming, Walter L., 159 *n.*, 160 *n.*
Fletcher, Robert S., 140 *n.*
Foner, Eric, x, 160 *n.*
Ford, Henry, 276
Ford, Henry Jones, 78 *n.*
Formisano, Ronald P., 150 *n.*
Foss, Philip O., 269 *n.*, 294
Fox, Dixon Ryan, 233 *n.*
Frank, Jerome, 285, 290
Freehling, William W., 60 *n.*, 61 *n.*, 64 *n.*, 71 *n.*, 88, 89 *n.*, 91 *n.*
Freidel, Frank, 140 *n.*, 185
Freud, Sigmund, 227 *n.*, 228
Friedman, Milton, 292
Fulton, John F., 140 *n.*

Gabriel, Ralph Henry, 139–40 *n.*
Galambos, Louis, 281, 296
Galbraith, John Kenneth, 285, 298
Galloway, George B., 284, 290
Gannett, Deborah, 36
Gardiner, John Sylvester John, 49
Gardner, John W., 127
Garfield, James Abram, 156 *n.*, 181 *n.*
Garner, John Nance, 280
Genlis, Stéphanie de, Mme., 42
George V, King of England, 250
Gibbs, Oliver Wolcott, 131
Gladden, Washington, 142 *n.*
Glazer, Nathan, 338 *n.*
Godkin, Edwin L., 176 *n.*, 186, 204
Godwin, William, 52
Goldman, Eric, 188, 189 *n.*
Goodman, William, 78 *n.*
Goodrich, Carter, 293
Gould, Jay, 189
Govette, Francis, 247–8
Graham, Hugh D., 257 *n.*
Graham, Otis, xii
Grant, Ulysses S., 180, 187
Greeley, Horace, 166, 179–80
Green, Ashbel, xiii, xiv
Green, Fletcher M., 70 *n.*, 82 *n.*
Green, George Walton, 192 *n.*
Greene, Jack P., 66 *n.*, 81 *n.*, 359 *n.*
Greene, Theodore P., 126
Greenleaf, William Willis, 113
Gregory, Francis W., 191 *n.*
Gregory, John Milton, 150 *n.*
Griffith, Ernest, 284–5, 290
Grodzins, Morton, 85 *n.*, 295, 298
Gross, Bertram, 296
Gulick, Luther H., 270 *n.*, 294
Gusfield, Joseph R., 339 *n.*, 340–2

Hackney, Sheldon, 60 *n.*
Haddow, Anna, 195 *n.*
Hadley, James, 141 *n.*
Hale, Nathan, 225 *n.*
Hall, G. Stanley, 196 *n.*, 227 and *n.*
Hall, Sarah, 37
Hamer, Philip M., 64 *n.*
Hamilton, Alexander, 13, 18, 31, 354
Hamilton, J. G. de Roulhac, 180 *n.*
Hammond, James H., 91–2 *n.*
Handlin, Oscar, 232, 324 *n.*
Hansen, Alvin, 295
Hansen, Terrence Leslie, 102 *n.*
Hardin, Charles, 269 *n.*, 293
Harding, Thomas S., 200
Harding, Warren G., 251
Hardy, C. DeWitt, 332 *n.*
Harris, Joel Chandler, 96, 108 *n.*, 110 *n.*, 112, 119
Harris, Joseph P., 295
Harris, P. M. G., 151 *n.*
Hartz, Louis, 91 *n.*
Harvey, William ("Coin"), 338 and *n.*, 359 *n.*

Index of Names

Hawke, David, 326 *n.*, 346 *n.*, 359 *n.*
Hawley, Ellis, 292
Hawthorne, Nathaniel, 150, 345
Hayek, F. A., 299
Hayes, Carlton J. H., 233 *n.*
Hayes, Rutherford B., 158 *n.*
Held, R. Burnell, 293
Hendricks, Luther V., 209 *n.*, 210 *n.*, 212 *n.*
Henry, Joseph, 140 *n.*
Henry, Patrick, 5
Herndon, William, 312
Herring, E. Pendleton, 299
Herskovits, Frances S., 98 *n.*, 100
Herskovits, Melville J., 98 *n.*, 100
Hesseltine, William B., 165 *n.*
Higginson, Thomas Wentworth, 186
Higham, John, xiii, 201 *n.*, 208 *n.*, 209 *n.*, 229 *n.*, 324 *n.*, 328 *n.*
Hinsdale, B. L., 181 *n.*
Hislop, Codman, 139 *n.*, 144 *n.*, 146 *n.*
Hoar, George F., 181 *n.*
Hofnagle, Warren, 170 *n.*
Hofstadter, Beatrice K., xiii, xiv, 308 *n.*, 360 *n.*
Hofstadter, Richard, x, 85 *n.*, 153, 188–9 and *n.*, 190, 194 *n.*, 229 *n.*, 338 *n.*; *Age of Reform* (1955) 313–17, 319–23, 338, 353; *America at 1750* (1971), 362–7; *American Political Tradition, The* (1948), 307–8, 310–13, 330, 346, 353; *Anti-intellectualism in American Life* (1963), 333–7, 348–9; and Columbia crisis, 343, 348–53; and "consensus history," 310, 324, 327; criticism of, 323–8, 332 *n.*, 333, 339–43; *Development of Academic Freedom, The* (1955), 330–2; "History and the Social Sciences" (1956), 361–2;
Hofstadter, Richard (*continued*)
Idea of a Party System, The (1969), 353–7; influence of Mannheim on, 308–10, 315, 317; influence of Progressivism on, 301–3, 313; influence of R. K. Merton, 317–18; literary influences on, 359–61; and Marx, 310; and McCarthyism, 330, 336 *ff.*; as "mediator" in life of ideas, 359–63; *Paranoid Style in American Politics, and Other Essays, The* (1965), 337–8; personal characteristics, vii–viii, xii–xiii, 307, 351; *Progressive Historians, The* (1968), 343–8; Pulitzer Prize, 314, 336; relations with students, viii, 351; *Social Darwinism* (1944), 303–6, 307, 308; on "status politics," 338–9, 343; writings on, 301 *n.*
Hollingsworth, J. Rogers, 324 *n.*
Hollis, Daniel W., 140 *n.*
Holmes, Oliver Wendell, 220 *n.*
Holst, Hermann von, 210
Hoogenboom, Ari A., 192 *n.*
Hoover, Herbert, xi, 257–9, 264, 280; attack on New Deal, 252–4; and banking crisis of 1933, 253–4; conception of order, 238; enters public service, 250–1; on labor, 240–4; on mining, 245–9; and relief, 254
Hopkins, Albert, 141 *n.*
Hopkins, George E., 278
Hopkins, Mark, 137 *n.* 140 *n.*, 147 *n.*, 150 *n.*, 196
Hopkinson, Emily, 37
Howard, Oliver O., Gen., 168, 170 *n.*
Hower, Daniel Walker, 196 *n.*
Hulme, T. E., 239
Hume, David, 13 and *n.*, 354
Humphries, Richard, 50 and *n.*
Hunnicutt, James, 178–9

Index of Names

Huntington, Samuel P., 62 *n.*
Hurston, Zora Neale, 119
Hutcheson, Francis, 198
Huthmacher, J. Joseph, 325 *n.*

Jackson, Andrew, 73, 84, 87–90, 92–3, 186, 312
Jackson, P. W., 56
Jahn, Janheinz, 98 *n.*
James, Henry, 347, 359
James, William, 209, 215, 216 and *n.*, 217–19, 223, 226, 361
Jefferson, Thomas, 7, 15–18 *passim*, 20, 93, 227, 258, 312
Jenckes, Thomas A., 168 *n.*
Jencks, Christopher, 128 *n.*
Johnson, Andrew, 168–9
Johnson, G. Griffith, 292
Johnson, Gerald W., 290
Johnson, Guy B., 107 *n.*
Johnson, Lyndon B., 298
Johnson, Samuel, 196 *n.*
Johnson, William, Justice, 137
Johnston, Mrs. William Preston, 111 *n.*, 119
Jones, Charles C., 103 *n.*, 104 *n.*, 105 *n.*, 107 *n.*, 108 *n.*, 111 *n.*, 112 *n.*, 117 *n.*, 118 *n.*, 120 *n.*, 121 *n.*
Jones, Howard Mumford, 37 *n.*
Jones, M. G., 43 *n.*
Julian, George W., 159, 160 *n.*, 162, 166–7, 170

Kames, Henry Home, Lord, 198–9
Kariel, Henry, 287, 299
Karl, Barry D., 297
Kazin, Alfred, 301 *n.*
Kelley, Brooks M., 157 *n.*
Kelley, Robert, 257 *n.*
Kelley, William D. ("Pig Iron"), 166–7, 169, 179–80
Kendrick, Benjamin B., 161 *n.*
Keniston, Kenneth, 128 *n.*
Kennedy, John F., 298, 335
Kenyon, Cecelia, xiii
Kerber, Linda, ix
Kersey, Harry A., Jr., 150 *n.*
Key, V. O., Jr., 62 *n.*, 68, 72 *n.*
Kibler, Lillian A., 64 *n.*, 81 *n.*
Kimmel, Lewis H., 291
King, Stanley, 136 *n.*
Kirkland, John Thornton, 195, 196 *n.*
Kleppner, Paul, 150 *n.*
Knox, Samuel, 45
Kohlmeier, Louis, 294

Lambrecht, Winifred, 95 *n.*
Lasch, Christopher, 301 *n.*
Latham, Earl, 294
Laurens, Henry, 365
Lawrence, D. H., 120
Lecky, W. E. H., 211
Lee, Robert Edson, 52 *n.*
Lehmann, Fritz, 291
Leiserson, Avery, 62 *n.*
Leitner, Ethel Hatton, 122 *n.*
Lepawsky, Albert, 293
Leuchtenburg, William E., xiii, 257 *n.*, 293
Levine, Lawrence W., x, 115 *n.*
Levy, Marion J., 296
Lieber, Francis, 140 *n.*
Lincoln, Abraham, 155, 159, 181, 311, 313
Lindbergh, Charles A., 278
Lindblom, Charles, 286, 298–9
Lindsley, Philip, 133, 134 *n.*, 137–8, 140 *n.*
Linn, John Blair, 42 *n.*
Lippmann, Walter, 259, 299
Lipset, Seymour, 338–9
Locke, John, 7, 198
Loo Etong, 242 *n.*
Loomis, Louise R., 233 *n.*
Loring, W. J., 248
Lorwin, Lewis, 291
L'Ouverture, Toussaint, 67
Lovejoy, Arthur O., 224
Lowi, Theodore, 287, 299
Lundberg, Eric, 270 *n.*
Luther, Martin, 226–7
Lycurgus, 3, 12–13
Lynn, Kenneth S., 333 *n.*

Index of Names

Maass, Arthur, 269 *n.*, 293–4
Macaulay, Catherine, 42 and *n.*, 48
Machiavelli, Niccolò, 12
MacVeagh, Franklin, 204
Maddex, Jack P., 179 *n.*
Madison, James, ix, 87, 354–6; on Antifederalist fears of usurpation, 26 *ff.*; on broad construction, 21–2, 25; on dangers of frequent conventions, 11 *ff.*, 25; on energy in government, 31–2; on legitimacy of Constitutional Conventions, 6–11; on Rhode Island, unstable conditions in, 29–30
Mahan, Asa, 140 *n.*, 142 *n.*
Maintenon, Françoise de, Mme., 42
Malone, Dumas, 140 *n.*
Manhart, George B., 149 *n.*
Mann, Horace, 201
Mannheim, Karl, 306, 308–10, 315, 317
Mansfield, Harvey C., 298
Marat, Jean Paul, 154
Marx, Karl, 194, 310 and *n.*
Mason, Priscilla, 47–8, 53, 55
Mayo, Elton, 276
McAlister, John T., 257 *n.*
McCarthy, John, 242 *n.*
McCarthy, John J., 167 *n.*
McCaughey, Robert, xiii
McClure, Alexander K., 156 *n.*
McClurg, J. W., 168 *n.*
McConnell, Grant, 287, 292, 299
McCormick, Richard P., 60 *n.*, 61 *n.*, 62 *n.*, 78 *n.*, 82 *n.*
McFarland, Gerald W., 190 *n.*
McFeely, William, 170–1
McKinley, Albert E., 81 *n.*
McKitrick, Eric L., 86 *n.*, 157 *n.*, 158 *n.*
McLachlan, James, xi, 200 *n.*
McPherson, Edward, 155 *n.*
McPherson, James M., 173 *n.*
McSeveney, Samuel, 328 *n.*
McVay, Henry W., 178 *n.*
Meiklejohn, Alexander, 126
Mencken, H. L., 361 *n.*
Mendoza, Daniel, 50 and *n.*
Meredith, Gertrude, 37, 48–9
Merriam, Charles E., 290
Merriam, George S., 161 *n.*
Merritt, Elizabeth, 92 *n.*
Merton, Robert K., 317–18, 340
Metzger, Walter P., 330
Meyer, Donald Harvey, 196 *n.*
Meyers, Marvin, ix, 3 *n.*, 20 *n.*
Meyerson, Martin, 128 *n.*
Michels, Roberto, 296
Middlekauff, Robert, 94 *n.*
Miller, Perry, 228
Miller, Samuel, 198 *n.*
Millett, John D., 291
Mills, C. Wright, 202, 359
Milton, George Fort, 155 *n.*
Mode, Peter G., 132 *n.*, 134 *n.*, 148 *n.*, 149 *n.*, 151 *n.*
Moley, Raymond, 259
Montagu, Lady Mary Wortley, 42
Montesquieu, Baron de, 33, 36, 198
Montgomery, David, 182 *n.*
Moody, Dwight L., 334
Moore, Clement H., 62 *n.*
More, Hannah, 42, 43 *n.*
Morgan, Donald G., 137 *n.*
Morgan, J. P., 189
Morgan, Robert, 293
Morgenthau, Henry, 263, 291
Morison, Samuel Eliot, 85 *n.*, 146 *n.*, 149 *n.*
Morrill, Justin, 156
Morris, William, 236
Muelder, Hermann, 147 *n.*
Mundy, John, 359 *n.*
Munsterberg, Hugo, 276
Murphy, Gardner, 216 *n.*, 228 *n.*
Murray, Judith Sargent, 36–8, 40, 42 *n.*, 43–5, 53, 55–6, 59

Nash, Gerald D., 295
Nash, Roderick, 136 *n.*
Nast, Thomas, 186
Naylor, Natalie A., 152 *n.*
Neale, J. A., 44 *n.*

Index of Names

Nelson, Ralph, 275 *n.*
Neu, Irene D., 191 *n.*
Neumann, Sigmund, 62 *n.*
Nevins, Allan, 150 *n.*
Newton, Isaac, 224
Norris, George, Sen., 268
Norris, Thaddeus, 103 *n.*
Nott, Eliphalet, 139 *n.*, 144, 146, 199
Nugent, Walter T. K., 328 *n.*

Oberholtzer, Ellis P., 181 *n.*
Otis, Harrison Gray, 85 *n.*, 86
Owens, William, 103 *n.*, 111 *n.*, 117 *n.*, 122 *n.*

Pace, C. Robert, 153 *n.*
Paley, William, 197
Parrington, Vernon, 302, 305–6, 314, 321, 329, 343–5, 347
Parrish, Michael E., 295
Parsons, Elsie Clews, 104 *n.*, 107 *n.*, 108 *n.*, 109 *n.*, 110 *n.*, 111 *n.*, 112 *n.*, 117 *n.*, 118 *n.*, 119 *n.*, 120 *n.*, 122 *n.*
Parsons, Talcott, 338 *n.*
Patten, Simon, 210, 259
Patterson, James T., 295
Paul, St., 233 *n.*
Pearce, James T., 101 *n.*
Peirce, Cyrus, 140 *n.*
Pendleton, Louis, 103 *n.*
Perloff, Harvey, 295
Perry, Benjamin F., 64 *n.*, 87–8
Peterson, George E., 144 *n.*
Peterson, George R., 186
Petigru, James Louis, 64 *n.*, 88, 89 *n.*
Phillips, Wendell, 162, 164, 172, 311
Pierce, Edward L., 162 *n.*
Pierson, George Wilson, 151 *n.*, 196 *n.*
Pinchot, Gifford, 206
Plimpton, Francis T. P., 126
Poe, Edgar Allan, 346
Pole, J. R., 301 *n.*
Polenberg, Richard, 297
Pollack, Norman, 189 and *n.*, 324 *n.*, 328 *n.*
Polsby, Nelson W., 340 *n.*
Pomfret, John Edwin, 140 *n.*
Pope, Christie Farnham, 170 *n.*
Porter, Noah, 201–3
Post, Truman Marcellus, 132–3
Poteat, William Louis, 129–30
Potter, David, 200, 232 and *n.*
Potter, J., 69 *n.*
Price, Hugh D., 62 *n.*
Proctor, Jenny, 122
Pursell, Carroll, 257 *n.*
Putnam, George Haven, 186, 203–4

Radom, Matthew, 297
Rammelkamp, Charles Henry, 148 *n.*
Randall, James G., 159 *n.*, 160 *n.*
Randall, John Herman, Jr., 233 *n.*
Rapaport, David, 228 *n.*
Raper, Arthur F., 292
Ratner, Sidney, 291
Rattray, R. S., 97, 98 *n.*
Rayback, Joseph G., 91 *n.*
Rea, J. H., 178 *n.*
Reagan, Michael D., 287, 299
Reese, John H., 298
Reich, Charles A., 294
Reid, Ira, 292
Reid, Thomas, 197
Reisch, Anna L., 293
Rhett, Robert Barnwell, 64 *n.*
Rhodes, James Ford, 187–8
Riddleberger, Patrick W., 160 *n.*, 162 *n.*
Riesman, David, 128 *n.*, 338 *n.*
Riker, William H., 296
Ripley, George, 149
Rippy, J. Fred, 64 *n.*
Robespierre, Maximilien, 154, 155 *n.*
Robinson, Benjamin, 209
Robinson, James Harvey, xi; Darwinian influences on, 208–10; education and early career, 209–10; psychology,

Robinson, James (*continued*) sources of his ideas on, 209–10, 215–20; shortcomings of his work, 221–5, 234; theory of history, 213 *ff.*
Rogers, George C., Jr., 81 *n.*, 89 *n.*
Rogin, Michael P., 340 *n.*, 341–2
Rohfeld, Rae Wahl, 209 *n.*, 211 *n.*
Roosevelt, Franklin D., xi, 184–5, 252–4, 258–9, 260–1, 263–5, 267, 271–3, 277, 280–1, 287, 290, 307, 312, 335
Roosevelt, Theodore, 251, 273, 335
Rose, Lisle A., 63 *n.*, 71 *n.*
Rose, Willie Lee, 163 *n.*
Ross, Dorothy, xi, 208 *n.*, 215 *n.*
Ross, Earle D., 166 *n.*, 191 *n.*
Ross, Edward A., 259, 303, 304 *n.*
Rourke, Constance, 100 *n.*
Rousseau, Jean-Jacques, 12, 51, 198
Rowson, Susanna, 37, 44, 56
Rublee, Horace, 204
Rudolph, Frederick A., 137 *n.*, 140 *n.*, 147 *n.*, 148 *n.*, 150 *n.*, 194 *n.*
Rudy, Willis, 145 *n.*, 146 *n.*, 147 *n.*, 149 *n.*
Rush, Benjamin, 36–7, 39, 44–8, 53, 56–9 *passim*
Rusk, Dean, 349
Rutherford, Thomas, 198
Rutledge, John, Jr., 63 *n.*

Samuels, Ernest, 139 *n.*, 195 *n.*
Sauvy, Alfred, 292
Say, Benjamin, 47 *n.*
Schaper, William A., 70, 71 *n.*, 72, 79 *n.*, 81 *n.*
Schattschneider, E. E., 85 *n.*
Scheiner, Irwin, 94 *n.*
Schickele, Rainier, 292
Schlesinger, Arthur M., 233 *n.*
Schlesinger, Arthur M., Jr., 189 *n.*, 301 *n.*, 341 *n.*
Schmidt, George P., 140 *n.*, 145 *n.*, 196 *n.*
Schorske, Carl, 207 *n.*
Schultz, Harold S., 90 *n.*
Schultze, Charles L., 299
Schurz, Carl, 155 *n.*, 165, 186
Schwartz, Anna J., 292
Scott, Andrew M., 325 *n.*
Scott, Walter Dill, 276
Sherman, Richard B., 325 *n.*, 326 *n.*
Shonfield, Andrew, 292, 299
Seigel, Jerrold, 207 *n.*
Senghor, Léopold, 98
Sewall, Albert C., 141 *n.*
Seward, Frederick W., 200
Shalhope, Robert E., 187 *n.*
Sharkey, Robert, 166 *n.*, 168 *n.*, 181 *n.*
Shays, Daniel, 7, 17, 30
Shepard, Edward M., 204
Sherman, R. B., 189 and *n.*
Sherman, William T., Gen., 159, 169
Shotwell, James T., 233 *n.*
Silliman, Benjamin, 50 *n.*, 52, 140 *n.*
Singer, Charles G., 66 *n.*
Sirmans, M. Eugene, 66 *n.*, 79 *n.*
Skotheim, Robert Allen, 209 *n.*, 228 *n.*
Sloan, Alfred P., 275
Sloan, Douglas Milton, 129 *n.*, 195 *n.*, 332 *n.*
Smith, Adam, 198
Smith, Preserved, 223, 226, 228, 233
Smith, Richard, 108 *n.*
Smith, Samuel Harrison, 44–5
Smith, William, 92
Smith, Wilson, x, 196 *n.*, 332 *n.*
Snider, Clyde F., 295
Snow, Louis F., 196 *n.*
Sokolsky, George E., 242 *n.*
Solberg, Winton U., 150 *n.*
Solon, 3, 13
Soule, George, 259, 263, 290
Spencer, Herbert, 215, 303–4

Index of Names

Sproat, James, Rev., 46 *n.*
Sproat, John G., 190 *n.*, 202–3
Stafford, John, 113 *n.*
Stampp, Kenneth, 94 *n.*
Steffens, Lincoln, 322
Stein, Herbert, 291
Stephenson, N. W., 64 *n.*
Stern, Fritz, 301 *n.*
Sternsher, Bernard, 290
Stevens, Thaddeus, x; death of, 181; and first Confiscation Act, 159; and Freedmen's Bureau Bill, 169–70; on goals of confiscation, 162–4; on Negro suffrage, 161, 171; as political "dictator," 156–7; radicalism of, 154–5, 182–3; Republican opposition to views on confiscation, 165–7
Stewart, Dugald, 197
Stewart, Sadie E., 117 *n.*
Strong, George Templeton, 131, 141 *n.*
Sturtevant, Julian M., 149 *n.*, 150–1
Sumner, Charles, 162 and *n.*, 172, 173 *n.*
Sumner, William Graham, 201, 204–5, 303, 305–6
Sunday, Billy, 334–5, 350
Sundquist, James L., 295
Swain, Donald, 294
Swift, Mary, 140 *n.*
Sydnor, Charles S., 67 *n.*, 78, 79 *n.*

Talbott, John E., 257 *n.*
Tardé, Gabriel, 217
Tate, Allen, 237
Taylor, Alrutheus A., 179 *n.*
Taylor, Frederick W., 276
Taylor, Rosser H., 67 *n.*, 69 *n.*, 71 *n.*, 73 *n.*
Tewksbury, Donald G., 152 *n.*
Thanet, Octave, 94, 112–13
Thelen, David P., 325 *n.*
Thomas, William I., 229 and *n.*, 230–2
Thomson, Elizabeth H., 140 *n.*
Thorndike, Edward L., 210, 216 and *n.*, 217, 218 *n.*, 224
Thorndyke, Lynn, 233 *n.*
Thorpe, Francis Newton, 79 *n.*
Ticknor, George, 139
Tocqueville, Alexis de, 135, 136 and *n.*, 237
Todd, John, 151 *n.*
Tong Sha-li, 242
Tong Shao-yi, 242 *n.*
Tönnies, Ferdinand, 296
Toombs, Robert, 157
Trescott, William Henry, 175 *n.*
Trilling, Lionel, xiii, 301 *n.*, 308 *n.*, 321, 322 *n.*, 360
Trotter, Wilfred, 218
Trow, Martin, 340 *n.*
Truman, David B., 85 *n.*
Trumbull, Lyman, 169
Tucker, Beverly, 91 *n.*
Tucker, St. George, 54
Tugwell, Rexford G., 259–60, 273, 287–9, 290, 296, 299
Tumin, Melvin M., 126
Turner, Edward Raymond, 55 *n.*
Turner, Frederick Jackson, 184–5, 232, 314, 343–5, 347
Turner, Nat, 67
Tweed, William Marcy ("Boss"), 186
Tyler, William S., 136 *n.*

Unger, Irwin, 324 *n.*

Van Buren, Martin, 73, 76–7, 91–2, 356–7
Vanderbilt, Cornelius, 189
Van Hise, Charles, 259
Vattel, Emmerich de, 198
Veblen, Thorstein, 219, 220 *n.*, 222, 251, 259, 304 *n.*
Vesey, Denmark, 67
Viereck, Peter, 338 *n.*
Voltaire, François Marie Arouet de, 211
Voorhis, Jerry, 285

Wade, Benjamin F., 176
Wagstaff, Thomas, 165 *n.*

Index of Names

Wallace, David D., 67 *n.*, 70 *n.*, 72 *n.*, 78 *n.*, 82 *n.*
Wallace, Henry A., 267
Wallace, Molly, 48 *n.*
Wann, A. J., 297
Ward, Lester F., 259, 303, 304 *n.*
Warner, W. Lloyd, 277, 296
Warren, Mercy Otis, 42 *n.*, 43 *n.*
Waterman, Richard A., 99 *n.*
Wayland, Francis, 131, 133, 137–8, 139 *n.*, 144, 196, 198
Weber, Max, 296
Webster, Daniel, 90
Webster, Noah, 37, 44–5 and *n.*, 49
Weinstein, Allen, xiii, 359 *n.*
Weir, Robert A., 65, 66 *n.*, 67 *n.*
Wells, David A., 205
Wengert, Norman, 270 *n.*
Wertenbaker, Thomas J., 140 *n.*, 146 *n.*
West, Andrew F., 139 and *n.*
West, Thomas, xi
White, Andrew Dickson, 139 and *n.*, 147, 148 *n.*, 211
White, Gilbert, 293
White, James C., 141 *n.*
White, Laura A., 64 *n.*
White, Morton G., 142, 208 *n.*, 215 *n.*, 220 *n.*
Whitehurst, P. H., 178 *n.*
Wiebe, Robert, 251, 296, 314, 327 *n.*
Wild, Philip F., 80 *n.*
Wildavsky, Aaron, 299
Willard, Samuel, 148 *n.*
Williams, Charles R., 158 *n.*
Williams, T. Harry, 159 *n.*, 168 *n.*
Williams, William Appleman, 323
Williamson, Chilton, 81 *n.*
Williamson, Joel, 163 *n.*, 168 *n.*
Wilson, Henry, Sen., 175 *n.*, 179–80
Wilson, James Q., 294
Wilson, R. Jackson, xiii–xiv, 305 *n.*
Wilson, Woodrow, 273, 313, 335
Wiltse, Charles M., 64 *n.*, 90 *n.*, 91 *n.*
Wise, Henry A., 91
Witherspoon, John, 197–8
Wolfe, Bernard, 113 *n.*, 121
Wolfe, John Harold, 63 *n.*, 70 *n.*, 71 *n.*, 82 *n.*
Wolfinger, Raymond E., 340 *n.*
Wollstonecraft, Mary, 42, 51–3
Wood, Gordon S., 70 *n.*
Woodburn, James A., 156 *n.*, 157 *n.*
Woods, Gordon, 187 *n.*
Woodward, C. Vann, xiv, 189 and *n.*, 301 *n.*, 313 *n.*, 328 *n.*, 341 *n.*
Woodworth, Robert S., 216 *n.*, 220 *n.*
Wooster, Ralph A., 77 *n.*
Wright, Frank Lloyd, 240

Young, Alexander, 196 *n.*

Znaniecki, Florian, 229 *n.*, 230 *n.*, 231 *n.*
Zornow, William F., 176 *n.*

A NOTE ON THE TYPE

This book was set on the Linotype in a face called PRIMER, designed by RUDOLPH RUZICKA, who was earlier responsible for the design of Fairfield and Fairfield Medium, Linotye faces whose virtues have for some time now been accorded wide recognition.

The complete range of sizes of Primer was first made available in 1954, although the pilot size of 12-point was ready as early as 1951. The design of the face makes general reference to Linotype Century—long a serviceable type, totally lacking in manner or frills of any kind—but brilliantly corrects its characterless quality.

The book was composed, printed and bound by Kingsport Press, Inc., Kingsport, Tennessee.

Typography and binding design by